CRY

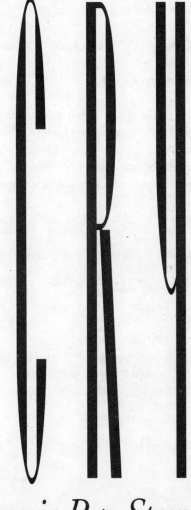

CRY

The Johnnie Ray Story

JONNY WHITESIDE

BARRICADE BOOKS INC. / New York

Published by Barricade Books Inc.
61 Fourth Avenue
New York, NY 10003

Printed in the United States of America.

Library of Congress Cataloging-in-Publication Data

Whiteside, Jonny.
    Cry: the Johnnie Ray story / by Jonny Whiteside.
        p.   cm.
    ISBN 1-56980-013-8
    1. Ray, Johnnie, 1927-1990. 2. Singers—United States—Biography. I. Title.
    ML420.R288W55 1994
    782.42164'092—dc20   94-25582
    [B]   CIP
                                                               MN

Designed by Cindy LaBreacht

First printing

ACKNOWLEDGMENTS

The origin of this book lies with Johnnie Ray himself, the late result of a 1989 meeting and interview session with him conducted when Johnnie was toying with the notion of writing his autobiography. Seeking a collaborator, his booking agent recommended me. When Johnnie was claimed by death months later, telling his story became almost an obligation; after his sister Elma informally gave me her blessings, the course was set. This is not as Johnnie would have told it, but is a fair accounting of an extraordinary life, laid out, tears, blood and all, as it actually happened.

To those who knew him, Johnnie was a friend of irresistible charm and rare loyalty, a fact reflected in the exuberant urgency all of them used when speaking of his adventures. Also common to these folks was a profound resentment at the way Johnnie Ray's towering contributions to popular music have been obscured; it's a sentiment common to anyone, original fan or curious newcomer, who is exposed to his music.

A biographer is necessarily an interpreter and editorialist. The few presumptions found here are colored primarily by firsthand comments from Johnnie himself. Measuring his statements (from my own tapes and forty years of press interviews) against everything his weird notoriety projected, cross referenced through the inevitable conflicts found in the memories of forty-four different individuals provided my framework of reckoning.

Sympathy is an ingredient dismissed as the hagiographer's, but in Johnnie Ray's case it is an essential. Publicly guarded, he became a past-master at the art of standardized disinformation. He often straight out lied to journalists. Only by becoming posthumously familiar with his character can one accurately interpret many of his public statements. And unless one has cooperation from the key players, the people whom Johnnie loved, forget it.

Without the generous and accommodating assistance of his sister, Elma, her husband David and son Roger, all these presumptions would have misfired. Elma's blunt candor and deliberate, meticulous manner were invaluable. Bill Franklin's intimate recollections were equally helpful and candid, and for these I am deeply grateful. Alan Eichler acted as mentor, tireless boon, unrivaled source of contacts, and offered both an extensive collection of Ray material and badly needed encouragement. Mr. Charles Ostergrant's rigorous assistance, both by following this book's line-by-line evolution and offering priceless information on the context and alliances of the era's Cafe Society and night club characters, was, like the man himself, a dream come true.

Don Ovens also proved to be a fount of knowledge and illumination, as did Mitch Miller, Danny Kessler and Bernie Lang. I would like to also thank Dixie Evans of Exotic World and the Copacabana's Arthur Meola, who went out of their way to accommodate me. Others who assisted in minor but thoroughly indispensable ways were LaVern Baker, Christine Chisler, Thelma Carpenter, Toni Carroll, Jim Dawson, Andy Schwartz and the staff at Columbia Records, Peter Guralnick, Jimmy McDonough, Nick Tosches, the incomparable H.D. Hover, George Schlatter, Marilyn Doff, Jimmy Angel, Bob Merlis, Bill Bentley and Greg Geller at Warner Brothers, Seymour & Billie Heller, Greg Langston, Big Jay McNeely, Chris Morris at Billboard, Gloria Pall, Alan Betrock, Arnold Rogers, J. Kevin O'Brian at the United States Department of Justice, Toni Morrison, Hadda Brooks, Renita Lorden, Athena Pope, Sam Butera, Margaret Whiting, Tito Adami, Sylvia Weiner at Roskin & Friedman, Jimmy Scott, Beck Stiener Gordon, Mary Lou Brady, Tina McCarthy, Gordon Stokes, Daniel Whiteside, Candace Callaway, Gary Stokes, Derek

Dickerson, Bud Dain, Rex Reed, Hugh Fordin, Jack Bean, Jane Powell, Chip & Tony Kinman, Kit Rachlis, R.J. Smith. Assistance from staff members at AGVA, AFTRA, The Lincoln Center Library for the Performing Arts, the Academy of Motion Picture Arts & Sciences Margaret Herrick Library, and the Hollywood Musicians Union was also greatly appreciated.

Oregon is untamed country. To the west, a coastline shaped by Pacific storms affords little comfort, while its Eastern deserts and mountains offer even less. Most residents prefer life within the central Willamette Valley, a broad, sheltering swath running from Ashland in the south straight up to where the Columbia River marks Washington's border. A land of low, roving hills and hectic stands of evergreens, cedar, cypress and ash trees, the Valley divides the entire state.

Bristling at the center with a scattershot column of towns and cities that seem like insignificant human annotation on a vast, indecipherable parchment, the

Willamette dominates attempts at civilization. Hemmed by the Coast and Cascade mountain ranges and scored by a network of rivers, much of the Valley still has a remote quality, despite the fact that Polk County, at the northwest end, was one of the first areas developed by settlers. This part of the Willamette is a kaleidoscopic tangle of uneven contours, a course of topographical humps and depressions that manages a lush appearance even in the dead of winter.

Here, Salem, the state's small, undistinguished capital spreads out like a comfortable pygmy edition of Portland. Both cities radiate from the banks of the Willamette River, as if buildings had somehow dragged themselves whole from the nurturing ooze and the streets evolved around them. Polk County borders the Willamette's west bank at Salem, and fifteen miles west of the capitol lies Dallas, an even smaller version of this river-centered configuration.

Dallas lies along the forty-fifth parallel,[1] placing it exactly halfway between the Equator and North Pole—an appropriate point of geographic origin for Johnnie Ray, the untamed song stylist who ignited a pop music furor mid-way between the band crooners' fall and rock idols' ascent. Simply by baring his emotions and following impulsive whim, Johnnie Ray smashed a hole through early 1950s American culture's grey ideological wall, creating a leak that swiftly grew to a torrent.

That the Willamette's Polk County produced Johnnie Ray is on one hand a surprise yet, on the other inevitable. Its citizens are models of Oregon's parochial, smug attitude. Desirous neither of pursuing worldly knowledge or inquiring if such holds any worth, the Oregonian thrives almost solely within the social dimension of his local context. Incongruity was always the hallmark of Johnnie Ray's life, and the Willamette provided it.

One of the area's earliest and most effective European settlers was George Gay, a British seaman born in Gloucestershire in 1796, who jumped ship off the Oregon coast in the early 1800s. Gay drifted inland; not only was the weather milder and trapping better, so too was distance from the coastal ports teeming with ships full of his former countrymen and whatever salty authority they could muster. Gay would have none of that. By 1843, he had constructed the first brick house west of the Rockies, a rudimentary one and a half story building located in a field near Hopewell, near what later became Salem.[2]

By contemporary standards, Gay's home was an extraordinary land-mark. The vision it presented to arriving wagoneers was a mind-twisting shock of recognition and disbelief, and it naturally became the site of much local revelry. He regularly held forth as host to an unlikely combi-nation of trappers, settlers, traders and Indians. The natives, yet to suffer the comforts of Christian conversion, were more than welcome in Gay's home, and he took a series of Indian wives, apparently preferring women of the Chelamis tribe.

Still, Gay's Indian women were a stain upon him in the eyes of many. Among his detractors were the Simkins, a family of English extrac-tion that travelled the punishing track across the plains, coming all the way from Pennsylvania in 1849. Eventually the Gay and Simkins blood commingled, but judgmental shame over "Gay's mating, or mis-mating," as Johnnie's sister Elma wryly put it, would remain for generations.[3]

"Our mother, Hazel, was a Simkins," Elma said. "She was a snob and did not want to admit there was even a trace of Indian blood in the family. If we kids ever brought it up, she'd always say, 'Oh, you cut your finger and it all ran out.'" Years later, one of Johnnie's press agents circu-lated a ludicrous story that his childhood Indian name was 'Little White Cloud,' title of his biggest record hit; at the height of explosive fame, he was queried during an interview as to which tribe he was descended. Johnnie, who had no idea whatsoever, stared down at his gleaming loafers and replied "Blackfoot." It became a press bio staple. Poor Hazel.

Moral issues aside, George Gay's stature as one of the first settlers and Lord of the Brick Castle, an impressive chunk of civilization set out in the middle of a bleak wilderness, overrode the indignity and gossip. His role in establishing the provincial government won him a spot in the his-tory books and eventually merited erection, by the squaw-snubbing Daughters of the American Revolution, of a historical bronze and stone marker at the building's Hopewell site.

Today, no such stone marks the Polk Station birthplace of Gay's great-great-great grandson John Alvin Ray. On January 10, 1927, at a farmhouse just a few miles from Gay's brick building, Elmer and Hazel Ray welcomed their second child, a son. The couple were both natives of the Northern Willamette Valley; Hazel was raised in Dallas and Elmer in nearby Zena. Wed nine years earlier, their first child Elma was born

January 13, 1922 at Spring Valley where Elmer worked for a prosperous local farmer/land baron named Stratton.

Elmer Ray was a typical, hard-laboring son of the Oregon soil whose background remains a mystery even to his own family. "It's devilish trying to track it down," Elma said, "I don't know what bloodlines come from my father's side of the family. Kids in the family have tried genealogy as a hobby, and they always run into blanks when it comes to my father's side of the family. My cousin's daughter says, 'They've got to be criminals; surely they rode with someone like Jesse James and assumed a false identity,' because you get to a certain point and then you can't find anything else."

Elmer returned to the Willamette after serving in the Great War, went to work for Stratton and indulged himself on weekends by playing fiddle with the string bands that entertained at dances regularly held on the Stratton spread. His desire to learn music was intense, a deep-rooted need that manifested itself during childhood. "My father was very young when he decided he wanted to play the violin," Elma said. "He walked miles through the forest to get to where lessons were taught, and after he saved enough money to buy a bicycle, he would ride probably twenty miles for his lessons. And he learned Americana—cowboy songs, mountain folk songs. My father played for dances, in the top of the barn, things like "Turkey In the Straw," the "Virginia Reel," square dances. It was his life."[4]

It was there, up in a hayloft with fiddle and bow in hand, that he first noticed 18-year-old Hazel Simkins. "They met at the neighborhood dance held in Stratton's fruit barn," said Beatrice Henry, Hazel's younger sister. "After they got married, they settled in Spring Valley, because Stratton had built several homes out there for his workers. They lived among those houses and that's where Elma was born. When she was three or four, they moved to Dallas."[5]

Elmer saved enough of his service pay and wages from Stratton to obtain their Polk Station spread, located two and a half miles east of Dallas proper. One hundred and sixty acres producing a diversified crop of cherries, pears, prunes and walnuts, it also featured a large vegetable garden and a small troupe of assorted live stock. At the farm's heart was a rambling ten-room house, copious with windows and porticos, encircled by a covered porch and shaded by a stately cypress tree. To Elma and Johnnie, as they watched Elmer clearing the land and dynamiting stumps from the earth, it seemed that those one hundred and sixty acres were not only the entire world, but theirs alone.

It was here that Johnnie shocked Hazel and Elmer by toddling over to an old pump organ which had stood in the house since long before the family arrived. Completely unprompted, the child worked the pedals and coaxed a melody, perhaps "Rock of Ages," from it. "I can remember him playing," Elma recalled. "He was of a size where he could pump with his feet and pick out things with his fingers, so I'd say he was probably three years old. My folks were astounded."

The children's days at Polk Station were a dreamy reverie, spent climbing the cypress tree, raiding neighboring apple orchards, and chasing after turkeys to hear their strange howling gobble. A favorite pastime was frolicking with Dinah, the Rays' Holstein cow. Johnnie would flop down in the dirt, grab Dinah's tail, plant both feet on her hind flanks and take a ride across the fields. "Let go! Let go!" Elma would shout frantically. "She'll shit!" Apparently charmed from the start, Johnnie never suffered that smothering indignity. It was picture perfect, a life spent roaming the countryside accompanied by a German shepherd mix named, of course, Rover. Elma and Johnnie's earliest feelings there were of complete, unrestricted freedom.

By the time Johnnie was old enough to enter school, a nearby one room affair (which like the farmhouse still stands), the family's store of blessings began to slip away. The swift toxicity of the Great Depression strangled Elmer's ability to make payments on the land. Compelled to move into Dallas, Elmer managed to get a job at a lumber mill. Yet their charmed life style, as far as Elma and Johnnie could see, continued unabated. After the move to town, they grew up unconcerned and largely unmolested by hard times that ravaged families all over the nation.

"Dad was a farmer at heart but after he lost the farm and was driven to the saw mill for a living, we didn't suffer at all," Elma said. "We were much more fortunate than most. My mom was a fabulous cook and we always sat down to a beautiful table of food, and really wanted for nothing. Johnnie and I were probably very typical kids. We didn't get everything we wanted, but what kid does?"

"My folks realized that he had some kind of talent, and an ear, so they sent him to a man who played organ in our church, 'Uncle' Will Caldwell," she dryly recalled. "'Uncle' Will would have liked to have taught Johnnie, but Johnnie was a source of consternation to 'Uncle' Will because if Johnnie heard something once, he could play it. He wouldn't exercise the discipline to learn what 'Uncle' Will wanted him to learn, because it was easier for him to do it by ear. Anyway, 'Uncle' Will did try, and Johnnie did learn."

Although the children dutifully played along with the Sunday routine, it was just that. Elma recalls "Boy! If Johnnie and I could do anything to get out of going to church, we did it." Nonetheless, Johnnie got his first public musical experience there; Uncle Will Caldwell, like the Rays, was affiliated with Dallas's First Christian Church, and the boy was soon tickling ivories in the Lord's house. Beulah Curtiss, the Sunday school primary superintendent recalled, "It always gave me a lift when I would see Johnnie willingly and faithfully open the worship of our class by playing the organ."[6]

About the same time, when Johnnie was five or six, he and Elma (who had girl singer aspirations early on) would appear at local elementary schools; she sang, he played and they performed "pop, only pop music" at these. Johnnie, as he accompanied Elma at the Zena schoolhouse seemed to one student to be "a very solemn little boy."[7] That solemnity was the earliest stirring of an entertainer's chameleon ability. Elma was serious about her singing and Johnnie accordingly played the stone faced accompanist.

Left to his own designs, Johnnie preferred mischief. Dallas native Naomi Brown recalled "One Sunday, his mother Hazel asked me to go from church to their house for dinner. I was 'going' with Johnnie's cousin Earnie who lived with Johnnie's family for a short time. After we had eaten, Johnnie played some little pieces on the piano for me. He was about four and had just started taking lessons. After he played, he climbed up onto a big chair next to me and kissed me on the cheek, then peeked around at Earnie, who acted very upset. Johnnie giggled and kissed my cheek again and told Earnie, 'I kissed your girl—again!'"[8]

His musical gift and natural performing instinct collided with the movies shortly before they left the farm. "When I was about five years old," Johnnie said, "Dad took me in the car one night, into town, to the movie house. Just Dad and me, and we saw 'Murder On the Blackboard.' It was a mystery with Edna May Oliver and I remember that so well—it was just like somebody hit me over the head with a baseball bat, I thought

'That's what I want to do with my life.' I saw all this going on, up on that screen and that's what I wanted to do. So from about five years of age on, I knew what I'd do with the rest of my life. I've been living with it all my life, just waiting for something to happen."[9]

One of Johnnie's closest boyhood friends in Dallas was Jim Low, who "moved to Dallas about the same time they moved in from the country, so of course we grew up together, played ball together, had rubber gun fights, and so on. He lived on one end of Hayter Street and we lived on the other.[10]

"That son of a gun could play the heck out of a piano, he really could." Low continued, "When he took lessons from that teacher, who was strictly classical, the guy used to go bonkers when John would start jazzing it up, and Johnnie used to love to drive the guy crazy. He used to drive my father crazy, because we had a piano at our house and he'd come over and just pound it out, for hell, oh, an hour, an hour and a half. My dad would just leave the house."

Johnnie was a well known prankster. Once he, Elma and one of her girlfriends from school went to the Majestic Theater and saw James Whale's "Frankenstein." The film terrified Elma, or at least she claimed that as grounds to persuade an older boy to walk them home. Johnnie ran ahead, hid behind a bush, then, howling and mugging, leapt out as the trio passed by. Elma was so surprised she screamed and flung her pocket book into the shrubs. Johnnie was delighted, but to ensure peaceful relations, returned with her the next morning to help collect her scattered property. Johnnie looked to and loved Elma with fervent devotion. From his earliest days she was his reference point and guide, protector and teacher, the most single important figure in his life.

"No one today can imagine what a beautiful life we had, growing up there," Elma emphasizes. "In the summer we'd climb Mount Pisgah two or three times a week, just go up there, build a fire, bury some potatoes, climb a tree and wait for them to cook. It was wonderful."

Two forces always held both power and mystery for Johnnie Ray: nature and music. The geographical mid-line where Dallas stood perhaps enhanced what unknown effects the moon and stars have, stirring the blood, coloring temperament and perception, setting the rhythmic pace of metabolism and emotion; his relationship with nature was lifelong, an innate, almost pagan connection to these forces. Music, too, was in his blood, a deft facility inexplicably natural to him. Johnnie's songwriting, later in life, always drew from and relied upon images of nature.

His father's country fiddle provided a natural mix of both—the simple folk music of the rural West was dominated by nature's influence. From the lyric beauty of "Red River Valley," to topical ballads like "Collin's Cave," the musician's environment and setting shaped his sound and approach as actively as did the catalog of European ballads, dance hall, military song and Church psalms which came to America with the settlers. One of the earliest commercial country recordings made on the West Coast was by Laam's Happy Hayseeds, a family string band from John Day, Oregon, some 400 miles to the east of Dallas,[11] and there were plenty of other hayseeds happily making music all over the state.

Taken with Johnnie's church-related musical efforts, he had a perfect background, gospel and hillbilly, to produce an understanding of music as a form of personal expression. "My basic background in music came from gospel and country & Western," Ray later said. "There was a lot of Western music around Oregon. When I was a kid, I was taken to square dances, where dad used to fiddle. We were well aware of the Roy Acuff things and far out people you wouldn't expect us to hear, like the Maddox Bros. & Rose, Homer & Jethro. I sang in church a bit. Don't know whether you'd call it gospel. It depended on the spirit in which you sang it. After all, you can take "Bringing In The Sheaves," which is basically a hymn, and make a gospel out of it. Basically, it was a combination, a wedding of the two kinds of influences."[12]

This sensibility was heightened all the more by contemporary pop music's seductive charms. Elma was a voracious pop fan who kept the family radio tuned to exotic live broadcasts from the Coconut Grove and innumerable hotels and ballrooms back East. The sounds of Bing Crosby and Russ Columbo added a hint of more sophisticated psychology to the mix on which Johnnie was weaned.

Then Johnnie discovered black music, a riotous cornucopia of jazz, boogie-woogie and blues. And again it was Elma's interest that exposed him to it. "When I go back and think about pop music," Johnnie said, "I always identify Duke Ellington's 'Take the A Train,' as one of the first records I ever recall hearing. It was one of my favorite songs when I was a kid, because Elma, who had a large record collection, brought that home. We had a portable at that time and we used to go out in the timber, into the woods and play records. So I got into Duke Ellington very young, because 'Take the A Train,' was one of her favorites. I wasn't really exposed to a lot of pop music, so I depended an awful lot on what my sister brought home."[13]

Thanks to her, Johnnie grew up a rural swinger. Boogie, already a popular novelty sound in the white pop world, was finally (almost) made respectable at John Hammond's historic 1939 "From Spirituals To Swing" Carnegie Hall concerts, when Kansas City pianist Pete Johnson romped the 88's with blistering agility. Boogie was a natural for Johnnie (who was left-handed anyway), a driving, arousing style that all the local kids dug.

"John would come down to my house, where we had a big old upright piano and he would play the boogie-woogie," said Marciel Shepard, who became friends with Johnnie in their sixth grade class. "It just fascinated me, because I was taking lessons and wasn't very successful, but John sure could play. And he would come down and play boogie-woogie until my mother would have to say 'Johnnie, it's supper time. It's time for you to go home.'"[14]

Betty Woodman, who lived two doors down from the Rays on Hayter Street, remembered Johnnie spending "many hours in his classmates' hay mows, singing to the top of his voice. We could hear him all over the neighborhood."[15] "He'd sing 'Elmer's Tune,' all those pop songs that were big before the war," Marciel Shepard continues, "and he would make up songs at that time, too. He wrote a song for one of our friends, Jane Cryder, entitled 'Jane.' I was a little bit jealous of that. He wasn't looking for special attention from the guys, or for a lot of girlfriends, he was just a good friend, a buddy."[16]

Jim Low, after Elma, was his most trusted friend. "Because we always seemed to understand one another," Low recalled. "We could spend hours sitting under a tree, by the creek down there in the park, and just talk about anything and everything." But theirs was no simple idyll; the Depression threatened everyone.

"They didn't have a hell of a lot of money, when we were kids." Low said, "I was fortunate in that my Dad managed the J.C. Penney store in town, so I always had clothes and stuff like that. John's parents were not that well off, and times were tough for everybody. We'd both go out and pick bushels of prunes for three cents a bushel, or hops, for a penny a pound, and that's a lot of hops to pick for just one penny. They would let school out for summer vacation when the prunes were ready, and we would go back to school when the hops were done—that's the way our school operated. So you might end up having two and a half months off, or even four months."

"In Dallas," Johnnie said, "from the time I was seven until I was twelve or thirteen, every summer I had to go to a farm several miles away and pick hops with other children. Usually we slept and boarded there. It was hot, hard work and I hated it, except for Saturday nights when they'd give me pennies to sing and play. I made up my mind that I wasn't going to be a farmer or laborer. I was going to be a movie star like Clark Gable or Tarzan."[17]

Johnnie often commandeered Hazel's sheets to rig a curtain out in their backyard for an ongoing series of performances, or to use as a movie screen. "He had an old eight millimeter projector, and a strip of film about three feet long of a cartoon, a Betty Boop or something," Jim Low said, "he'd have everybody sitting around, with a goddamn sheet hanging up and he would start this projector and it only lasted about ten seconds, and that was it. Everybody would yell and boo. He would do those things all the time." His original programs ranged from melodramas to musical offerings to hatchet throwing exhibitions, a pursuit more in keeping with the Northwest's rugged lumber-jack image.

Johnnie didn't shy away from rough and tumble pastimes. At the edge of town, Dallas High School's playing field was surrounded by bleachers built upon an existing, and not inconsiderable, grade. The neighborhood children gathered there regularly, and one of their favorite pursuits was coaxing Johnnie to ride his bicycle, arms extended, feet off the pedals, at full tilt down the steep earthen aisle between bleachers and directly into a drinking fountain at the bottom. He would careen momentously, yelling "Look Ma, no hands!" limbs flapping, barely able to maintain his balance, more often than not cartwheeling end over end before smashing into the concrete fountain. He performed this feat as often as interest dictated.

While this may have been a compensatory act of tribute to his peers to make up for his otherwise anomalous interest in music—something only girls like Marciel and Jane seemed to really appreciate—Johnnie's own reckless nature was of a sort that he likely did it alone, without an audience. A natural aesthete, equal parts prodigy and urchin, he grew up careless, wild and unafraid. Johnnie never learned caution.

By the time he started junior high school in Dallas, Johnnie had grown to an angular, slim, hyper-animated boy. A blond wraith with cool blue-grey eyes, careless grin and a contradictory raw-boned yet delicate appearing facial structure, he moved through Dallas like a musical flame. "At parties, Johnnie was always sittin' down at the piano, he loved to do that," Jim Low said. "And of course any kids that could play piano or guitar were the ones you had to your parties, so they could help entertain. He loved to play, and sing too. When he started playing boogie-woogie on the piano, it was great, very enjoyable."

"Johnnie was born smiling. He had the charm in the family," Elma said. "Everybody liked him, females of all ages, from the youngest to the oldest." Between soda counter dates and time spent grinding out boogies at the piano, Johnnie gorged himself on show business ephemera. He studied at the movie house and at the Dallas library, where he was such a regular visitor that librarian Hulda Smith became a friend for life. Johnnie kept tabs on Hulda, visiting at the retirement home where she spent her last days whenever he returned to the area.[18]

"Show business was his obsession, all the time," Elma explained. "There wasn't a time in his life when he wasn't pursuing musical interests. It was his single interest in life for as far back as I could remember, and the obsession always showed itself in one way or another."

By 1940, Johnnie felt as if he was just marking time, that childhood itself was of secondary importance, an unavoidable delay. Life up to that point was merely a series of experiments and rehearsals. He had no doubt as to his goal, describing it as "a burning ambition to be in the business, which is strange in itself, given my environment. But it was something like a calling. I had to become what I had to become."[19] Beyond the church, school room, and his backyard theatrics there was little opportunity to pursue the business. He waited.

Unconventional as he was even then, Johnnie was well liked in Dallas. The small town is pre-disposed to accept eccentricity if it comes from one of their own, and Johnnie tested the limits. "He didn't pay much attention to the way he was dressed. He had other things on his mind. Once he showed up at a high school dance wearing an old fuzzy sweater with great big holes in the elbows, and one of the girls took him aside and told him that he'd have to go home and change his clothes," recalled Jim "Snuffy" Smith, a schoolmate, "but he just didn't care."[20]

At another school dance, Johnnie appeared with a startling new look. "He showed up at a Rainbow Girls dance, and he had dyed his hair green—I mean GREEN," said Jim Low. "And everybody there was saying 'Jesus Christ, John, what have you done?' It was just a crazy goddamn thing, it wasn't for Christmas or for any reason you could figure. He got an inclination to dye his hair green. As a matter of fact, I believe he used food coloring to do it, because his hair was blond anyway, very light, and it was bright, bright green. Oh, it was crazy, but like Snuff said, he would just do those things. Quirks. Crazy things."

It was for the girls. Low recalls the green hair episode as leverage used to beat him out of a date with Jane Cryder that night, a peacock maneuver which surprisingly worked to his advantage. "We used to fight like dogs over Jane Cryder,"[21] Johnnie said. Low, beaten, fled the dance in disgust and drowned his teenage sorrows in orange gin. Another crush was Rosalie Johnson, whom Johnnie took out for a roller skate date at the Armory building. "I was twelve or thirteen and I promptly fell in love. I never saw poor Rosalie again—but I did get to kiss her goodnight."[22] Johnnie dated both Jane and Marciel with ritualistic enthusiasm, responding in kind to Elma's own growing parade of suitors. He looked to her for every aspect of life.

In the summer of 1940, Dallas was site of a Boy Scout Jamboree, with troops from all over the Pacific Northwest flooding into the area, setting up their tents in a field behind the Dallas City Park. Thirteen-year-old Johnnie, himself a Scout, wandered through a sea of boys, digging the clamor. His own troop, including Snuffy Smith and Jim Low, were organizing a blanket toss.

"Not far from the old swimming hole," Snuffy recalled, "a bunch of us scouts were taking turns tossing each other up in the air by using a half a canvas pup tent, the scouts holding it around the edges in a circle. Johnnie came up there, I don't think he was even a scout at the time, but we got to throwing him up in the air on one of those tents. We must have tossed him too high, he was up about ten or twelve feet, and when he came down he almost missed the canvas and we lost our grip and he fell into the dry grass."

He landed hard, slamming the side of his head onto the ground, running a dry straw into his left ear. It severely traumatized the ear canal and punctured the ear drum membrane. Johnnie suffered a concussion and immediately lost fifty percent of his hearing. "It was a hard fall, and when he hit the ground, he was pretty shaken up," Snuffy continues, "I remember that he held his head, held his ear on that side."

"When it was Johnnie's turn in the blanket, some kids let go of their corner and he landed on his head," Jim Low remembered. "It was pretty serious, he obviously had a concussion, but nobody was concerned about it." There was no blood, no first aid was sought; Johnnie, disoriented senses churning vertigo, his equilibrium struggling to find a center, managed to pick himself up and walk away.

Johnnie was not at all sure just what was wrong, the degree of the problem, or whether he should even mention it to his parents. The natural instinct to avoid dissension and trouble within the family, and a child's faith in his own indestructible nature—which he had certainly tested many times before— led him to conclude that this accident should not be publicized. No one was aware of the fall except the boys who had witnessed it.

Scared by the inexplicable change in his perception, bitter over being slammed into the dirt and never really sure whether someone had accidentally-on-purpose let go of the canvas, Johnnie waited to see if he would return to normal. Half-convinced that it was a temporary condition, the shock of impact, Johnnie retreated into patient silence. He waited. And waited.

There was to be no recovery. The ear is an intricate construction whose operation hinges on the eardrum membrane itself. When sound waves hit the membrane, located mid-way between the ear canal and the middle ear, vibrations are transmitted into the inner ear's cochlear duct where a techtoral membrane vibrates against minuscule hair cells. These hair cells' movements are converted into nerve impulses which travel to the brain. The trauma to Johnnie's ear canal, drum, cochlea and stapes was severe, and damaged the delicate physical apparatus so badly that the vestibulocochlear nerve, which conducts aural information to the brain, received nothing it was able to comprehend or translate into recognizable patterns.[1]

"He told me he didn't even realize it was his hearing," said Bill Franklin, who later lived with and managed Johnnie for almost ten years. "It was just like BONK! and the whole world was different. And even when he started thinking 'maybe there is something wrong with my head,' as he put it, he didn't say anything to people because he wanted to be like them. He didn't want to be, as he said, 'a weird kid.'"[2]

"There was a definite change in John after that accident," Jim Low said. "He wasn't as much of an extrovert as he was before, he became much more the introvert, he really did. Because we were always close friends, I can say there was a definite change in him. After that incident, from then on, John was sort of, well, he spent a lot of time with himself and his music. When it came to his music, he wasn't the introvert—he always took the front, always promoted himself. Any kind of music and he was right there, all the way through."

Still untreated when school resumed that fall, Johnnie realized it was a bigger problem than he wanted to admit. He could not hear most of what the teachers said in class, and his grades, which had always been fair, degenerated rapidly. More and more confused by the murky rumbling signals that his brain could not decipher, he drifted farther and farther away from every aspect of life in Dallas. Once a celebrated local wise guy, he now became the town odd ball.

Suffering from the "hey, fellas wait for me" syndrome was nothing compared to this. "That period made things even worse. When I couldn't understand my teachers, I landed at the bottom of my class. So, I was the dumb bunny of the crowd, who was left out of play periods because everyone got tired of hollering at me," he told an interviewer years later, "I was a mighty sad and lonely boy who needed something to keep me going, to make me feel adjusted to the narrow little world into which I had been shoved."[3]

Nonetheless, he never spoke of this to anyone, not Elma, Jim, his parents, Jane, Marciel. No one else was told because Johnnie himself was incapable of understanding why this had happened.

"My folks didn't realize it at first, and neither did I or anyone else," Elma said. "And he was having a terrible time at school, until his teachers began to ask 'well, is he retarded or just plain dumb?'" Weeks stretched into months, and Johnnie withdrew even further into himself, accepting his new role as "the loneliest boy in the world."[4]

Forced introspection compounded the problem. When he failed to hear a remark made to him, it appeared he was ignoring the speaker. This was marked up to teen age pre-occupation or simple bad manners. Many people quit trying to talk to him altogether. Johnnie thought he was being ignored.

These were the conditions under which Johnnie went through puberty. A confusing and strange enough period in life even under normal circumstances, Johnnie experienced it without any social reference points, from peers or otherwise. A difficult and potentially devastating combination of misfortune for an individual's self-image and emerging sexuality, he left childhood behind as an enigma, misunderstood by everyone he knew, on every conceivable level of inter-action. Strange, dark days for Johnnie. He was probably unaware of when his voice changed.

This adolescent half-life was the Cry Guy's origin, a tortuous season of pain, mystery and deepening alienation which Johnnie was unable to recognize and release until years later as a public figure, steeped in terrible loneliness and isolation, who wrenched out and battled his worst fears and weaknesses. The accident was the first substantive blow landed against what had been a charmed life, and the result was a strand of neurotic unhappiness.

"When I was a kid and started to lose my hearing," Johnnie said, "I would sort of seclude myself from people. I used to go for long walks, take my dog with me and we'd go walking down in the park, where the swimming hole was, we'd walk out in the woods, out around the mountains and creeks and backroads . . . and I was alone an awful lot.

"I don't think 'lonely' is quite the correct word, but I was extremely aware of isolation at a very young age, and so therefore, being from a very happy, emotional, loving, giving family, you learned to love very openly, and learned to give, and to think about the things around you. And I don't think that, as a kid, I would've developed into thinking as sensitively or emotionally as I do now, as a man, if it hadn't been for that." This was an admission of rare candor.[5]

Judging from the way he always lied about his hearing loss in later years, Johnnie apparently never completely reconciled himself to his misfortune. He spun outrageous fabrications to journalists, claiming that after the accident his condition went undiagnosed for five years, and later changed the story entirely, claiming there was no accident involved, that it was a congenital problem which had manifested itself much earlier in life, and that he had been under medical care for it from early childhood. Even with intimates, decades later, he rarely gave a consistent accounting. As Johnnie presented himself to the world, the only solid fact was that he had wandered alone, "feeling very sad inside."

"He was poorly understood, probably totally misunderstood," Elma said. "Even after they put him right up in the front of the classroom, he still had a terrible time." Almost a full year later, it finally struck Hazel and Elmer that something was wrong. "We didn't realize that he was hard of hearing until he started snuggling up to the radio. Johnnie would curl up on the rug and put his ear right next to the speaker," his sister said. "We noticed that and it finally dawned on us, 'the kid can't hear!'"

"It put a limit on a lot of things that Johnnie would have liked to have done," Elma reflected, "and he became more introverted than most, which was completely foreign to his nature. The loss of hearing changed things for him in a way that you or I could not imagine. There were times when I thought I really didn't know or understand his pain."

At this point an exasperated teacher told the Rays to send him to a school for the deaf, and the family immediately brought Johnnie to a doctor. "A teacher suggested I be sent to a school for the Deaf and Dumb— that's what he actually said to my parents," Johnnie said. Such a possibility terrified him. "Those were imperative years for my emotional development. I'm still too sensitive for my own good. That's me and I can't change it."[6] Even after treatment began, progress was agonizingly slow. "The doctor tried to help Johnnie with some sort of therapy where he forced the eustachian tube open with air, or water," Elma continues. "They tried to keep it open, but it always collapsed again."

Inadvertently, his parents contributed to Johnnie's sense of isolation. "Whenever my folks wanted to exchange a piece of gossip, they would lower their voices to a whisper, but Johnnie could see their lips moving and he'd get really angry and yell 'Now cut that out!'" With his own family appearing to take advantage of his condition, the psychic bruises Johnnie suffered were ugly.

But there was a saving grace, the factor that helped him "adjust to the narrow world into which he had been shoved," and that was radio. Radio and the records which Elma collected. At the time she was dating a local trumpeter, "a powerful musician" with whom she occasionally sang at club dates and was soon to marry. Johnnie was already familiar with Duke Ellington, Count Basie, Jimmy Lunceford and now tuned into hepwise whites like Bunny Berrigan, Gene Krupa and Anita O'Day. It was the era of Krupa's million-selling hits "Let Me Off Uptown," "Thanks For the Boogie Ride," and of Johnny Mercer's "Blues In The Night," some of the earliest incorporation of black musical style into mainstream white pop music. Johnnie was enraptured—and nurtured—by it.

In the fall of 1941, Johnnie got his first hearing aid, a heavy battery-operated piece of crude audio equipment that not only looked weird, when the earpiece was not properly connected, it squawked with feedback, an unfamiliar phenomenon that seemed straight out of Buck Rogers and Flash Gordon. The schoolyard teasing which the awkward gadget brought him paled to insignificance beside the joy of his renewed ability to hear. "Johnnie told me he was so moved when he got his hearing aid," Bill Franklin said. "He thought 'Wow! This is it—I've got the world back!'."[7]

"When he got his hearing aid," Elma said, "boy, he'd turn that thing up full blast so he wouldn't miss a thing. He'd be snooping around, listening to everybody's conversations." The hearing aid became such a natural part of Johnnie that Jim Low can not even recall when he was first fitted out with one. When the rains came shortly afterward, Johnnie was thrilled by the sound of it. "We were all deeply touched when he heard the rain on the roof, because he hadn't heard that in a long time. That really did something to our sensitivities. See, we just didn't realize what all he had missed," she explained. "And we all cried."

*   *   *

"There came a war," Elma said with typically dry Ray understatement, "and we moved to Portland for the defense work." Or as Johnnie described it, "We were all hustled off to Portland, where I lied about my age and became a welder in the shipyards, working with my father." It was a distinct turn for the better; Johnnie only labored at Uncle Sam's forge in the summertime, and Portland had radio stations, theaters, nightclubs, beer joints, burley houses and dance halls. It was exactly what he needed.

He was fortunate, too, in that the Lows also followed. "We moved to Portland about the same time. He lived on South East 48th and we lived on North East 39th. We went to different high schools, but we would still get together from time to time," said Jim Low. "And he was writing music of his own at the time, I mean, it was some pretty good stuff, but who the hell am I to say?" Johnnie did everything he could to be heard: "On one occasion he needed twenty-five dollars to have a publisher look at some of his music," said Low, "and he played a couple of songs for me that day, and asked if he could borrow the twenty-five dollars from me, but I had to tell him, 'John I don't have that kind of money.'"

Johnnie attended Franklin High school ("I was a lone wolf there," he said)[8] and began at last to seriously develop his primary goal, show business. His ambition to be an actor, fired by "Murder At The Blackboard" almost ten years earlier, was further encouraged with appearances in high school plays (he was an elderberry wine victim in "Arsenic & Old Lace" and in "The Night Of January 16," an Ayn Rand melodrama, he portrayed a district attorney).[9] Performing before a live audience was even more fulfilling than he dreamt.

But it was in music that he excelled, and Johnnie wasted no time in becoming involved with the Starlight Club, a community organization that sponsored youth dances every weekend at the Y.M.C.A., where he entertained and hawked war bonds. In short order, he became a regular on "Uncle Nate's Stars Of Tomorrow," Portland's answer to Major Bowes for the junior set. Soon he enjoyed a wide range of settings in which to perform and hone his craft, from dances held at the "Y" (he was subsequently elected President of the Starlight Club) to a variety of department stores and car lots where Uncle Nate held forth, making promotional appearances for the program's sponsors.

Performing gratified Johnnie immensely, and the bleak silent year he suffered in Dallas instilled a powerful ability to express himself in song, to express himself well, with a depth of emotion that previously had been inconceivable. Once Johnnie got his first taste of cosmopolitan applause in Portland, he was hooked.

The accident that damaged his hearing had no effect on his musical ear. It did not diminish his ability or instinct in the slightest. In that sense, Elma "considered Johnnie phenomenal. I have been walking down the street with him and he'd say, 'I hear things . . . how does this sound?' and then he'd hum something for me. I don't know where that came from, it seemed to spring from some Artesian well in his consciousness. But I've never forgotten that, when he said 'I hear things.'"

Her record collection inspired him even further. Despite wartime shortages of shellac, she and her husband got hold of what notable new releases there were, and in 1944, provided Johnnie with an epiphany. "Billie Holiday had just recorded 'Lover Man,' and 'That Old Devil Called Love,'" he later said. "My sister had it laying around the house, and I happened to run across it and played it. At first I kind of cocked my head and thought 'what is she saying?' Played it again, and it was like being possessed by something. I became a Billie Holiday fan, and started collecting all her records . . . Jazz came into it then."[10]

"He felt a real kinship with Billie Holiday and her style," Elma explained, "and he did love Kay Starr, and I'm sure they were an influence in that Johnnie thought 'I want to do what they're doing.' Johnnie always seemed to have his own particular purposes and they didn't seem to hinge on anybody else's endeavors. He didn't pattern himself after anyone."

The Stars Of Tomorrow was an important first step, with each successive broadcast, his smoky, gentle readings of pop standards matured. Also, The Starlight Club was inevitably affiliated with every war bond stumping star that came through Portland. "Every time a celebrity would come to Portland to sell war bonds," he said[11], "we would play on the show, so I got experience that way." It exposed Johnnie to real name talent, like Sophie Tucker, who, when asked by young Johnnie what her advice would be to an aspiring talent such as himself, replied, "If you want to make it in show business, kid, get the hell out of Portland."[12]

That struck a chord. Johnnie never questioned, wondered at or faltered in his pursuit of stardom, a fantasy which seemed to him the preordained conclusion of what had begun at the dusty keys of the pump organ back at Polk Station. "I had to become what I had to become," he said, "and it never occurred to me that given the chance, I would not succeed."[13] Every step forward in his by then consciously developing interpretive style was matched with a commensurate upswing in musical activity.

Another vital aspect of what Johnnie was bound to become, an aggressive drinker, had already entered his life. Elma and Johnnie were first introduced to booze by a father and son team of Polk station moonshiners, and the siblings explored alcohol use with all the pioneering spirit they used when scaling Mount Pisgah. "He probably started drinking, hell, it had to have been around '41 or '42," Jim Low said. "We used to always drink beer, as much as we could get. One time, around 1944, my brother and I were flying back from Seattle, where we had gone to a wedding, and Elma was on the same plane with us. Then we all met Johnnie in Portland, when we got back and went out and got drunker than hell that night. That was the last time I saw him in Oregon, because I had joined the Navy, and John couldn't join the service, of course, because of his 4-F classification. I'll never forget when John threw up his booze in Laurel Hurst Park. He was sick."

Sick, hell. He was rehearsing.

Immediately upon graduating from high school, Johnnie, after nosing around the fringes of the Portland theater crowd, got his first professional job. He was hired to sing "Look For The Silver Lining," in a production number at Portland's Four Star Theater, a burlesque house, home to shake dancers, peelers, rum-dum comics and seedy musicians.

Johnnie lied to his parents about the job, a two-week engagement, and Elma convincingly backed him up, saying he was at a Starlight Club event, or dinner at a friend's, anything to keep Hazel from discovering that he was sharing a stage with strippers and hard drinking vaudevillians. Hazel had decided that her son ought to become either a minister or baseball player, and would have been devastated if she knew where he really

was. The Four Star was Johnnie's first taste of greasepaint and curtain call
and he gorged on it. As he described it, "I was the kid they goosed to get
laughs."14

His next engagement came at "a crummy after hours joint in
Portland," Elma said. A second floor gin mill filled with defense workers
from the swing and graveyard shifts; the fact that he was underage made
little difference. It was an illegal operation that had the tacit patriotic
approval of local police. "It was dark and rather dingy," she recalled, "and
he'd just sit there at the piano and sing whatever they wanted to hear." A
true proving ground for Johnnie, having already developed a taste for
liquor, he now began to adapt to nocturnal life.

Attempts at other forms of gainful employment proved as disastrous
as his show business calling was intense. After the war ended and defense
work wound down, the Rays re-located to Salem. Elmer took a job as mill-
wright at the Oregon Pulp and Paper Mill, a huge, steam-belching, tree-
shattering operation perched atop the bank of the Willamette River on
downtown's Front Street.

Shortly after starting there, Elmer managed to get Johnnie work as
relief man on the night shift. "He did a lot of little things around the mill,
cleaning up, things like that. He wasn't very experienced," explained Dean
Knupp, a co-worker of Johnnie's. "And we became friends. I didn't know
a lot about him, except that he was a friendly guy and that he was goin'
into Portland every weekend for talent shows and stuff."15

One night Johnnie relieved the signal man, who worked at the slip,
a long steel chute running down to a slew on the Willamette. "We saw the
guy runnin' the donkey, ole Ed Petersen, standin' there scratchin' his head
and grinnin'" Knupp recalled. "Apparently Johnnie had lost his balance,
gone right into that slip and down into the river. Ed said all he heard was
kind of long 'eeeeeaahh,' and then they were fishin' him out. That slip was
pretty steep and he must've been goin' some miles an hour—he was lucky
there wasn't a log in the slip or he'd have hit that, instead of the river."

The terror Johnnie experienced apparently matched the degree of
luck he was graced with, and he came even closer to accidental death a
week or two later. "Johnnie was a little clumsy," Knupp continues, "and
somehow or other, one night he slipped into a conveyor that carried all the
heavy junk—sawdust and bark—up to another conveyor, which dumped
into another conveyor. He was knocked unconscious and got carried along

clear up to the point where he was just a hundred feet or so away from getting dumped into the hog, which would just chop you up so fast there'd be absolutely nothin' left, but the guy tending that saw him coming, rang the bell and shut it down. It was right after that they said, 'Hey, we better get this guy something else to do, and put him on the day shift.'"

Nearly every weekend throughout 1947, he borrowed Elma's car and drove to Portland (an adventure in itself—Johnnie never felt comfortable behind the wheel and later quit driving altogether, unless he was drunk), either to work what sporadic jobs he was able to book for himself or to see and meet name entertainers appearing in the city. When it was announced that Kay Starr was appearing, Johnnie was outside the theater hours before anyone even arrived to open the box office. "I remember when I first heard Kay Starr," he said. "It was on a jazz record, very early in her career, and I didn't know who she was. I'd never heard of her before, but there was something about her phrasing that was just magical to me, and she was to become one of the few people who influenced me vocally, as far as phrasing is concerned."[16]

Starr had just began recording for Capitol Records, but was already a familiar stylist through her countless broadcasts with fiddling band leader Joe Venuti. The Oklahoma-born singer laid a gleaming jazz varnish onto a lyric with an undertone of purring vibrato, and her coolly driving approach to rhythm numbers enthralled Johnnie. Hours later, when he was ushered, completely tongue-tied, into her dressing room, Starr was struck by his wraithlike appearance. "He was so slender, his skin was so pale, and with that fine blond hair he looked almost like a ghost."

He somehow managed (Johnnie remained in awe of Starr for the rest of his days) to tell her of his ambitions and explained how his parents, Hazel especially, were unsure that a show business career suited him. Johnnie finally relaxed enough to sing for Starr, and she told him, "With a God given talent like yours, it would be a sin not to pursue show business." That was all he needed to hear.[17]

For the remainder of his days in Salem, Johnnie was restless and uncomfortable. Even after his twenty-first birthday, his family remained a tribal unit which thrived on each other's support and mutual regard. "They were a very affectionate family," said Dean Knupp, "and they demonstrated it quite openly." Knupp had met Hazel, Elmer and Elma when Johnnie invited him to accompany them on a weekend fishing trip on the Oregon coast.[1]

It became increasingly clear to his parents that Johnnie was not long for the Willamette Valley. Despite the routine catalog of white lies and deceptions that exist in any family, the Rays were, as Johnnie said, "A very close-knit, very affectionate family. We were touchers, huggers and kissers, stuff like that. My family was like that and I'm very much like that. It gets misunderstood a lot, because if I like somebody, I don't hesitate to tell them, whereas, on the other hand, if I don't like someone, I generally keep my mouth shut. I take after my dad like that, he was sort of the Gary Cooper type, tall and lean and strong and he didn't have a heck of a lot to say. But when he spoke, he spoke. The rest of the time it was all silence. But he sure loved a lot."[2] Elma concurred. "My father didn't talk much. He was the most self-contained man that I have ever known. I didn't know him that well, but he was a wonderful man."

"Hazel was a very domineering woman," said Jim Low. "She totally dominated that family from what I remember. And Elmer was just a guy whose attitude was like 'Well, if it rains today, so what? I'll pull the weeds in the garden tomorrow.' I got to know Hazel and Elmer much better in later years, but she always was a very, very strong-willed woman, I'll tell you, and Elmer was just the opposite, he was a very easy-going guy, Salt of the Earth."

This family structure—pairing a strong-willed, dominant mother with a quiescent, soft-spoken father, from a working class, deeply religious background, with little money to spare—is one common to several of America's greatest pop music stars. It's the same basic framework, albeit played out in entirely different social settings, which produced Frank Sinatra, Hank Williams and Elvis Presley.

An exceptional family factor was Johnnie and Elma's relationship, an extraordinarily close bond whose ongoing inter-action strengthened and elaborated the natural creative process Johnnie was bound up in. Elma, by example, constructed the basis of Johnnie's female ideal. Throughout his life, Johnnie was drawn to women who, like his sister, were free-spirited, intelligent, out-spoken and free-pouring drinkers.

"It became crystal clear to my mother that I was not going to become a baseball player," Johnnie recalled. "That's what she wanted, she wanted me to be a lefty pitcher, but I didn't have any big eyes toward that. Football was my sport, but I couldn't play because of the hearing aid, and baseball left me a little bit disenchanted. But when I was growing up, I knew what I wanted to do with my life, and that meant leaving home and coming to Los Angeles."[3]

Although Hazel's dream of her son becoming either a minister or ball player was persistent, "Johnnie could pretty much twist Mama around his little finger," Elma said, "I think she would have been happier with the idea that he didn't work in some dirty little night club where they sold booze. Mama was very domineering, and if she could have called it, she would have kept him in her little world, tied by the apron strings.

"But Johnnie was not so constructed and show business had been his single ambition for as long as I recall Johnnie," she continued, "He was of such a single-purposedness that he couldn't do anything else. He'd had other jobs and was a total flop. He had to entertain. And when offers came, I remember my father saying 'Do it. If that's what you want to do, do it. Go as far as you can go, and if when you get there you don't have the money to get home, I'll help you.' When I heard my father say that it was very touching. It was the stamp of approval and moral boost that Johnnie needed." It was also a radical break from the family's established division of power. When Elmer recognized Johnnie's needs he spoke out, essentially for the first time, against Hazel.

Shortly after his twenty-second birthday, Johnnie boarded a Greyhound bus for Los Angeles. A couple of friends from his Starlight Club days, Carl Schmidt and Kenneth Johnson, had already moved to the city and provided him with enough of a sense of the familiar to ease his country boy anxiety.[4] Once in Hollywood, Johnnie made the *de rigueur* rounds of agencies and studios, sneaking onto movie lots, going from nightclub to nightclub, waiting for the big break.

Johnnie's goal was to get legitimate representation, and he sought out the top agencies. At MCA, a prestigious outfit who booked Sinatra and most of the remaining big bands, they "couldn't see him at all." His call at the William Morris office was more encouraging. Morris talent broker Dave Scher auditioned Johnnie, was impressed enough to try to get the office brass to listen, but was unsuccessful. Johnnie realized that booking himself was the only way to get work.[5]

His first job came at a Beverly Boulevard nightspot, playing piano for $7.50 a night. Decent money, but the gig was short-lived. Johnnie, like hundreds of other would be entertainers, sat down at any piano he wouldn't be chased off of, and begged to be allowed to play for tips in a series of attempted auditions at a variety of joints. He found himself part of an endless tournament of marginal talents, all jockeying for position in a search for recognition— "discovery." He finally found out about an opening on a bill at a joint in South Central Los Angeles, the Yacht Club, and managed to land the job.

"Johnnie used to work at the Yacht Club down there on Western Avenue, at Florence," recalled honking R&B saxophonist Big Jay McNeely. "It was a mostly white neighborhood. I remember we were the second black family to move into that area. The whole community was much different then."[6] (It was three blocks west and forty-two years later that the Los Angeles riots of 1992 exploded.)

"It was run by a couple of older Jewish guys, and they used all kinds of entertainers: comics, singers, burlesque artists—strip dancers, both black and white. The comedian was black and they had thousands of girls, black and white, coming through there," McNeely said. "The Yacht Club is where Johnnie Ray got his start. He was a regular there."

Dixie Evans, a stripper who later parlayed a resemblance to Marilyn Monroe into a successful burlesque career, worked at Hollywood's Mayflower Waffle and Donut Shop. She recalled, "A bunch of kids I worked with were all saying, 'Oh, there's this great guy working at a nightclub on Western Avenue, let's go down and see him.' It was a popular club way out on Western. By the time we got off work and got down there it was already around nine o'clock, and I remember seeing his name on the bill, like a lobby card, that they had out front. When we got to the club it was so crowded that we didn't even get a seat at a table. Johnnie Ray was all the rage when he played there."[7]

Whatever degree enthusiasm reached, Johnnie's acceptance and credibility at the Yacht Club hinged (as far as the management was concerned) on a "knock about" comic duo from the Midwest who worked the shrinking *vaude* circuit and at nightclubs all over the country, Jan Grayton and Bob Mitchell. Something sparked among the three as soon as they met. The showfolk incorporated Johnnie into their act, and into their Hollywood bed.

There were two exceptional aspects to this booking: Johnnie was paid $40.00 a week, his best pay rate so far, and Grayton and Mitchell's intense interest, verging on fascination, with this unusual waif-like creature. Johnnie became intimate with both; so intimate, in fact, that he would later say "Jan and I were practically engaged at the time."[8] They worked up special material, using Johnnie as accompanist and straight man, and he was also featured in his own brief set, appearing between more established acts.

After Grayton & Mitchell moved on to other bookings along the West Coast's "burlesque wheel," Johnnie's welcome at the Yacht Club wore out. Falling back on his soda jerk experience, he was soon dispensing shakes and sundaes, even working as a car hop. But the law of gravity was never kind to Johnnie, and as at the saw mill, it conspired against his temporary career choice. Next, he worked as bell boy. He hated all of it.

Free from the stultifying small town atmosphere he was raised in, Johnnie's awkward sexuality developed over the course of his stay in Hollywood. Beyond the platonic school girl steadies and brushes with libidinous Rosie the Riveters who toyed with him in Portland, Johnnie struggled with an increasing awareness of his desires. He tried to ignore them earlier, but in Hollywood, these things made more sense. Starting with Grayton & Mitchell, Johnnie became entangled with a series of men and women, as the ambivalence of his painful adolescence led him to reach out to whatever prospect seemed most desirable.

"There were women and there were men," Bill Franklin said. "He was a cute little kid with a big dick—he liked to talk about that and people liked to hear about it. He was getting a lot of invitations and going in a lot of different directions. Years later in Vegas, a press agent named Phyliss something or other turned up. She was really good to Johnnie and he told me that she used to give him a lot of blow jobs in the early days in L.A. People like that kept popping up. Johnnie actually continued to be bisexual, I think, all his life, except the percentages kept changing."

This was Hollywood, and Johnnie loved every minute of it, despite the fact that he was soon near broke. Coffee and donuts became a daily ritual, if he had 15 cents, at Coffee Dan's on Sunset Boulevard, followed by hot dogs at stand up joints or whatever cheap specials were offered in the cafes he and countless like-minded others drifted past while out searching for a gig. Johnnie sneaked onto the 20th Century Fox lot, where "Father was a Fullback," with Maureen O'Hara and Fred MacMurray was shooting on an exterior set, and managed to hang around only because the scene used college boy extras; later, his press agents claimed that he worked one day as an extra on "A Place In The Sun," but Johnnie never mentioned this to anyone.[11]

When he had money, he would gladly pay the weeknight $1.50 cover at Ciro's, and hang around for hours watching the show, watching the crowd, hunting for a break.[9] He strolled along Wilshire Boulevard, gazing at the fabled Coconut Grove, which seemed to erupt out of the dignified Ambassador Hotel edifice. It was a scented garden of glamour and passion and success; that's where Crosby made it, where Rudy Vallee reigned triumphant. The marquee announced Tony Martin.[10] Johnnie wondered how his name would look up there.

At twenty-two, Johnnie was a striking figure. A lush head of thick dark blond hair that tended toward the shaggy was parted on the side and combed back to frame a face that was rough and angular, with prominent ears and nose. Yet there was an almost incongruous softness and delicacy in the structure of his eyes, cheeks, lips and jawline.

Energetic and lithe, Johnnie was a creature of gentle but deep emotion, an androgynous mix of ragamuffin country boy and torch-singing gamin. His speech was soft yet husky, an unmistakable speaking voice which remained entirely unaffected by his hearing loss. Johnnie was always the first to laugh at a joke and even faster to cry in the movies; even "Ma Perkins," a fifteen-minute radio soap opera, could move him to tears. His hearing aid set him apart from the troop of show biz hopefuls, but it was no advantage.

Soon, his savings dwindled and he walked the boulevards with cardboard stuffed in his shoes to plug the holes. It started to grind him down. Despite his innate confidence, Johnnie didn't know what he had in himself. "I wasn't setting out to be a singer, I wanted to be an actor," he said in 1989, "but the only way I could stay in show business was to sing and play the piano. I wasn't handsome—I knew I wasn't going to be getting any leading man parts, so I did what I had to do to stay in the business, which was sing and play the piano . . . I was just singing in bars, upholstered sewers."[12]

Los Angeles was nothing like Portland; the clubs teemed with hustlers, grifters and shady promoters. When not bought off, law enforcement was aggressive—any L.A.P.D. narc who busted someone of stature, a Woody Herman or Gene Krupa, was automatically promoted to sergeant. Anything could, and did happen, in the clubs.

At Billy Berg's on Vine Street one night, Duke Ellington, lyricist Don George and Nat Cole were listening to Ella Fitzgerald, "when a man came staggering out onstage with a knife protruding from his chest while Fitzgerald was singing. Between the cigar-smoking hoods at a front table, blowing smoke up in her face and the blood spattered on the stage, Ella was getting much the worst of it . . . she stuck it out and finished the set."[13] It was not an easy place for a hayseed like Johnnie to get an even break. At the Yacht Club, just when he started to make a name for himself, he was shown the door. Johnnie needed an inside line, a native guide, coat tails to ride. He missed Grayton & Mitchell. He kept moving.

*　　　*　　　*

Hollywood in the summer of 1949 was an unprecedented musical Eden, lush with explosive new sounds, styles and trends. Palatial spots like Ciro's, Mocambo, the Coconut Grove hosted the biggest names, but in the black clubs on Central Avenue, the Hollywood jazz joints and the okie bars of the San Fernando Valley, American music was undergoing near total transformation.

Rhythm & Blues was, for all intents and purposes, invented in California; Johnny Otis, Big Jay McNeely, Joe Houston were rocking their vehement back-beat-driven sound as hard as they could push; Los Angeles was home base to country music's most sophisticated and brash purveyors, Merle Travis, Tennessee Ernie Ford, Joe Maphis, the Maddox Brothers & Rose, richly idiosyncratic performers who left Nashville behind in an artistic cloud of dust.

Pop music was a rich, overlapping blend of jazz and Tin Pan Alley, elevated by the likes of Les Paul and Mary Ford, Kay Starr, Nat Cole. Black variety artists like Charles Brown, Nellie Lutcher and Hadda Brooks plundered the shadowy borders and back streets of blues, gospel, jazz and novelty, creating a singular pop/R&B hybrid. But jazz was the ruler, and as the big bands went into demise, countless small combos featuring the most driving, experimental players constantly expanded the language and rhythm of the music.

Significantly, all of it converged at one point or another in Los Angeles. One night Ciro's presented steamy chanteuse Peggy Lee, the next, it would be singing cowboy star Eddie Dean, whose oaters were so popular that Dean was featured in his own weekly comic book. The Palomino, North Hollywood's country music showcase, had just opened and almost immediately instituted a regular weekly jazz jam.[14] In the Hollywood clubs, a new breed of black-influenced white performers laid down a bafflingly hip array of new sounds. There was Ricky Jordan, a white cat who romped the 88s like a black man and let rip with frantically emotional ballads. Many on the club scene say he strongly anticipated Johnnie Ray; after Jordan disappeared in 1950, everyone assumed he died. Too, there was Harry "The Hipster" Gibson whose addlepated novelties and viper mad blues piano also foreshadowed Johnnie.

Most important of all these, though, was Frankie Laine, a big white lad with "steel tonsils" who belted out torch blues while stomping his size twelve foot in joints like Billy Berg's, Club Hangover and the Bandbox. Laine was discovered at the Bandbox three years earlier, singing Hoagy Carmichael's macabre blues "Rockin' Chair." Signed to Mercury shortly afterward, he recorded "That's My Desire," a 1931 chestnut which Hadda Brooks had recently revived on Los Angeles R&B indie label Modern and got his first hit. Laine's intense vocal style owed nothing to Crosby, Sinatra or Dick Haymes. Instead he drew from Billy Eckstine, Joe Turner, Jimmy Rushing, and with it Laine had sown the seeds from which an entire new perception and audience would grow.

By early summer, Johnnie had fallen in with an aspiring singer/disk jockey named Eddie Smardan. A magnetic character familiar with the Hollywood rigmarole, Smardan took Johnnie in, fed him, housed him and hipped the anemic-looking boy to the best potential outlets for the potential goldmine he carried with him—his songs. Frankie Laine was the natural first choice to pitch material at. They wasted no time in arranging an audition for Seymour Heller, whose Gebbe, Lutz & Heller agency represented Laine (and Liberace, at the time an in-house regular at Las Vegas' Last Frontier Casino).

Heller's offices were located at 6274 Sunset Boulevard on the southeast corner of Sunset and Vine Street in a small converted house. Gebbe, Lutz & Heller had the ground floor; upstairs was Leon Rene's Exclusive Record Company (which had been cutting R&B hits since 1945 with the likes of Joe Liggins & the Honeydrippers and Johnny Moore's Three Blazers, the trio which introduced Charles Brown; Exclusive also recorded Ricky Jordan). Across the street was Glenn Wallich's Music City and Capitol Records. To the east was the Earl Carroll Theater, radio station

KFWB and Warner Brothers Studio. To the west were the NBC studios, and further along the boulevard, Ciro's and the Mocambo. Just up Vine Street was Billy Berg's, Club Morocco, Columbia's recording studio, and the Bowling Alley Building, Hollywood's answer to the Brill Building. Around the corner, Hollywood Boulevard was bristling with various other jazz, juke and hillbilly joints, among them Club Hangover, where two years earlier, bandleader Red Nichols helped persuade Kay Starr to sign with Capitol.

The streets teemed with musicians, singers, record men, flacks (trade jargon for publicist), song publishers, song sharks and song pluggers. Most of them were like Johnnie—broke. Paper boys had to watch their stacks like hawks, and spent a lot of time chasing down sticky fingered hopefuls who helped themselves. At the corner of Hollywood and Vine was the Mayflower Waffle and Donut Shop. "The song pluggers would come into the Mayflower," Dixie Evans said, "wearing rain coats just loaded with nickels and dimes, and they would plug the heck out of records on the juke box. I heard 'Rose, Rose, I Love You,' and 'Mule Train,' over and over. They really were song pluggers in those days." Laine reigned supreme among "boy singers."

This was the setting, a kaleidoscopic course of hope and failure, faith and despair. Smardan and Johnnie opened the door at 6274 Sunset. "Johnnie came around with his songs to try and get Frankie Laine to record them." Seymour Heller said, "Eddie Smardan brought him in. He was feeding him at the time. We listened but Frank really didn't care for any of them."[15]

Heller's partner, Sam Lutz, kept a small piano in his office, which was directly across from the desk where receptionist Billie Rosenfield worked. "I was running Frankie Laine's fan club, all that junk, and Eddie Smardan brought Johnnie in, they were friends," she said. "Eddie was very good looking, a kind of a brash guy with a very nice voice, he was quite handsome, and after he first brought him in, Johnnie used to come in on his own when everyone had gone to lunch. Sam's office was right across from my desk and when you opened the door there was a piano right there. And Johnnie would come in because it was free use of a piano and I was a good audience. He would sing me all his songs, just for the hell of it, and to get my reaction. I became quite fond of him.

"For him, it was wonderful because he could holler and sing as loud as he wanted since nobody was there. And he was kind of composing as he went along, he would mess around with the lyric, and if I didn't like a particular lyric, why, he would work on that," Billie continued, "I remember him singing 'Mountains In The Moonlight,' and 'Tell The Lady I Said Goodbye.' I don't remember him doing any particularly 'up' numbers - they were all sort of romantic and, it seems to me, very soulful. Johnnie had a very deep nature. His style was not as intense as it was later with 'Cry,' but it was very emotional.

"At that point, it seemed he wasn't trying to be a singer so much as he was concentrating on his writing. He was an awfully nice person, always up, always hopeful. He was just hanging around, trying to plug a song, get discovered, do something. 'Pounding the pavement,' as we used to call it. And when everybody'd come back in from lunch, he would disappear again."[16]

Smardan mentored Johnnie in the ins-and-outs of pavement pounding and some additional, more intimate activity. Neither aspect of his relationship with Eddie Smardan amounted to any significance. Even taboo explorations of the flesh and other worldly pursuits paled beside Johnnie's ambitious aspirations. He kept on doggedly making the rounds and replenishing the slips of cardboard which kept gravel out of his shoes. He ground dozens of them to sodden pulp.

It was difficult to evade frustration. Uncle Nate's Stars of Tomorrow alumnus Jane Powell was already a bona fide movie star, since her debut three years earlier in MGM's "Mexican Hayride," playing exactly the type of role that Johnnie dreamed of, an innocent who broke into song every twenty or so minutes. Faced by her example, he tried not to lose heart. Subsequent jobs at the 49ers at Fifth and Main in Los Angeles and El Sereno's El Capitan Club were short-lived.[17]

By the end of the summer, Smardan threw in the towel and had a friend help move Johnnie into Schmidt and Johnson's Huntington Park apartment. The Oregonians vowed they would not let him accept any job unless it somehow related to show business. "I was starving to death in Los Angeles," he said, "working in night clubs and just trying to keep a job. And I couldn't keep a job, people kept saying 'You're too weird for us,' and they'd fire me on the spot. I sweated out all of 1949 there, and of course, nothing happened. Starved to death, literally—I remember stealing lemons for breakfast once. It was not a pretty year."[18]

Schmidt and Johnson made regular drives to Baja California, and always returned with a trunk load of illegal lobsters. It was a household staple, so much so that "Johnnie could never stand the sight of, let alone eat lobster again for as long as he lived," Elma recalled. That was the least of his worries. Johnnie's deep sense of pre-ordained stardom was getting the bum's rush. He hated himself, and Hollywood, for it.

"On Thanksgiving I was standing in front of Coffee Dan's at Sunset and Vine. I didn't even have the price of a cup of coffee," Johnnie said. "And when I did, it burned me up that it cost a dime."[19] He was at the end of his rope. The notion of a lobster dinner on Christmas was unbearable, and he started hitchhiking back to Oregon. He got as far as San Luis Obispo, a sleepy hick town eighty or so miles north of Los Angeles, "when I suddenly got very hungry, and called my folks, collect," he said. "Dad wired me money for a bus ticket."[20]

Shortly before leaving town in December 1949, Johnnie borrowed his roommates' car for a final meeting with Dave Scher at William Morris. It was fruitless. Johnnie drove it up into the hills of Griffith Park, where he parked and gazed teary eyed over the sprawling city. Brooding over Hollywood's thwart of his mission he loosed a final shot, screaming at the top of his voice, "Just wait! I'll show you! I'm going to come back here as the biggest star this town ever saw!" Then he tucked his tail between his legs and split.[21]

* * *

"He was there for a year, or less," Elma said. "He had tried but he became disenchanted, unsuccessful. So, he came on home and worked around the Portland area as much as he could, catch as catch can. Our folks had moved to Roseburg, Dad had got another job in a saw mill down there, so Johnnie also worked around the clubs in the Roseburg area [about 150 miles south of Salem], I remember one in Medford, and Ashland and on the coast, at Coos Bay. Then he would come home, find another job, then go work that for awhile."

It was a kingsize drag. Portland agent Norman Anderson tried to book him, but failed. He worked at Ernie Paluso's in Eugene, at Portland's

Club Tropics on a bill that included Joan Brandon, a "femme hypnotist" who would, after hours, put Johnnie in a trance state and implant positive messages to give him extra confidence and dispel frustration.[22]

Johnnie was frustrated—artistically, emotionally, sexually. The crummy provincial joints he worked in during this period seemed distressingly familiar, and his performances were as cut-and-dried regulation as the worn banquettes and watered-down cocktails each provided. And Johnnie was downing a lot of them.

More often than not, he found himself alone in a Coos Bay flop at three in the morning. Booze became a loyal pal. When the hearing aid came off, these cheerless rooms became forbidding and full of dread; with a gut full of cheap bourbon and tap beer, he could concentrate on the noises from within and count on them to lull him into sleep. There was plenty to hear.

By now Johnnie was writing more songs than he had at any other time in his life, over 140 by his own later reckoning. After the discouragement of Hollywood, he did not write with the notion that he was attempting to create a pop hit, he did not write material tailored to prevailing styles nor even necessarily for himself. It was more like emotional transcription, an outgrowth of his desperate need to sort through his subconscious mind's messages. In a sense. Johnnie's songwriting was an exorcism of his pubescent isolation. Haunted by the dread silent year when he felt completely cut off from his fellow humans, Johnnie now directed all his bristling, perplexed energy toward the only nurturing, familiar and uncritical force in his life, music. It served him well.

One day in early 1950, he and Elma were visiting at their parents' Roseburg home. Johnnie was depressed about his career that afternoon, particularly over a Portland booking which had fallen through. While Hazel prepared dinner, he excused himself and wandered outside to amble the countryside. Presently he found himself at the nearby Umpquah River. Johnnie lay down on the riverbank. "I just took every idea out of my mind," he said, "and sort of thought 'Lord, you'll have to take over from here. I just don't know what to do next. I guess I'm licked.'" He gazed into the blue expanse of sky and addressed a cloud that drifted overhead. He "heard things." A lyric came into his mind, a melody to his ear and he began scrawling words down even before he got back to the house. "It was all there," he said. "The title, the words, the tune."[23]

"Johnnie went for a walk," Elma recalled, "and he came back in and said 'I went walkin' down by the river and I got a new song. I want to play it for you.' He sat down and played 'The Little White Cloud That Cried,' just like that. What I heard then was almost exactly what I heard on the record."

A contemplation of his painful adolescence, the song was an anthemic summation of Johnnie's experience, drawn both from agonies past and the present struggle to understand his sexuality. "The Little White Cloud That Cried"'s child-like simplicity reflected the country music he was weaned on, imbued with traces of the gospel background which had been his earliest direct musical experience. The lyric is inextricably linked to the countryside, a mode he would return to in virtually every song he wrote, and was not dissimilar to "Look For The Silver Lining," the Jerome Kern song which was the first number he had been paid to sing.

But mixed into this was a world weary grimness and a near mystic sense of destiny that lent the ballad a strange quality, a conflict between hope and desperation that reflected his own unsettled character.

Song writing was Johnnie's only refuge after he returned to Oregon, and became the sole and single context he fit in. Scant refuge though it was, he clung to it.

This metaphoric, fragmented reality took hold of Johnnie in Roseburg. He was close to none save his family; his only other close friend, Jim Low, had disappeared into the Navy and out of his life years earlier. Elma, divorced while Johnnie was in California, re-married and was often unavailable to him. Separated too by his altogether unconventional sexuality, Johnnie's only other reference points were natural forces. The cycles of the moon and turn of the seasons were as significant to (and more closely observed by him) than most of the other trappings, logistics and responses which his life as an entertainer brought him in contact with.

To sing "Little White Cloud" was a relief, his only one, and the song codified and ingrained this almost dissociative way of self-absorbed thinking to Johnnie once and for all.

An essentially simple piece of work whose complexity came through in his performance's depth of expression and emotion, Johnnie had finally nailed it. With "Little White Cloud," he found the voice and artistic persona that not only provided him a basic framework for his entire career, it also turned out to be a voice and stance to which the public responded.

When he learned of an upcoming appearance at the Four Star by Jan Grayton & Bob Mitchell, Johnnie was delighted. He re-united with them in Portland, and both re-affirmed their apparent devotion to him. The trio soon grew closer than they were in Hollywood, and would not be separated. Grayton & Mitchell, with upcoming bookings in Ohio, called their agent, Sid Friedman. He balked, but before the team's Four Star engagement was up, Friedman managed to get Johnnie, a sight unseen property, a two-week engagement in Ashtabula, Ohio, at an unprecedented salary of $150.00 a week.[24]

From there, Johnnie intended to stick it out with his friends, booking themselves, if need be, all the way back to New York, the show biz paradise Johnnie read about in Walter Winchell and Cholly Knickerbocker's columns. He longed to prowl the Brill Building and land a publishing deal, dreamed of performing at the Baby Grand, Barney Josephson's Cafe Society, the Copacabana, Latin Quarter, Paramount Theater. Any trace of doubt was erased from his mind. This would be it.

Overjoyed when Friedman confirmed the date, Johnnie received some last instructions from Jan and Bob on how to travel on the cheap. He felt complete confidence that when he next returned to Oregon, it would be on vastly different terms from those under which he had slunk back from Hollywood.

True to his word, Elmer loaned him $50.00 for bus fare and Johnnie was gone. The two weeks in Ashtabula were another visit to a peripheral show business arena of faux sophistication and hard drinking natives. It was almost enough to make him long for the bright lights of Portland.

Shortly after arriving, the experience withered into a painfully familiar blur of cocktail lounge drear. He talked about it for years afterward. "You think you know about show business?" he would crow whenever a band member waxed lofty, "You? Have YOU ever played two weeks in Ashtabula,

Ohio?"[1] He craved escape. Johnnie reacted by turning inside himself and profoundly altering the way he worked.

He wrenched increasingly physical performances from within himself. Johnnie began breaking out into torrential, wailing cries, an automatic, almost reflexive, musical spasm. He surrendered completely to the music, let its rhythm and mood command him. Once Johnnie tasted the joyous freedom it brought, he could not tame the impulse.

He grew more and more unconventional; each show became an increasingly bold, defiant and startling display of unchecked expression. Johnnie was developing a performing style that had as much to do with breaking the monotonous routine of Ashtabula night club etiquette as it did with his need to exorcise his personal alienation and confusion—balladeer therapy.

Naturally, the club owner told him to knock it the hell off or get out. "I've had more than one boss say, 'Look, kid, you're too weird for this room,' and I'd get fired," he said later. "My work was very physical and demonstrative, it was something unheard of and unseen at that time. It seemed quite natural for me, but it caused me quite a lot of problems because I had difficulty keeping jobs."[2]

He managed to run the two-week course. With what little money he had left—Johnnie routinely drank up most of his salary—he happily rode a bus to Akron and joined Grayton and Mitchell. They were determined to oversee his career, for no more reward then the considerable pleasure which Johnnie's company provided both. Neither ever requested anything more of him, for Johnnie provided them deep mutual satisfaction.

Sid Friedman was hardly encouraged by reports from Ashtabula, but under pressure from Grayton and Mitchell, agreed to let them know if jobs came up. Johnnie's careless self-confidence took a blow. He was almost flat broke, and hopes of working his way to New York seemed slim. He knocked around the city for a couple of weeks, landing an occasional club job, but was almost always fired. On several bookings he worked as part of in-house trios but "I could never get along with the musicians," Johnnie said. "One of them would tell that I wasn't going to make it and I'd blow up. Most of the times when working as a single I'd get fired for being too radical or noisy."[3]

The only ones he did get along with were his protective partners. The relationship with both Jan Grayton and Bob Mitchell intensified. They fed him, shared their hotel room with him, taught him, rehearsed him, introduced him to club owners, agents—they did everything a team of personal managers would, and did so despite weeks of marginal poverty and unemployment.

The weeks stretched into long cold months of hardship. As a trio, they worked together as much as possible, and with Mitchell acting as agent, Johnnie also often appeared in a duet with Grayton, billed as "Jan & Johnnie Ray." There was no reason for an audience to think that they were not a married couple. This, indeed, was an intimate act.[4]

In October of 1950, Johnnie was working at Cy's Bar, a joint on State Road in Cuyahoga Falls, Ohio. He became friendly with a local radio record spinner, Jerry Crocker, one of the first to spot Johnnie's talent. He promoted Johnnie, scouted jobs for him, and offered at one point that autumn to sign him for a management contract. Even after Grayton & Mitchell put the kibosh on such small potatoes, Crocker regularly let Johnnie sing and play for fifteen minutes on his radio d.j. show broadcast on Akron's WCUE.[5]

The platter spinner helped Johnnie get work at George Senior's Yankee Inn, where Johnnie accompanied Devina, a stripper who worked submerged in a glass tank full of water. Devina invariably sloshed water all over Johnnie as she went through her routine.[6] He also had his own spot on the bill, but that was soon restricted to playing piano only. Nix on the yelling and screaming routine, Senior told Johnnie.

While in Akron, Johnnie met a local performer who made a deep impression on him. "The greatest influence on me was a blues singer named Maude Thomas," he said in 1952, "I first heard her in Akron. She had the same feeling about songs I had. She gave me confidence."[7] Little is known of Thomas, who apparently never recorded, but Johnnie rarely named anyone other than Billie Holiday and Kay Starr as an influence. He was learning the blues at street level.

It was Grayton and Mitchell, though, who did the most for him. They were an exceptionally close group. That winter, Mitchell and Johnnie shared one top coat between them. Although Johnnie established his name on a limited circuit of mob-controlled clubs in Cleveland and

Akron that gave him work now and then, the trio was almost invariably broke. Johnnie was compelled to wire home for rent money at one point; they all spent a meager Thanksgiving together in a Cleveland hotel room. Christmas was no cause for celebration.[8]

By early 1951, despite the support and encouragement Johnnie got from Jerry Crocker, Maude Thomas and his own strange vaudeville menage-a-trois partners, it was obvious that nothing was happening for him in Cleveland. Grayton & Mitchell had bookings of their own in the East and, unhappily, left Johnnie behind. He had just turned twenty four, an Oregon rube whose only connections were to Jerry Crocker—not counting his tenuous alliance with Cleveland's Mayfield Road Gang. For some reason, they, too, helped the singer.

"I was starving in Cleveland, literally starving. But I got a job at the Biscayne Lounge, a hooker hangout," Johnnie recalled. "Innocent John. I used to wonder 'what are those girls doing here every night? why are they dressed the way they are?'."[9]

"I remember him talking about the Biscayne Lounge," said Bill Franklin. "Johnnie always said he was very popular with the mob. He used that expression and he always did this when he said it." (Franklin pushed his nose to one side with his index finger) "Crooked, you know? He wasn't a threat to these guys. They liked him as a son, or something . . . "[10]

Grayton and Mitchell, through Friedman, monitored Johnnie's shambling progress and knew he was in a jam. Moreover, they missed him. The team was appearing at Detroit's Flame Showbar, a sizzling room that featured three full shows six nights a week. They persuaded Flame owner Morris Wasserman and floor manager Al Green to audition their unconventional friend. Green reasoned the kid had to have something after the way they pushed for the audition, because the Flame Showbar rarely used white musicians. Wasserman deferred to Green's judgement.[11] When they consented, Jan telephoned Johnnie in Cleveland and told him to take the next bus out. He had just enough money left for a one-way fare.[12]

*   *   *

The Flame Showbar was as different from an Ashtabula cocktail lounge as night is from day. Although white owned (with backing from Detroit's notorious Purple Gang, a mob that scored big bringing Canadian whisky over the border during Prohibition and still controlled vice in the city) the Flame had established itself in just a few short years as the Midwest's leading showcase for jazz, rhythm & blues and black variety artists. "In those days, Detroit meant the Flame Showbar and Al Green," said Detroit born R&B singer Jackie Wilson, whose career was launched at the Flame in 1956.[13]

The Flame was unique. A black and tan club, that is, one patronized by both blacks and whites, it enjoyed a prominent reputation in the scheme of Detroit's club world. The Flame was no joint. It had class. Frequented by blacks who worked on Motor City's assembly lines and by the white upper class liberal and avant garde social set, all of them dressed to the nines, it was the most successful of Motor City hot spots.

Located in an all-black section of the city, wedged onto the corner of Garfield and Canfield streets, "Flame Showbar" was spelled out in huge neon letters on either side of a diagonal corner marquee and entrance. The exterior walls were plastered with additional hand-lettered bills announcing the various acts; when Johnnie arrived in early 1951 they read Mabel Scott, Carl Van Moon, Little Miss Sharecropper, Maurice King & the Wolverines. These were posted beneath wide, high-set batteries of glass brick alternating with windowed alcoves wherein beckoning tongues of neon fire seductively flickered and shimmied.[14]

Its interior was lavishly appointed, with a long bar ringing a sunken nightclub floor, and dozens of tables crowded in a semi-circle around the stage. Its five-hundred-seat capacity was reached almost nightly. Flame audiences signaled approval of an act not by applause, but by rapping gavel-like wooden "knockers" on the table tops. This singular practice originated several years earlier at Club DeLisa, Chicago's top R&B nightspot and was quickly adopted and installed at black clubs throughout the Midwest.[15]

The Flame presented the biggest national names in black music, Billie Holiday, Dinah Washington, Louis Jordan, Ivory Joe Hunter, T-Bone Walker. Its eight-piece house band, Maurice King & the Wolverines, blew a sophisticated brand of urban R&B. Detroit was home to transplanted Delta bluesman John Lee Hooker and honking saxophonist Paul "Hucklebuck" Williams, and both worked there frequently. Later, Jackie

Wilson and Della Reese came out of the Flame, under Al Green's nurturing aegis, to enjoy national popularity. Berry Gordy's sister ran the photo
concession and Gordy, as a young man, was a fixture there.

"I was almost at the end of my rope when I got a booking at the
Flame," Johnnie later told an interviewer from Ebony magazine, "Jan
Grayton had persuaded me to come to Detroit and had called Morris
Wasserman, the owner of the Flame, and asked for an audition for me. It
took us exactly one half hour to get to the Flame after he said he would
listen to me. Wasserman, Al Green, the floor manager, and Maurice King,
the bandleader and musical director at the club auditioned me. It was
Maurice who turned out to be my closest friend and most stubborn boost-
er. Maurice told Wasserman that I was an exceptional discovery, and he
followed through, backing me up."[16]

Green was impressed enough with the young singer that he not only
signed him up for two weeks at $75.00 a week, with an option, he also
offered Johnnie a personal management contract, which he was very
happy indeed to sign.

"When I started at the Flame," he said, "they told me, 'the louder
you sing, boy, the better!'"[17] Johnnie wailed the blues with such conviction that he was quickly accepted, if not downright adopted, by the Flame
Showbar's regular performers. Already surprisingly conversant with black
music (thanks to Elma), he became immersed in black culture, taking up
their language, manners and lifestyle.

Among them was singer LaVern Baker, billed at the time as Little
Miss Sharecropper, as a rival to the Little Miss Cornshucks, who worked
at the nearby Frolic Showbar. Originally from Akron, Ohio, Cornshucks
was a huge hit at Harlem's Apollo Theater, one of the first high profile,
post-war R&B women who blazed the way for the likes of Baker, Ruth
Brown, Esther Phillips and Etta James. Cornshucks "was a little black
chick, in rags, with two buckets and pigtails, came out of the Apollo
Theater, and sang her ass off," said record man Lee Magid.[18]

Johnnie, who caught her act at the Frolic, described her as "bizarre,
is the only word I can use . . . "[19] and extolled her virtues for the rest of
his life. In Harlem Cornshucks had, according to Baker, "fallen in with the
wrong people and had to come out to Detroit to work." Still, her reputation was strong enough that Al Green opted to capitalize on it by creating
his own Little Miss Sharecropper. Detroit, after all, was home to tens of

thousands of Southerners drawn north by the automobile industry job market.

LaVern Baker was relatively new to the business herself. As a teenager, she made such a sensation at Club DeLisa in 1949 that her one-night booking was extended for six consecutive months. Al Green heard of the powerhouse belter and when she was released from her contract at Club DeLisa, wooed her to the Flame. She also made a hit there and by 1953 was a national star, with Atlantic Records hits "Tweedle Dee," and "Jim Dandy". Not yet twenty one, Baker had an earthy yet ingenuous sex appeal and a romping, overwhelming level of volume that lent her a commanding stage presence.

"It was always a real production at the Flame, with an opening act, a comedian second, then a dancer, and then the principal act, followed by a closing act. I was the opener and Johnnie Ray was hired to close the show," Baker recalled. "And this was his first time out here, you know what I'm tryin' to say? So, I started watchin' him every night, and this kid, by way of not bein' able to hear properly, he could get away with not bein' in tempo, he could get away with murder! The band had to help, they would even wait for him, Maurice King and all of 'em would just go with him. Pretty soon, everybody loved him. And we became friends, we just sort of adopted each other. We would go out almost every night after the show, they had all night movies and we were up, so we'd go."[20]

After Grayton and Mitchell moved on to other eastern dates, Johnnie became particularly close to Baker. She recalled that he would often show up outside her apartment after he had had a few, stand out front and call out "Sharecropper! Share-Cropper!" It was a wild, carefree time, and Johnnie readily embraced the Flame cast as family. Johnnie naturally identified with their alienation and separation from mainstream culture, and this common ground soon formed a decisive alliance, personally and artistically.

As Johnnie said, "Detroit had a lot of guts. We drank too much, partied too much, and set off too many fireworks."[21]

With his long-established love for Basie, Ellington, Lunceford and Billie Holiday, Johnnie plunged into the burgeoning R&B idiom. He grew particularly fond of Ivory Joe Hunter's sophisticated blues numbers and added "Pretty Eyed Baby" to his established repertoire, and became a solid interpreter of Rhythm & Blues. "He had just started there when I met him, and he was good—did it nice," recalled blues singer Jimmy Witherspoon, who shared a bill at the Flame with Johnnie, "And he did it with dignity, too. He didn't clown or bullshit."22

He also got help from LaVern Baker. "After I started watchin' him every night," she said, "he already was goin' over fantastic, due to the fact that he was handicapped with the hearing, but it was still missing something, and I felt that he could still receive more from the audience, because I was sittin' out there, and in this business you'll have a lot of people who see you doin' wrong and will tell everybody but you.

"He was so new to it, that when he'd take a bow, there was still somethin' missin', so I told him 'tomorrow night, try the Jolson bow,' and he didn't even know who Al Jolson was at that time! So, we did our homework on Jolson, and he saw that most everything was down on one knee, and he started goin' over real big after that." Without aid and encouragement from Baker, Maurice King and Wolverines drummer and baritone player, "Crazy" Dagwood and Stringbean, he might have remained a simple novelty, the handicapped honky cat trotted out for a few laughs at the end of night, perhaps, at first, even calculated to clear the room. But now Johnnie was a cat. He was in.

Once Johnnie was acclimated to the Flame's knocker walloping audiences, once he began to savor the sense of disimprisonment which made the R&B movement such a potent and affecting one, he began to cease thinking about his performances at all and instead simply felt them. The results were dramatic, and made all the more so because for the first time in years, likely the first time in his adult life, Johnnie felt as if he belonged.

"I was really content when I was in Detroit," he said. "The Flame Showbar was a very popular nightclub, every night was like New Year's Eve and the Fourth of July. I remember it so well, doing three shows a night, starting at seven and continuing 'til two a.m. It was pure madness.

"A lot of that new stuff, the way I worked at that time, everything about it was wild," he continued, "I was so undisciplined—the piano bench would go flying across the stage, draperies would be coming down, the piano would get beaten, the music scattered everywhere. I was all over the place." A pause. "And I would have to say it was all me. It was pure John."

At the end of each performance, a bemused Maurice King would observe the chaos Johnnie left in his wake, and dispatch a waitress to search for Johnnie's cufflinks. They invariably shot right out of his sleeves and went sailing twenty or thirty feet across the floor. "And I was very sincere about all this," Johnnie said, "I thought, 'doesn't everybody do it this way?' I didn't think there was anything unusual about it. I knew it was different, it was pretty wild, but it was just me, and after the show was done, I was just a regular guy."[23]

As regular as a skinny white cat could be who shouted the blues and wore a hearing aid, who could be seen nightly escorting Little Miss Sharecropper to all-night movies and after-hours joints. "Yeah, we'd go out together every night," Baker said. "We even went to jail together, one night when we had gone to an after-hours spot and the cops raided it. We weren't booked and were only in jail a few hours. And the next night, he sang "They Raided The Joint," but he changed the lyric from 'They raided the joint, took everybody down but me," to 'They raided the joint, took everybody down—including me!'

Baker laughs at the memory, an incident that goes beyond a forty-year-old inside joke to underscore Johnnie's vicarious participation in the harassment of blacks by white cops. He had now truly come to the center of their life and experience. Unfortunately he had also come to the attention of the Detroit Vice Squad, a development that at the time seemed unimportant to everyone except the officers who conducted the raid. The Vice boys all took a turn past the drunk tank, surreptitiously eyeballing him. He was pegged immediately by Vice: Nigger Lover. Fruit. Trouble maker. Neither Johnnie nor Baker was charged with anything, but the scrawny white queer with the gizmo stuck in his ear was not easily forgotten.

Johnnie went over so well at the Flame that his option was picked up and he worked four weeks straight. Al Green was pleased with his new property, and set to spreading the word on the strange, exciting new talent. Green got Johnnie additional dates, "some bookings in Canada—not successful bookings, either," Johnnie said. "Most of them ended abruptly. Then I went back to Detroit, to the Clover Club. The reception there was the greatest. After that it was back to the place that had given me my big thrill, the Flame again. That's when things started to pop."[24]

When Johnnie arrived back in Detroit in early April, Bob Mitchell and Jan Grayton were waiting for him. Mitchell arranged a session so Johnnie could make some demonstration records. He cut a couple of his original songs onto acetate, and Mitchell sent them out to Dave Dexter, A&R head at Capitol Records, an acquaintance from vaudeville days when Dexter had emcee'd a show, headlined by Peggy Lee and featuring Grayton and Mitchell at Seattle's Palomar Theater. Cozied up in their room at Detroit's Berkshire Hotel, the trio awaited Dexter's response.

No one knows what songs Johnnie chose for this demo, but it is likely that "Tell The Lady I Said Goodbye" was one of them. Johnnie had passed out copies of his tunes to various and sundry performers who were bound for New York, and several Brill Building firms would later grouse about passing on the tune (but who pitched it there remains a mystery).[25]

He kept working around the Midwest, most often in Ohio, where he had established a somewhat different kind of family. He worked for Devina on numerous occasions. But at the Flame, where he periodically returned, Johnnie could perform in the wild, kinetic style that suited him best. The very fact that he was such a social anomaly is what led him to feel content in Detroit.

"He talked about the Flame a lot," recalled Bill Franklin. "He was very proud of his start in the black and tan joints and said they were great, exciting days. I think, all in all, he was a much wilder, much broader and much more secure performer in those days."[26]

Johnnie crossed a line very few dared to even acknowledge in 1951. The number of white cats working in or even able to grasp the R&B idiom at all—Johnny Otis, Frankie Laine, Harry Gibson, Ricky Jordan—could be counted on one's fingers. But Johnnie walked it and talked it just like his black brothers and sisters. Through the soul-nurturing stoicism and message of the blues, Johnnie was starting to reconcile himself to fate's shattering blow upon his person, the twin hoodoos that being deaf and bisexual forced on him.

Through the liberating release of blues charged with rhythm, he not only reconciled but overcame it. He accepted both. Through the blues, Johnnie realized that social concession and propriety was a losing game, one he swore off playing ever again. It was one of the very few conscious decisions that he made and stuck with. While it brought him more fame, success and glory than even he dreamt of, it also nearly killed him.

*　　*　　*

Rhythm & Blues, forced into remission by wartime shortages of shellac, exploded in Los Angeles in 1945 when a mediocre independent label, Gilt Edge, took a gamble and released "I Wonder," a blues ballad by black Tennessee-born R&B crooner Pfc. Cecil Gant ("The Sepia Sinatra"). It sold out within a week. To parent company 4 Star Record's astonishment, records could not be pressed fast enough to meet demand. Dozens of other small operations sprung up immediately and in no time at all, the "race market" was one of the hottest-selling fields in the American music industry.[27]

The established majors wanted to cash in. Decca, of course, had been recording preeminent R&B master Louis Jordan with great success since 1938, and his 1945 smash "Caldonia" (inspired by the gyrations of formidable shake dancer Esther Young) cemented R&B's growing reputation as a gold mine, all the more so when Woody Herman's cover of the Jordan hit went to the top of the charts.

By 1947, R&B spread like wildfire, a phenomenal popular response heightened further when Los Angeles independent Black & White released Jack McVea's "Open The Door, Richard." McVea's novelty went to number one on Billboard's Honor Roll Of Hits in March and was swiftly covered on no less then fourteen different records (by everyone from Jordan to Basie to pop group the Pied Pipers to country singer Hank Penny). The song became so ubiquitous that New York super station WOR, hoping for a respite, banned all versions of the song.

Columbia Records, home to Frank Sinatra and Gene Autry, assigned the song to two groups, the Three Flames and the Charioteers, a lapsed gospel quartet, but these failed. "Being on a major label was a hindrance at the time," Columbia A&R head Mitch Miller said. "The mythology was that the only good R&B was on smaller labels out of the inner-city."[28]

In their corporate possession was a long inactive label, Okeh. Okeh issued one of the very first blues ever recorded, Mamie Smith's "That Thing Called Love" cut in February of 1920. Okeh thrived, in various hands, throughout the 1920s with both race and hillbilly releases. The records sold like crazy and by the mid-1930s Okeh became almost respectable, featuring name jazz artists like Billie Holiday and Duke Ellington.[29] At that point Columbia bought it outright.

By 1942, with a severe shortage of shellac and Musician's Union strongman James Petrillo's 18-month "juke box strike," Okeh was scrapped in order to allow them to concentrate on releases on the flagship red label. But the Okeh name would still have recognizable credibility in the race market of 1951, and Columbia shrewdly reactivated it. Once that was achieved, their only problem was finding a white man able to run the damn thing. Luckily, he already worked for them.

Danny Kessler was a twenty-five-year-old R&B freak, a rarity among white record men. He worked his way up the food chain and by 1950 was heading Columbia's regional distribution office in his home-town of Philadelphia, Pennsylvania. When Columbia's national sales director, Paul Wexler, decided to bring Okeh back, it quickly became obvious that Kessler was prime choice for A&R head. He was happy to oblige. Slight of build, with jet black hair curled over an intent wedge-shaped face, Kessler's typical expression was one of focused, perpetual enthusiasm, beaming out along either side of a formidable proboscis.

"I'd been given the job because of my background in the black record business. I knew the business, I was a great fan of 'race records,' as they were unfortunately known then," Kessler explained. "I was probably as well versed in black music as anybody at Columbia in those days. There were many times when I was the only white face at Club DeLisa."[30]

He wasted no time scouting talent and cutting records; one of the re-activated Okeh's earliest releases was by Maurice King & the Wolverines. Kessler initially seemed to have more blind luck than instinct working for him. He stumbled across the Treniers rehearsing in a Philadelphia theater and signed them on the spot. A high-powered seven-piece vocal group fronted by twin brothers Claude and Milton, their "Go, Go, Go," became Okeh's first national R&B hit. Tipped by an Atlanta, Georgia disk jockey, Kessler signed Chuck Willis, whose records were strong regional hits. (Willis went on in all his be-turban'd and dark eye-glassed glory to score big with dance smash "The Stroll," becoming one of the first black performers to appear on Dick Clark's "American Bandstand.") Kessler was prowling for talent full time in the spring of 1951. He arrived in Detroit in late April, for another Wolverines session.

"And along the way," Kessler said, "I had heard about Little Miss Sharecropper. So I flew to Detroit to see if I could sign Little Miss Sharecropper, who was working at the Flame Showbar. My best friend in Detroit was a white disk jockey named Robin Seymour who worked at WKMH out of Dearborn, Michigan. He also mentioned that 'there's a kid out there playing piano who is terrific, but nobody in the world knows it because as soon as the headliners finish, the place empties out.'

"So we went out there, and there weren't too many white people in the club, by the way, and Little Miss Sharecropper did her thing, and I flipped over her. Then out came a white kid wearing a hearing aid, who played the piano. There was no name introduction. I really didn't know this was the kid Robin was talking about—I assumed he was talking about a black singer. But I was probably more overwhelmed with what I heard and saw than by anything else I had ever encountered artistically in my life. [31]

"He killed me. He was different, he was exciting." But Kessler kept a cool A&R head. "So, I then went back and talked to Johnnie Ray and said, 'I heard a couple of things I liked, and I want to hear more.'" He arranged the use of a piano in the ballroom of his hotel and asked Johnnie to come by the next day and run through his material. Johnnie, on Grayton and Mitchell's advice, played it just as frosty. "I held out, because I still wanted to be on Capitol Records," he said. "It's amazing the guts you have when you're twenty-four years old."[32]

The next morning at Hotel Berkshire, Bob Mitchell received the letter they were waiting for, postmarked "Hollywood." Dated April 25, 1951, it read:

The records of Johnny Ray that you sent to Dave Dexter were forwarded to me at this office because all new talent is played by me. I have played the record and feel that Johnny Ray has a definite style and possibly could fit in some record companies catalog, but at present I feel there is no place in our artist's roster for him. Signed, Voyle Gilmore[33]

Mitchell was crestfallen. Johnnie was furious that his name was misspelled. Puzzled, too. "Capitol was the groovy label I wanted to be on, they had Kay Starr, Peggy Lee, Stan Kenton, Nat Cole," he said. "But I finally got a letter back from them which I have never forgotten, because at the time I did not know what the word 'roster' meant."[34] When he asked for a definition, the tension was broken. All three howled with laughter. For all Johnnie's newly acquired jive-talking cool, he was still very much the innocent hayseed. They called Danny Kessler.

Johnnie sat down and played for him. "I heard three or four things that knocked me out—so much so that I signed him on the spot. His sound was very special, his style of performing was so physical, so free and so new. Johnnie Ray was not a fake performer, he gave his all, every time. There was a freedom, a very special quality."

Kessler had arrived just in time. Although Johnnie was going over well at the Flame, his engagement was up, and he was going back to Ohio to work some dates with Devina. "I knew Johnnie had to have direction," Kessler said. "Here I am, signing a guy who I think is going to be a major star, and he's telling me he's leaving the Flame Showbar to go work in 'some strip joint'!"

Panicked, Kessler wasted no time booking a session at "some little studio in Detroit, it may have been in the back of a radio station, I just don't remember." It was set for May 29, three weeks off, with Maurice King and the Wolverines to accompany.

"I signed him for four sides with options over five years," Kessler said. "At that point I was so absolutely overwhelmed with Johnnie Ray that I wanted to sign him for management, which I wasn't supposed to do." Nonetheless, Kessler produced, along with the Okeh contract, a pro forma management contract. Johnnie signed both of them. Al Green was unaware of this aspect of the deal, just as Kessler was unaware that Green had paper on the boy. He returned to New York, still wound up over Johnnie's talent, and carrying a dub of the acetate Johnnie recorded for Capitol.

"I also knew that my job at Columbia was much more important to me than being a personal manager," Kessler said, "so I called Rosemary Clooney's manager and I said, 'Joe, I just found a guy who's gonna be a star,' and I played him Johnnie's dub, but he said, 'It's not my cup of tea.'" Stymied, Kessler didn't know where to turn. "I knew that I had to get somebody in there who would take tender loving care, and then I thought of Bernie Lang," he said.

"Bernie was a song plugger for Larry Spier Music in New York, and he used to occasionally show me songs Spier was publishing and try and get me to record them. All of these guys used to cater to me, but Bernie and I became great buddies," Kessler explained.

"Now, Bernie had no experience as manager, but there are certain guys you believe in, who are much more talented and better than what they're doing, and I felt Bernie Lang had that kind of potential. That's why I called him and said 'you are now a manager.' And Bernie came out to Detroit to meet Johnnie." Kessler paused. "Instant relationship."

Lang was an average song plugger who went from town to town, ballyhooing Spier titles to A&R men and records of tunes Spier published to d.j.'s, hunting for new titles, new talent, hustling all over the Eastern half of the country. Precisely why Kessler chose him is unexplained; he may simply have run out of prospective handlers. Perhaps it hinged on some favor that left Lang beholden to him and assured Kessler future collection of under-the-table management commissions which he had no legal right to. Lang explained Kessler's find to Larry Spier and begged a loan for trainfare to Detroit. He arrived on the 29th, just in time for the record date.

They went in and cut four of Johnnie's songs, "Whisky & Gin," a stomping R&B number, and "Tell the Lady I Said Goodbye," a torchy ballad. The other two, "She Didn't Say Nothin' At All," and "I'm Just A Shadow Of Myself" have never been released.[35] While both "Whisky & Gin," and "Tell The Lady," were firmly within the rhythm & blues idiom, Johnnie was not aping the style so much as he was defining his own assimilated version of the form.

"Tell The Lady" throbs with a mournful late-night cafe gloom. "Whisky & Gin" is a hard socking record—Dagwood's drum kit was set up right next to him to ensure he stayed in time—and his vocal is dramatic, fraught with emotion yet fluid, almost winsome.

Even in this distinctly urbane formula, Johnnie brought some of his innocent Oregonian nature to the lyric. Ironically, the mildly titillating verse, "She kisses me good night / she hugs and squeezes me tight / oh Lord I love her so / and then she turns off the light / there ain't a cloud in sight / she leads me to the river where the still waters flow . . . " would keep the song off the air. The record was "Pure John." Cloudless night skies, rivers, and in one particular line, a telling glimpse of Pure John, "who knows how love begins / or where it ends?"

The booze theme was certainly in keeping with his lifestyle. "I knew that he was a heavy drinker when I signed him," Kessler said, "I'd been told that he would have five beers for breakfast. He only got about $38 dollars at the end of every week because of his bar tab."[36] The soaring, untamed quality in his vocal was not the drunk's euphoria, it was a cry from the long-muted voice of the pained teenaged Johnnie now, finally, loosed.

The record pealed. It rang out a force unlike anything in white pop, the force of undeniable, individual power. That power was derived from his freedom, and the freedom imbued him with overwhelming power. That day Johnnie took an artistic step forward that, at the time, no one else considered possible or was able to follow. In the booth, Kessler and Lang's palms began itching.

Bernie then presented Johnnie with a management contract. He was smart enough to delay signing until seeking the advice of Jan Grayton, a significant example of Johnnie's relationship with Jan in particular and women in general—he looked to them for a wisdom he felt bereft of. The deal was sweetened by the fact that any song-publishing money generated by Ray originals would be his alone. Only after Jan read and approved it did Johnnie call Lang and arrange a meeting at the club where he was appearing. Johnnie was preparing to sign his third management contract in as many months.

"The first time I saw Bernie was at the record session. Danny Kessler somehow got ahold of him," he said. "It wasn't long after that I signed with him. We hit it off right from the beginning. The papers were actually signed at Club Forty Niner in Detroit." The propitious moment unexpectedly soured. To Bernie's dismay, "I got fired from the spot," Johnnie said, "because the owner thought I was too noisy."[37]

Al Green was out in the cold, but Johnnie thought little of it. He never mentioned that paper to anyone. Grayton & Mitchell headed for bookings in upstate New York. Johnnie went on to another engagement at the Flame. These lives would never again be the same. It was May 30, 1951. Mario Lanza was the most popular male singer in America.

Kessler returned to New York, "just completely knocked out by this superstar I had found. I played the record for the sales force at Columbia, and almost in unison they said, 'we don't think she's  gonna make it.' They all thought I was pitching a girl who sounded like Dinah Washington! Finally, I convinced them that she was a boy, and then I had to break the news that she was a white boy. I know they all felt that I had lost my head completely." Nonetheless, "Whiskey & Gin" backed with "Tell the Lady I Said Goodbye," was scheduled for a July 27 release.

Shortly after that disappointing episode, Kessler made a key appearance at a Columbia sales convention in Chicago.

"Paul Wexler was solidly behind me, asked me to come to the convention and play my new artist. 'We won't give any advance hype,' he said. 'We'll just introduce you as the head of A&R at Okeh and you'll play your product.' So I got up, made my little speech and played this new record." Kessler relishes the story, "The reaction was overwhelming—they literally stood up and cheered. Then I had to break the bad news about Ray's being a white boy. At that point they didn't care if he was green or purple."

With any doubts about Columbia's acceptance of the record wiped out, Kessler and Bernie Lang began to operate. Also twenty-five years of age, Bernie Lang was the walking visual definition of average. Slightly heavyset, his thinning hair and thick-lensed spectacles lent him a rather owlish appearance. He was a pure product of Brill Building/Tin Pan Alley school of hustle, with some germane contacts of his own. Bernie took a dub of the record to Tom Seat at General Artists Corporation, a fast rising talent agency. Unlike Voyle Gilmore and Clooney's manager, Seat was wise enough to foresee stirring winds of change. Ten percent of this might be worth a little effort. Seat agreed to book some dates on Johnnie once the record had hit the marketplace. The only thing left to do now was to wait.

*   *   *

For his part, Johnnie didn't fret or wonder about the reaction his record might get. His self-faith was such that it hardly even crossed his mind. As far as Elma and the rest of family back home knew, there was no anticipated upshift, no imminent breakthrough. But in his mind, success was a given. All he thought about was his performances.

It was a big time for Johnnie. The evening that he learned Billie Holiday was in the house, he flipped. "She came in to see the show and I was so nervous because Billie Holiday was in the audience that they literally had to take me upstairs and push me onto the stage," Johnnie said. "I was scared, just as scared as any kid could be, because this woman I idolized was sitting out front. But I went on, and later that night we were introduced, and in years to follow, we became friends."[1]

"Some funny things happened at the Flame, too," he said, "I was the only white singer on the bill but sometimes, because of makeup, you'd never know it. Once I posed for a picture with Joe Louis. When the print came back it showed me darker than Joe!"[2]

Johnnie used cosmetics heavily, not to darken his skin, and not just to make himself him look better (he was unable to consider himself handsome) but also because he enjoyed it. It was part of the theatrical ritual he cherished, one reinforced by the presentations of glamorous black singers like Billy Wright, Savoy's colorful "Prince of the Blues," and Little Richard, then four months away from his record debut.[3]

Johnnie finished work early at the Flame on June 5, took several drinks at the bar and left the club wearing full makeup, base, powder and lipstick. He returned to his hotel, the Park Avenue. Restless, he changed clothes and went down to the street. He was dressed entirely in black.

Johnnie made his way to the Stone Theater on nearby Woodward Avenue. The Stone was a burlesque house, and the marquee announced "Live Girl Show Onstage! Men, This Is It! Adult Fun! Twenty Five cents!", a familiar setting for Johnnie, where the lavishly costumed peelers always provided a diverting hour or two. The mix of libidinous theatrical glamour and a crowd of men with erections was irresistible.

Shortly after 1 a.m., he took a box office raincheck and repaired to an adjacent saloon, where he knocked back a few more boiler makers. Back at the Stone, he went downstairs to the men's toilet and found himself in conversation with a loiterer. He was Officer Francis Demmers of the Detroit Police, sent there by the Vice Squad's Chief after receiving "complaints about the fact that homosexuals congregated at the Stone." As soon as Johnnie entered the men's room, Demmers knew his work at the Stone was going to end for the night. The smart-ass nigger lover. Vice had counted on running into him.

According to Demmers' colorful testimony, it was 1:45 when his target breezed in. "Hi," Demmers greeted Johnnie.

"Hi . . . hot isn't it?" he replied.

"Sure is," Demmers said.

"I know where it's cool," said Johnnie. "Real cool."

"Where might that be?" the plainclothes cop asked.

"My place," Johnnie said. "The Park Avenue Hotel, room 310."

"What could we do at your place?"

"We'd get cool, man, get cool," Johnnie said. "We could open a bottle and have a couple of blasts."

It was payback time for Johnnie. Demmers would testify that Johnnie offered him a blow job; Johnnie confided to friends that

Demmers rousted him. Either way, out came the cuffs. Johnnie fought back; his jaw bore two ugly scratches as a result. Any blow landing on his hearing aid sent excruciatingly amplified lightning bolts of pain through his skull. It was pointless to resist. He was booked at 2:20 a.m.

Johnnie was charged under Section 448 of the Penal Code of the State of Michigan, Soliciting and Accosting: "Any person who shall accost, solicit or invite another in any public place, or in or from any building or vehicle, by word, gesture or any other means, to commit prostitution or to do any other lewd or immoral act, shall be guilty of a misdemeanor."

He glared back at the camera when they took his mug shots, look-ing feral, scared, angry. Desk Sergeant Michael Van de Keere noted Johnnie "had trouble hearing what was said although he was wearing a hearing aid." He had turned it off, a typical Ray move when a situation worked against him. Van de Keere asked Johnnie why he had accosted Demmers. "This is a result of something that happened to me years ago," the Sergeant claimed Johnnie replied. If anything, he probably said "weeks ago," referring to the after hours raid when he was brought in. He had presence of mind enough not to speak further.

At his arraignment the next morning before Recorders Judge Joseph A. Gillis, Johnnie said he didn't wish to have a lawyer, waived trial by jury and summarily entered a guilty plea. Gillis ordered an immediate trial. Demmers appeared and told his story. Johnnie was convicted and sen-tenced to either thirty days in the Detroit House of Correction or a twen-ty-five dollar fine. Johnnie paid it and returned to his hotel.[4]

Detroit Vice was not through with Johnnie Ray. But Johnnie was through with Detroit. He finished his engagement, left the Flame and returned to the Ohio lounge and nightclub circuit. The cops there, he knew, would not dare bug him.

As scheduled, Okeh released "Whiskey & Gin" on July 27, aimed at and marketed solely in black record outlets. As expected, it began with good sales in Detroit, Boston, and Pittsburgh. The record was hot in Buffalo, where disk jockey Joe Rico gave it heavy play, and Cleveland, aired frequently by WERE's late night record spinner Phil McLain, who had already heard about the singer from Jerry Crocker.[5]

Kessler targeted each of these cities, links in a regional chain of rec-ognized music industry "litmus towns," key locales (with large black pop-ulations) for establishing a foothold in the record field which then allowed a disk to break out nationally. Kessler worked overtime to establish rapport with the reigning disk jockeys in each of these. Except for one notable exception, he was in; WERE's top jock, Bill Randle, refused to play it.[6]

None of this was lost on Al Green, the man who originally signed on as Johnnie's personal manager. When he discovered the extra paper his singer consented to sign, he was furious. Detroit nightclubbing was a tough business, and Green was no softie. He called his friends in the Purple Gang and explained what was going down. They prepared to dispatch a "convincer" to New York, under instruction to kill Danny Kessler unless he and Green reached an immediately satisfying understanding.[7]

The dawning of Johnnie Ray's record career was marked by chicanery, rage, threats of violence and intimidation. He knew nothing about it. Just as he knew nothing about Kessler's speech and reception at the Columbia sales force convention in Chicago. Just as he knew nothing about his record sales in the east. Just as he knew nothing about Bernie Lang selling him to GAC.[8]

*   *   *

At Akron's Yankee Inn, Johnnie worked at a fever pitch, and made quite an impression on another up-and-coming belter, signed to Okeh's parent, Columbia. His name was Tony Bennett, who knocked around New York and already "had tried to be everything from a race singer to Mario Lanza" with little success. At Columbia, Bennett finally hit upon the correct formula: "We decided to get some strings behind me and I'd just sing sincerely," just as the label was losing interest in him.[9] Bennett's latest release "Because of You," a syrupy Percy Faith orchestrated ballad, had broken out of the Eastern music towns and was starting to scale the Billboard pop charts. Bennett was headlining at the Yankee Inn when Johnnie returned there in late June.

"I had already heard about him, this great performer who did anything and everything onstage, who broke every rule possible, and when we were in Akron together, we became great friends," Bennett said. "I used to call him up onstage and we'd knock the audience for a loop. One night we had a conga line with the whole audience that went all the way through the club, outside around the whole front and rear of the club, then back inside through the kitchen.

"Johnnie did something that was completely different," Bennett explained. "Music, in those days, was still a kind of sweet, long line of singers like Dick Haymes, Bob Eberly, and, of course, Frank Sinatra, who sang very sentimental, lovely, well-written songs, done very sweetly. But Johnnie became a visual performer. He was the first to charge an audience. He had to rip the curtain down, bang away on the piano, or jump on the piano because he just couldn't stay cool enough not too. And I really consider Johnnie Ray to be, in that sense, the father of rock and roll."[10]

His presentation was as revolutionary as Elvis Presley's—perhaps, at the time, even more so. Johnnie was the first white pop singer to stand at the piano; the first to send a piano bench flying with a swift backwards kick; the first to wrest a microphone from its stand and carry it about the stage with him, the while vibrating through a kinetic series of convulsive, violent gestures, each wild movement instinctively calculated to emphasize the lyric. He tore at his hair, shot his arms out at the audience, spasmodically clenched and flexed his fingers. He bent over backwards; he went down on his knees; he crouched; he leapt; he rolled on the floor. His was a performance in the truest sense.

His singing style was equally radical. Like Jimmy Scott, the Cleveland, Ohio jazz singer who began recording with Lionel Hampton in 1949, Johnnie stretched out the words of a ballad so outrageously that he necessarily created his own meter; like Kay Starr he burnished rhythm numbers with an urgent vocal momentum. He was also phrasing on each individual syllable, something no one had ever done, introducing a lyrical delivery technique that became standard in rock and roll. Johnnie's voice rose to an anguished roar, subsiding to an almost pitiful, gasping near-silence. As desperate as he seemed it was nonetheless immensely appealing.

He broke tempo, rules, piano lids, music stands and hearts every time he performed. More and more, his audiences responded in kind.

For Johnnie, the earliest blush of success came when GAC entered the picture. "After we recorded those two songs nobody sat around waiting for fireworks to happen," he said. "I wasn't aware of the dictates of the record business, and I just sort of forgot about it until GAC sent me to Chicago, where I worked in a little bar across the alley from the Chicago Theater. And when this big agency that had signed me sight unseen sent me to Chicago for $350.00 a week, I thought 'this is the most money I'll ever see in my life.'"[11]

While it seemed to Johnnie as if Okeh had forgotten him, too, the long green GAC managed to get was consolation enough; and the Capitol Lounge was choice. Louis Jordan made his name in the room years before, and the Capitol was home to Maurice Rocco, a popular black pianist who stood up at the keyboard. Johnnie kept on doing what was natural—tearing up the piano and downing gallons of beer. The engagement, while lucrative, was not well received. Johnnie was such a marathon boozer that he actually drank up his entire $350.00 salary in just a few nights and, after buying rounds for the lounge's congenial barflies, wound up owing a sizable bar tab.[12]

"We got this date for Johnnie in Chicago," Bernie Lang said. "At the Capitol Lounge, right next to the Chicago Theater, we had a week's engagement there. And Johnnie was very physical in the sense that he'd bang on the piano and sang a lot of original and black blues material which was an integral part of his sound, more so than anything else.

"But Joe Swartz, the owner, closed us down. He fired Johnnie after three nights. And the record was making a little noise in Philly, in Buffalo, but not in Chicago. Never did anything in Chicago." Danny Kessler arrived to cut his latest discovery, Joe Williams, then a Club DeLisa regular, and also take up the slack in Johnnie's career. "He ended up playing at the Brass Rail, which was just a little bar, and he wound up owing a $260 bar tab," Kessler said. "I put him into a couple of rooms friends of mine owned, just to keep him going. He was very naive."

"I finally called Columbia," Johnnie said, "and asked when they were going to release my record. And they said 'Well, we already released it, a couple of weeks ago.' I used to go all over Chicago looking for a Johnnie Ray record."[13]

Even though Johnnie couldn't find a copy of his own disk in the Windy City (top jock Howard Miller had not yet warmed to Kessler), it was stirring up more and more action elsewhere in the Midwest and Northeast. Within weeks, it became evident that Ray's appeal on record was not limited to a black audience. In Buffalo and Cleveland, dozens and dozens of white kids were calling radio stations, bugging record store clerks—they wanted more by Johnnie Ray, despite the fact that black record retailers were assumed to be well off the beaten path. Columbia's distributors were perplexed.

Cleveland, already a crucial make or break "music town," was also one whose white youth embraced Rhythm & Blues with uncommon, avid zeal. An ideal site to parlay any pop comer's name to heights of fame and fortune, Cleveland was tailor-made for a white R&B-based performer like Johnnie.

Kessler was still trying to get Bill Randle on the record. Fortunately, he was not the only one promoting Johnnie Ray in Ohio. "I had a pipeline to Bill Randle and Phil McLain," Tony Bennett said. "I called them and said 'wait 'til you see this guy—he is going to explode the town of Cleveland.'" It seemed as if Fate was always stepping in to Danny Kessler's advantage that year.

When Bennett called, Randle had just discovered that WERE's switchboard was lighting up during Phil McLain's late night slot and not on his show, and he embraced Johnnie Ray. Faced with a popular trend he failed to initiate, Randle claimed it as his own before the whole affair got too noisy. Once he entered the picture, the walls came down.

The cult of broadcast celebrity, the Personality Jock, was just forming and Randle was its most vociferous pioneer, several steps ahead of another Cleveland d.j., Alan Freed. Randle was emerging as the city's most influential and effective voice on the air, to the point where record distributors would accept new titles from a label only after they got an affirmative response to a question that was becoming more important: "Is Randle behind it?" His support was imperative to a new artist's success.

"I would not be where I am today," Tony Bennett said, "if it were not for Bill Randle." Time magazine featured him that year, asking "Is this the most important man in radio?" Just as Randle later played a vital role in nationally breaking Elvis Presley beyond the regional Southern circuit, so too did he introduce Johnnie Ray. And Johnnie would never forget his first meeting with Randle.[14]

"Columbia called me back and asked if I would mind going to Cleveland to promote this record," Johnnie said. "I didn't know what that meant. I thought I'd be going to some cocktail party and shaking hands or something. I didn't know that it meant disk jockey shows and live broadcast interviews and all that. But they said someone would meet me at the station and I said, 'Sure, I'll go.' I got on the train in Chicago and arrived in Cleveland early the next day. No one had told me that my record was the number one song and that Johnnie Ray was the biggest name in town. They never said a word to me.

"I remember getting off the train, there were hundreds of teenagers outside and I thought to myself 'There must be a movie star on this train, Ann Sheridan or Hedy Lamar, or at least Perry Como!' I got off, and nobody knew what I looked like except this one guy, Bill Randle, who walked up and said 'You're Johnnie aren't you?' and I said 'yes.' And all of a sudden I realized all these kids were here to see me.

"There was instant pandemonium. These kids were all over me. Randle was the number one disk jockey at the time. I did not know any of this, but he had gotten a copy of my record and said he'd been playing it all the time. The few days that I spent there, I learned real fast how to do promotion. Going to all these school dances and record hops, and being surrounded by screaming kids," he paused and laughed softly. "I got used to that real fast, too, I thought 'this is more fun than chocolate sundaes!'"[15]

The fuse was lit. A chain reaction began, touched off by a wild recognition and embrace of Johnnie's unique quality. He evoked paroxysms in his listeners, an unlikely idol who sated the unspoken needs of a generation. The fact that Korean War conscription siphoned off three million able-bodied young men further helped create a climate that served to elevate his appeal (as with Sinatra's during the Second World War). Ohio became Johnnie's first and sweetest proving ground.

Bill Randle took Johnnie on the rounds of record clubs and school functions, making in-store appearances at stores like Eli Mintz's Record Rendezvous (one of the first white retailers to stock and promote race music: "We've got the jazz and the pop and the rhythm and the blues—get 'em at the Vouz on 10th Avenue!") and kept plugging the record on his WERE show. Despite the fact that "Whisky & Gin," was too suggestive and raw for broadcast at any other time than the wee small hours (although Phil McLain still pumped it after midnight), it posed no problem for Randle. He simply played hell out of "Tell The Lady," because as Johnnie said, he knew that "the kids were smart enough to buy the record and turn it over."[16]

Cleveland went Ray crazy. Randle arranged appearances at neighborhood block parties, community centers, more high schools and youth clubs—Johnnie even appeared for the benefit of the Cleveland Police department at Saints Philip & James Church. The first Johnnie Ray Fan Club was chartered in Cleveland that summer.[17]

A typical promo visit was recalled by Jack Brooks, a singer turned broadcaster, who came into the booth at San Francisco's KGO during an interview with Johnnie decades later:

"This man performed at the Showboat in Lorain, Ohio, and I was the opener," Brooks said, turning to Johnnie. "Then I took you over to the high school and you performed at our assembly program. We had, God rest his soul, an old man named Driscoll who had a music store, and I ran over to Mr. Driscoll and said 'We want a brand new grand piano for Johnnie Ray!'"

"That was his first mistake," Johnnie murmured. "I can see it coming."

"And Johnnie used to get pretty carried away when he did some of his numbers," Brooks continued, "so he was rolling on the floor, crying and tearing his hair out, but that's not the worst—he then stood up, took off one of his loafers, which had a metal cleat on it, and commenced banging out the rhythm on the top of this brand new, uninsured grand piano! And the audience was going crazy, absolutely crazy."[18]

Coincidentally, as Johnnie arrived in Cleveland for that first p.r. tour behind "Whisky & Gin," Tony Bennett was appearing at Moe's Main Street, a small but prestigious room on Cleveland's Euclid Avenue. Main Street run by Moe Nahas, a small, shrewd man with bulging eyes, whom Bennett recalled as "a terrific guy—very smart. He had the 'in' club, because you could see a very famous artist on a very intimate basis. I followed Billie Holiday and Art Tatum into Main Street, he had people like that in his club."

Nahas also had people from Cleveland's Mayfield Road Gang, who ran prostitution, drugs and illegal casinos throughout the Midwest. In partnership with "The Big Four," the city's Jewish mob faction, they owned sixty-four percent of the nearby Thistledown track. Several notorious names came up with the Mayfield gang, men like Moe Dalitz, an old school bootlegger who was running the Desert Inn in Las Vegas, and his boyhood chum, Jimmy Hoffa.[19]

Moe's Main Street was a steamy, zebra-print-draped gathering place for both upper crust and underworld elements of Cleveland society, and an important setting for any performer working the Midwest. GAC and Bernie Lang were unable to get Nahas to hire their boy, but Tony Bennett was still looking out for him, and arranged Johnnie's debut at Moe's with ease.

As considerate and generous as he is talented, Bennett actually needed Johnnie on this occasion. On the eve of his first marriage, an elopement, Bennett was unprepared to fulfill his commitment at Main Street and decided to substitute Johnnie. After settling up with Nahas, Bennett called a local television station and also arranged to have Johnnie fill in his own scheduled slot on a local Friday night program. The show was "Soupy's On" hosted by Soupy Hines, a young comedian soon to gain national prominence in his own right as Soupy Sales.

"I was supposed to have Tony Bennett on the show that night," Sales said, "but Tony called and he had something going on, he said 'Look, I can't make it, but I got you Johnnie Ray. He's really fantastic, he's going to try out for Moe Nahas tonight after your show. Put him on the show and we'll all go down to Moe's afterwards.' So I said, 'OK,' and Johnnie came on the show. Oh, God, he had holes in his socks, and he had this record 'Whiskey & Gin,' and he came on and lip synched to the record. And then we went down to Moe's Main street to see him that night.[20]

"Tony couldn't stay and do the whole show for whatever reason. He came on, did three or four numbers and then he introduced Johnnie Ray. Tony was really like his discoverer. He said, "I've got this young man who is really great, I know you're going to like him and so without further ado . . ."" Sales paused, searching for the context. "And Cleveland was a jumping town, with lots of clubs—everybody came through that town. But he just blew everybody away, and you knew that this kid was going to be the biggest star in the world. Johnnie was magnetic in his talent. He wasn't a brilliant piano player, but that voice of his was sensational, that raw emotion, it just thrilled . . . I mean he was the most exciting nightclub performer I had ever seen."

"It's just that he smashed all the rules," Bennett said. "He did everything. He jumped up and down, jumped onto a curtain. He hit the audience with that piano, standing up at the piano, no one ever did that, everybody sat at the piano. He loved to perform, but he had this tremendous problem of not being able to hear himself, and hoping that he was singing in tune, and not being sure of that—but when he wasn't sure, something would take over. As they say in Japan, some aikido would set in, and it would become a great performance, a great visual performance."

"Tony Bennett brought him onstage," Bernie Lang recalled. "And he absolutely tore the fuckin' place up, he ripped the place apart. Moe Nahas got on the floor, said 'I want to book him. When is he available?' And the only other booking we had at the time was one in Washington D.C. that Don Seat had got for him." Bernie struck a deal with Nahas then and there, letting him have Johnnie for $500.00.[21]

After that night, Johnnie Ray, who virtually no one in the business had yet heard nor even seen a picture of, became a prime subject of discussion and speculation. In August, Billboard Rhythm & Blues reviews said of "Whiskey & Gin," *"Warbler has an extraordinary sound, a cross between Kay Starr and Jimmy Scott, on this finely constructed rhythm novelty."* On "Tell the Lady I Said Goodbye": *"Ray does another sensitive ear arresting job on an unusual classy ballad."*[22]

Despite the terse trade jargon, this capsule summation was quite eloquent: extraordinary; sensitive; unusual. And how. Moe's was packed every night for Johnnie's two-week stand there.

The Washington date was a stiff. After a fair two-week club engagement in Pittsburgh, he went to Buffalo, for his "theater-cafe debut" at the Town Casino. In comparison to the Flame and Main Street, Harry Auburn Long's Town Casino was huge. The fifteen hundred-capacity room had thrived for years and drew customers from as far away as Rochester and Toronto.

Johnnie's first non-club date since being goosed onstage at Portland's Four Star theater, this would be a real test of his drawing power. It was still a see-saw, touch and go. "I'd go into Cleveland or Pittsburgh and cause a real crazy riot," Johnnie said. "Then I'd go in Washington and I might as well have stayed in bed. It was enough to give me a complex."[23] The on-air word of mouth campaign which Buffalo's Joe Rico initiated and Bill Randle's influence ignited with other Eastern jocks was paying off.

"Buffalo was unusual," said Bernie Lang. "When he went to play Buffalo it was with Ethel Smith, the organist, and another singer at the top of the bill. Johnnie was the third act. It was a Monday, which was Ladies Night, and it was freezing but the women were lined up all the way around the block. So after the first night, the bill was re-arranged and

Johnnie wound up closing the show. At the time, I was still working for Spier Music, and after that my boss there said, 'Quit your job. Have your wife quit her job.' It was getting to that point."

Danny Kessler came up for the shows at Town Casino to gauge the fever and hang out with a pal of his, Cy Kertman. He worked as Mercury's Eastern sales manager, but was considering taking a job at Capitol. "They came to Buffalo to work, and the Town Casino, that was my home." Kertman said, "I knew Danny, and I saw Johnnie work. He really was a very exciting performer. Then I met him, got acquainted with Johnnie and Bernie, and what happened actually, was Johnnie was going back to Cleveland, Bernie was going back to New York and Danny said, 'would you go along and take care of everything in Cleveland?' because I had been in the business for years.

"I went to Cleveland with him and it was no job, I was just taggin' along. Then we went to New York and I don't even know if it was Johnnie or Danny who said 'why don't you come along—stay on and travel?' because Bernie had to stay and take care of business and they wanted somebody to be with Johnnie. We got along well and I said 'Fine.'"[24]

Cy accompanied Johnnie for the next four years, another Kessler-chosen "handler." The Ray situation was unstable, potentially explosive. Still dogged by Al Green's threat, Kessler had to both cover himself and make sure Johnnie didn't get drunk and freaky and thrown in the jug. Another source of worry was fear that news of the accosting and soliciting arrest in June would leak. Image and survival, in Johnnie's case, were inextricable. And, on top of it all that damn hearing aid—they had Johnnie take it off after a Billboard piece noted "Odd thing about Ray is that he works with a hearing aid; is deaf has to play his own piano. Can't hire an outside pianist because he can't hear."[25]

"He was working without his hearing aid," Kertman said, "but one of the problems that occurred was that he'd have trouble hearing the bass, that was why he started carrying his own drummer." He worked with New York drummer Sammy Fede, who essentially served as conductor—when Johnnie got lost, he would fall back towards the kit and wait until he felt the drum's physical vibration and regained proper tempo.

Johnnie's next date was choice, an engagement at Hartford, Connecticut's State Theater, which Louis Jordan described as "a white theater for the hep college crowd,"[26] on a bill with Count Basie and Steve

Lawrence and Eydie Gorme. Even in staid New England, pandemonium ensued. Back in Detroit, Bernie Lang and Art Franklin, a hustler they signed on as Johnnie's flack man, finally settled Al Green up, with assistance from Savoy Record's A&R man Lee Magid. "Me and Al Green were very close," Magid said. "He had paper on Johnnie Ray . . . Bernie Lang, who managed Johnnie, and Danny Kessler, who signed him to Epic [sic], got into some kind of swindle with Al. Bernie was given Johnnie through Danny Kessler, but Danny had no right to take him because Al Green had him. It was that kind of situation. Al was the one who brought Danny to Detroit. I like Danny and I always liked Bernie—he used to hang around my office when he had nothing to do. Al Green and me became pretty close because Al knew I was close to these guys. And I made them settle the thing. When Johnnie hit, they deposited thirty-five thousand dollars in Al's account." The settlement also included booking Johnnie a 1952 date at Olympia Stadium, with all the b.o. receipts going straight to Green.[27]

GAC, with Bernie Lang's heartfelt encouragement and full-time assistance, kept driving Johnnie's price up. Club owners were baffled. In a few short days, it went from $500.00 a week ("Steep for an unknown . . ." they grumbled) to $750.00 ("For this Ray guy?"). Another few days passed and they were asking for $1,500.00 ("And I still haven't heard of him!"). By the end of September it reached $1,750.00.[28] The trade's prevailing attitude towards Johnnie is best summed up in three words: What the hell?

None of the sharp operators stopped to wonder. Exploitation was in their blood; Johnnie Ray cried out for it.

Columbia Records' New York headquarters at Fifty-Second Street and Seventh Avenue was churning out pop hits driven by an earthy new sound drawn from folk music, a hitherto unex-

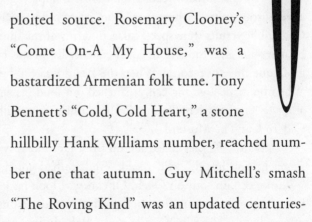

ploited source. Rosemary Clooney's "Come On-A My House," was a bastardized Armenian folk tune. Tony Bennett's "Cold, Cold Heart," a stone hillbilly Hank Williams number, reached number one that autumn. Guy Mitchell's smash "The Roving Kind" was an updated centuries-old English folk ballad. Columbia Records began to feature new concepts of instrumentation and arrangements, using

6

harpsichord or french horn, cracking bull whips, honking geese and barking dogs.

These wildly fresh ideas came from Columbia's new Artist & Repertoire director, Mitch Miller. A graduate of the Eastman School of Music and accomplished oboist who still found time to perform with symphony orchestras, Miller's modus operandi was as unorthodox as the sound effects he piled onto his records. He eschewed the A&R ritual, lunches at Lindy's, Toots Shor's and the Plaza's Oak Room, preferring to work through lunch while raiding a small refrigerator stocked with cheeses and health foods. Stalking from his office to the studio in rumpled shirt sleeves, stroking his bristling russet goatee, burning an endless series of long black cigars, Miller was a peerless character.

He first made waves as head of Mercury's A&R department and had produced the hits that made Frankie Laine a national star. When Columbia's long-time A&R chief Manie Sachs defected to RCA Victor in 1950, Columbia's executive head of operations Godard Lieberson, himself an Eastman School alumnus, brought Miller in. Song pluggers had to be at Columbia at an ungodly eight a.m. to pitch him material—Miller got to work the same time the elevator operator did, when most of his colleagues were at home nursing hangovers. After "The Beard" hit Tin Pan Alley, things were never the same.[1]

A consummate record man with a superb musical ear, Miller's adventurous spirit set him apart from every other A&R man on the East Coast. The results were spectacular, in terms of the number of hit records by new stars and, too, for an equal casualty list of spectacular misfires and grotesque novelty records. When the Beard was on, he ruled pop music. When he made a wrong call, it smelled out loud (as with Rosey Clooney and Marlene Dietrich dueting on the Carlisle's salty hillbilly novelty "Too Old To Cut The Mustard").

"Danny Kessler called me up from Detroit, very excited about this singer he had heard," Miller said. "And we had got the masters and put "Whisky & Gin" out on Okeh. Of course, I look back now, and say that it was probably the very first rock and roll record, or, one of the first black-oriented styles sung by a white man. Nobody knew who he was, but it caused a murmur at first, and then even more noise. The point is, it caused enough noise that Johnnie came to New York and, being the head of the department, I decided that I would look for stuff that would suit him."[2]

Miller's song acquisition also broke routine in that he would try anything and actively flouted the incestuous song publisher/label bedmate arrangement. He appropriated tunes from any source at hand—even from within his own company. No one ever learned how Miller, in New York, somehow heard a dub of "Come On-A My House," set to be recorded in Los Angeles by Charmin' Kay Armen. Clooney's record was being pressed only a few days after Armen and Ross Bagdassarian delivered a demo record at Columbia's Hollywood office. He also encouraged his own hand-picked troupe of independent writers to pitch him new material as often as possible.[3]

Among these were Terry Gilkyson ("Cry of the Wild Goose"), Bill Engvick ("Song From Moulin Rouge,") and most notably, Alec Wilder. An eccentric who wrote stark, beautiful songs like "I'll Be Around" and "Where Do You Go?", Wilder was a brilliant slob "always rather unkempt in appearance,"[4] who hung around with both jazz men and long hairs, counting Miller and Peggy Lee among his closest friends. When Johnnie arrived in New York, Wilder had just presented Miller with his latest, "Give Me Time."

It became clear to Bernie that the Beard (when he travelled out of town to see Johnnie work) was seriously considering recording the boy. When Lang saw a way to potentially cut off under-the-table commissions Kessler received by going over his corporate head, he started moving. "I hustled Johnnie off to New York," Lang said. "I borrowed a thousand dollars from my father and bought Johnnie a tuxedo and a couple of nice suits." He had to borrow the grand because all Johnnie's money was in Al Green's bank account.

"What happened was, I was between dates and they sent me to New York because Columbia had heard about this weird kid and they wanted me to do a short," Johnnie said. "I shot a seven-minute short with Delores Hawkins . . . I don't even know what happened with that." (Filmed at Eddie Condon's joint in New York on September 10, 1951, it featured Johnnie singing "Tell the Lady," and eventually wound up as a segment in 1951's "Cavalcade Of Broadway.") "Then we went to a studio where I met these Canadian kids, the Four Lads, and all these great Columbia musicians. But the point is, Mitch didn't have any idea of how to record me."[5]

"Mitch recommended the Four Lads vocal quartet and arranger/conductor Jimmy Carroll," Bernie said. "And he gave us a song by his close friend, the famous songwriter Alec Wilder, called 'Give Me Time.' He also asked Alec to come by, before the date. They lent us a studio so Johnnie and the Four Lads could woodshed the material, and Alec came in to run over 'Give Me Time' with Johnnie.

"He sat at the piano and Johnnie started singin' his song. Alec fell out. He just flipped, ran downstairs and told Mitch that Johnnie was 'the most fantastic, creative singer he had ever heard,'" Bernie said.

"Mitch came up and he went bananas, jumpin' up and down in the booth, he flipped out, too. And during a break he asked Johnnie and me to go to his office, and he played the record of 'Cry,' by a girl singer [Ruth Casey] on some little label [Cadillac] and told us the story of the night-watchman [Churchill Kohlman] who had written it and had this dinky record made. It was a great song and Mitch asked Johnnie to do it."

They were ideal vehicles. "Cry" stands as one of the most intense, empathically powerful pop records ever made, a work of true interpretive genius. He took Kohlman's lyric soaring into blue strata of hopelessness, then plunged them into a vermillion pit of blood-churning emotion. No one in the room had ever heard a pop singer make such visceral impact.

Johnnie was also bowled over. Manhattan. His first tuxedo. The Beard's caterwauling. Alec Wilder's exotic, rumpled boho appearance. His first time in a legitimate working situation with such professional studio musicians—and they all heaped enthusiastic praise upon him. But when he sang, none of the nervousness one would expect from an Oregon farm-boy was apparent. They set a date, three weeks off, to start recording.

When they began, on October 15, 1951, Johnnie transformed every song to a work of soul-deep magnificence. Everything was cooked up that same day and night by Jimmy Carroll, the band and Johnnie. Carroll basically arranged only the vocal quartet and gave the band, pianist Stan Freeman, guitarist Mundell Lowe, bassist Ed Safranski and drummer Ed Shaughnessy, skeletal lead sheets. "All the lead shots showed were the chord changes," said Freeman, "and we'd just improvise it."

Essentially, they followed Johnnie's vocals, which were as unpredictable as they were unorthodox. During "Cry," he suddenly began drawing out each word to impossible lengths, dramatically phrasing each sustained syllable. It was as much a shock to the band as it would be to the public. "Mitch was the boss, but the whole concept of how it came out was Johnnie's," Bernie said. "On that last chorus, where he started doing that up and down thing with his voice—nobody else could've even tried that. But Johnnie was an interpreter of song."

"We picked 'Cry,' 'Please Mr. Sun,' 'Brokenhearted,' and did them all as head arrangements, just knocked them off," Johnnie said. "The only time we did a third or fourth take was when one of the Four Lads decided to try a different note or switch their parts around. When we found we still had time on the session, I said, 'well, I've got this song I've written, "The Little White Cloud That Cried," that I do in the club when it's quiet enough,' and Mitch liked the idea."[6]

That Johnnie managed to slip in this intensely personal anthem is no surprise. It was the final step, he hoped, in the exorcism of his darkly neurotic adolescent mystery. The deaf loner triumphing over personal adversity and fate's backstabbing through sheer heartfelt expression and considerable lung power. Music's innate power was no secret to Johnnie. What he poured out that night in the studio was so intimately personal, so redolent of pain and fear, desperate for succor and his need to belong— his searching for a place in the world—that it struck a raw nerve deep inside any who heard it. They responded strongly; as Johnnie often said, "You either became a Johnnie Ray fan for life, or you hated my guts."[7] "Everyone was very excited about it, particularly Mitch, who was jumping up and down and screaming. We all felt that we had a hit," Stan Freeman said.

Even Johnnie, always his harshest critic, found it exceptional. "The night we recorded 'Cry,' I knew something was going on," he said. "There was an electricity to that recording session that nobody could put their finger on."[8]

*   *   *

The strength of Johnnie's singing, its captivating quality, lies in several factors. Foremost is his unusually gentle, smokey androgynous tone. Drawn from the feline pride and warm sensitivity of Dinah Washington and Lady Day, offset dramatically by Johnnie's brash male bite and perpetual adolescent energy and somehow fused as one, it was, despite a completely unconventional sound, a contradiction which rang true.

This sense of conflict, his blurring and cross-circuiting of image and emotional messages was an instinctive, sophisticated musical psychology.

It insinuated and pervaded the listener's subconscious in a way no singer managed since Bing Crosby's shrewdly delivered cartoon erotica of 1931. Bing's purring croon reached femmes with a moistening effect that liberated pop singers (and audiences) in a subtle way that escaped Columbo and Vallee. Crosby's was all implicit longing, intimacy and desire, never stated outright but profoundly sensed, thoroughly understood. While Johnnie eschewed the Crosby subtlety, his entire stance was based on the same sort of intimate and inescapably personal communication.

Johnnie got frantic with it. He unleashed a torrential cascade of expression. Tellingly, it was ballads that drove him to his wildest, hammering interpretations. And it was that unorthodox blend of male power and female sensitivity which drove him. What enabled Johnnie to conquer and transcend recognized pop styles was his unique, radical use of rhythm. When he would apply a soft, nurturing Dinah Washington caress to his own wailing, drawn-out phrasing, he often broke the tune like a stick and created his own meter, following a sudden, weird twist separate and above that assigned a lyric by sheet music's annotated melody and tempo.

"Cry" becomes revelatory when he hits the third verse repeat. Each syllable is extruded, put through an agony wringer. The meter is totally altered. He stretches, bends and dominates the lyric in a tumultuous release of desperate psychic information. And it is put across not only by a voice charged with anguish and emotion, but by a dramatic shift in rhythmic pattern. That is the Kay Starr influence, yet Johnnie's application of Starr's rhythm melodrama differs in that he would jam it when no one could have possibly anticipated him to. Billboard recognized it: "a cross between Kay Starr and Jimmy Scott."

Dissection of Johnnie's hodge-podge of influences is helpful only in identifying which musical wells he drank from. How he came to assimilate and assemble this sound is far more significant. What began in Los Angeles and climaxed in Detroit was a process of self-invention on all levels—artistically, sexually and as physically demonstrative as he could—that vigorously challenged and re-defined his entire stock of psychic need and impulse. On stage.

Retaliatory in nature, confrontational by design and marked by urgent desperation, Johnnie went from affable honky tonk ingenue to become a frantic conduit through which flowed the pent-up longing and emotions of his deepest self and, as it turned out, most of Western Civilization.

This extraordinary transformation was an equal product of his native gifts and a then culturally necessary process of survival through identification with society's untouchables: the blacks, whose supremely expressive music thrilled him, and created the primary spark in his personal reconstruction. Almost as important, through the working situations he was compelled to partake in, were the strippers. The exotic dancer's strutting refutation of society's numbing moral code, carried out under the authoritative color of beplumed, erotic luxury and seamy theatrical glamour, spoke directly to his own awkward, impulsive sexuality.

Johnnie's eager acceptance of and by these two separate outcast tribes is a textbook example of reflexive embrace which historically manifested itself among disenfranchised Americans as far back as the blackface minstrels of the 1840s, and even farther in the theater's unspoken status as a benign, welcoming haven for homosexuals. Between the blues shouters and peelers, Johnnie was provided with an instantly recognizable, and recognized, sanctuary.

Influenced and nurtured by these two essentially underground strains of popular art, Johnnie was able to complete his reconstruction. Without encouragement, without precedent, he ignited to become America's first culture-shocking misfit, the earliest nationally recognized prototype model for those the press tagged, as de-mystifyingly and unemphatically as possible, "anti-hero": Brando, Dean, Presley. But the genesis of this heretofore unimaginable phenomenon was entirely personal: the howling, bloody carriage of his conflict-ravaged psyche, ripped untimely from its cerebral womb and cosmetically altered in a wild process of purification and compulsion.

While the results of this psychic re-creation soothed and settled his tangled personal wilderness (and, God knows, made for boffo box office) the process was never carried to completion. Just as Johnnie felt he had finally found a way to adjust—by going berserk—the vortex of activity which "Cry" touched off suddenly, without warning, whisked that delicately established thread of contentment off into a cataclysmic dimension he was completely unprepared for.

Cleveland was the chosen epicenter. Randle built the hype up to a boiling point even before "Cry" was released, orchestrating it like a master with a relentless advance tease: "In two weeks, I am going to play a record that I know is going to sell a million copies."[9] When he dropped the needle in late October of '51, everything changed. The record went to number one on Billboard's Pop and R&B charts in little more than a month's time.

Johnnie kept playing the same rooms, with each successive appearance garnering more and more excitement and larger and larger crowds. But none of them, Bernie Lang, Danny Kessler, Mitch Miller, nor GAC, knew how to sell a misfit. Especially one that (unlike Elvis four years later) was openly bisexual. Johnnie was wild, but not stupid enough to push it. Bernie thought only of pushing Johnnie's price higher and higher. Kessler, an R&B man with sympathy for the outrageous, wasn't sharp enough to keep Johnnie under his control, save for the commissions Bernie was still paying him under a contract as valid and binding as Johnnie was mild and conventional onstage. So they all carved Johnnie up, doling out the morsels of shock and genius that Johnnie threw upon the musical landscape like careless thunderbolts from his Olympian funhouse.

The only man to merit involvement with Johnnie was Mitch Miller. He simply turned Johnnie loose in the studio and captured what occurred on tape. Miller was not smart enough, though, to take Johnnie all the way, to continue pushing the borders and trampling the established fashions. It was too early, too radical a notion to allow Johnnie to expand, if not completely transform, America's understanding and expectation of pop music, to take it from staid bandstand entertainment to violent mandates on emotion and freedom.

Johnnie rocked the sensibilities and very structure of the nation's self-perception and public character. It was the first time any one other than a politician or religious idealogue had done so. Johnnie cut across every established line of behavior and self-control. He did so entirely naturally; his intensity and depth of feeling were matched by guileless, straight-forward honesty. His was an attitude totally foreign to the 1951 model, a collective persona essentially mired in a repressive, parochial moral swamp.

Johnnie's agenda was simple: "I just show people the emotion they're afraid to show. People are too crowded inside themselves these days. They're afraid to show any love. And boy, what is the primary existence for existing? It's beauty and love."[10] Johnnie's boozy beatitude, with all its undeniable impact and pervasive, evocative allure, was utterly sincere—and it was because of that sincerity that he was perceived as either a threat or a savior.

A radical like Johnnie, if talented, is always heard first and best by other performers. Two iconic figures in American music and their initial reactions to Johnnie Ray demonstrate the changes already going on and those which the Cry guy engendered. One, Hank Williams, was poised to become one of the most influential singer/songwriters country music had ever produced; the other, Frank Sinatra, was in the midst of a horrifying career slump.

Hank Williams symbolized pop music's post-war trend toward the single—the dynamic individual whose style and message are rooted in a common, undiluted populist sensibility. The Hillbilly Shakespeare admired the Cry Guy out loud, naming Johnnie Ray (along with another white piano pounder, Louisiana boogie man Moon Mullican) as one of his favorite entertainers in Country Song Round Up magazine # 18's "Witness Box" Q&A interview format.

Williams was more eloquent when interviewed by Ralph J. Gleason in Oakland, California shortly after "Cry" was released. "I like Johnnie Ray. He's sincere and shows he's sincere," said Hank. "That's the reason he's popular—he sounds to me like he means it." When Gleason showed surprise, Williams elaborated. "What I mean by sincerity, well, Roy Acuff's the best example . . . He's the biggest singer this music ever knew, and he'll stand up there singin', with tears running down his cheeks."[11]

Frank Sinatra represented perhaps the highest flowering of a quarter century tradition of crooning but suddenly found himself an anachronism. First Frankie Laine, then Tony Bennett, and now Johnnie, dubbed "the Belters" and "the Exciters," came along with a brash vibrance and vulgar beat that made the old bandstand routine which Frank meticulously perfected seem almost invalid. He had elevated popular song interpretation as no one since Crosby, and now it seemed as if the public was defiantly turning their backs on him.

After Manie Sachs left Columbia, Sinatra's sense of betrayal was deepened by Mitch Miller's desperate attempts to sell product. The two never saw eye to eye in the studio, and Sinatra's fall from grace was, he felt, precipitated by the novelty songs Miller suggested. What saloon singer would feel comfortable with material like "Cry of the Wild Goose"?

After novelty duet "Mama Will Bark (Papa Will Spank)" (with Dagmar, television blond bombshell who never spoke on camera), Sinatra grew to loathe Mitch Miller. He placed much of the blame for his predicament squarely on the Beard. Either way, Sinatra's records stopped selling. (He has still never forgiven the producer. "A good Mafioso blood feud," is how Miller described it in 1992.)

All this left Sinatra numb. Begging wife Nancy for a divorce (so he could chase Ava Gardner full time) intensified his misery. Shortly before Nancy conceded in late 1951, Broadway columnist Earl Wilson visited at Sinatra's California home (he was wrapping work on his latest doomed-to-flop picture "Meet Danny Wilson"). They talked about this belter business, of Frankie Laine and Johnnie Ray.

"What do you think is happening?" Sinatra, clearly disturbed, asked Wilson.

"It's a pendulum," the columnist replied, "it'll swing back."

"I'm not throwing in any sponge to Johnnie Ray!" Sinatra snarled, then shouted it, like a curse, "JOHNNIE RAY!"

The Voice reacted by pursuing other avenues of artistic expression, as Wilson wrote, "desperately looking for some new interests to soften the disappointments he suffered in his nose dive." Frank announced to Wilson that he was taking up painting and had, in fact, just completed his first effort, which he proudly displayed. It was an oil portrait of a clown.[12]

*   *   *

The pace at which Johnnie's fame grew was astonishing, made all the more so by the distinctly unusual quality of a voice which arrested the pop music audience. Their embrace of that strange voice assumed a vehement acceleration. "It wasn't moving too fast for Johnnie," Cy Kertman said. "He told me that he always felt he was going to be a star and that was what he planned for from the time he was a youngster. When we'd talk about it, he would say 'I always knew I would attain stardom.' And knowing him, knowing the way his feelings and reactions were, why, it wasn't like he was being presumptuous, it just seemed like a natural flow of things, the way things were meant to work out." Johnnie's was a dizzying fate—ghetto knockabout in spring, "one of Tin Pan Alley's sizzling Newcomers" in autumn.

"I came back from Korea on the U.S.S. Missouri in October of 1951," Johnnie's old friend Jim Low said, "and went to Washington D.C.; my wife and I got a place there. A little while after, we were in the apartment listening to the radio and I heard 'Little White Cloud That Cried.' I had never heard the song before, but I recognized his voice immediately. That song *was* Johnnie Ray. He really had a classic way of doing it— there was no mistaking him for anybody else.

"'That's Johnnie Ray,' I told my wife.

"'I know,' she says. 'I've heard it before.'

"'No, no, you don't understand, I grew up with the guy for Christ's sake!' I said.

"'You have got to be kidding.'

"'Hell, no,' I said, 'We grew up together and we've known each other since the third grade.'

"'Well, he's down at the Capitol theater right now,' she said, 'he's performing there.'

"'I have got to go see him.'"

Low was ill prepared for what awaited him. "So I went to the Capitol theater," he said. "And there had to be ten thousand screaming, delirious females down there! I thought 'how in the hell am I going to get to see John?' I walked around to the stage door—which wasn't easy—and the old guy at the door says, 'what can I do for you?'

I said, 'I want to see Johnnie.'

'You and ten thousand other people,' he says, jerking his thumb at the crowd.

'No, no, you don't understand, I know him. We grew up together.' And just then Cy, the road manager, happened to walk by and he says,

'Where do you know Johnnie from?'

'Dallas, Oregon,' I said.

'Come on in,' he says, because nothing had been printed about Dallas. It always said Portland or Roseburg, so when I said Dallas, he knew immediately. Cy was a hell of a nice guy."

"Johnnie was on, he was performing at the time." The memory is a rich one; Low is still awed by the moment's fated propinquity. When Johnnie noticed Cy in the wings next to a man in uniform, he probably thought it was another bust in the making. Then it hit him—Jimmy Low. "That damn fool," Low said. "He looked over and when he saw me, shit, he came running over, jumping, with that big lanky form and those long arms flapping, and he jumped right on top of me! We both fell down. Oh, shit, it was something else . . . unreal, just unreal."

Surreal is perhaps a more appropriate word. When Johnnie worked he wore so much pancake that off stage and under normal light, he looked positively orange.[13] Johnnie slathered it on to the same degree Sophie Tucker did, as if putting on armor. After he loped back out on stage, Low stood in the wings, mesmerized. The crowd, band, Johnnie's voice are a crescendo he will never forget. Johnnie writhed through his remaining numbers and the two enjoyed a monumental reunion.

"We went out that night and got so goddamn stone drunk it was terrible," Low said. "He told me how he had been playing in this one booze house night club, and things had just gone up from there." It was a manicured account of a complex chain reaction, but Low had known of Johnnie's fated stardom for so long that it struck him as neither curious nor exceptional.

His friend's understanding was well suited to the occasion; Johnnie knew it and tendered Low's confidence an intimate admission. "John and I stayed out 'til about four or five in the morning, and we were walking down the street, we had our arms around each other and he told me, 'Jim, you know I'm homosexual.' I really wasn't that surprised, because I remember hearing rumors, back in Portland, about these tendencies he had. It didn't make a goddamn bit of difference to me. 'Johnnie,' I said, 'we're still the best of buddies.' And I meant it. John and I were friends and that was all that mattered."

Low is completely sincere. A plain-spoken and simple man, he got no vicarious charge from Johnnie's amazing new celebrity, save for an intense personal pride. The glamour and cast of big-name characters meant nothing to him. Low, a career Navy man, did not follow or even listen to pop music. "We were out all night," said Low. "And I had to go straight into work."

Shortly after his D.C. stint, Johnnie returned to Columbia's studio on November 29th and recorded two of his most remarkably personal compositions. "Mountains In the Moonlight" graphically relates his experience wandering the woods after the 1940 accident. "Mountains," Johnnie sang, "seem to call my name to me / never fear the darkness / never fear the black of night / for mountains in the moonlight will fade the shadows from your sight." Nature was his only ally: "panic all around me / the black of night surrounds me / like a child who's been left alone / but mountains in the moonlight / whisper softly / never fear."

"Paths of Paradise" is a remarkable essay on morals, faith and mortality, with a strange ambivalent twist; while overtly metaphysical, with lyrics more suited to the seance and sinner's bench than bandstand, it bears no relation to his Jubilee show closer or any conventional gospel number.

It tours a shadowy personal Limbo, where he absolves himself of Earthly accountability, decries sin and craves death. His haunted, emotional wail enhances a mood of fear, detachment, and resignation, a disconcerting sensibility heightened by the song's totally unconventional structure. "Paths of Paradise" has neither chorus nor bridge and is, in effect, a single rambling verse—a chant of confession, prepared for the day of reckoning.

The message is one of doom, a tour of the dark half of Johnnie's personal matrix—it is the spiritual flipside to "Little White Cloud." Where "Little White Cloud" evoked hope and "Mountains In the Moonlight" spotlights his blind pagan faith, "Paths of Paradise" delineates the confusion and guilt that gnawed at Johnnie's soul. Strange tales coming from one who sat atop the world, with all his dreams realized.

Having gotten these off his chest at long last, Johnnie thought little about anything except his next performance and his next drink. When the show ended he did not experience the horrible tailspin and sense of emptiness many performers dread. He never thought about the void between an onstage high and the reality of his life as Ray, citizen.

Johnnie's personal life was extremely unconventional but was in no way based upon his stage persona. That was what made him such a remarkable showman—the spontaneity and emotional surge translated into a presentation as much guileful pose as it was an honest expression of beauty, abandon and joy. It was a celebration of life, his personal realm of utter liberation.

Johnnie was alone there. He had little understanding of what was going on around him as a result of this expression. Intuitively, he felt it was all natural, but the release of "Cry" brought on a flaming reaction beyond anyone's comprehension. How could he know that Sinatra railed against him, or that Hank Williams listened intently to the disk, revelling in the vermillion throb and shattering impact of Johnnie's voice?

The cloud of ignorance which Danny Kessler and Bernie Lang established earlier in the year still hung over Johnnie's blissfully unconcerned head. But from coast to coast, operators, exploitation men, show biz flacks and gangsters were acutely cognizant of Ray. While Al Green, Jerry Crocker, Jan Grayton and Bob Mitchell watched from a distance, the trade insiders and their mob backers schemed on how best to use this sensation. While Bernie worked "the morning line," his daily price-inflating ritual, bamboozling night club bookers with his implacable and outrageous demands for an ever-increasing guarantee, the

players were lining up on either side of the singer, a gauntlet of ravenous traders who smelled wall-to-wall cash.[1]

In December, jazz bible Downbeat did the first substantive print interview with Johnnie. The magazine chose an unusual format: they sat down with Johnnie in an office at Larry Spier Publishing and asked him to debunk, line by line, the litany of myth which his official GAC biography sought to establish.

He corrected inaccuracies and explained, with fierce self-depreca-tion, how little he thought of himself and his talent. Preferring to plug Kay Starr and Little Miss Cornshucks, Johnnie allowed as to how "this whole thing might go over like a lead balloon and I can always go back to the movie extra deal," a job, of course, which he never had. The myth blossomed all around him. As per Bernie's instructions, Johnnie played the hayseed Uriah Heep, and spoke of how "All I want anyway is to have a wife and kids and a nice home where I can sit down and sing to myself."[2]

The knowledge that his arrest in Detroit six months earlier could derail the entire business colored Bernie's orchestration of every public move, but the public's embrace of "Cry," softened the need to control and dis-inform. Johnnie made money and that alone was enough to ensure a degree of respectability.

But the ascension had not even half-way begun. Johnnie ground it out with a wrenching intensity and thousands of fans responded just as emphatically. His crowds grew wilder and more unpredictable; police became fixtures at many of his appearances. Earlier in the month, Johnnie had been back at both Moe's Main Street and Buffalo's Town Casino, jam-ming the rooms and turning away patrons who stood on line for hours. Bernie was in overdrive; Johnnie's price at Buffalo was $7,500.00, having jumped upwards over the past two and a half months until it seemed as if it would never cease rising.

Lang was conducting an astonishing juggling act of dates booked earlier at lower salaries and new ones which commanded successively higher and higher fees. There was a mixture of bald greed and self-pre-serving tact here. While the Town Casino paid through the nose it was, after all, Nowheresville. What the entire future of Johnnie's career depend-ed on was his reception in Manhattan, and Bernie and GAC had begun courting and negotiating with the glittering center stone in Gotham's gem-laden crown: the Copacabana.

The haggling began in September, even before Johnnie met Mitch Miller or heard "Cry." The first ripple on the surface of New York's consciousness came when Johnnie appeared at Ben and Doris Maksik's Town & Country in Brooklyn, a cavernous nightclub at the time with a 2,000 capacity, where Tony Bennett once again introduced Johnnie—a crucial move in terms of acceptance.

A subsequent Ray engagement at the Boulevard Club in Queens gave the GAC brass opportunity to drag the Copa's Jack Entratter out to see Johnnie work. "Drag is the word," Entratter said. "They almost had to put a gun in my ribs. I didn't want to go. And after I got there and watched the kid, I was so doubtful that I pulled one of the biggest skulls in my career—it was a mistake that cost me $3000."[3] Entratter offered Bernie $300 a week for Johnnie; the Copa was worth a price concession and he gave Entratter a standard GAC contract to sign and return to the office for Johnnie's signature. Entratter signed it the next day and promptly forgot about the whole deal. He also forgot to send it back to GAC.

Bernie knew that Entratter was not a man to be pushed, and didn't bat an eye when he was informed of the measly terms. Shortly after the Copa's original proprietor Monte Proser had been muscled aside by the controlling interests of Lucky Luciano sub-capo's Frank Costello and Joey Adonis, Entratter, with the approval of Copa manager Jules Podell, had gone from bouncer to maitre d' to nominal entertainment director, an unusual ascension he enjoyed through his long-time association with Costello and Adonis. Following Luciano's Cuban exile in 1947, these two came into control of the entire organization. Seasoned bootleggers and some of the very first mafiosi to branch out into the narcotics trade, these men defined power in New York City. When J. Edgar Hoover played the ponies, Costello covered his bets.[4]

Thus Bernie was in no hurry to grouse at the Copa's offer. Johnnie himself made that unnecessary as each successive appearance drew more and more attention and more and more money. When the contract never arrived, and Billboard announced the deal—an unknown at the Copa was news—Bernie knew the re-negotiation would take care of itself.

It was Johnnie who needed minding. His drinking was ferocious, and his unorthodox presentation aroused as much suspicion as it did enthusiasm.

The potential for disaster was softened by the typhoon of money that followed Johnnie. And Bernie kept him working: of his next fifteen engagements each broke box office records. Such a smash of successive victories was unheard of; suddenly, Martin & Lewis were small time after Johnnie. His explosive impact and the near riots he caused after "Cry" gave rise to a rolling fireball of rumors about the singer: that Johnnie was a black woman (a natural enough assumption for the casual listener to make; his success was so sudden that no one had time to photograph him); that Johnnie was a deaf mute somehow able to sing; that Johnnie was dying of throat cancer; that Johnnie as a result of some bizarre trauma had a steel plate in his skull. "Man, I heard all those stories about me being somebody else, or a dead man," he said, "and I give you my right hand I began to believe them myself." Only one thing was clear, that here was a figure as strange as he was powerful.[5]

*   *   *

America spent a lachrymose Christmas in 1951. "Cry" poured out of phonograph and radio sets. Already a number one pop record, with "Little White Cloud," at number two (the first time in Billboard history that both sides of a single disk held those spots) it hit the top of the Rhythm & Blues charts on the 26th. Johnnie returned to Cleveland for two weeks at Moe's Main Street. Despite harsh weather fans lined up hours in advance. Although Bernie originally booked the date at $1,750.00 a week, Variety reported that Johnnie worked there at a "salary concession," agreeing to a $1,250.00 fee.[6] Publicizing such an arrangement was standard public smoke-screen for a private financial arrangement, the under-the-table bonus, a hefty percentage skimmed from bar receipts. Bernie was learning management as fast as Johnnie's records were selling.

"Cry" sold 200,000 copies during the first two weeks of January 1952 alone, making it a smash comparable only to Gene Autry's "Rudolph, the Red Nosed Reindeer," at the time the biggest seller in recording history. "Cry" was a monster hit and implied a prestige beyond that which the Okeh label merited. So too did the terms of Johnnie's contract.

His original Okeh contract called for their standard royalty and advances for one year with two one-year options; but as Danny Kessler said, "After Mitch called me and said, 'Let me produce that kid who cries and kicks the piano,' and 'Cry' went to number one, and 'Little White Cloud' went to number two, on the Okeh label, we had a big meeting at Columbia. And since Okeh was supposed to be a black label and Johnnie was white, they said 'We're moving Johnnie to the red label,' which was fine by me, because you've got to remember that I had signed a management contract with Johnnie, which I was not supposed to do." The move reduced a potential conflict of interest hassle which could land him in trouble. Johnnie's new contract, settled in January, gave Columbia a seven-year stretch with the singer.[7]

Johnnie's move to the red label couldn't have come at a better time; prior to the Beard and Autry's "Reindeer," Columbia suffered a series of minor set backs; their established stars had stopped selling. In 1951 they considered shutting down their country division entirely—its "Big Three," Roy Acuff, Bob Wills and Gene Autry, were, like Sinatra, commercially all but forgotten. And Sinatra was into the label for more than $250,000 worth of unearned royalty advances he needed to keep the IRS off his back. Came "Cry" and Columbia's coffers were churning with cash; Johnnie's sales made even Rosemary Clooney's and Tony Bennett's seem comparatively tame.

With the record deal straightened out, the Copa booking in the works, Columbia sent their wonder boy West. The trip was a combination promotional tour and vacation put together by the label's West Coast promo man Jack Devaney. Johnnie savored the notion of his triumphant return to Oregon, and Devaney cooked up a splendid itinerary.

When Johnnie and Cy landed in Portland, the entire town was at fever pitch. Mobs at the airport, official proclamations, even a parade with Johnnie perched atop the back of an open Cadillac convertible, basking in the tumult. He adored the mobs. He shook hands with the Mayor. "I arranged for him to get the key to the city," Devaney said, "and then we went over and he gave a speech at the assembly hall of his old high school."[8] He could not perform there—the Union and American Guild of Variety Artists took a very dim view of name artists who performed without fee.

It was the first time he saw his family in some eighteen months. "We were not in that close touch with Johnnie during that time," Elma said. "He would write home occasionally, saying that every job he got paid a little more money, that every time the pay scale was a little better." There was so much that he could not tell them, his correspondence had naturally been limited. It happened so rapidly that Elma couldn't even find her brother's records until he arrived and Devaney gave her some.

"We had an inkling when he got the recording contract, and we knew that his records were strong in the East, that it had built up by degrees. And suddenly, you'd turn on the radio and there would be a Johnnie Ray record—it was absolutely unbelievable. And then he came back and all formed an entourage to follow him around." Even his family acted like fans.

Johnnie wowed Elma with tales of meeting Lady Day. "I loved Billie Holiday, loved her," Elma said. "And Johnnie developed his ear for song by listening to her, just like I had. We both loved her and Johnnie told me that he met her at the Flame, that she carried a little dog and wore a gardenia in her hair." He regaled Elma with his tale of a Holiday appearance in Windsor, Ontario where she left Johnnie to take care of her chihuahua during the performance. He accidentally let the dog off his lap and wound up crawling on his hands and knees under the tables trying to grab her.

"And he brought me a picture of Billie, with Johnnie sitting beside her and told me that he had said to her, 'Billie, come home with me. I'm going on vacation and one thing I'd really like to do is walk up to my sister's door with you, knock on it and have her look out and see you standing there.' I was very touched by that."

There's no doubt Johnnie said precisely that. Once he was able to calm down enough to find his tongue. Facing his primary artistic female icon it is natural that he would speak of the only other woman in his life who rivaled Holiday's exalted position—his sister, the woman who exposed him to Holiday in the first place.

Johnnie's "vacation" was a three-day visit to Portland and one day in Dallas, where he wallowed in his new found glory. By Mayoral proclamation it was "Johnnie Ray Day." Mostly, it was also a hectic go-round of Portland d.j. shows. Before leaving, he went to dinner at his Aunt Bea's home there, where one of his teenage cousins sheepishly admitted to boasting all over school of his famous relative's planned visit. When the phone rang, Johnnie was asked to speak to the caller. It was a high school girl calling to find out if he was truly the Cry Guy.

"Hello?"

"Who is this?"

"Johnnie Ray."

"Who is this *really?*" The girl demanded.

"Johnnie Ray. Who's this?"

"Rosemary Clooney!" she shrieked and hung up.

He broke up laughing. Johnnie Ray was already bigger than life, far too large for any modest Portland home to accommodate.[9]

Johnnie made his goodbyes, but not before promising to fly Hazel and Elma, who dreaded nightclubs, out to New York for his Paramount Theater engagement in June. Devaney rounded him up and they went south. Back to Hollywood.

There were no appearances booked in California; it was strictly more promo stuff and, most importantly, a record date, set to produce Johnnie's first full-length album, a still-new concept that Columbia was one of the first companies to introduce. Johnnie's first red label release, "Please Mr. Sun," backed with "(Here Am I) Brokenhearted," was just entering Billboard's Top Ten, but could not get past "Cry" and "Little White Cloud."

*   *   *

Johnnie returned to Hollywood just as he predicted before hitchhiking out of town in 1949, as the biggest name in the business. He gloated to the press: "Hollywood plain told me to get lost. They didn't like me because I wore a hearing aid. I was told to forget about a career," he said to a reporter from the Daily News. "I told 'em to go to Hades. I proved the public will accept me."[10]

Bernie wanted to ensure that his boy's fame grew even greater; only one thing concerned him more than the steady escalation of Johnnie's price—that Johnnie's free-handed sexuality remain unquestioned, and the best way to ensure this was through the press. Lang made some inquiries, searching for a suitable package of female to link Johnnie with.

He found an ideal specimen in Tempest Storm, a red-headed Georgia farm girl of stunning voluptuosity who would rise to prominence as one of America's most successful peelers. Storm was just coming into her own as an exotic dancer, a profession loaded with familiar appeal for Johnnie. As one of a sisterhood which watched over and nurtured Johnnie she would enjoy instant rapport; as a still green country girl she would not question the more outre elements of Johnnie's character. It was a flack man's dream caper. The shots would look great in the papers.

"I had just arrived in Hollywood in 1952," Storm said, "and I remember I was in the Mocambo one night when Rock Hudson walked in with about four other guys and I said 'My God, there's a fantastic-lookin' guy!' And my friends told me 'Forget it. Hands off—he doesn't like women.' And I said 'What do you mean?' 'Well, he likes boys,' they said. 'Well, excuse me!' I thought. I just didn't understand that at all."[11]

"So, my press agent at the time was Ed Devere and he knew someone who worked with Johnnie. Ed told me, 'It would be good publicity if you and Johnnie Ray got together.' And he took me down to Florentine Gardens and I met Johnnie there. I had already heard rumors about him, but I was very naive. They had a fabulous show there, big chorus lines, and Johnnie was a very charming man. He was really a gentleman and a straightforward person, very respectful. He knew how to treat a woman—he had a lot of class and a lot of talent.

"He was very charismatic," she said, "I did not want to believe these rumors. He even made a pass at me, as a matter of fact. I could have fallen in love with him very easily, but because of those rumors, I just did not want to get into that."

No matter. The shots looked great in the papers.

At the Yacht Club, his former bosses griped inconsolably. At the highbrow joints wanting to book him, things were considerably more heated. The Sunset Strip's most prestigious rooms were Mocambo, owned by Charlie Morrison, a warhorse showman out of New York, and Ciro's, run by nonpareil operator H.D. Hover. Both desperately wanted Johnnie. They each got their first look at him when Jack Devaney hosted an introductory party for the press and radio at The Interlude, a chic cocktail lounge adjacent to Ciro's.

Apart from the industry crowd, very few outside the business attended, with one notable exception, Charlie Morrison's daughter, Carol Elizabeth Morrison. A lively, twenty-one-year-old brunette party girl, she had taken a name more in keeping with her swinging Hollywood self-image: Marilyn.[12] Marilyn's dark feline eyes spoke of heat, hunger and frolic. She could not take them off Johnnie. His pensive yet intense manner, offset by a rural ebullience, was charming. His soft, purring speaking voice soothed her ear. Her smoldering gaze cut through the smoke-filled room full of boozing Fourth Estate hacks, and its warmth was not lost on Johnnie. He dug it.

When a guest approached Devaney and asked whether the star was planning to sing for them, he said it was out. But Johnnie overheard the exchange, and as eager to please as when he went to teen birthday parties in Dallas, he gladly sat down at the piano and performed several numbers. Marilyn was hooked, irrevocably attracted to the singer. And, to her delight, Johnnie was in the mood. They left the party together.

This development was not lost on Mocambo's Morrison or Ciro's Hover, either. "I had spotted Johnnie immediately as a comer," Hover said. "I used to spot these attractions before they became too famous and tried to sign them at a reasonable price. And when he came down from Portland, Charlie wanted him and I wanted him. So, we had a little problem."[13]

Herman Hover was a rara avis among club operators. He began his career as a chorus boy in Earl Carroll's Vanities on Broadway during the late 1920's and became one of the Great White Way's youngest directors, attending Yale's law school at the same time. After he passed the bar, still directing for Carroll, Hover also authored a book "The Fourteen Presidents Before Lincoln," commercially published in 1940. He came West and opened Ciro's on December 26, 1942; the next seventeen years brought prominence.

Hover also owned the Earl Carroll Theater at Sunset and Gower, and held interests in Las Vegas' Last Frontier, and later, the Silver Slipper. Hover was scrupulously legitimate. Hollywood was teeming with the likes of Mickey Cohen, and Johnny "Stomp." Whenever the mob boys "asked" to buy into Ciro's Hover ran a standard response: "Well, I've got two partners," he would say, poker faced, "and I can't make a move without them, I can't blow my nose without their consent. I will be happy to call them and explain the terms of your offer. They are lawyers, employed by the Department of Justice in Washington. I'll call them right now." The boys would vanish before he could pick up the telephone. Hover was the sole owner and proprietor.

He was a master at the fine art of "romancing an attraction," as he put it and was not afraid to gamble. "When I first put Sammy Davis Jr. into Ciro's, everyone asked me 'why do you want to have anything to do with that nigger?' I told them, 'Because he is one of the greatest entertainers alive.' And see how he turned out, one of the biggest names in the business.

"And the next thing I know is that Charlie Morrison's daughter Marilyn is really romancing Johnnie, and that is something that is pretty tough to overcome," Hover said. "When you go after attractions, there is no limit to the extent to which you will go. I won't say that Charlie asked his own daughter to get intimate with Johnnie, but he did everything he could. He'd take them out to dinner at every opportunity. And everytime I talked to Johnnie, he was with Marilyn. They used to come into Ciro's but I could never talk to him alone, I could never use all the nice gestures that I normally do to romance an attraction. To sign him." When Johnnie left Los Angeles for a couple of days, for a press party in Del Mar and additional radio interviews, Hover was stymied and anxious.

Even more important than Marilyn, Mocambo or Ciro's was the record date. Mitch Miller flew in after arranging to use the Buddy Cole Quartet (guitarist Nick Botkin, bassist Dick Whittington and drummer Nick Fatool).[14] The session was cast in the same mold as Johnnie's first Columbia date—an intimate clubby sound, this time minus the Four Lads. The band's spare backing gave Johnnie's voice free reign and he turned in a vocal performance as heady and emotional as Miller had hoped for.

The songs included Johnnie's fine, pleading version of "All Of Me," and an exceptional reading of "Don't Take Your Love From Me." Both were standards—none of Johnnie's original material was included, although at the time Bernie was setting up Carlyle Music, Johnnie's own publishing firm. All 150 odd songs Johnnie had penned went into the catalog, yet ultimately less than a dozen of these were committed to wax.

In typical Miller style, the entire affair was casually assembled. "I was at the session," Jack Devaney said. "Johnnie was very disciplined—he cared. There were no real preparations, no big long rehearsals. There were no rhubarbs or anything like that. Johnnie had a very, very good musical mind. He went in, they set the mike up, the musicians would start and he sang. It was very off the cuff. They did the whole album in one afternoon."

Johnnie's singing on the album is markedly black-influenced, laden with Rhythm & Blues phrasing and emphasis, more so than anything he had yet recorded. Yet that style, ingrained as it was to him, was not one which he concentrated on or sought to establish as his forte. During a break, Johnnie's reverence for Tin Pan Alley antiques came through and he suggested they include "Walkin' My Baby Back Home."

"'Walkin My Baby Back Home' was a song that I heard in my youth," Johnnie said. "Me and Buddy Cole were recording on the coast, and just off the top of my head I said 'Let's do Walkin My Baby Back Home,' and we just winged it."[15] The performance is a throwback to the hokum of his Portland and Coos Bay lounge days. A distinctly conventional reading, it is an almost total reversal from the churning approach of "Give Me Time," or the track that follows "Walkin" on the album, "Don't Take Your Love From Me."

On that song, his searing intensity and extravagant phrasing reaches a stratospheric plane of forlorn pleading. With a powerful, indigo-hued wail, he altered the lyric ("would you take the wings / from *little* birds / so they can't fly?") and transformed it into an even more powerful metaphor. He could stretch a line as far as conceivably possible, and at this session whatever he reached for, no matter how distant and unlikely an artistic goal, was grasped and caressed by his voice.

This ability, despite the radical nature of his overnight introduction to the public, was starting to gain recognition from the more sophisticated corners of the American mainstream. After "Please Mr. Sun" was released as a single, Johnnie received an important nod from the legitimate New York press. On January 30th, Dorothy Kilgallen, a second generation Hearst reporter who became Broadway's first female columnist in 1939, featured a tellingly personalized item in her nationally syndicated column:

"A simply awful thing has happened to me.

"How am I going to say it?

"Goodness, it's too frightful really. (Steel yourself, girl. Get it off your bodice once and for all.)

"All right. Here it is.

"I've come to just love Johnnie Ray's record of 'Please Mr. Sun.'

"Now will anybody ever speak to me again?"[16]

Bernie was overjoyed. Kilgallen, at the time, rivalled Walter Winchell in terms of influence and power. Their influence was such that press agents with a recognized ability to get items into her Voice Of Broadway or Winchell's On Broadway were "retained" annually by publicity-hungry celebrities for high five-figure sums. Let Entratter chew that one over, Bernie thought, gleefully cognizant of the fact that their Copa contract had never been signed.

Hover was still trolling. "To have a big attraction is very important to us operators—we lived on attractions. Since his girlfriend was my competition's daughter, I decided to romance Bernie Lang and his wife," Hover recalled. "I'd have them in as my dinner guests and I would make the nice gestures, but always planting the seed. 'Charlie himself is a former agent, a very good agent,' I'd say, 'and as soon as anything serious happens between Johnnie and Marilyn, naturally Johnnie is going to work for his wife's father. You're going to lose Johnnie Ray.'"

"Someone told me that Johnnie was homosexual, but I didn't place any weight in that," he said matter of factly, "because most of your top attractions are homosexual. It was so prevalent that it didn't matter. It's like having black hair—so what?" But Hover knew that Bernie was duty bound to see the public romance with Marilyn through. Very few others shared Hover's liberal attitude. The Langs desperately needed Marilyn.

Hover played on. "Every night we'd have the Langs to dinner. My wife was developing into a showman's wife, so she helped a little too. We would talk to Bernie and Gloria, and then Johnnie and Marilyn would come in." Bernie's head must have spun. He did the best thing he could: nothing. Let it take care of itself.

Johnnie's image, however, could not. He and Marilyn's nights on the town defused potential scandal but the Negro issue was another potential stain on their property's already unstable public persona. Billboard[17] ran a feature on the impact and prevalence of Rhythm & Blues on pop music that drove the perception home: "The influence of R&B disks on the pop market both as tunes and artists has been of great import over the past year. Johnnie Ray, at present a 'hot' personality in the pop field, with a singing style close to R&B vocalists, sells just as well in both fields."

Mitch Miller was also acutely aware of the undesirable connotations such an understanding might bring to the public. "Of course, there is no great white singer who was not influenced by a great black singer. The white audience, at the time, just couldn't accept it from a black artist— like Big Maybelle, Little Richard—but I didn't want Johnnie to be noted just for his black-inspired singing," Miller said, "I knew he was an original, and obviously the sales of the records proved it. But you'll notice, in the rotation of releases, that on the next record I came out with a standard

'Walkin' My Baby Back Home.'" And of course it was Johnnie himself who decided to record the song. Miller's instinct was sound. The single went gold later that year.

* * *

While the almost unprecedented sales of "Cry" bespoke his achievements, the truth was that everyone making money off of Johnnie— Bernie Lang, Cy Kertman, Sol Lazarow, lawyer Halsey Cowan and GAC—were fearful that the bottom could drop out at any moment. That was what made the Copa engagement so crucial. It was all well and good to draw hysterical adolescents and sex-starved women whose husbands were away in Korea, but unless Johnnie sold his wailing, piano-kicking style to the Cafe Society set any future career would remain limited to the teen-age crowd's attention span.

Not all the press Johnnie received was positive. New York columnists frequently threw jabs ("Anytime the Little White Cloud That Cried wants to become the Little White Cloud That Died is fine by us. And the sooner, the better.")[18] Britain's Melody Maker called Johnnie's style "uninhibited and tasteless," adding "If an artist has to descend to this level to capture the masses, then the outlook for popular music is bleak indeed."[19]

They were not alone in their thinking. As it stood in March 1952, Johnnie's career could still go either way. After Ray appeared twice on Perry Como's ABC television program in January and February, Ed Sullivan booked him on his "Toast Of The Town" show. Johnnie received one thousand dollars for each appearance.[20] His performance style, a convulsive series of sweeping gestures, deft poses, and agonized contortions, all given emphatic visual punctuation by his grinding jaw and spasmodically clawing hands, completely conquered the national audience.

After the Sullivan show, "Cry" sold an additional 480,000 copies in a matter of days.[21] Once America saw Johnnie at work, the natural reaction was parody. Comedians everywhere added Ray impersonations to their acts; one burly comic did a routine where he would remove his shirt and shred it to ribbons while lip-synching to Johnnie's records. Sammy Davis Jr. did a hilarious Ray impression. When Capitol Records released "Try," Stan Freberg's "Cry" send-up in late March, it only heightened the general public's picture of Johnnie as a grotesque curiosity, an anomalous freak. (Freberg perfected his stylized Ray phrasing by cutting the record with Buddy Cole, who counseled him on the nature of Johnnie's gaspy breathing.)

"Try" went to number fifteen on the Billboard pop chart. Freberg, for years after, would run away from Johnnie every time their paths happened to cross. "Cry"'s publishers threatened a lawsuit, which Capitol's Cliffie Stone settled out of court, agreeing to split the royalties 50/50.[22] None of it bothered Johnnie, though. "I get the biggest kick out of take-offs on me," he said in 1952. "Particularly Stan Freberg's record and the stuff that Jack E. Leonard and Sammy Davis Jr. do."[23]

Johnnie returned to Buffalo's Town Casino for a two-week stint that month. Once again, he sold out two shows nightly and the club turned away thousands of "Ray's Slaves" as the Buffalo bobby soxers rather luridly designated themselves. Life Magazine sent a crew out, the first substantive national coverage Johnnie received outside of pieces in the trades and gossip column items.

A teaser page showed two huge shots of Johnnie's back, snapped from behind as he leaned down into an enraptured mob of young girls. "Again—Shrieks and Swoons" it said. "A tearful new singer leads his young followers to the brink of frenzy. To see who he is, turn page." (As if no one could figure it out; "hmmm, mama, it's maybe Mario Lanza?")

"Johnnie Ray Sings and Sobs His Way to a Quick Fortune," the headline read. "Not since Sinatra set the style for cadaverous Casanovas in 1943 has any young singer moved his audience to such tantrums of woe and joy. Whereas Sinatra and his army of imitators made other people moan and squeal but remained fairly restrained themselves, Ray has renounced restraint. He pants, shivers, writhes, sighs, and above all, cries. He is America's Number One Public Weeper."

It also featured the very first photograph of Johnnie wearing his hearing aid, which Bernie strictly forbade him to wear onstage. Life re-told the Boy Scout blanket toss tale and identified him as being half-deaf explaining that although "Ray wears a hearing aid . . . he takes it off while performing because it might distract his fans." A sequential flurry of photos showed him working at the piano ("Ray grimaces, clutches his temples and pounds the piano") and at a recording session—flat out on the floor, surrounded by musicians. "Finally prostrated by the emotions of a new song Johnnie Ray lies on his back in Columbia Records studio and sobs out a sad refrain." Johnnie played it cool with the Life reporter. "Ray is not impressed by his financial success . . . Nor is he impressed by his singing voice. 'Ridiculous,' he calls it." A three-page spread in Life; not bad.[24]

While legitimate coverage (or as legitimate as Johnnie could expect to get) like that was impressive, it placed him solidly in the tenuous teen idol vein. No one knew what the hearing aid revelation might do for him. He didn't care. "There was a time when I did not wear the hearing aid onstage," he said years later. "Because people thought it was a gimmick to get the audience's sympathy. That I did not think was right. But it did get me to take the hearing aid off for awhile, and I was still doing business without it. But time doesn't tick off in my head like it does with some jazz singers, so I was constantly fighting to stay in tempo.

"I remember it was in Buffalo one night that I decided to put the hearing aid back in. They were taking pictures for Life Magazine and I said, 'For the picture should I wear the hearing aid or take it off?' They said, 'Do whatever you want.' So I thought 'What the hell? I can't spend the rest of my life with people not knowing I wear a hearing aid.' I really couldn't hear the band without one. Without it, I always had to maintain a sight line with the conductor."[25] The way Johnnie worked, moving around the stage like he was dodging tomatoes, made that a difficult prospect.

The recording session where Life photographed him produced "A Sinner Am I," one of Johnnie's most volatile originals. A torturous glimpse into his sexuality, "A Sinner Am I" ("for falling in love with you"), reads as a slice of the "Love Which Dare Not Speak Its Name" barely passed off as a conventional love triangle. Even on the DeSylva Brown and Henderson oldie "(Here Am I) Brokenhearted" when Johnnie sang "It's bad enough that I lost her / I had to lose him, too" the implication was an eyebrow lifter, but "A Sinner Am I" was such a declamatory and confrontational wail that it left little to the imagination.

It seemed all the more unusual coming from a man deep in a serious romance. In March, Marilyn arrived in New York and took a suite in the Warwick Hotel near Johnnie's. They became, on Johnnie's few nights off, an inseparable pair who could always be found drinking in one of Gotham's high-toned niteries. Whatever hesitancy he felt about the course this relationship was taking, Marilyn's air of power and familiarity with the show business world that Johnnie suddenly dominated was a boon and reference point he welcomed.

He was still green, a rube whose urban acclimatization was limited to low-rent communities in mid-size cities. Marilyn's ease and native disregard for the rules Johnnie was still learning made it smoothly euphoric for him. The sexual percentages shifted. Marilyn and Johnnie spent a lot of time in bed together.

In the first week of April, Elma, now Mrs. Art Haas, flew into New York with her husband and two kids. She was the only person to whom Johnnie deferred, and he happily spent every moment he could with his sister. A planned highlight of the visit was when Johnnie took them out to see Frank Sinatra at the Paramount, where he had made his greatest success almost a decade before. This time he was performing between screenings of his latest bomb "Meet Danny Wilson."

The very climate which allowed Johnnie to rise so swiftly had eroded Sinatra's popular foundation with equal alacrity. The engagement, which had opened on March 26th, was a disaster. Even after Earl Wilson staunchly peppered his column with items about how Sinatra was singing better than ever, naming the host of stars attending (most of whom Wilson himself hand delivered to the front row), it was a dismal flop. MCA had just announced they no longer represented Sinatra. Columbia was preparing to announce they would not renew his contract. Fan clubs were disbanding.[26]

Sinatra's sole comfort was his new bride, the long-sought-after, indescribably lovely Ava Gardner. They had married just weeks before. When Johnnie, Art and Elma were invited backstage between shows to greet the Voice (the two singers were, though not for long, label-mates), Sinatra acted the gentleman, but it was Gardner who really appreciated their visit. As with Marilyn, Johnnie's incongruity of image—his rough yet delicate features, so tall and long of limb yet hopelessly delicate, such a powerhouse on record yet so soft spoken and gentle in manner—fascinated Gardner.

It was an unremarkable meeting until Sinatra was momentarily called out of the dressing room. As soon as he exited, Ava impulsively slung herself onto Johnnie's lap and began petting him. Elma recalls it as a distinctly uncomfortable moment. When Sinatra returned, he froze. Without a word, he yanked Gardner off of Johnnie and briskly hustled her outside. They did not return.

Johnnie and Elma tried not to laugh. "And I don't think that Frank ever forgave Johnnie," she said. "He never forgave Johnnie for being attractive to Ava." It was the second time Johnnie Ray had pissed off Frank Sinatra.

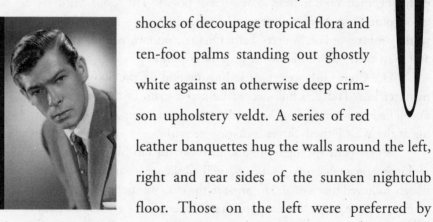

Located at 10 East 60th street, the Copacabana's six hundred and ten person capacity is accommodated within an airless subterranean grotto dense with curved metal fixtures, coarsely rendered shocks of decoupage tropical flora and ten-foot palms standing out ghostly white against an otherwise deep crimson upholstery veldt. A series of red leather banquettes hug the walls around the left, right and rear sides of the sunken nightclub floor. Those on the left were preferred by celebrities, the most exclusive members of New York's 400 and The Five Families.

The table-crowded floor itself seemed almost impossibly small. As the dozen or so Copa Girls sashayed out upon it, their scent and rustling nearness was hypnotic. When the stage's built-in extension risers were rolled out to accommodate big bands, patrons necessarily tucked their feet beneath their tables.

Even at mid-day, hours before opening, the crowded feel was enhanced by a rather low ceiling and the perilous angles of the half dozen lumpy chalk-colored decoupage palms. Every square inch of wall was either blood red or featured garish murals of lush jungle growth. Lit after a dim fashion by several banks of recessed colored spot lights which ring the step down to the floor, it had a tangled, exotic atmosphere that, after dark and a few cocktails, challenged depth perception with its swirling red/vermillion print carpet and multi-leveled pillar and palm-spiked layout. The Copa was nothing if not an ideal realization of an adult fun house. It bespoke power and fame, hosting extremes of both, from J. Edgar Hoover to Frank Costello, Walter Winchell to Frank Sinatra.[1]

In April 1952, the Copa cover was $3.50, with a $5.00 minimum and shows at 8:30, 12:15 and 2:15. On the bill with Johnnie were Betty and Jane Kean, ventriloquist Jimmy Nelson, and of course the World Famous Copa Girls,[2] often belittled by other entertainers for apparently knowing only three dance steps, their hands extended before them as if each fingernail bore a fresh coat of nail polish. The Copa Girls were wholesome, fresh-faced country girl/cheerleader types—not at all like the worldly minxes at Lou Walters' Latin Quarter, who wore mink underwear and dyed their hair exotic shades of pink or purple.

The Copa Girls were kept in line, on and off the floor, by general manager Jules Podell, a bull-necked hulk of a man. In bootlegging days, Podell had been arrested for Volstead Act violations (and survived a shooting at the West Fiftieth Street speakeasy he ran).[3]

When Podell wanted attention, he would rap his huge diamond pinky ring on a table top or water glass. Total silence invariably and immediately followed that signal. His pride in the club was fierce and he haunted every square inch overseeing its smooth operation. Between his patrols of the floor, Podell usually lurked on a bar stool in a small pantry just off the kitchen's entry hall. The Copa Girls always tip-toed when they had to pass it, lest he call them in for a paternal kiss. After Podell died in the early 60s, the club was never quite the same again.

On April 10th, the velvet ropes were already up outside on East Sixtieth Street, and they, like the lines down the block, would remain there for the rest of the month. By eight o'clock the room was packed with even more Very Important types than usual. Mitch Miller, Rosey Clooney, Frankie Laine and Tony Bennett were there. Also Winchell, Kilgallen, Igor Cassini a.k.a. Cholly Knickerbocker, Hy Gardner, Ed Sullivan, and a dozen others from the press corps. Yul Brynner, the Broadway star of "The King & I," and Marlene Dietrich, then smitten with Brynner, came in. Tallulah Bankhead, and Ava Gardner, now Mrs. Sinatra, with her husband, were there. Great Britain's Duchess of Windsor also attended.[4]

The show began. The Copa Girls, fingers extended, somehow executed their routine on the packed floor. The band played, a boy and girl sang "Don't Put A Tax On Love." The ventriloquist did his turn, followed by the Kean Sisters, Betty and Jane, two young Broadway dames prone to deep cleavage and sardonic topical humor.[5]

Reaching the area just outside the dressing room at the back of the club, the sisters were greeted by their manager/handler, a consummate no-nonsense stage mother. She gestured at the phone booth where the star attraction huddled inside. Beads of perspiration already dotted his make-up and his hands were tightly clasped as if in . . . prayer? Several Copa Girls joined the Kean huddle. No one knew what to make of this. Mrs. Kean spoke. "Haven't you heard?" she said. "He's got a direct line to God."[6]

The house lights dimmed. In the audience, Elma tensed. The prevalent mood was clearly one of cynical disbelief, heightened further by Sinatra's presence. No one believed this latest bobbysox idol could possibly deliver goods any more tempting than those which they had already gorged upon. It was, as Billboard reported, "a typical, cynical Copa crowd that was prepared to jeer" a singer "preceded by press controversy . . . [whom] even the Copa management had qualms about."[7]

When the emcee called his name Johnnie loped out to the piano and launched into a straight reading of "Walkin' My Baby Back Home." Elma, elated at hearing Johnnie's voice, was nonetheless puzzled. She had yet to see him perform in, as she said, "the style developed," since he left Oregon in 1950.

This was hardly a performance of a sort to generate the mystery and ridicule which glutted the press and airwaves. Johnnie finished the number to polite applause and made some comments on how nervous he was, adding, "and to the people who are sitting behind the pillars and can't see me, I want you know you are not missing a damn thing."[8]

Then he sang "The Little White Cloud That Cried." Johnnie turned on, shifting instantaneously from bashful boy singer to a man scouring the deepest truth from his lyric, one that represented his essential self's totality of emotional understanding. The audience was, as he counted on, completely unprepared.

His performance, coming after such a mild opener, shocked the house. He flexed, vibrated, shivered. Every broad, frantic gesture and dramatic pose emphasized the lyric with a physical spontaneity that was electrifying. His voice exhilarated them. It filled the collective ear and struck the collective mind like a skyrocket bursting into a multi-colored flurry of sparks. When he finished the crowd "was torn from its 'show-me attitude' into wild enthusiasm."[9] When he rose from the piano and dashed onto the floor, pencil mike in hand, they gasped.

The rest of the show spun by like the hectic view from a carousel, with Johnnie here, now there, now back on stage at the piano, leaping off the drum riser, suddenly dropping to his knees. When he sang "Give Me Time," solemn and alone with a single pin spot the sole illumination in otherwise total darkness, a trance set in. On the closing line, the pin spot shrank down to his hands, extended in a dramatic grasping gesture, until they alone were visible. As his voice trailed to silence, the light snapped off. Wild shouts and screams pierced the darkness. "I could not applaud. I could not even move," Elma said. "It was one of the greatest pieces of staging I have ever seen." When he subsequently introduced her to the audience as the "woman who has contributed so much to my life and to my art," Elma, not Johnnie, cried.

"It was no longer a song session," Billboard noted. "It was a masterful display of showmanship that evoked mass hysteria resembling a Holy Roller meeting. Ray gave all he had, his Columbia waxings, his new album, even his first record 'Whisky and Gin.' When he sang 'Cry' there was sheer pandemonium. It was hard to say who screamed more—Ray or the customers. When he finished, beat to a pulp, dripping perspiration, he was exhausted. So was the audience, but yells of 'more,' threatened the second show."

His prayer was answered; Johnnie had arrived. He limped back towards the dressing room. Then Podell, whose qualms had been strong indeed, suddenly bundled Johnnie into the kitchen where the entire staff —cooks, waiters, dish washers, bus boys, bartenders, all the Copa Girls— had pensively assembled. Johnnie thought he was going to be fired on the spot. Instead, Podell introduced him with patriarchal courtliness, informed them he thought Johnnie was "the greatest," and landed a numbing slap on the singer's back.

Bernie had capitalized on Entratter's contract gaffe by refusing to discuss terms until that night; now he and Johnnie argued about it. Johnnie was all for doing the run per their original agreement. Bernie wanted to ream them. Podell and Entratter, accompanied by several Costello goons, hedged Bernie in by the walk-in refrigerator. Johnnie was already in the elevator that went up to his suite in the adjacent Hotel Fourteen.

"So we got your boy in here, doing good business but still no contract," Entratter said.

"We're going to have to do something about that," rasped Podell.

Someone threw open the walk-in's heavy iron door. "Think about it." Podell barked as the boys shoved Bernie inside and slammed the door. "It was a joke," Bernie said forty years later. He was not smiling.[10]

Before the room cleared, one topic dominated conversation. Brynner and Dietrich were addicted. They rushed to stand in line for the elevator to Hotel Fourteen. The Duchess of Windsor was flushed. A reporter asked Tallulah Bankhead, "a confirmed jazz buff with violent opinions on music," for her opinion of the boy. "He's adorable," she purred, "I want to adopt him."[11]

Earl Wilson approached the Sinatra table and asked Frank what he thought about Johnnie. "I'd like to tell you but my girl won't let me," he said, barely managing a grin.[12] "He sends me," murmured Ava. "In what direction?" Frank shot back.[13] All three rode up to the dressing room where, to Frank's disgust and Wilson's horror, Gardner again physically displayed her enthusiasm.

"Ava was a wonderful lady. She came backstage at the Copa, and flung her arms around Johnnie," Mitch Miller recalled. "She was very voluble about his performing and artistry. I can't prove it, but a friend of mine told me he was getting off at the Hampshire House later that night, when Ava came out the door. She was crying and her face was bloody. Her mouth was bleeding because Sinatra had bopped her."[14]

*   *   *

Johnnie had established his place in Cafe Society. It was, by all press accounts the next morning, a glorious one. Earl Wilson's New York Post column said "he pulled one of the greatest stunts in show business history at the Copa." The New York Journal's Gene Knight called him "A phenomenon of show business." Hy Gardner of the New York Herald Tribune was dumbstruck by Johnnie's "phenomenal rise to stardom." The Daily News' Bob Sylvester said he "raised more commotion than all the other crooners put together." In the same pages, Sid Shallett called him "the Atomic Ray, that phenomenon, that sensational Eighth Wonder of the World." Dorothy Kilgallen's Voice of Broadway described Johnnie as "Endsville. He held the town's toughest audience spellbound (or maybe it was paralyzed with astonishment)."[15]

Billboard's final word echoed the conclusion of all there: "If there was any doubt Ray was a box office phenomenon, it was erased at the Copa. Kid should be able to write his own ticket."[16] Johnnie owned New York. And New York's favor made him the biggest singing star in the world.

The next day, Elma went to Johnnie's suite at the Warwick Hotel for breakfast. She walked in, saw the notices scattered around. It was still, almost silent. She found Johnnie, head in hands, on a window seat, gazing down upon Manhattan, a city that now, in all truth, lay at his feet. Johnnie was crying. Elma held him, waited for the tears to subside. "Well," he whispered, "I said my prayers . . . I said my prayers." He rose and they sat down to eat. Johnnie, suddenly, was back to his regular cheery self.

The next two weeks were a whirl of action, sweat, tears and booze. One night Johnnie collapsed between performances. Another found him drinking until dawn with Jackie Gleason and Salvador Dali. It was a memorable morning after; Gleason, demanding five million dollars for renewal of his CBS television contract, nodded off during a meeting with William S. Paley, who said "If that's his attitude, just give him the money."[17]

Bankhead made good on her promise and literally kidnapped Johnnie for an extended bender, characteristically hosted in the nude. Billie Heller heard later that "Tallulah kept him locked up for about three days." Jane Kean says he missed only one Copa show as a result of the "adoption."[18]

Jack Entratter eventually agreed to pay $1,750 a week for Johnnie's debut, and offered $5,000 a week on his return. Having scraped the egg off his face, he was quite happy with Johnnie. "Who can argue with an overflowing cash register?" Entratter said.[19] Johnnie had dwarfed Martin & Lewis' Copa attendance records and sold $230,000 worth of food and drink in two weeks. He was rewarded by Podell with a brand new, two-toned blue Cadillac convertible coupe with an engraved plaque mounted on the dashboard solemnly memorializing his drawing power. A fabulous gesture, but Johnnie had lost any desire to drive. The Copa Caddy was just another toy; essentially it became Cy Kertman's personal ride.[20]

*   *   *

Johnnie created such a stir, even among the high culture set, that the New York Times dispatched its classical music critic Howard Taubman to the Copa. Highbrow Taubman was dubious, and his review set a trend for dime store psychologizing that plagued Johnnie for the next several years.

"Ray sings like a man in an agony of suffering. Drenched in tears . . . he tears a passion to tatters and then stamps on the shreds. His hair falls in his face. He clutches at the microphone and behaves as if he were about to tear it apart.

"It is to be noted that, possessed or not possessed, tortured or not tortured by spasms of movement, he never forgets to bring his lips to the microphone when the time comes to sing a phrase. The most convulsive writhings occur in the pauses between notes."

His summation: "This young man's style speaks for young people beset by fears and doubts in a difficult time. His pain may be their pain. His wailing and writhing may reflect their secret impulses. His performance is the anatomy of self-pity."[21]

It was much more than that; much more than someone like Taubman could understand. Most every newspaper writer identified Johnnie as a "phenomenon,'" but it was a combination of his interpretive talent, totally unrestrained by social and moral convention, fortuitously timed to ascend during the severe ebb which American popular culture suffered during the early 1950s that enabled him to reach that status.

It was not an ebb of creativity or quality but an overall dwindling interest. The public had effectively disconnected itself from established forms. Johnnie's radical style and frightening sincerity retained just enough of a connection to pop bandstand tradition that he fit within the existing context, yet still threatened to destroy it.

A double edged ambivalence, typified by his androgynous appeal and extreme readings of ancient hokum like "Brokenhearted" and "Walkin' My Baby Back Home" (when he broke tempo on his record, musicologists and band men everywhere took it as an affront) seemed a contradictory and incomprehensible approach. The fact that he looked affectionately to the past while apparently hacking and trampling contemporary aesthetics with merciless zeal baffled arbiters from coast to coast.

Like Taubman, many saw Johnnie as a vehicle of self-pity, a freak thriving on nihilism, a cannibal gorging himself on a musical canon at the expense of the business. His style was perceived as a psychological aberration, subject to merciless dissection that never yielded answers.

This mystery is what led Cafe Society and the bobbysoxers to pledge Johnnie their affection so staunchly. Each faction thrilled at the recklessness that urged Johnnie on. For each, his stated goals of "expressing beauty and love," and "yanking the deep, buried stuff up and bringing it to the surface,"22 made Johnnie Ray a vehicle of liberation. In that sense there was little difference between Johnnie's sole predecessor, Al Jolson, and his most effective successor Elvis Presley. These three are inextricably linked by use of that power, which was key to their success.

Popular music relies on gauging and defining an audience's self-image and desires, the unspoken urges which lie at the soul's core. By speaking to and gratifying the needs of its audience, pop music goes beyond entertainment to offer spiritual glamour.

Jolson was the first who brought that soaring shock of exuberant power and freedom to the public; his plummy emotional wail was so contrary to the accepted norm that Jolson was compelled to work in black face. There was, at the time, no other option. No white performer faced by the post-Victorian Judeo/Christian ethic dared express himself so openly. In blackface, a performer no longer needed to toe the cultural line—he could leap across it. Ironically, it freed him, and the entire historic blackface minstrel tradition was built around that leap.

From the cornerstone of blackface (the earliest commercial 50-50 blend of African rhythm and European melody) popular music grew in entirely new and different ways. The general acknowledgement of such personal freedom brought with it a sense of individual power. That response led to a craving for the long denied taboo of primal independence. Jolson brought it to the Twentieth Century; Johnnie tore off the theatrical mask and offered it to the people; Elvis gave it a threateningly tangible accessibility.

When Bing Crosby stepped out of this line with his jaunty, collegiate who-cares ethic, it was a brilliant re-assessment of the popular psyche, one much more easily accepted and identified with. Rudy Vallee's "Vagabond Lover" typified this cozy side step: Bing and Rudy were all about getting laid, and their ability to glorify it without shattering the cultural context was deeply satisfying. But it was tame, mild.

Subsequently, Frank Sinatra and Dick Haymes necessarily ignored the quality of freedom and unchecked emotion Jolson offered; throughout the Second World War their lullabies were a welcome respite. When Johnnie took up where Jolson left off and threw it all back in our face, it was a high voltage shock.

Johnnie brought back the personal power and sense of disimprisonment that Jolson disguised under his greasepaint. He reinstated it with bolts of musical lightning. The shock of Johnnie Ray was the forced recognition that everyone struggled to bury emotion but really yearned to free it.

He defied routine, frustration and behavioral constraint with every breath. This is precisely what Elvis would do four years later. Unlike Johnnie, Elvis had a ready-made context behind him, the earthy framework of Southeastern country music, already a morass of tortured self-expression and bald emotion made acceptable by Hank Williams; Elvis also had a mainstream national audience primed by the shock of Johnnie Ray.

When Johnnie brought it to the Copacabana crowd in 1952, he had absolutely no context whatsoever to bolster acceptance or understanding. By driving home a message of raw emotion and disregard for convention—redefining self-perception—Johnnie's career was almost overtly political.

The shock of Johnnie Ray was the shock of recognition. His personal power mirrored the suppressed power of the nation's citizenry. It was radical, dangerous and Johnnie was completely alone.

"There are too many hypocrites in the trade," Johnnie said shortly after his Copa opening. "I'm not happy with some people. Everyone now says that they knew it would happen all the time. Too many are taking bows. As a result, the people who really helped me are getting pushed into the background. Some hate me because I made it big."[23]

*   *   *

By conservative estimates, Johnnie was going to earn one million dollars in 1952. Bernie did everything conceivable to ensure it was not a ceiling figure. Of one million dollars, Johnnie would get six hundred and fifty thousand, the balance making up Bernie's twenty-five percent (half of which was supposed to go to Danny Kessler) and GAC's ten. Of that six hundred and fifty thousand, after taxes Johnnie would be left with one hundred thousand dollars. He also had to pay drummer Sammy Fede, Cy Kertman, Art Franklin, accountant Sol Lazarow and lawyer Halsey Cowan. It was rumored that Larry Spier also got a cut. Another on the payroll was Nat Lorman, a well regarded flack man who was in charge of administering operation of the eight hundred and fifty Johnnie Ray Fan Clubs already in existence.

Together, these men formed Johnnie Ray Enterprises, Inc., the first business venture in pop music history to aggressively develop and market merchandise that capitalized on a star's name. The notion originated with Larry Spier, who had already seen to the production of "the Johnnie Ray Cry-Kerchief," a sheer hankie emblazoned with Johnnie's screen-printed image in the center and on each corner, bordered around with musical notation and the titles of his record hits. They sold like mad, along with eight by ten photographs peddled at every appearance. Spier had stumbled onto one hell of a good thing.

Prior to the "Cry-Kerchief," eight by ten glossies were the only souvenirs available at any pop star's dates, and commercial product endorsements the only extra-curricular resource to which stars sold their names. With Johnnie Ray Enterprises, Inc., Bernie virtually invented merchandising, now a multi-million dollar cash cow trotted out by every rock and roll band able to draw a crowd. It was a swell racket.

Johnnie Ray Enterprises' incorporation papers listed Bernie Lang as President, Cy Kertman, Treasurer, Halsey Cowan, Secretary and Sol Lazarow, the only one with any financial expertise, Assistant Treasurer. Les Persky Product Services was franchised on a sales percentage basis by Johnnie Ray Enterprises to issue licenses. Johnnie would receive the same split he got under his management terms with Bernie. Exactly what Larry Spier, Nat Lorman and Danny Kessler were to get from this new cash source no one said. One thing was certain—plenty of money came rolling in.

Every license Persky issued to a manufacturer brought a substantial cash advance against royalty earnings. The Kallen Blouse & Sportswear Company gave them $2,000 up front for rights to produce a Johnnie Ray ladies' blouse and men's sport shirt. The advance was based on a five percent royalty rate, and Kallens announced they expected to sell 250,000 items of Ray apparel that year. A Johnnie Ray compact also brought $2,000 up front, with the same royalty terms.

A license was issued to Westberg Clothes, who were set to manufacture a "Johnnie Ray Teardrop" men's suit. This was an even better deal—Westberg advanced them $5,000 and obligated itself to an annual $20,000 sales guarantee. Esquire Bobbysox agreed to identical terms; by July, they were selling 30,000 dozen pairs of Ray bobbysox every week, and were soon paying Johnnie Ray Enterprises an additional $1,000 every month.

There were plans for "a finger puppet character in the Ray likeness," and it was also announced that Johnnie would author a book "on the subject of religious faith." Persky was besieged by offers from another industry, but when Johnnie learned of it he emphatically killed them all. These came from hearing aid manufacturers.

Johnnie stood to make anywhere from $50,000 to $75,000 from these products in 1952 ($550,000 from personal appearances, $300,000 from record royalties, and additional monies from song publishing and investments made up the balance of his million dollar income for '52). As Billboard noted, "the income producing potential of Johnnie Ray Enterprises, Inc. is, in itself, a fabulous story of capitalization on a star's popularity."24

Fabulous, and like the singer himself, completely without precedent. Johnnie Ray became instantly recognizable not only as himself, but also under more than a dozen handles the press churned out and dumped on him: the Cry Guy; the Prince of Wails; Mr. Emotion (Bernie was dubbed Mr. Commotion); the Atomic Ray; the Nabob of Sob; the Golden Tearjerker; the Anguished Bard; the Cheerful Tearful; the Howling Success; the Violent Ray; the Million Dollar Teardrop; the Song Wringer; the Master of Misery; the American Sob Singer; Johnnie Jolt 'Em; the Man the Girls Strip; and, most hated of all, the Guy With the Rubber Face and Squirt Gun Eyes.[25]

Johnnie's life was still conducted on the simplest terms. After GAC's Sol Lazarow left the agency to work full time as Johnnie's accountant and business manager, all Johnnie saw by way of financial reports was his personal bank statement at the end of each month. He knew that it looked bigger every time and never gave it a second thought. He trusted Bernie, he told Billboard, "implicitly."[26]

Bernie, for his part, was toughening up. Ten minutes in the frigid darkness of Podell's walk-in made him stop and think. He was Johnnie Ray's personal manager—nobody to push around. Bernie was making long-term, big-money deals: a tour of Britain, and more importantly, Johnnie's Las Vegas debut. Jack Entratter wanted Johnnie for the grand opening of the Copa Room at the still-under-construction Sands Hotel. There was no bigger name in show business. With the prestige of the Sands opener, the unparalleled success of Johnnie Ray Enterprises, Inc., the continuing smash record sales, the whole operation was running smooth as silk.

Bernie stopped paying Danny Kessler anything. Danny was busy romancing a Copa Girl who had caught his eye during Johnnie's engagement and whom he would soon marry. Between that and his Okeh A&R duties, they rarely saw each other anymore. After handing over $35,000 to Al Green, Bernie wanted little to do with the man who had brought him Johnnie—especially after discovering that the contract Green had was legally invalid.[27]

The revelation led to some hot talk between Lang and Kessler. That's what the AFM said, Bernie groused. Tell it to the Purple Gang, Kessler snapped. He was the one who discovered Johnnie in the first place. Or had he?

Jerry Crocker was the first to kick up a fuss. When he told Billboard that "a number of people have asked whether I'm going to sue Johnnie Ray. I wonder how I should answer," Johnnie suggested "See my doctor." The question of who found him became a hotly contested battle for credit. Officially, to shield Kessler from conflict-of-interest charges, Bernie Lang was named as the one. Al Green claimed he told Kessler. Kessler cited Robin Seymour. Crocker said it was only after he talked Johnnie up to Columbia Midwest distribution rep Ted King that Kessler heard of the singer. No one could settle it.

Asked if it was Kessler who first approached him, Johnnie (who now alternated black jazz lingo with high faluting society grandeur) replied "We don't know or care. We just decided that, from the beginning, Danny should get the credit. If someone did tell him to record me, he'd be an idiot to admit it." Al Green's beef was the only one with any degree of urgency to it. Of that settlement Johnnie rather cryptically said "It hasn't cost me a cent and it won't cost me a nickel."[28]

The only ones not falling into line, hands extended, were Jan Grayton and Bob Mitchell. The team split in early 1952, with Jan doing a single in the New York area and Mitchell concentrating on two new "boy singers." Though he mentioned Jan's name in a Saturday Evening Post profile, Johnnie never spoke of his relationship with the two or the help they had so faithfully given him. He never confided anything about the threesome to Elma or Jim Low. Publicly, he spoke only in the most general of terms: "I don't think I owe anything to anybody. Nobody has given more to me than I have given to them. In helping to build me, they've built themselves." Jerry Crocker never called an attorney. Ted King remained silent. Al Green said he and Johnnie were friends. Grayton and Mitchell remained silent.[29]

Herman Hover followed Johnnie back to New York, arriving shortly after the Copa engagement ended, only to discover he had the same problem as in Los Angeles. "I took a plane to New York,

checked into the Plaza and again, wherever Johnnie went, Marilyn was with him," Hover said. "I couldn't get a chance to talk to him alone." Back at Mocambo, Charlie Morrison chuckled over the situation. He well knew how much Hover detested having to leave Ciro's for more than 48 hours, and hoped to wear him down through Marilyn's benignly daunting presence.

After squandering several days trying to operate around his competition's daughter, Hover grew increasingly frustrated. With time growing short, Charlie and Marilyn took the offensive. On April 30th, Louella Parsons revealed on her nationally syndicated radio show that Johnnie Ray and Marilyn Morrison had announced their engagement. Hover saw black. It was the first Johnnie or anyone else in his entourage heard of it, and none welcomed the surprise bulletin.

"That was the end as far as I was concerned," Hover said. "I figured 'He's going to marry this girl. It's over.' I went back to the Plaza and was packing when the phone rang. It was Bernie Lang. He said 'Do you still want Johnnie? Come on over to the GAC offices and I'll give you a contract.' It was a shock—Johnnie had just announced his engagement, but I figured that my tactics had worked, the idea of romancing Bernie and his wife. I went over to GAC, Bernie Lang gave me a contract and naturally I signed it.

"And then he said to me, 'You probably want to know why we're signing with you instead of Charlie Morrison.' Gloria Lang was there, too, and she said, 'When Johnnie moved down to Los Angeles and he was broke, he used to go into Ciro's and stand at the bar. No one ever hustled him for a drink, no one ever hustled him to spend any money and he made up his mind that if he ever hit it big, he was going to repay you by working at Ciro's.' And Bernie said, 'Well, the time has come. Johnnie is very appreciative, so we are giving you the contract.'"

Hover was touched by the deal's ingenuous sentimentality. Ciro's itself had "romanced the attraction" three years earlier, and, too, Charlie Morrison's long distance manipulation helped make the decision. Johnnie signed for two weeks at Ciro's in October, and better still, Hover said, "His price was not excessive, not at all excessive."

What did Charlie Morrison say about this? "I didn't care what he had to say," Hover answered. He flew back to California, a prince among Operators. When Charlie Morrison initially leaked Marilyn and Johnnie's engagement to Parsons, her announcement would be, he assumed, the coup de grace in his rivalry with Hover. He had bungled; worse, the entire caper backfired. Stung on discovering Hover held the paper, Morrison publicly announced his opposition to the marriage: "No daughter of mine is going to marry ANY singer," Parsons quoted him as saying.[1]

Johnnie and Marilyn. Marilyn and Johnnie. Theirs was a backstage romance; as such it was always fitful, but this feudal goof turned it even more so. And there was precious little time to attend to anything but work. After Johnnie closed at the Copa he went into Atlantic City's Steel Pier Theater, playing a record-breaking 38 twenty-minute-shows-a-day engagement, starting at nine a.m. until 10 p.m. The money had bulk. Fans lined up during the pre-dawn hours, while the star was still boozing it up in his hotel room. Johnnie thrived on the tumult—even flew to Philadelphia for a charity show during this punishing engagement.[2]

The course of the romance was in Marilyn's hands. She began a bi-coastal campaign to re-claim the suddenly tainted affair, flying back and forth from New York and Los Angeles, stringing along both her father and lover boy. Marilyn would do anything to make Johnnie hers.

From Steel Pier Johnnie went into Chicago's Oriental Theater in May, on a five-shows-a-day bill featuring Billy Ward & the Dominos, (the great R&B vocal group that produced Clyde McPhatter), acrobatic act Billy Wells & the Four Fays and the ubiquitous Gary Morton. The picture screened between performances was titled, appropriately, "Flesh and Fury."[3] Marilyn flew in for the first shows.

It was a frantic springtime mob scene; an ocean of wound-up teenagers, screaming their heads off, stormed his opening on May 2nd. Billboard's review noted the unusual qualities of both performer ("tearing hair and torso tossing") and audience ("it was a race to see who could outscream who"); Johnnie started a near riot when he announced he would be available for autographs.[4]

A trio of star-struck teenage broadcasters from a small Aurora, Illinois radio station were escorted in by a policeman. Dressed in their Sunday best, little white gloves and veils on the girls, the boy in an askew bowtie, they were struck dumb. Between the chorus of adoring shouts wafting up from the alley and Johnnie's tangerine-toned pancake makeup, their gee-whiz nerve evaporated.

Johnnie greeted them like old friends. Zeroing in on sixteen-year-old Charles Ostergrant, Johnnie all but ignored Marilyn and the other two girls. He took the boy's hand and asked "Would you like to see my fans?" He led him to the open window, and as they gazed out on the mob, Johnnie's hand dropped from around the kid's shoulder to his behind. "Here was someone I idolized—a star—and I was dumbfounded, but delighted, too," Ostergrant said. "I was very embarrassed. He had just introduced me to Marilyn and I tried not to look at her, which was awfully hard because the dressing room wasn't that big."[5] Tell Louella about THIS, Johnnie thought. At the makeup table, Marilyn silently poured a glass of whiskey and drained it. A billfold sailed through the open window. Johnnie laughed, stuffed an autograph into it, draped his arm back around the teenage visitor's shoulder and tossed it back out. Marilyn poured another drink. Come arrests, riot, sodomy, scandal, or worse, an exclusive lifetime contract at Ciro's, she was determined to marry Johnnie.

*   *   *

Louella continued on as public matchmaker. No matter how hard Morrison pleaded for its burial the story was too meaty to abandon. On May 14, her headline officially let the cat out of the bag: "Cry Girls Cry: Johnnie Ray To Wed." Noting that "When I first printed the news (and had it on the air two weeks ago) her father heartily denied it . . . ," Parsons could not resist adding "An amusing angle is that Ray is booked to appear at Ciro's," but quoted Charlie as saying "Any time he wants a job at Mocambo, it's his."[6] Marilyn was back in Beverly Hills, shopping for her wedding gown. According to Louella, the date was set for May 25.

That same day, a reporter from the Chicago Herald American rushed down to interview Johnnie. The singer was "in a mental tailspin," and showed up at the theater in a disheveled state unusual even by Johnnie's careless standards. "I'm the most confused guy in the world," Johnnie said. "I am in love for the first time and I'd like to get married but how can a guy tell if it's the real thing? I'm really scared."

He confirmed the Parsons report, saying, "I am confident I'll marry eventually but . . . " and here was Bernie talking, "I'm also worried about the responsibility I have to the teenagers who helped put me where I am." Johnnie added that "May 25 is definitely out," as he was booked in Albany May 24, Newark on the 25th and set to open at the Paramount Theater the morning of May 26.[7]

In Beverly Hills that same day, Marilyn told reporters "I talked to Johnnie for about twenty minutes this morning and he agreed that we'll be married on the twenty-fifth. Johnnie proposed to me on the telephone *about ten days after I returned from Chicago* where he opened at the Oriental Theater. We hoped to keep secret our plan to be married but Louella Parsons learned about it and broke the story.

"That was all right with us," Marilyn added, "because Louella is a very good friend."[8]

On May 15, Marilyn called a press conference at the Beverly Wilshire Hotel. Wearing a radiant smile, polka dot blouse with a large black bow that she toyed with constantly, she told them, "Johnnie proposed to me *about five or six weeks ago in New York*—without tears! Daddy met Johnnie over the phone the other night and liked him very much. I know when he meets him he'll like him." Reporters reminded her that Daddy had heatedly announced his opposition. "That's all cleared up," she said.[9]

Marilyn had played her ace in the hole; having missed a period, she told Charlie that she suspected she was pregnant. There was no other way. After four months of scheming (a showman's daughter after all) Marilyn knew a little bit about romancing an attraction. The fix was in. Johnnie was hers. Publicly at least. He no longer resisted; appearing in Cincinnati, he told reporters "I'll say we're getting married—she's the first woman who ever made me feel like a man!"[10] Later, Johnnie would bitterly regret his choice of words.

The whole affair took a staged, public turn. In New York on the twentieth, Marilyn and hordes of reporters waited for Johnnie's flight in from Cincinnati. Rehearsal could not have rendered a more touching tableaux. When Johnnie, clad in a plush black topcoat, appeared on the ramp, Marilyn burst from the gate like a shot; he began racing towards her and the pair collided with an audible smack that sent change flying from Johnnie's pockets.

He swept her into his arms, hoisted her off the ground and spun her around a half dozen times, planting kisses on her cheeks with each revolution. They beamed at each other. Cradled in his arms, her finely turned legs posed beneath a smart cocktail suit, they presented a romantic ideal. Reporters clamored when? when?

"Ask her," Johnnie said. "She's the boss." "Get that on paper!" Marilyn crowed. "I have four or five tentative plans for our wedding and we'll announce details as soon as a decision is reached."[11]

There were no further formal announcements. On the twenty-fourth, Johnnie and Marilyn applied for their license. She listed her occupation as secretary. Marilyn returned to the Warwick.

Johnnie flew to Albany; he was appearing before a sold out crowd at the State Armory. His performance that night was so inflammatory that thousands broke past security barriers and rushed the stage, nearly capsizing the makeshift bandstand.[12]

It rained all day on the twenty-fifth. Hazel and Elmer had arrived the previous night. In the Warwick lobby, fifty or sixty damp and disconsolate bobbysoxers loitered sullenly. In the twenty-first-floor bridal suite, several dozen guests including New York's Mayor Vincent Impellitteri and his wife, were already "drinking champagne by the bucket."[13] Judge Hyman Barshaw, to Hazel's chagrin, officiated. Cy was best man; Marilyn's half sister Toni was maid of honor (Cy and Toni planned to marry within two weeks).

Johnnie wore his favorite suit, "midnight blue, with a beautiful weave."[14] "Man, I'm so nervous, I'm paralyzed," he said. "I feel like I'm going to go down on my knees." Marilyn appeared wearing a pale lilac taffeta cocktail suit with full accordion pleated calf-length skirt; her satin shoes, tulle hat, and the baby orchids and lilies of the valley she carried were all dyed a matching lilac. Barshaw backed them up against a mirrored wall whose white fireplace was banked with white gladioli and peonies. No one in the room was able to hear Johnnie's "I do."

Barshaw pronounced "I sentence each of you to a life of health, contentment and happiness." Johnnie, to compensate for his inaudible vow, took Marilyn in his arms for a kiss that lasted nearly two full minutes. He told a reporter how much better he felt, that he "couldn't get over how nice that 'Mr. & Mrs.' sounds," and considered a "real honeymoon to be a week on the farm, but we've only got two or three days together right now. We're going to be thoroughly by ourselves this summer for a whole month."[15]

A delegate from the bobbysoxers was brought into the room. Fourteen-year-old dungaree clad Rennee Magrisso, Johnnie Ray Brooklyn Fan Club President, was introduced to Johnnie (swoon!) and Marilyn (*eeeew*). Johnnie led Magrisso to the piano, sat with the teen upon his lap, and gave her a sip of champagne. He sang "Cry" and Magrisso did exactly that. When he finished, Johnnie "gave her a kiss almost as long as the

Johnnie, age 1.

ge 3, with Rover.

Age 17, with a cousin in Portland.

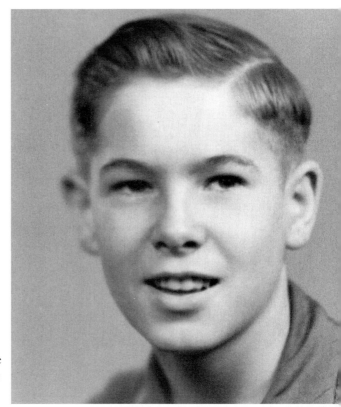

Johnnie around the time of the blanket toss accident.

"My arrival in Philadelphia," he noted. "It was windy."

Breaking attendance records in Hartford, Connecticut, fall 1951.

Blood, Guts and Thunder: onstage at the Palladium in London, 1954 (left), and at the Town & Country, Buffalo, New York, 1951.

eveland goes Ray crazy.

Whiskey & Gin" at Moe's Main Street, Cleveland, Ohio, 1951.

Johnnie returns in triumph to the Willamette Valley, January 1952.

...siness as usual in Buffalo; note graffiti at right.

...stant pandemonium, 1952.

Wedded bliss? Johnnie and Marilyn tie the knot, May 1952.

Christmas with Hazel and Elmer, mid-'50s.

Hospital even before the engagement closed. (Her condition was not so serious as to keep her from re-joining Johnnie on the road within a week.)

The emotional and physical reality of Johnnie and Marilyn's relationship remains guarded. With Johnnie gone and Marilyn silent, only press accounts and his friends' recollections remain. These are rough guidelines, tainted by the strange relationship this couple enjoyed. As Jim Low said it seemed that theirs was "not a loving relationship, but a more formal type of friendship."

"All I know is what he told me," said Jimmy Campbell, who worked as Johnnie's musical director in the early 1960s. "I think he got shoved around pretty good with that marriage, but that baby was supposed to be his legacy, you know?"[30]

Whatever the veiled truth of the matter, it was a decisive blow against Marilyn's dreams of life with Johnnie. This tragedy, real or imagined, accident or abortion, conveniently sealed their romantic fate. As time passed, the story grew uglier through embellishment and circulation. "Marilyn was a drunk, a complete lush," Campbell recited. "What I heard is that she got drunk, fell down a staircase and lost the baby."

There was little to be done except call it quits. "It was not a pretty picture at all," Johnnie said decades later. "Something had to give."[31] They separated. It had not lasted a year. They agreed not to file for divorce until 1954. Initially, the split was not announced but word spread throughout the trade.

Johnnie went on to play another stand in Cleveland, where fans pitched a tent in freezing weather, remaining there all night in order to get into the theater the next day.[32] Then he went back to Boston. When the engagement closed, Cy had taken off for advance promo duties, leaving Johnnie in Bernie's care. They went to Logan Airport for a flight to New Orleans; Johnnie was drunk, and Bernie exhausted—fighting through those crowds was no small task, nor was keeping track of all that money. Johnnie wandered off to find a men's room.

Unable to locate one he compromised, rather carelessly, by watering a potted plant at the edge of a terminal concourse. He then lay down on the floor and passed out. "It was all a mistake," Johnnie said. "Pretty soon someone came along and told me to come with them. I thought they were my managers. I woke up two hours later and wasn't in a plane at all. I was in jail."[33] The charge: common drunk. Released the next morning,

Johnnie was surrounded by a handful of smiling cops and dozens of small children, mostly little boys. Fine photo opportunity. Johnnie looked pleased with himself.

Fortunately, his reputation (and what remained of his and Marilyn's union) was set to be renewed in a spectacular fashion on the West Coast. More specifically at 1007 North Beverly Drive, Beverly Hills, one of the addresses of Marion Davies, "widowed" mistress of the late William Randolph Hearst. The austere engraved invitations had gone out weeks earlier:

> Marion Davies
> invites you to greet
> Mr. & Mrs. Johnny Ray
> at a
> Cocktail and Buffet Supper
> on Thursday, the second of October
>
> Black Tie.

It was to be a one nighter so outlandishly sumptuous that Orson Welles would have rejected such a sequence from "Citizen Kane" on the grounds that it simply defied comprehension. This was extravagance beyond Xanadu. It was Hollywood.

Johnnie arrived at Los Angeles International Airport on Wednesday, October 1 and made a big show for the gaggle of reporters. "Where's my wife?" he asked no one in particular. "I think she's goofing off." Marilyn, delayed by traffic, made her entrance ten minutes later. Another flash bulb display, and Johnnie, as if on cue, crowed "I didn't see her for six days. It seemed like six years!" Marilyn wept. The couple drove to the Beverly Hills Hotel.[1]

If Mocambo had lost out to Ciro's on Johnnie Ray as a star attraction, and Marilyn's bid for romantic permanency seemed rocky, Charlie Morrison would ensure that folks in the movie colony knew who had the real show business clout—the star attraction's father-in-law, and his pal Marion Davies whom Morrison knew from his theatrical agent days. She was so close to the Morrisons that Marilyn was considered her niece. Just married to "former ship's mate" Captain Horace Brown following Hearst's 1951 death, Davies was ready to kick up her Hollywood heels.

Mocambo, with its small 220-person capacity would barely accommodate the staff this celebration would require. Davies pulled out all the stops. More than 30 years later, it is still widely and quite fondly regarded as the last of the true, old Hollywood school examples of the party as wretched excess.

The three-story pink Mediterranean mansion's exterior front wall was torn open and tented, the driveway re-routed and extended so that arriving guests drove their limousines directly into a huge front room where a battery of valets awaited. In this reception area was a long bar, a scattering of tables and an ancient Roman sarcophagus, freighted down from San Simeon, scrubbed, re-lined and filled with magnums, jeroboams and Methuselahs of champagne.[2]

From that auspicious entry, guests passed through a series of rooms done up as replicas of New York's top night spots, authentic in every detail—the tableware was flown in from El Morocco, the Stork Club and 21. These rooms opened onto a sweeping terrace with a one-hundred-foot-long three-tiered pool running through a formal garden. The affair spilled out onto the grounds, where a circus tent was erected near a fish pond. Even the garden paths were decorated with synthetic grass.[3]

Three orchestras, the Eddie Oliver, Freddy Karger and Harold Stern organizations, played. Parisian florists were hired to create centerpieces for the fifty tables; each consisted of seventy-two American Beauty roses. Eight uniformed Beverly Hills Police provided security, there were a dozen parking attendants and sixty caterers serving fifty pounds of caviar, four hundred pounds of filet mignon, seventy-five turkeys, three hundred and fifty chickens, and fifteen hams.[4] The guest list was reported variously as being five hundred, seven hundred and fifty and one thousand celebrities strong, who polished off fifty cases of imported liquor.[5]

"Everything about it was so off the wall—Johnnie Ray and Marilyn Morrison! People just said 'oh, they got married, isn't that interesting?' and went to the reception," said actress Jan Sterling, who attended with her husband, Paul Douglas. "It was the most incredible party I have ever been to in my entire life. You drove into the living room, and there was this great long sarcophagus, and the bushes all wired with gardenias.

"I looked at the bar and the first person I saw was Gary Cooper. There wasn't one person there who you didn't recognize immediately as a movie star, or as someone in the business prominent enough that you thought you knew who they were. It was extraordinary because every single table was nothing but stars. I never saw anything like it. I thought 'This is it—*This* is Hollywood.' It was amazing. Astonishing."[6] As Debbie Reynolds said, "It was like being in a museum and a nightclub all at the same time."[7]

Davies' entrance was a moment of high drama; she appeared at the top of a grand staircase, clad in a velvet and lace Don Loper creation, augmented by over half a million dollars worth of jewels. The guests cheered and applauded as she descended. "People were thrilled," Debbie Reynolds wrote. "It was like 'Look, she's actually *walking*!" Johnnie and Marilyn waited at the bottom and the trio formed a receiving line, greeting the likes of Joan Crawford, Charlton Heston, Gary Cooper, Red Skelton, Lena Horne, Jack Benny, Merle Oberon, Gregory Peck, Clark Gable, and Dinah Shore.[8]

Ed Wynn said it reminded him of the Diamond Jim Brady days in New York. One unnamed star, standing at one of the sixty-foot-long bars told a reporter "I could retire for life on what Marion is spending tonight."[9] It became wild: British actress Diana Dors "accidentally" fell into the fishpond and was promptly surrounded by photographers. Broderick Crawford "was doing alcoholic acrobatics on the veranda." Even Ava Gardner, on her best barefoot behavior, was there.[10]

Johnnie was in heaven, a heaven precisely as he had fantasized it all his life. He mingled with lifelong idols; he danced with Sammy Davis Jr. A Newsweek reporter asked Johnnie's opinion on the proceedings. "It's the craziest," he replied. "I don't get it, but it's wonderful."[11]

"It was fabulous, the last of the old guard Hollywood parties," said Jack Devaney. "Marion had the whole place fixed up, and tented and catered and every movie star in Hollywood was there. I've never seen so many movie stars in one place in my life. It was a ball, a once in a lifetime experience."

"It was huge. It was overdone." Cy Kertman said. " Everybody that was anybody was there, loads of celebrities, Life Magazine sent a crew out to cover it. There were so many people that I don't think I saw Johnnie more than once that night. Charlie Morrison had spent something like a million dollars just for flowers." What a son-in-law. The Hollywood wise guys said, "He hasn't lost a daughter—he's gained a daughter."

Not to be outdone, Hover threw a preview of Johnnie at Ciro's the next night, where many of the same stars came limping in, only to have their hangovers erased by the shock of the Atomic Ray. "Ciro's was the same as the Copa in New York," Bernie said. "Every major star in town was there." Merle Oberon was particularly taken with Johnnie. Sammy Davis Jr. came in to get pointers for his impression.

"We gave him a two-week house," Hover said, "and no one had ever seen anything like Johnnie, the way he worked. He'd sing 'Cry,' get down on his knees and bang on the floor." Ciro's belonged to Johnnie for the next twelve nights—just as he had sworn it would three years earlier. "He was a hell of a performer," said George Schlatter, who worked as Hover's assistant long before launching his television production career, "The total commitment of it was dynamic. The only one you could compare him to was Jolson, for the emotional involvement with a lyric. It was like what Garland had, but Johnnie Ray was very unique, super high energy, very dynamic, and it was amazing because he wore the hearing aid."[12]

Even in this hour of triumph, though, whatever dark forces were conspiring against Johnnie with gas bombs and razors took a hand; on October 6, the two-tone Copa Caddy convertible was stolen off of Ciro's lot. Johnnie wept as he failed to recall the license number to police.[13] Hover does not recall that night but said, "That is quite strange. Our cars were always very well protected at Ciro's."

Neither does George Schlatter remember any particulars, "But," he said, "you would have to be pretty stupid to steal a car that Jules Podell gave someone. He was not a peaceful man." Stupid, or perhaps, someone on good terms with the Copa powers-that-be. Long after the insurance company paid off, the car eventually turned up in New Jersey, but neither Bernie Lang nor Cy Kertman can shed any light on how it got there.

In Hollywood, no one mentioned the baby or its tragic loss. Johnnie worked half the night at Ciro's, partied at Hover's, and was in the studio with Mitch Miller recording most every day; they were stacking up material every chance they got. Miller scheduled sixteen sessions with Johnnie over the first twelve months of their association. When he finally got a night off with his new bride, all he could talk about was another woman—one he was set to record with the very next morning: Doris Day. Another high Miller concept, pairing the Man the Girls Strip with Les Brown's dreamy, virginal girl singer. For a raver like Johnnie who idolized Lady Day and Misses Cornshucks and Sharecropper, it seemed an unlikely pairing. Johnnie was overjoyed and intensely nervous at the prospect.

Doris Van Kappelhoff, from Cincinnati, Ohio, had left Brown's organization in 1946 and by age 27 when she met Johnnie in Hollywood, had appeared in twelve motion pictures. Johnnie had adored Day's singing since hearing "Sentimental Journey" as a teenager. Late in life, he would name "Secret Love" as one of his all-time favorite records.

Despite an almost full year of stardom, Johnnie was paralyzed at the prospect. "I couldn't really talk to her, because my mouth was full of marbles, so to speak. I was a big fan and here I am in a recording studio with Doris Day!" he said. "I wanted to watch my mouth, to make sure I didn't use any profanities, and I remember telling myself, 'No—you cannot smoke in front of Doris Day, you can't do this, you do that . . . ' but all of my inhibitions, all of that, were for no cause, because Doris is sweet, a very sweet lady."[14]

The October 16 session—one year to the day that Johnnie had recorded "Cry," was to cut "Full Time Job," an Eddy Arnold hit and "Ma Says, Pa Says," a featherweight novelty; Miller envisioned it as a country music spectacular. "I did the very first pop crossover with country in '50 and '51," Miller said. "Most people then were concerned with what category a song belonged in, but I looked at them as just plain good songs. Both Johnnie and Doris had single hits out at the time, and the market could not absorb another single, but if you had a duet, it was like a whole different kind of record. Like I had done with Frankie Laine and Jo Stafford on 'Settin' The Woods On Fire.'"

Miller used the same unorthodox studio configuration on this Ray/Day date that he had with Jo and Frankie. "What Mitch came up with was the idea to have seven guitar players sittin' in a circle with one Telefunken mike hangin' down off a boom right between them," said Speedy West, California's top steel guitarist. "It was me, Alvino Rey and a bunch of the other top players. They were all unamplified, there was no amplifier except on me, and they had two drummers, one playin' a regular kit, and one playin' with brushes on a piece of paper settin' on a piano bench. I was the only lead instrument, I done all the intros, fills, turnarounds, endings, everything."[15]

West was so highly regarded by Miller that he got double scale for these Columbia sessions (despite the fact West could not read music and it was two years before he came clean to Miller. "He'd say, 'okay, scratch bar 48,' and I'd grab my pencil and rub somethin' out. I didn't even know where in the hell bar 48 was!"). A brilliant improvisatory stylist, his adventurous playing skipped atop the full rhythmic strum of seven guitars, creating a unique sound. The Beard's conceptual mind was fascinating.

Equally arresting was Johnnie's behavior in the studio. If he meant to act restrained and well mannered, his was a strange notion of polite conduct. "He was different—a complete wreck as far as bein' nervous. He was wound up tighter'n a nine day clock," West said. "Someone told me, 'You might see him climbin' the walls,' but he was bouncin' off the walls! Johnnie was great, no problem to work with, but hyper. He was hyper as hell. I don't know if it was his natural way or if he was on dope or what, but he had energy galore." (West has also described seeing Johnnie get down on all fours at this session and actually start chewing on an arm chair.) "It was sure different from what I was used to, playing country," he said.

Alcohol and amphetamine use was nothing new to country musicians. But when Johnnie dropped dexedrine into his already booze-amped system the results were spectacular. And he was using; Jim Low recalls one late night carouse in Philadelphia when he complained of being tired. Johnnie whipped out a fat shiny capsule: "This'll take care of it," he said. Johnnie was going up, up, up and out.

Johnnie already was, as Danny Kessler said, "the most natural wild man I have ever seen." His combination of liquor and speed kept him in a state of completely unchecked and unpredictable behavior. In that sense, and in his sexuality, his performing style, even his appearance—long, slicked back hair, his androgynous manner, that contraption stuck in his ear—Johnnie was a publicity nightmare who could wake up, screaming, at any moment.

Hence Miller's pairing him with Doris Day on a country music record was about as far away from "his black-influenced singing," which Miller "didn't want him to be noted for," as he could have taken Johnnie.

Despite Johnnie's folk music background, and a wonderful blend of two voices, the results were undistinguished (but the single did, after all, make the Top 40).

The beginning of a series of Miller experiments on Johnnie, searching for a new sound, a fresh pop style, heralded a major shift in Johnnie's output. Everything, bar "Walkin' My Baby," that Johnnie recorded during his first year with Okeh and Columbia, was markedly black-influenced, a wedding of R&B's earthy phrasing to the great American pop standards, a style which was, at the time, prominent among black singers. Even as the pure R&B style ascended, most blacks affectionately recorded and performed standards. Singers like Billy Eckstine, Hadda Brooks, Thelma Carpenter specialized in them.

It was a blurred musical line throughout 1952-54, and A&R men began consciously separating the idioms to establish distinct markets, in the same process Miller now began with Johnnie. The abandoning of this bi-racial pop dialogue is a loss which has subsequently given rise to grave misperception of pop music's natural growth. While Hadda Brooks recorded "That's My Desire," before Frankie Laine, she decided to do so only after hearing Laine sing it at Billy Berg's club[16]. In a Washington D.C. housing project, adolescent Marvin Gaye was doing a note-for-note "Cry," falling on his knees and weeping exactly as Johnnie had done on "The Toast of the Town." Gaye kept the move and the tears in his act for years, on the ballad "Distant Lover."[17]

Johnnie was set to kick off another theater tour, with his first date set for Los Angeles' huge Shrine Auditorium. After the lukewarm reception Gary Morton received over the summer, GAC suggested one of their new acquisitions, local R&B honker Big Jay McNeely, "The Deacon of Tenor Sax." McNeely was a six-foot-plus black man who favored holding a single wailing note for forty or fifty bars, blown while lying flat on his back, or strutting from table top to top, even leading his audience, pied piper like, out onto the street, playing all the while.

He exercised a shamanistic, almost hypnotic power over an audience. At the time, McNeely said, "I was drawing six thousand white kids every week in L.A., and my manager had just gotten me signed with GAC, and we were all set to do this tour with Johnnie Ray, which was going to be great exposure." With McNeely's gift for reducing his listeners to howling, writhing fiends he was an extremely tough act to follow.

Bernie had his own reasons for de-emphasizing Johnnie's ties to Rhythm & Blues. They led inevitably back to the Flame Showbar, which led back to the Detroit Police blotter which led to utter disaster. Prior to the Shrine date, Bernie bet McNeely's manager a new suit from Sy Devore's Hollywood tailor shop that the sax man could not bring down the house and stop a show the way his boy could.

During the first show at the Shrine, McNeely got the sign from his manager: do it. Within ten minutes, the wild honker whipped the sold-out house into such a thrashing mob that police were called and the show, indeed, temporarily halted. McNeely's manager got the suit, and Big Jay got the boot. He was off the tour, and Morton was on.

Before leaving town, Bernie finalized negotiations at 20th Century Fox, and Johnnie signed a long-term, seven-picture contract. They would begin shooting his debut, tentatively set as a tailored vehicle with the working title "All Of Me," to be produced by Leonard Goldstein,[18] following Johnnie's Spring tour of Great Britain. One final business problem was yet to be settled—the matter of Johnnie's Las Vegas debut. Construction delays plagued the Sands Hotel, and Entratter was forced to keep pushing the date back; first two weeks, then two months, three months, six months. By the time the Sands was ready to open in the fall of 1953, Entratter and Bernie were at bitter odds.

*   *   *

"Johnnie never acknowledged any trouble in his life," Jack Devaney said. "He always walked away from dissension. He lived for the moment." Without the shackles of public decorum which Marilyn's presence nominally required, Johnnie also turned farther from convention and plunged into an intensified after-hours life, scouring action in every city he worked. Jim Low fell in with him for a few days after the separation. "We were in Philadelphia," Low said, "and he took me to one of these, what they called, 'purple places,' an absolutely gay after hours club. I couldn't believe it. It was about three a.m. and the place was full of gays and lesbians. Look over here, see two men huggin' and kissin', look over there and see two women huggin' and kissin'. It was a real eye opener. Strictly underground type of spot. But we just had a drink and that was about it."

Back in New York, Johnnie attended a jazzman's reefer party with a couple of musician buddies. "I was havin' a little party at my apartment on West 71st Street and a couple of the guys in Anthony's band asked if they could bring Johnnie Ray," the host recalled. "I told 'em, 'Shit, yeah. C'mon over.' Had about thirty people in this tiny studio apartment, no worries 'cause the manager was there, too, he was smashed," the host recalled.

"In comes John, he says 'where's the booze?' We raged 'til the wee hours, and of course, being musicians, they were all smokin' pot, and I had a bunch of construction paper, all different colors, and crayons. Everybody'd get high and doodle. Just whatever came off the top of your head, y'know? I didn't see Johnnie smoke any, but he must have breathed enough in. And he did do some doodles with the crayons. Used to have 'em hangin' on the wall . . . don't know what ever happened to those."[19]

It was an ideal spot for Johnnie—a room crowded with adults behaving like children. His spirit was that of a perpetually carefree kid, and was finally able to try and set up a life style that catered to his impulsive nature. He returned to his suite at the Warwick, and soon welcomed one of the male model set to share it with him whenever he was in town. A tall, striking man named Stan Halpert ("he was one hell of a nice guy," by Jim Low's reckoning), he kept up a steady, intimate relationship with Johnnie for the next two years.[20]

On the precious few off days Bernie's scheduling permitted, Johnnie was free for the first time in his life to indulge himself in any manner he chose. For the last two years, the true, child-like John had been subjugated by the Cry Guy's fireworks and the, humble, God-fearing front he attempted to maintain as a public figure under constant scrutiny from reporters and disk jocks.

This Johnnie was a carefree slob who kept an open house stocked with plenty of liquor. After dark he would order several limos to ferry him and his clan around various night spots. It was the first time Johnnie, since leaving the Flame, could be himself. The Warwick staff buckled down for the usual fireworks. They got them.

Reality, and the road, however, kept interfering. Apart from a spate of club dates in Texas earlier in the year, Johnnie had made few appearances in the South, and none which capitalized on his teenage following. Bernie, not considering the fact that his boy drew more of a mixed crowd than anyone else in the business, sent him on an auditorium tour that kicked off in the heart of Dixie. "I played a ballpark in Mobile, Alabama, and they built a stage right over home plate," he said in 1983. "Over by first base there was a separate section and I asked them what that section was for. They told me 'That's where the niggers sit.' So I said, 'Look, these people are going to pay their money. I don't mind your segregation, I'm not here to change your entire social structure but this won't do! If you want to rope off part of the main bleacher section, that's alright. Otherwise they are going to watch the entire show looking at my back.

"So they agreed to that, but what they did was rope off what they thought would be the worst seats. Well, they had never seen me work before, I guess they thought I was a stand up singer, they didn't know that I moved around. Those seats they had given to the blacks turned out to be the best seats in the stadium!"

He played the entire show to them, and tension grew the longer he was on. "After I finished the jubilee number at the end of my act, it was all a blur. I was not even allowed to take a curtain call, they rushed me into a waiting limousine—I was not even allowed to stay in the city of Mobile!" Innocent John. Nearly ignited a race riot.

"Then I played the Fox Theater in Atlanta, Georgia. That's when I first saw 'black' water fountains and 'white' water fountains. At the Fox, all the blacks had to sit up in what was called 'nigger heaven,' the balcony," he said. "There was nothing I could do about that. I couldn't cancel the engagement, and I felt that the balcony really wasn't the worst place to see me. That's how I became aware of prejudice in the South. Later on, Ebony Magazine got ahold of me to do an in-depth interview, and blasted hell out of the white community, without using names."[21]

The piece appeared in Ebony's March 1953 issue, a spectacular four-page spread titled "Negroes Taught Me To Sing, By Johnnie Ray." "Famous Cry Crooner tells what Blues Taught Him" read a sub-head, with a double spread photo of Johnnie, Billy Ward and the Dominoes 'crying,' together backstage at Chicago's Oriental Theater. It was an unprecedented move that even Frankie Laine would not have tried to get away with. For someone like Eddie Fisher, it would have been career suicide. For Johnnie, it was natural.

Put together by veteran black journalist Bill Lane, the story did not exactly "blast hell out of the white community," but it was an impressive gesture for one in Johnnie's already vulnerable, if not downright tenuous, position. Other photos showed him hanging out at Club De Lisa with Joe Williams, Illinois Jacquet, re-united with Maurice King at the Detroit Fox Theater, and posing with Nat Cole and Billy May backstage at the Paramount. Johnnie was one hip, freaky little mother of a white piano cat. Cool beyond Frankie Laine, beyond even Johnnie Otis—his natural sense of belonging and grasp of the blues idiom did not rely on promotion or exploitation; Johnnie was drawn to the black musical community by necessity. He had a ton of hip thrust upon him.

"From then on, I remember I could drive around Harlem and the people used to come out of their apartments and wave at me," Johnnie said. "I could go into the toughest nightclubs in Harlem and feel very protected. It wasn't anything I had earned. I had just told the truth."[22] The truth was a mighty dangerous thing; he was lucky to escape a whipping in Mobile. No other pop star so explicitly flouted the rules of segregation—Sinatra's "The House I Live In" was about as developed and outspoken as pop's social conscience had gotten.

Although Johnnie never made the Rhythm & Blues chart again, he was a strong favorite among black audiences. The annual 1953 Theatrical Poll in black community newspaper The Pittsburgh Courier ranked Johnnie fourth, behind Arthur Prysock, Joe Medlin and Nat Cole. After that incendiary 1952 tour, Bernie did not book any more stadium shows in the South.

*   *   *

Fat settlement or no, Marilyn had little interest in money. She was as desperately in love with Johnnie as Charlie Morrison was desperate to finalize negotiations with Halsey Cowan. By November the strain of losing him landed Marilyn back in Cedars of Lebanon. That she was fifteen pounds underweight and miserable with the realization that she and Johnnie were splitsville was common knowledge in the trade. When columnists began reporting the marriage's demise, Marilyn fought back. She telephoned Louella Parsons, who ran their conversation under the headline "Johnnie Ray Rift Denied."

"Johnnie and I are not separated except by distance," she said in a prepared statement. "He's in San Francisco, where he's appearing and I'm in here in the hospital. I'm very much discouraged by my ill health which keeps me from him. I love him and he loves me. He telephoned from San Francisco to wish me a happy Thanksgiving. He feels badly, as I do. I am unable to travel but as soon as I regain my health I'll be by his side. It's unfortunate that such stories about us are being printed. We have had no fights or battles. I feel sorry that I've let him down."[23]

In late November, Johnnie returned to Hollywood for his screen test at Fox, which was screened and personally approved by Darryl F. Zanuck. The latter had nixed Leonard Goldstein's "All of Me," and planned to cast Johnnie in a different, as yet undecided, picture. Johnnie was suddenly Zanuck's golden boy, and he performed at a post-premiere party for the "Snows of Kilimanjaro" at Romanoff's.[24] The picture starred Gregory Peck, Ava Gardner and Susan Hayward (who had not known Gardner was in the picture until after shooting was completed).

Marilyn, still in Cedars trying to whip her "run-down" condition, fumed at the prospect of Gardner and her husband together. Johnnie played another sold-out engagement at the Shrine Auditorium and flew to Hawaii for a four-night stand. By then, Marilyn was well enough to see him off at the airport, but the fact he went alone inspired more rift rumors.

Charlie realized the entire caper was reaching critical mass, and that it was time to up the ante. Privately seeking to end the on-again, off-again marriage his daughter was fighting to preserve, Charlie was banking on a big pay-off. He was compelled, publicly, to uphold what tattered honor Marilyn had left, while working behind her back to get Johnnie where he wanted him—over a barrel. On December 7, he phoned Louella for a "Parents Squelch Report Ray, Wife Separated" headline, again citing his daughter's frail health as the only reason the pair was apart. He made some other calls, sat back, and waited.[25]

Things suddenly got a lot tougher for Johnnie. On December 12, "The Hollywood Life Newsweekly of the West: San Francisco-Los Angeles," a vanity trade newsletter that promised "the real INSIDE-the TRUTH behind the news," published by broadcast demagogue Jimmie Tarantino, arrived on the desks of many in the broadcast trade with a screaming front cover headline: "Johnnie 'Cry' Ray Arrested on Homosexual Charge."

Someone had tipped Tarantino on Johnnie's Accosting and Soliciting bust two and half years earlier and rang in a favor by getting the charge in print. The page one attack used the words "homo" or "homosexual" no less than eighteen times and noted, by way of introduction, that "the absolute most dangerous homo is the one who combines his sex weakness with drinking sprees."

Tarantino claimed he learned of the arrest months earlier and that he "had planned to investigate, but was deterred by the news that Johnnie Ray and Marilyn Morrison were marrying." Yet Tarantino suddenly felt compelled to recount the incident in all its back alley sleaze, and added "if anything his homo habit increased . . . he's continued right on with his hit and run, thrill and drinking kick."[26] Fortunately, this was a strictly inside, subscription only sheet and while it went to both Hedda and Louella (and hundreds of other broadcasters), none in the fourth estate dignified the revelation by repeating it. Johnnie's need for damage control mushroomed all over again.

When Johnnie flew back to Hollywood, he went straight to Marilyn's suite at the Beverly Hills Hotel. A reel of Johnnie's silent eight-millimeter home movies segues from footage of Waikiki Beach to a shot of him awakening Marilyn in her bed there; the relief on her face is matched only by the melancholy tension etched on Johnnie's; they embrace, he lights cigarettes for both of them and reclines beside her. It is a pensive, bittersweet tableaux.[27]

Toni Kertman, Marilyn's half sister, took up the cause and phoned Earl Wilson. "Johnnie Ray, Bride Reconciled," Wilson duly reported. Toni was quoted as saying the pair was "completely reconciled. Marilyn will definitely join Johnnie in New York. They'll be living together at the Warwick before Christmas. The only problems they have are problems of health. Marilyn lost fifteen pounds since she lost her baby and when she gains five or so pounds everything will be all right again."[28]

It was her desperate last stand. Johnnie had returned to the Capitol Theater where (between screenings of Errol Flynn's "Against All Flags") he gave six shows a day (and pulled down $25,000 a week). An audience member recalls Johnnie pounding the white baby grand piano so hard that a chip of wood splintered off and flew into the audience.[29]

Marilyn joined him, just as Toni prophesied. But Johnnie had had enough of the chase. His deliberately gay New Year's Eve revelry proved too much even for Marilyn. She was through; on the first of January, she called Charlie from the Warwick and said "I'm sorry, real sorry, Daddy, but our marriage is definitely over." He was overjoyed.

The next day she marched into Johnnie's dressing room and told him she was leaving. Then, true to form, she called Earl Wilson. "It's all over," Marilyn told him. "Completely through."

Wilson scampered over to the Capitol. While most of the nation pondered headlines announcing Hank Williams' untimely death, the Ray split, by Broadway standards, was meatier by far. Wilson found Johnnie backstage, sitting on a trunk, head in hands. "Man, it wasn't that chick's fault, because that chick tried," he told Wilson.

"In this bebop and hepcat lingo," Wilson reported, "the 26 year old crying crooner took all the blame for permanent bust up of the seven month marriage." He described Johnnie pacing as he spoke, so agitated that he waved his arms exactly as he did performing. In fact, he was performing. "Man, I love that chick more than the day we got married," he said, "but she deserves a man who can do a lot more for her than I can."

Wilson asked if it was due to his career. "Well," Johnnie waffled, "it just didn't work out. When she lost the baby, she took it so hard. *I just thought it was an act of God.* But man it never had a chance . . . this . . . ," he gestured disconsolately about the cavernous theater. Errol Flynn swashbuckled at barely audible level.

"And on top of that, no home except for the next hotel. Plenty of people told me it wouldn't work but I thought I could make it work . . ." his voice trailed off almost completely. "And man, she tried . ." Wilson thanked him and prepared to leave. Johnnie explained that they were never able to recapture "the few hours of enchantment of our honeymoon," and begged Earl to ask his "BW" (Beautiful Wife) to "have a cup of coffee with her. She doesn't know many people here and she'll be lonesome." The split was so onerous that at the time Johnnie did not dare, or perhaps did not care, to personally see Marilyn. Charlie Morrison told Earl that his daughter would return to Hollywood within a few days.

Wilson's exclusive ran down the marriage's bizarre chronology, reprinted the "only woman who made me feel like a real man" quote, cited the previous summer's arrests in Boston and Minneapolis, the September miscarriage, Johnnie's return from Hawaii and the past three weeks' reconciliation. It was a mess Johnnie desperately wanted to forget, and

Marilyn had just as desperately longed to see straightened out. Only Charlie was happy. The talk about it was ugly.[30]

"They met, fell in love and got married in just a few months' time," said Tad Mann, a road manager Johnnie confided in years later. "But it was a Hollywood deal. They didn't even know each other. That marriage was window dressing—strictly damage control. She was married to Johnnie but he wasn't sleeping with her. And once the damage control didn't work out, they made her a fat settlement. 'Okay, that's it. Here's your money. Take it and go.'"[31]

The loss of face for Charlie Morrison was nowhere near as profound as it was for Marilyn; only the amount of money wasted on the affair bugged Charlie. So much so, that in April, Mocambo's controlling corporation, Maguire Inc., sued Marion Davies for $11,582, charging that she neglected to pay her share of the Ray party costs.[32] Davies was appalled.

Through her amanuensis, she issued a statement, claiming that "Mr. Morrison stated he would pay the expenses of the party and that he felt the success of the party would be augmented by my sponsorship. I gladly complied with his flattering request. Five months later Mr. Morrison asked me to pay for the food, liquor and servants provided. I was astounded."[33] The Morrisons were evidently not as well heeled as they appeared.

When Charlie died five years later, uninsured and heavily in debt, Mocambo was near closure and his widow was nearly forced into bankruptcy. "Charlie had thousands of friends, but we had about four dollars," she told Earl Wilson. "Then Frank (Sinatra) called me up. He said, 'Mary, I don't have anything to do for two weeks. How about me coming into Mocambo with Nelson Riddle's orchestra?' He had never sung at any club in Hollywood and it was like New Year's Eve every night. We took in over $100,000 in those two weeks, and I gave old Charlie a millionaire's funeral."[34]

Johnnie and Marilyn's marriage had been a complex construction based on fame and power, desire and fear, put over in all earnestness through the era's typical Hear No Evil, See No Evil, Speak No Evil fashion. Its final stages were played under the same rules of conduct. Whatever emotional integrity that existed between the two was forced to take a back seat to the considerations of public image, private paranoia and the amount of cash Johnnie stood to lose as a result of the split. The pair remained friendly and Marilyn often turned up in posed press photos—opening nights, greeting her ex at airports—for the next several years. But the pain both felt over such failure and loss also remained.

Being tossed in the drunk tank and kicked around by journalists was nothing. This was the first real downturn, a harsh nose dive, that Johnnie had suffered since his hearing was destroyed. Fame darkened, seemed to turn against him. Without the implicit Morrison clout Johnnie was considerably more vulnerable. And he never did appear at Mocambo. Nearly four decades later Marilyn told Jane Kean, "I would marry him all over again."[35]

In the wake of his split with Marilyn and Jimmie Tarantino's revelations to the trade, Johnnie, with his veil of domestic respectability torn away, was a walking bullseye. "I became very guarded and

very suspicious of the press. I didn't have any friends, I didn't have an entourage," Johnnie explained. "There was no one to tell me what was right, what was wrong, what was a mistake, or to advise me. I was a setup for every lawsuit or cheap article that wanted to take a crack at me."[1]

To his detractors, the Ebony feature only emphasized his low character. To Johnnie, it was positive, the best kind of publicity: it had conscience. He was sincere about it, willfully taking an overt controversial stance which pre-dated the Civil Rights movement as significantly as his brand of extreme pop anticipated rock and roll.

When things began to sour between him and Marilyn, Bernie and Art Franklin schemed endlessly on how to bring respectability, or at least, legitimacy to the public's confused understanding of Johnnie Ray. With such a high and outside national profile, the Cry Guy needed an anchor to society, to normalcy. Realizing there was nothing normal whatsoever about him, the choice was as obvious as it was solid, natural: "The Johnnie Ray Foundation for Hard of Hearing Children." Outside of his family and the trade, the only other people Johnnie really gave a damn about were the deaf—a tailor-made group of losers for a flack man to feed off.

In a perfect combination of legitimate concern and press-garnering activity, Bernie arranged a Christmas visit to Brooklyn's PS 47, a school for hearing-impaired youth. Costumed as Santa Claus, Johnnie handed out over 100 presents there, beginning an annual ritual he repeated each year (road schedule permitting). Back on the Ed Sullivan show in February, Johnnie announced that he was officially establishing the Ray Foundation with the donation of his thousand dollar fee. Ever the master showman, he even went so far as to "don his hearing aid on camera," a dramatic act which dropped more than a few jaws.[2]

With gossip about the sordid truth behind his split from Marilyn spreading like septic gas, Art Franklin seized upon the inherent decency Johnnie was exhibiting. The nearly 1000 Ray Fan Clubs across the nation joined in raising funds. Johnnie was genuinely inspired to establish the Foundation. His empathy ran deep, and his emotional reaction to the kids' grateful response (to such an improbably wraith-like Santa Claus) was intense. He ultimately donated hundreds of thousands of dollars, not only to his own foundation but numerous other organizations, and continued the work for the rest of his life.

Johnnie returned to the Copacabana, opening on February 5, an engagement that coincided with the first days of Lent—a period when New York night club floors often resembled a barren No Man's Land. Johnnie, of course, did the same kind of "you couldn't get near the Copa" business as his debut run. He drew such enthusiastic turn-away crowds that the New York City administration, alarmed by the manic atmosphere

Ray fans seemed to generate, suddenly proclaimed "Mental Health Awareness Week."[3]

Before the opening, Johnnie stopped by the Latin Quarter to catch the Kean Sisters' act. The club's new wardrobe assistant, unfortunately, was an incompetent. As the orchestra played the sisters' introduction a third time, Johnnie sensed a problem. Unprompted, he leapt on stage.

"We were frantic, we could hear the band playing our music, but she couldn't get me into the costume. So, Johnnie jumped up and did about ten minutes of material, until we were ready to go on," Jane Kean said. "Betty and I already considered him a friend, but after that, we both fell in love him. There aren't many entertainers who would do that in a similar situation, especially one of Johnnie's stature."

He was living the Rooney/Garland silver screen fantasy of one cheery show biz family, always ready to pitch in and make sure the show went on. Johnnie accepted every sugar-coated myth the trade presented about itself to the public (and laughed off backstage) as gospel.

Johnnie became particularly close to Betty ("she did enjoy drinking a lot more than I did," Jane explained) and lavished both with expensive gifts. He associated them inseparably, as he continued to do with ventriloquist Jimmy Nelson, with the ecstacy of April 10, 1952. To Johnnie's delight, the Keans, a Copa mainstay, were held over and featured (along with tap dancers the Nicholas Brothers) on Johnnie's engagement.

It was a replay of the previous Spring's sensation, despite the threat of more pious Catholic members of the theater set staying home and observing their ritual. "Ray Effect on Gotham Saloon Set is Little Short of Mass Hysteria," read Billboard's opening night review. After the show, Johnnie posed in the kitchen with Podell's young niece and nephew, then rode the elevator up to Fourteen, where he was joined by the Keans, Milton Berle, Jan Murray and a dozen others. His show biz family billed and cooed. Johnnie soaked it up hungrily. He loved them all, and they pledged their love to him.[4]

Bernie was not enjoying himself at all. Since canceling the Sands contract some months earlier and refusing Entratter's continual demands they commit to the hotel's Copa Room grand opening, tension had mounted steadily. Phone calls from Las Vegas to Bernie's offices at 1650 Broadway grew more and more acrimonious.

The fact that Johnnie was booked months in advance and contracted to shoot his Fox screen debut made no difference to Entratter. That he could not confirm the Sands opening date was equally trivial. Entratter's fumble of Johnnie's original contract (having personally paid the price difference) charged the situation further. Very touchy situation.

Copacabana prestige was what really broke Johnnie on a national basis; the fact that "Cry" had sold over two million records even before he arrived there was insignificant to Entratter. Johnnie was, to the Copa way of thinking, beholden to them. Bernie refused to cancel any dates for the Sands, promising only to appear in Vegas as soon as their schedule and, he stressed, construction delays permitted. To Mr. Commotion, business was business, not favors and concessions.

Entratter became furious. Although he was, as Earl Wilson wrote, "100 percent clean all his life . . . Entratter knew about the other world because he had a brother, Charley Green, who was killed by the Vincent 'Mad Dog' Coll mob in the post-Prohibition era and found under a bridge."[5] As a figurehead and front man, Entratter was ideal. The power behind him, Frank Costello, operated as ruthlessly as any one in the Charlie Lucky fold.

Competition between Las Vegas' Flamingo and Last Frontier had always been fierce. Intensified by the Desert Inn's August 1950 opening, the Sands appearance on the Strip raised it to a new pitch. Entratter realized that Johnnie and Bernie would not bend and that he needed a name entertainer with a strong draw. In early 1953, though, Johnnie had no rival.

The Sands powers-that-be were out for blood. "This is a creepy story," Lang said. "Jack Entratter threatened my life, threatened a lot of people's lives. We were really playing hard ball. I called Moe Dalitz and Moe settled the whole thing." This was as close to bedding Johnnie down with the mob as Bernie had come so far, but there were few options. Anyway, as a Cleveland Mayfield Road boy, Dalitz was predisposed to favor Johnnie.

Fortuitously, the autumn release of "From Here To Eternity" reinstated Entratter pal Frank Sinatra (who affectionately nicknamed Entratter "Jew Feet") as a top attraction all over again. It was the one occasion when anything pertaining to Sinatra boosted Johnnie's career. In this case, without Frank's return to public favor the Cry Guy's prospects were grim. But unfortunately for Entratters Sinatra was at the time exclusively contracted to the Flamingo.[6]

As construction dragged on, Copa Room hopes for a boffo headliner dimmed. The situation changed dramatically in mid-1953. Over at the Flamingo, Earl Wilson noted, "the atmosphere wasn't too cheery. Owner Gus Greenbaum and his wife had just been mysteriously slashed to death with a large carving knife at their ranch house outside Phoenix.

"'There's an understanding among the boys that you never murder anybody in Las Vegas,' they would tell you there. 'It would give the town a bad name.'" As the Flamingo's Bugsy Siegel was gunned down in Los Angeles, so too did Greenbaum get his elsewhere.[7]

The case was never solved, but Sinatra's exclusive at the Flamingo apparently expired along with the Greenbaums. He opened the Sands that fall, triumphant initiation of a new era in Vegas' swinging culture. He was followed by Martin & Lewis (who were also previously Flamingo exclusives), Sammy Davis Jr., and eventually, Johnnie. Just as they were almost back in place, Entratter's ruffled feathers got mussed up all over again— Bernie was making a deal with the competition for the Cry Guy's Vegas debut.

After Sinatra opened the Sands, Bernie was contacted by the Desert Inn's Robert and Leonard Goldstein. Although Johnnie was to a degree obliged to Dalitz and the D.I., the Goldsteins offered something that Entratter had not: to break the price barrier, a hitherto inviolate $7,500 weekly scale (well-connected attractions, of course, always got hefty under-the-table bonus cash).

"The Goldstein brothers called me about Johnnie working at the Desert Inn and said they would break the price barrier," Lang recalled. "They did, too. We eventually settled on a deal to appear there three or four times a year for a lot more money than they had previously paid. We went to $15,000 a week the first time in, and after that, everyone threw the price barrier away."

The Goldstein brothers, nominal D.I. co-producers, had grown up with Dalitz in Cleveland. Prior to his arrival in Las Vegas, Dalitz' portfolio of infamy was distinguished by prohibition booze smuggling and illegal gambling credits. He made a fortune running Canadian whisky and had attended, along with Al Capone, Joe Adonis, Albert Anastasia, Meyer

Lansky, Frank Costello, Lucky Luciano and Lepke Buchalter, a May 1929 bootlegger summit at Atlantic City's President Hotel.[8]

Cleveland's Mayfield Road Gang had yearned for a piece of the action brewing in the Nevada desert as early as 1946, when Dalitz dispatched muscle (Tony "Ape Head" Torcasio) and front man (Wilbur Clark, a professional gambler who had drifted east from the Long Beach gambling ship Monte Carlo into the Gang's illegal casinos) to establish operations in Las Vegas. Once they were ready to open in 1950, Dalitz joined them. He became the Desert Inn's "Entertainment Director." ("Can you believe *that*?" Trade insiders joked. "Moe Dalitz calling himself an 'Entertainment Director!'")

Bernie's turning to Dalitz for settlement of the Sands hassle was a decisive move, one he avoided making for as long as possible. Johnnie had already come in contact with at least three separate organized crime factions, Cleveland's Mayfield Road Gang (as early as 1950), Detroit's Purple Gang and New York's Luciano family, headed in Lucky's absence by Joe Adonis and Copa backer Frank Costello. All three had made money off Johnnie. "The mob offered to buy my contract for $50,000 once, but my manager refused," he told Arnold Shaw years later. "We all thought we were going to be mutilated for a few days."[9]

Every aspect of such dealings was business as usual for any prominent entertainer of the day. Whatever alliance reached during this Vegas rhubarb was prompted more by the big money Johnnie made with or without mob backing. And Johnnie did indeed go into the Sands three months after his debut at the Desert Inn. But the plea to Dalitz and his intervention, caused significant problems for Johnnie's career years later.

*   *   *

In late March 1953, Johnnie, Cy, Bernie and drummer Sammy Fede flew to London for Johnnie's European debut. He was starting a three-week tour of Britain at London's Palladium. Located off the West End's Strand, the venerable red-velvet fuzzed and gold-fixtured theater had hosted England's music hall idols for decades. Few Americans had yet to make a splash there; Frankie Laine and Jimmy Durante had done respectable business, but Danny Kaye's engagement there the previous season drew the biggest accolades any Yank enjoyed.

Considering the negative reviews Johnnie's releases got in Britain, it was not to be a piece of cake conquest. Post-war England was still scrambling to recover; the economy was a shambles, and day to day survival for many still required their blood, sweat and tears. Shattered by bombs and rockets, London had barely started to rebuild. But if the tone of the popular press was hostile, Johnnie's record sales put the lie to Fleet Street's accounting. Nonetheless, things began to sour as soon as they arrived.

Bernie painstakingly ensured every aspect of the itinerary and paperwork were in order; both Johnnie and Fede held the requisite Ministry of Labor-issued work permits. The Musicians Union, however, inexplicably and emphatically chose not to recognize Fede's. During rehearsal at the Palladium on Friday, March 27, Union representatives demanded he get off the house band drum kit. A replacement set was hired, sent for and assembled; rehearsal resumed. Then M.U. officials told Fede he would not be allowed to perform. "We will not have it assumed," a Union spokesman sniffed, "that foreign musicians can wander into a British orchestra."

Although Kaye, Laine and Durante had all used their own accompanists there, Fede was barred at the Palladium. "We had gotten permission to bring our own drummer in lieu of a conductor," Bernie explained. "But the Union decided that Johnnie did not require him, and so we should hire a local drummer. Val Parnell, Lew Grade, everyone involved went to the Union and they turned them down."

Questioned by journalists, Palladium manager Parnell "went so far as to suggest that Johnnie Ray would be unable to appear."[10] No one ever decided what the genesis of this trouble was. "It may have been spite," Lang said. "It was an era of new pop styles. I don't think it was aimed at Johnnie personally but who knows? The whole thing came down to 'are we going to cancel the show or not?'

"Of course we weren't about to do that. Johnnie had worked without his own drummer before, and he had a lot of rehearsal then, was familiar with the whole setup. We carried our own equipment, too, the clip mike and monitors. We put our monitors on the stage, which was not considered the thing to do in those days. Johnnie just went out and did his thing."

Bernie had Fede slip into a cerise band uniform jacket and whisper instructions to the drummer throughout the first show there on Saturday night. The Union kicked him off and refused to let him back for the second set. By then the British drummer was familiar with the arrangements and there was no turning back; Johnnie's conquest was total. The sold-out house exploded when he hit the stage and howled throughout the entire two-week engagement.

"The Palladium was the wildest audience, in terms of response that I had ever seen," Kertman said. "He got a big reaction there." "No one there had ever seen anything like Johnnie, the violent movement of the way he worked," Bernie said. "He made superb impact at the Palladium."

As Tony Bennett described it, "They were all looking for something in Britain—they had no money, they had nothing, the people there. It was international news. He ripped the Palladium apart, it was the first time pandemonium hit that scene. I don't remember anybody outside of Danny Kaye who did a bigger job at the Palladium than Johnnie. He was huge."

There were near-riots at the night's end. Fans spilled out into the Strand, blocking traffic. Police were powerless. Johnnie was compelled to take to the theater roof, blowing kisses and waving them off. The crowd's roar, diminished by the poor quality of his hearing aid reception, was nonetheless a sweet tumult. No one had ever seen anything like it. Only after he disappeared from sight did they finally start to disperse. When the dust settled and the last cocktail was drained, Noel Coward noted in his diary: "Took Gladys [Calthorpe] to Johnnie Ray's opening at the Palladium. He was really quite remarkable and had the whole place in an uproar."11

The uproar spread throughout the British Isles. By the time he reached Scotland his entire street wardrobe had been shredded by the mobs of fans which awaited him everywhere on the tour. It was during that jaunt Johnnie began to purchase and wear only the cheapest, casual clothes. He carried dozens of Johnnie Ray sport shirts (a novel fashion item at the time; Fred Perry began producing his line in 1952 when Johnnie's was introduced; previously the LaCoste model was the only such item manufactured) and bargain basement slacks. These never lasted more than a few days, often only several hours.

"Man, I lost more wardrobe!" he said. "Especially in Europe, where not only the kids but grownups fought for souvenirs. They would've taken my ears if they could."12 Despite the volatile unpredictable mob nature—

or perhaps because of it—Johnnie adored pushing through the groping, manic crowds. Bernie capitalized on the frenzy by having Johnnie send dispatches to the press corps back home, a practice almost as unusual as the British fan's behavior was extreme.

One journalist who did not receive such a letter seemed surprisingly piqued by his neglect. "The boy ought to be his own press agent. In Scotland, he's frittering away the dull hours by writing to every columnist and disk jockey whose name he can recall. Despite the fact that the letter is the same for everybody and might as well have been mimeographed, it's amazing how many of the typewriter and microphone boys reported its contents to their followings as solemnly (or in some cases breathlessly) as if it had been a holograph from Albert Schweitzer."[13]

The offended scribe was none other than Dorothy Kilgallen of the Hearst Press. She had yet to meet Johnnie personally but it seemed that she not only "came to love" his recording of "Please, Mr. Sun," she inexplicably personally admired him.

*　　*　　*

Not all the press in the U.S. revered Johnnie. Shortly after he left the country, *Confidential* ("Uncensored and Off the Record") magazine's April issue hit the news stands. America's premiere scandal rag, it was the first of many to profit from lurid accounts of celebrity transgression. With Marilyn out of the picture and the scent of Jimmie Tarantino's first blood still fresh, *Confidential* cheerily took on the Prince of Wails.

"Johnnie Ray Scandal!" screamed a banner headline at the top. A photograph of Johnnie, face screwed up in angelic insouciance as he blew a kiss into a telephone mouthpiece (snapped in long distance conversation to his mother) was boldly captioned "Johnnie Ray: Is It True?"

Four pages of character assassination, couched in dime store psychologizing and purple pulp phraseology, it was the most concerted public assault on Johnnie to date. Focusing on his marriage (which was treated as an ongoing union) the lead zeroed in on his already oft-repeated prenuptial remark:

"The newsmen and others in the cramped room later vowed that Johnnie bubbled like a bottle of pop, or a high school girl on her first prom date, as he blurted out a confession that lifted the curtain, however briefly, on one of the best kept secrets in show business. 'Man, I'll say we're going to get married,' he fizzed. 'She's the first woman who ever made me feel like a man!'"

The next paragraph was set in bold face: "If Johnnie Ray ever had occasion to burst into tears this was it. For in the very gushing, over-whelmed way he said those words was the damning evidence that he spoke from his heart. He was 26 years old and discovering for the first time what it meant to be a man!"

It was a consummate hatchet job. *Confidential* accused him of begin-ning his career as a female impersonator, "donning a gown of billowing black, high heeled shoes and makeup, then mincing onto . . ." a Detroit nightclub floor where, an unidentified source said he "kept it up until the audience was limp as rags in their chairs. It was damn well hypnotic."

The story was peppered with comments from "eminent psychia-trist" Dr. Louis Berg ("here what we have is a case of a personality in which the 'war of the sexes' is waged within a single body.") He diagnosed Johnnie as "a split personality with hysterical overtones." Berg also dis-sected the hearing problem's effect on his adolescence and impugned Johnnie's relationship with Elma.[14]

Vicious and contentious as the story was, it pulled several key punches. The only arrest mentioned was the Boston airport pinch; it omitted the Minneapolis incident, his separation from Marilyn, and most importantly, the 1951 Detroit accosting and soliciting conviction (and these were already on the record). Held in reserve for future exploitation, the story was fleshed out by comments from its primary source, none other than Art Franklin, Johnnie's own press agent.

Since assisting in the settlement of Al Green's beef and arranging for Johnnie to be welcomed by Detroit's mayor and receive the keys to the city, Franklin had constantly been after Bernie for more money. Bernie refused. Stung, Franklin plotted revenge, and even assured Bernie the piece would be a legitimate profile, resulting in a rare (for *Confidential*) direct meeting between writer and subject.[15]

This was Franklin's warning shot, fired when both manager and attraction were half way around the world. ("Art Franklin said, 'No, no, the guy's going to do a great story,'" Bernie recalled. "And the guy didn't. So, we fired Franklin. Then he threatened to expose all these things, like the Detroit thing.") The whole matter grew increasingly ugly, and

Confidential established a new era of public perception, typified by this pulpy account (probably a verbatim statement from Franklin) of one of "the spindly wailers" 1952 Philadelphia appearances:

"A shaken observer of his performance reported: 'he ran up and down the aisles kissing the girls and shaking hands with the boys and crying like a starved baby, shouting and wriggling all the time. Then he scooted back on the stage. Behind him, girls were kissing each other and some actually scratching each other's arms. Then they jumped from their seats and went rolling up on that stage like a pack of love-starved panthers. Ray was dumped off his piano stool so hard that he was knocked unconscious. The cops broke it up and I went outside for a couple of shots of whiskey.'"

The article's close underscored Franklin's threat. "'Ray would seem to be making a success because of his abnormality,' Dr. Berg said. 'Erase the abnormality and he'd not only be average in behavior but no longer a star.' Put in Broadway's terms, Johnnie's like a lot of us—only more so. Dry those tears and you've also wiped away a million dollar showman."[16]

Apart from the fact that the story originated within Johnnie's own camp, its most threatening aspect was not that it implied Johnnie was homosexual, his marriage a sham and his performance's toxic effect on teenage fans, rather it was the impact that it made upon his general perception and public acceptance. The scandal sheet damaged Johnnie's credibility just as he was about to establish a foothold in the trade. While legitimacy was a goal to strive for more in hope than certainty, *Confidential* capsized the bloom of respectability Johnnie was near achieving with his British tour and upcoming motion picture.

The grim reality that he was nowhere near attaining a place in mainstream pop culture came as a slap, a reminder that he was a misfit, a freak whose public embrace might be relinquished at any moment—a fad personality who, despite the strongest record sales in his field might wake up a discarded relic.

And the fact that *Confidential* essentially stated that Johnnie was gay was no laughing matter. Although the prevailing social climate rendered any action over such a disclosure to a behind-closed-doors blacklist rather than up front public persecution, the gag which taboo status maintained was beginning to unravel.

1953 was the year transsexual Christine Jorgenson made international headlines and became the topic of choice at cocktail gatherings from the Waldorf Astoria to Ashtabula, Ohio. The release of Ed Wood Jr.'s transsexual exploitation drive-in special "Glen Or Glenda?" reflected the fact that even the great unwashed were abuzz over it. The first general acknowledgement that human sexuality was a malleable, widely varying behavior had staggering implications for American culture. It created a mood of disgust and delight, resentment and fascination. Johnnie was caught square in the cross fire.

"I've heard all those stories that I'm queer, that I'm an alcoholic," he said. "I pay 'em no mind, and keep on singin'."[17]

But just as he reached the height of fame and commercial success, to accept or endorse Johnnie Ray became something to think twice about; Tony Bennett, for instance, who ballyhooed Johnnie to every disk jockey and columnist throughout 1952, fell silent. No one had recognized—or at least publicly acknowledged—precisely why Johnnie seemed so "unusual." He had made people uncomfortable from the start but this cast a new light upon him.

Nonetheless, millions craved the oft indecipherable and exhilarating information which the very quality of Johnnie's voice seemed to broadcast. Johnnie's appeal was rooted in that strangeness, in his vulnerability and the metaphysical aura of suffering and emotionality he exuded. Eddie Fisher he was not. Bernie kept him out on the road, grabbing the cash as if there were no tomorrow.

The tilt-a-whirl lurched, roared and ground along its frantic course. Johnnie worked so much throughout 1953 that he did not enter a recording studio until December. Johnnie now required blackout curtains in his hotel suite bedroom. His nerves began to show the wear. Appearing at landmark Montreal nitery San Souci the microphone went dead in midsong. He snapped and threw it down in what Variety chidingly called "a childish display of temperament." Johnnie, born and bred an entertainer, whose onstage chatter was as courtly and formal as anyone in the business, was gritting his teeth through amphetamine and booze exhaustion. The abyss beckoned.[18]

*　　*　　*

1953 was all backlash, starting with the London Musicians Union incident, the *Confidential* story and a climactic pair of law suits from within

Johnnie's own camp. Art Franklin had to be dealt with. Bernie terminated his contract on July 31st. Not even a kiss-off check. Franklin, embittered and out in the cold, planned a litigious revenge.

Danny Kessler rankled also. He was not receiving any of the gravy Bernie promised and schemed for a way to bring a lawsuit—without raising any conflict of interest charges. Columbia named him A&R head of new subsidiary Epic in June, along with his Okeh position, and Kessler could not afford to jeopardize his record career. When Kessler was wooed to RCA after they offered him a spot heading their new R&B subsidiaries, X and Groove, he immediately threw paper at Bernie.

Attorney Lee Eastman filed a complaint in New York District Court on October 2, alleging that Lang had assigned him 50 percent of all monies received from Johnnie Ray on or about May 1951 but had paid Kessler only $1,800 thus far. To avoid any lingering conflict of interest stain, Kessler assigned his cause of action to a secretary, Miss Rochelle Lewis, and asked for $750,000, with interest, payment of all court costs and asked the court that "Johnnie Ray be directed to hold 50 percent of all monies payable by him to Lang pending final determination."[19]

Worse, they were demanding a jury trial, guaranteeing a high profile case where selecting the twelve men good and true would in itself be newsworthy. Bernie conceded, settling out of court for an undisclosed amount. Neither man today cares to speak of it except in the broadest, time-heals-all-wounds manner.

Art Franklin banked on intimidation, the implicit "I'll drag-it-all-out-into-the-open" threat. The scorned flack man's fury was considerable, and by December his breach of contract suit reached pre-trial examination in New York Supreme Court. He asked for a total of $75,000 having, after all, "worked above and beyond normal duties."

Franklin claimed the Johnnie Ray Foundation for Hard of Hearing Children as his own original concept; he got Johnnie the keys to the city of Detroit, where he also worked "to reverse unfavorable attitudes and counteract certain rumors." He claimed a hand in the settlement of Al Green's proposed $500,000 suit against Bernie.[20]

Franklin had all of the most gruesome skeletons in Johnnie's crowded closet. When Bernie heard their bones rattle he had no choice but to reach for the checkbook—it was either that or make another call to Moe Dalitz. Settling up these suits (and Marilyn's kiss-off) tapped the coffers of

Johnnie Ray Enterprises and dealt a crippling blow to the economic machine Bernie had worked so hard to build up since the winter of 1951. All this and Halsey Cowan's bill too.

The money was spread all over between GAC, Bernie, the corporation, and Johnnie. A great deal of it, Johnnie came to believe, was unaccounted for but he was never able to prove it. When the Internal Revenue Service took a look at the situation years later, their reckoning was a shock.

Small wonder Johnnie was booked 40 to 50 weeks a year; Bernie and Gloria were accustomed to the "nice gestures" learnt at Hover's Hollywood table and without him they were nowhere. Whenever any question of their business relationship arose—which was rare—Mr. Commotion told Mr. Emotion that they could tear up the contract and walk away, no questions asked.

Even though Johnnie had done sixteen dates with Mitch Miller between September 1951 and December 1952, putting live appearances before recording was a terrible mistake. But royalty checks were not so easy to siphon commissions off as box office money. The result was a loss of artistic momentum, exacerbated by the toll which *Confidential* and gossip took on Johnnie's image. Mitch Miller had his own ideas on how to re-create Johnnie, but few of them took advantage of Johnnie's native talent.

What Johnnie committed to wax at those sessions represented an extraordinary body of work. The mix of black-ballad phrasing, untrammeled emotion and his ingenuous, wide-eyed rural outlook created an astonishing, individuated pop music style. No one except Jolson had ever re-created the idiom as personally and successfully as Johnnie Ray, and only a very few of those who followed him matched this startling originality. Like Jolson, Johnnie was one of the last pop music performers who took an active hand as a stylistic leader rather than a follower.

His original songs, "Whiskey & Gin," "Tell The Lady I Said Goodbye," "Mountains In The Moonlight," "Paths Of Paradise," "A Sinner Am I," provide the most telling, incisive self-portrait of Johnnie available. Even with the deep urban passion-mongering of "Whiskey & Gin," Johnnie remained the wonder-struck country boy. Mountains called his name, clouds spoke to him, most all his lyrical action occurred, like so much of his life, on a riverbank; themes of despair, anxiety, faith and redemption dominated his songs.

"Paths of Paradise" remains the single most striking, unorthodox and remarkable articulation of his psychology. His songs were refuge, providing the sole satisfaction and context Johnnie experienced. Significantly, isolation and loneliness are never addressed unless they are being conquered, and the fact that he was compelled to convince himself such a conquest was possible—onstage—was what created the masterful performing style that made him famous. The nurturing quality of his music, the way he used it to quench desperation and hopelessness, imbued his 1951-1952 recordings with a strange, indefinable electricity. It fascinated Johnnie as much as it did his audience.

Even stranger was the control he exhibited even at the most intense, agony-wringing peaks his vocals strove for. A showman with impressive technical facility for injecting blood and thunder drama into a lyric, Johnnie's own personality—the essence of character—nonetheless came through. It was confusing and offensive to many, gratifying to others. The emotional impact was too concrete to get around, and the fact that it had to be faced, taken with his brilliant R&B-inspired stylistic upshift, is precisely what made Johnnie a revolutionary figure.

The demands of his career, the stomach churning momentum of non-stop road work, began to re-define Johnnie almost as rapidly as he re-defined the artistic parameters of pop music. He became lost. Ironically, it was Johnnie's force-feeding of raw emotion that created a context for Elvis Presley and for Frank Sinatra's breakthrough "No One Cares" album, the final word in glorious saloon song gloom.

But his confrontational aesthetic was being eroded with every press jab, lawsuit and malfunctioning microphone he was faced with. The faster Johnnie's career moved, the more his gift seemed to diminish. Business began to roll over Johnnie. When he finally got back into the studio in December, he and Miller chose an appropriately safe and symbolic title: "As Time Goes By."

Johnnie's back-to-back engagements featured one distinct advantage: a stage was the only place he felt secure. Once he hit the nightclub floor even his enemies became quiescent. Each night was a triumph. He flew back and forth across the country on an endless tour. Philadelphia's Latin Casino, Chicago's Chez Paree, the Town Casino in Buffalo, over and over. He made his hotel debut at St. Louis' posh Chase Club.

"Too much has been written already in an attempt to analyze his amazing exhibitionistic style of singing," a review of the Chase opener said. "Suffice to say that he held a pack jammed room in the palm of his hand from the moment he entered until he begged off. Some came to jeer and scoff, they went away impressed." The Ray rip-tide of musical blood, guts and thunder swept up everyone within earshot.[1]

Johnnie wept into New Orleans' Roosevelt Hotel; while in the Crescent City, he enjoyed the twenty-four-hour-a-day hedonism of the French Quarter. So much so, that it wound up costing him $1,000. At the Cafe Slipper, his presence created such an immediate sensation among the patrons that he felt obliged to leap onstage and knock off a powerhouse twenty-minute set. When AGVA learned of it, they hauled Bernie onto the carpet. Nobody gets away with free, un-contracted performances— particularly those occurring in one of New Orleans' humid gay *boites*. Somehow word of this "cuffo" spot reached their offices.

Bernie went to bat for his boy, telling AGVA that "upon entering Cafe Slipper, Ray noticed a riot in progress. Being a public spirited citizen, he sized up the situation, got on the floor and calmed the crowd by singing." Nice try, but AGVA nonetheless handed down a thousand dollar fine. ("It was not explained," Variety noted, "whether Johnnie Ray's entrance caused the riot.")[2]

Johnnie closed out the year at New York's La Vie En Rose. The room was operated by original Copacabana owner Monte Proser, his reward for letting Frank Costello muscle Proser out. Intimate and prestigious, Johnnie got a mere $7,000 a week there. Despite the Spring's unfavorable developments, Billboard assured the trade that "Johnnie Ray is still a topside attraction."

"His singing may be bewildering to purists, but there's nothing wrong with his salesmanship . . . his belt them in the belly method is as commercial today as when he first hit . . . there's no sleeping while Ray is on . . . he had everybody in the jammed room splitting their mitts. Sure he's flirting with a sock in the nose when he dashed around kissing femme ringsiders but so far nobody has objected and the gals don't find it objectionable . . . it adds up to a great performance."[3]

The final nail in his marriage's coffin now had to be driven home. After a full year of behind the scenes negotiation and wrangling over money, it was time for the public formalities. On January 12, 1954 Charlie Morrison announced that his twenty-three-year-old daughter was flying to El Paso as Marilyn Ray but would return to Hollywood as

Marilyn Morrison. She would file for divorce in Chihuahua, Mexico, Charlie said. Under Mexican law, Johnnie had to be present. He appeared on the Perry Como show in New York that night, then caught the next flight out. She and Johnnie met in the border city and traveled separately into Mexico, but not to Chihuahua. Juarez was the actual site, kept off the record to avoid a mob of El Paso bobby soxers.

This tears-and-tequila-drenched reunion was notable only for its brevity. It was the long overdue climax of much conference between Halsey Cowan and Marilyn's attorney, Harry Wechsler, both of whom toiled to avert the "threats of bitter recrimination and very sensational divorce case" Louella Parsons hinted at and which the newspaper boys had been counting on since the previous year. Johnnie was on hand for a final conference with local attorney Amador Y. Trias, which delayed the actual filing another day.[4]

The next morning when Marilyn's petition, on the grounds of incompatibility of character (the most accurate public accounting of their romance to date), was entered into the record, Johnnie wept. While the proceedings were mere formality, the emotion of the day hit both Johnnie and Marilyn. Photographs captured two distraught, pathetic figures, sagging and rheumy eyed. A United Press reporter cornered Johnnie, who said: "I'm sorry the marriage turned out the way it did. Love is as holy as religion to me. Someday I plan to marry again. Every man wants a home and children." Pure jive.[5]

This statement was little more than a running inside joke; Johnnie, after a good cry outside the court room, had clearly returned to his usual sly self. His religious conviction was ambivalent at best. The total extent and zenith of his faith was "I'm Going to Walk and Talk with My Lord," the show-stopping Jubilee number he closed every performance with. Singing gospel in a booze house was another radical first he introduced to pop music. "'Walk and Talk with My Lord,' was a fantastic number on a nightclub floor," Mitch Miller said. "The audience would go bananas."

Driving an audience bananas was Johnnie's true religion.

He enjoyed hornswoggling the public with theological flim flam. During his first Copa engagement, Johnnie, with Elma and her husband sitting by, told Hy Gardner, "My formula, if I have such a thing, consists of Billie Holiday for passion, Perry Como for peace, and Elma for God." Brother and sister must have strained to keep from laughing. Both detested church and the old-time religion Hazel had aggressively foisted off on them as children.[6]

Once the divorce was sealed and filed away, Johnnie flew to Oregon to belatedly celebrate his twenty-sixth birthday with Hazel and Elmer. It turned into an impromptu family reunion and public relations trip. He was followed constantly by a photo crew from the Portland Sunday News, who photographed him being awakened bright and early by Elmer, feeding the chickens, at the piano singing with Elma and Hazel, passing out popcorn to the nieces and nephews, enjoying a hamburger at a Dallas lunch counter. Wholly wholesome stuff, just the way Bernie wanted it. It was, as ever, a short visit.[7]

In early February, he was back in Columbia's New York studio on East 30th street, a converted church whose high, vaulted ceilings provided superb acoustics and quite a working atmosphere. Miller agreed to let him cut a "pure John" record, covering R&B hit "Such a Night," a raunchy, balling 'til the early bright song written by Lincoln Chase, whose "Jim Dandy" was a smash for LaVern Baker. "Such a Night" was launched by the Drifters as a tongue-in-cheek novelty, and while Johnnie always claimed to have consciously given it that type of reading, the results were a sock, dirty R&B disk. His education in the black and tans was right up front.

"Just the thought of your love sets me afire," he shouted. "I think of you . . . and I feel desire." His animal panting and primal groaning were a study in rhythmic arousal. Propulsive saxophone lines, pounding backbeat and Johnnie's hot, breathy vocal resulted in his truest R&B effort since "Whisky & Gin" (and the blackest-sounding record Mitch Miller ever had a hand in). Unfortunately, Johnnie's inflammatory approach came to the F.C.C.'s attention. The result was an airwave ban on both his and the Drifters' original within several weeks of the single's release.

In live performance, "Such a Night" was wild—a riot of pelvis thrusting, microphone stand acrobatics and plenty of his most startling stage moves, torso-tossing. Johnnie curved his spine, threw head and shoulders back and let gravity take over. As he let fly with a tom cat yowl, one long leg bent back and hooked a foot up under the piano, scuffled, kicked and wrapped around its wooden leg. He rocked, clawed and twitched, suddenly threw himself down to the floor, arms and legs flailing, groaning into the mike, then leapt to his feet and gave the piano lid a hinge-loosening slam.

Screaming came naturally to his audience. No other reaction would make sense. The dizzying swiftness with which he executed this deft series of radical poses always came across as utter spontaneous abandon. It never seemed like staged routine—although Johnnie was a monster choreographer, this mugging venery and unpredictable physicality were completely sincere and natural reactions. They were also more extreme, out-and-out dirty and threatening than any rock and roller who succeeded him.

*   *   *

From New York, Johnnie returned to Texas for several night club engagements, starting at Houston's Clover Club. The city was at its extravagant height as an oil-money-glutted playground for hardscrabble rednecks made wealthy. A typical Houstonian practical joke was arranging for a full-scale roller coaster to be erected on the grounds of a mansion whose owner had left town for the weekend. The Texans and their spouses thrilled to Johnnie's feral performances. Johnnie was just as impressed by their vulgar opulence.

"I remember down in Texas, some rich rancher said 'C'mon out to the house and we'll have some drinks,'" a friend of Johnnie's recalled. "And we get into this big typical Texas limousine with the steer horns, tooled leather seats, the whole bit and Johnnie says 'Wow! It must be nice to be able to afford one of these.' And I'm thinkin' 'Jesus, John, you could afford to buy a half dozen of these—he doesn't even know he's into money!'"[8]

Called back to the East 30th Street studio in late March, Miller was calling the shots, and insisted on a far safer brand of material—songs from Broadway's "Pajama Game." The Beard's shoehorning these onto the Cry Guy's recording schedule proved that, as Johnnie so often said, "Mitch Miller had no idea of how to record me." The doe-eyed syrup of "Hey There" suited his weeping style, but the lamentable tango novelty "Hernando's Hideaway" was strictly cringe material. The record oozed harmless respectability and mild intent, but did not hit the retail counters with any noticeable impact, unlike Rosey Clooney's "Hey There," whose chart-topping success Miller attributes to a special recitation he had written for Clooney. It was Johnnie's first serious artistic and (in comparison to Clooney's sales) commercial misfire.

With one great record that was promptly banned and another mediocre one which stiffed, Miller and Ray were no longer enjoying the eye-to-eye creative dialogue they had throughout 1952. Johnnie did not have time to dwell on it. But his version of "Hey There" led Clooney's on the British pop charts, a land where he apparently could do no wrong. In April, Johnnie returned to the Palladium where he was set to record, onstage, a long-player for UK release, one of the earliest "live" albums made.

When Johnnie's plane landed in England, he shook off the perpetu-ally encroaching flight time hangover and peered out the window. What he saw made him snap his hearing aid back on immediately. Britain was eager-ly awaiting his return—there were thousands of fans on the field. Cry-ker-chiefs waved and hand-painted banners fluttered in the propeller's draft.

As he appeared, the mob's collective throat wailed. Of all the fan gauntlets Johnnie routinely ran, the English were his favorite. While the Fleet Street press launched its fair share of missiles at the Little White Cloud ("In approaching a high note," J.B. Boothroyd wrote of his Palladium debut, "he is the school boy cricketer praying to hold a vital catch."), but few took the vicious tone of American pundits. The British fan's unconditional love set Johnnie's bones tingling.[9]

His cult there continued to gain force; when he returned the fol-lowing Spring, the crowds were even larger. At the Palladium, their "ecsta-tic squeals and hysterical fervor" reached fever pitch. Fans smashed the stage door barrier and dozens of additional police were called in.[10] At Edinburgh, over a thousand followed him from the airport to the Caley Hotel. Stepping from the limousine, "he only got about two feet as hands grabbed at hearing aid, hair, coat, jacket, tie, and collar." Transferred back into another car, Johnnie, nearly unconscious, was finally smuggled in by a side entrance. Half an hour later, he appeared on a balcony and sang "Cry" to the throng.[11]

This British adoration was captured on tape at the Palladium. Johnnie's live album, released as a ten-inch long-player in Britain, is the best available representation of his audiences' screaming response. The Palladium's polished-sounding compere got as far as "The famous

American singing star . . . " before being drowned by a torrent of swoony shrilling.

Johnnie was using new material for the first time since his original Cry staging and book of 1952. New only in the sense of being additions; he opened with "Please Don't Talk About Me When I'm Gone," a standard he favored in his lounge days and which, after *Confidential's* assault, became an almost mandatory number. He gave it an amped-up reading, a hep-wise come-on: "You're gonna miss-a your swingin' daddy from now on . . .". His thunderous "Glad Rag Doll" was followed by a beautiful ballad reading of "100 Years From Today." When he purred "Don't save your kisses, pass them around," the crowd moaned.

The material was shrewdly chosen. Perfect for Johnnie's style, the songs were non-threatening, yet imbued with a fresh interpretive coloration and emotion no one else could have brought the songs. Even familiar standards became far more visceral and raw than the music of Bill Haley & the Comets, his leading American competitor there. Haley's fabled 1955 reception and numbingly repetitious "rock rock" routine, pales in comparison to the lasting impact Johnnie Ray made.

There was one significant problem with the Live at the Palladium album—save for the requisite "Little White Cloud," he sang none of his own compositions. In fact, Johnnie had ceased writing altogether. Of the 154 Johnnie Ray compositions in his Carlyle song catalog, less than a dozen were ever recorded, and most of those began to disappear from his stage show by the mid-50s. While "Little White Cloud," and "Whisky & Gin" stayed in the book, titles like "Mountains in the Moonlight" and "Paths of Paradise," essential Ray numbers, slipped into limbo.

Considering the inference nightly performances of "A Sinner Am I" would inevitably yield it is no surprise these were being expunged. But his quitting song writing was symptomatic of a grave shift in Johnnie's creative self and his response to the career. It was a concession, the result of his self-deprecating and defensive "I'm an Entertainer not a Singer" armor, a stance brought on by the press and American public's turning tide. Johnnie alone was responsible for this slow withdrawal. As controversy rose, it was increasingly hazardous to articulate the messages his subconscious mind fed him; he began turning back, more and more, to the standards.

Johnnie's non-stop booking schedule was not exactly conducive to inspiration and composing. "I've been criticized for booking Johnnie, forty, fifty weeks out of the year but that is what he wanted to do. He wasn't one to go on vacations," Bernie Lang said. "And he didn't do something else that he should have done, which was write songs. All of a sudden he just stopped. Stopped cold. We all kept after him to write, Mitch wanted him to write, I wanted him to write, the arranger for the act wanted him to write, everyone kept after him.

"It was the lifestyle. Johnnie was up all night, almost every night. He didn't sleep in a bed unless he had to be up for an interview or something like that," said Lang. "And it was the times too. Johnnie was not conventional, on stage, or off stage either. He was a very strange person, or it seemed that way. Very unconventional for the time. And he tended to get into trouble, like the way that he would never drive when he was sober."

Johnnie's artistic response to the mounting pressure of his ongoing public dissection was to wilt. Having to play the wholesome public heterosexual, with all that gee-whiz piety, was fiercely debilitating. His personal response was to rage and rave, liquor-anesthetized, into the dawn with whoever was around and thirsty enough to keep up. If they tired, he fed them speed. If they bored him, he mixed such stiff drinks they would pass out cold. Only behind closed doors and after hours could Johnnie let his hair down and ball. It became a calling as full time and demanding as his stage work and he established a party crew in every major city where he appeared. This secret Ray, whose emotion and expression were necessarily subjugated, could not help but contribute to the atrophy and fragmentation of the artist Ray.

It all began to unravel simply because there was so little time to consciously address his situation, role and potential with any clear-headed logic. Johnnie lurched through engagements on his infallible performing instinct, refining his interpretations and unfailingly "whamming" the crowd. But the fan's constant jostle, the rigor of his itinerary, the vast amount of energy and concentration he burned on stage and the frantic release his partners-in-frolic brought in the dead of night, all became routine. The pattern was inescapable, a cut and dried rigmarole whose confines defied any hope for Johnnie to continue exploring the personal, idiosyncratic expression which was the backbone of his original material.

Everything he came up with was volatile. "A Sinner Am I," his best stab at Tin Pan Alley convention, was nonetheless, both proclamation and endorsement of his purest sense of self and sexuality. That was his entire artistic drift and basis—the articulation of soul-deep personal truth. Gritty, mesmerizing, often cathartic, it was far too strong for its day. It was impossible to put over. Johnnie saw that continuing as such was a damned total impossibility. He fought to keep the damnation from poisoning his soul, but did so in all the wrong ways.

There were more pressing concerns and dangers which had to be faced every day. The fan's adoration was exhilarating, but they were dangerous and prone to flare into unchecked mob hysteria. He had to concentrate on fighting his way out of the theater, assuming the barricades would hold, expecting both crowd and police to maintain emotional equilibrium.

Career demands negated debate; let Mitch and Bernie nag him to write new, tamer songs—who the hell had time for it? After the skirling, metal-on-metal spin of the Ray tilt-a-whirl had torn up the British Isles, it was back to Hollywood. Twentieth Century Fox Studio beckoned with full circle realization of his primary goal since childhood. "I had a seven-year contract with 20th Century Fox—my big dream as a kid!" he said.[12] Johnnie was going to become a movie star, "just like Clark Gable and Tarzan" at long last.

*   *   *

He was dying to get on the set. Determined not to screw this up, Johnnie had studied the script intensely, poring over it hour after exhaustive hour, and was beside himself at the notion of being projected up on the big screen. He had worked so constantly since "Cry" hit that he never even saw the film short lensed at Eddie Condon's. Now he could settle in and wallow in a sweet, celluloid fantasy life.

A wallow is precisely what "There's No Business Like Show Business" was. Its born-in-a-trunk vaudeville clan plot, familiar Irving Berlin songs and stalwart musical star players added up to an overwhelming sense of "this is where we came in" deja vu, but on an unusually grandiose scale. Johnnie received $100,000 for the job.[13] The cast, Ethel Merman, Dan Dailey, Mitzi Gaynor, Donald O'Connor, Johnnie and

Marilyn Monroe provided an interesting elemental mix—five million dollars worth to producer Sol C. Siegal's way of thinking. The unprecedented budget ensured a ton of glamorous ham.

Originally slated for shooting in the summer of 1953, director Walter Lang's illness halted the production. Merman loved Lang and insisted he was irreplaceable. Zanuck and Siegal had pitched numerous alternates. Every suggestion got the same response from Merman: "I'll wait for Walter."[14] The delay, meantime, led Zanuck to opt for debuting Johnnie as a supporting player rather than expect him to carry a starring vehicle. "There's No Business Like Show Business" was finally set to roll during the first week of June 1954.

The principals were called to Sol Siegal's office for a pre-production pow-wow. Johnnie, excited, scrubbed, buffed, perfumed and sober, arrived promptly. Merman was already there. Marilyn Monroe never showed up. As the minutes ticked off, Merman regaled the cast with vulgar jokes. "Did you hear the one about the two maids sitting on a porch?" she asked Mitzi Gaynor. "One of them said 'Do you remember the minuet?' The other one said, 'Hell, I don't even remember the men I've fucked!'"[15]

None involved knew what to expect from Johnnie. He was told he could wear his hearing aid during rehearsal, but they would, of course, be shooting without it. On the first day of rehearsal, he amazed both Lang and Siegal by revealing that he had memorized not only his own dialogue, but also that of his co-stars. "I can read lips, to a certain point," Johnnie explained, "and I thought the best way I could remember where my lines came in was to learn the others' lines."[16]

He idolized Merman, who grew quite fond of him. Johnnie's running joke was that with her powerhouse speaking voice he did not need a hearing aid at all. "Ethel was very helpful to him on the picture. I remember him telling a story about his very first close-up ever, and of course, Johnnie was extremely nervous because it was cinemascopic technicolor," Bill Franklin said. "Ethel played his mother, and he was supposed to hug her for the shot. So, he hugged her as you would a mother, and she said, 'No, darling, I want you to put your head on the other shoulder, so we can get a close-up of your beautiful face.'" At the day's end, he floated out of the studio.

Johnnie was friendlier with Monroe than anyone else in the cast. He first met her during his Ciro's engagement. "She had problems getting a date," Johnnie said. "Because, for most men, the fear of being rejected by Marilyn Monroe was just too much for the male ego. So they didn't ask. After the columnist Sidney Skolsky introduced us, I took her to a lot of openings and things."17

The pair enjoyed a mutual sense of private alienation; each represented an unbridled sexuality. Johnnie had rare appeal. As he said, "Women see reflected in me all of the emotion and tenderness that, unfortunately, the American male doesn't have time for today."18

This quality endeared him to Monroe, six months into her marriage with Joe DiMaggio, and increasingly disturbed by Joe's insistence they sleep in separate beds. DiMaggio was jolting balls all summer long, and Marilyn rarely strayed from the side of her eccentric mentor and drama coach Natasha Lytess. Theirs was a strange, intense relationship, off and on the set. At a rehearsal, Johnnie overheard Lytess whispering "In this scene you are a bubble, and you will float."19

When Monroe failed to show up for a promotional photo session, the stars were posed with a gap between them so her image could be matted in later. "The group shot was to be used in ads," Johnnie said. "All the stars had equal billing but Ethel's contract provided that her name come first. One morning the Hollywood Reporter ran the photo in a double-truck ad that listed 'Marilyn Monroe, Dan Dailey, Ethel Merman,' etc."

The Cry Guy's childhood thirst for mischief was unslaked. "I showed the ad to Ethel and said 'What do you think of that?' She read it but didn't say a word. I could tell she was angry. Her eyes became steely and her fists clenched. I don't know what she said to the studio manager but the billing error was never repeated."20 Johnnie acted out of deference to Merman, but he and Cy got a laugh out of it.

One of the job's most enjoyable aspects was that it allowed him to rent a home. The knowledge that he would be returning to it on a nightly basis for the next three months was welcome. Johnnie actually unpacked.

"We rented a house up on Tigertail, in Brentwood," Cy Kertman said. "It wasn't a really big place, three bedrooms, it had a pool and a view. It wasn't opulent, it was just somewhere for him to stay while doing the picture. And everybody came out at one time or another. I remember Dan Dailey brought Julie London up one night, there were always people around on Tigertail." As Jack Devaney, still based in Los Angeles'

Columbia office (and who became one of Johnnie's closest friends over these months) said, "We partied on Tigertail that entire summer, had a great time every single night."

But Johnnie never dragged onto the set complaining of a hangover. His dedication was fierce. The rudimentary ability to lip read served him well on the set, and shooting went smoothly. "Johnnie is a sensitive actor," Walter Lang said. "He's making his debut in fast company, but all of us were surprised at his innate grasp and understanding of his characterization. He'll do well in pictures—wait and see."[21] Johnnie relished everything about the project. Over lunch in the commissary he would play out entire scenes for journalists, taking his, Merman and Dailey's roles. Johnnie often moved himself to tears.

"I actually couldn't call it work," he said. "I was playing around the studio with these people. They were fun, particularly Ethel and Marilyn. I had already met Ethel in New York, and Marilyn was such a darling girl, so it was like going to a picnic."[22]

He remained dazzled by all of them. "It's not that I didn't have self-esteem, I just didn't know what in the world I had in common with these people. Ginger Rogers was making a picture on the next soundstage— Ginger Rogers!" he fizzed. "When Fred Astaire came on the set and said 'We should make a picture together,' I tripped over some cables. I just did not think this could happen to me. I thought 'what in the world would I ever do in a picture with Fred Astaire?'"[23]

As a hot jewel in Hollywood's crown, Johnnie drew all the players up to Tigertail at one time or another. Even following his spectacular introduction to the movie star set at the Marion Davies reception, he was still a wide-eyed farm boy. "I was thrilled meeting these people," Johnnie said. "Dan Dailey, Mitzi Gaynor, Donald O'Connor—and these were just the people I was working with! Marlon Brando was up at my house eating turkey, Merle Oberon was there, asking for an autographed picture. The last thing in the world I could even remotely imagine was Merle Oberon playing Johnnie Ray records."[24]

Another frequent visitor at Tigertail was Marilyn Morrison, whom Johnnie had not seen since Juarez. Charlie's manipulation and sabotage had only intensified Marilyn's passion for Johnnie, and they both got a kick out of spending evenings at Mocambo. They dropped in on Charlie twice, June 10 and June 28. When reporters demanded to know what was going on, Marilyn unhesitatingly "hinted that they'll try it again."[25] Pictures of them together ran in all the Los Angeles papers. It was good for his public image, but her ardor, in the wake of the vicious campaign Charlie waged against Johnnie, was unsettling.

In July, Johnnie with a break in his shooting schedule hightailed it to Las Vegas. Noel Coward was in the middle of his engagement at the Desert Inn. Yul Brynner had introduced them at the Copa, and Johnnie was eager to renew their friendship. At the D.I., Johnnie also re-united with more than a few familiar faces from his roadhouse days in Ohio. Only their faces were the same—they changed names almost as often as they did their underwear (it was a ball, except for one painful afternoon when Johnnie, padding barefoot around the Sands pool, stepped on a discarded martini toothpick).[26]

After wrapping up the picture in Hollywood, Darryl Zanuck announced, through Fox studio flack Wolfson, that "he was so impressed with Johnnie's performance" that the producer had picked up his option. The picture, "Pink Tights," would again pay $100,000.[27]

Johnnie returned to sweltering mid-August Manhattan and Mitch Miller, who was actively seeking to re-mold Johnnie's sound on record. On the 26th, they recorded several of the Irving Berlin numbers featured in "No Business," including a ludicrously overblown "Alexander's Ragtime Band." Johnnie, with the tinsel and celluloid charm still upon him, was happy to oblige. His black and tan frantic vocal bested a brass-heavy arrangement, and the record was a hit. Recording Johnnie was an experience.

"I always looked forward to working with Johnnie, because I knew it would be something different. He was something else," Columbia engineer Frank Laico said. "He did it as if he were in front of an audience. Johnnie was all emotion, all action. Those eyes were closed, the body was going—a lot of other pop singers were almost bland. They just didn't have that kind of inner energy that Johnnie kept exhibiting. And he made everyone play better than they thought they could, I think, because watching him, you kind of had to get carried away, too."[28]

On the 28th, though, he and Miller clashed for the first time. The bone of contention was "Thine Eyes Are as the Eyes of A Dove," a sickly sweet, faux-sacred ballad which Johnnie abhorred. "Mitch always picked songs for me, and I never questioned his choice of material. That was as close to ever having a fight as Mitch and I ever came. We locked horns over it in the studio, but I did what he told me," Johnnie said.[29]

Push come to shove, he trusted the Beard. "Everybody thinks I was this tyrant, but there are many ways to skin a cat," Miller said. "You can't pull someone into the studio and say 'sing this.' Psychologically, even if they sing it well, their heart is not in it, and you can't do that—you have to have one hundred percent cooperation."

Johnnie gave him that, but always gleefully pointed out, "I was right—the record did nothing. Even my mother didn't save a copy of that one."[30] The obnoxious flipside, "Papa Loves Mambo," was almost as bad. At least his model friends got a boot when Johnnie sang "Look at them sway with it . . . Gettin' real gay with it . . ."

*   *   *

In late September, back in Hollywood for movie promo chores, Johnnie could feel, as Bill Franklin put it, "the percentages changing." Despite the fact that he constantly wore a silver ID bracelet (inscribed W.L.F.Y.L.M., for "with love from your little man") which was a gift from Stan Halpert, Johnnie found he was hot for Marilyn Morrison all over again.[31] After they wound up in bed together, the relationship came to the fore again. "Man, she's the slickest chick I ever met. We goofed on the marriage," he told Sidney Skolsky. "We were too young, too unprepared, and there's too much career."[32]

When she returned to New York with Johnnie on the 22nd, Louella Parsons ran with it. "Johnnie's been wooing her for several months," she reported. "Her mother was in on the secret and helped Marilyn pack for what looks like an elopement. Marilyn telephoned Charlie Morrison from the Warwick Hotel and told him, 'Johnnie and I love each other and are trying to make a go of it.'" There was no public comment from Charlie, but Zanuck and Siegal breathed a sigh of relief.[33]

This was no elopement. It was simply a party. Marilyn was, unfortunately, trapped in a Hollywood flack scheme. The fact that Johnnie's unbridled emotion and desire currently favored her made it all the more difficult to break off when Johnnie left for his Australian debut. The subject of renewed romance was dropped as suddenly as it had come up.

When he appeared at Ciro's in November, Johnnie, cornered drinking beer in the Garden of Allah bar, was asked about Marilyn. "I may marry next month, or next year. It gets pretty lonely at the top," he said. "But Sophie Tucker gave some advice about that. Wonderful Soph. She said, 'There's two things in life you shouldn't be in a hurry about—marriage and death.'"[34]

Undaunted, the former Mrs. Ray never gave up hopes of a reconciliation. "Marilyn was just desperately in love with him," Bill Franklin said. "She really was, and probably still is. It was sad, because to Johnnie, the marriage had been strictly a convenience, but she wanted to go back to that. I heard a lot of things about how Charlie Morrison was aware of Johnnie's bisexuality and had tried various ways to break up their marriage.

"In later years, Johnnie spent a lot of time dodging her," Franklin recalled. "She would just drive him crazy. Marilyn surfaced in my life several times when I was managing Johnnie, wanting to get in touch with him. He asked me to lie for him, which I did, so that she couldn't find out where he was, or get the phone number. And she really begged me to help bring them together."

When "There's No Business Like Show Business" had its gala premiere on December 8, Marilyn accompanied Johnnie. He was on crutches—the toothpick he stepped on in Vegas deposited a minuscule splinter that had not been removed. Festering there for the last five months, a painful infection developed, but nothing could have kept him away. There he was—a real trouper.[35]

Johnnie's role in "Show Business" placed him hip deep in corn. His character ended up joining both the Army and the priesthood (driving Catholic-hating snob Hazel Ray positively mad with indignity). This institutionalizing made his character an unquestionable Real Man, albeit one sworn to celibacy. Such heavy-handed image-gilding did not help Johnnie's acceptance or the picture's success. Just as the Davies reception evoked an era of by-gone Hollywood ritual, "Show Business" was a relic, the gaudy death rattle of a flag waving, tear-jerking vaudeville hokum tradition.

Reviews of the picture were not particularly kind to Johnnie. Variety's did not even mention him; Time magazine said "Johnnie Ray, playing a priest as a singer, singlehandedly set back the cause of Catholicism fifty years."[36] Hollywood's natural reaction to Johnnie Ray was immersion in a familiar, highly structured framework, the while praying to God that he would not tear it down.

Fox, in the wake of *Confidential*, was less inclined to invest in a volatile animal like Johnnie Ray. Dan Dailey was a big enough headache; *Confidential* did a job on him in March 1954 ("Why Dan Dailey is Too Hot for the Gossip Columnists"). After their follow-up, "The Night Dan Dailey Became Dolly Dawn," he was washed up at age 42, appearing in only three more films. (This common ground led to a sincere friendship between Johnnie and Dailey, and they remained close until Dailey's death.)[37]

Shortly after the premiere, Zanuck abruptly resigned from Fox to develop his own independent production company. "Although I was his fair-haired boy," Johnnie said, "he had no plans to take me with him."[38] The new regime at the studio had little interest in Johnnie, and made it clear they would not follow up on the option Zanuck exercised for "Pink Tights".

It was one of Johnnie's most bitter regrets. Later in life, Johnnie regaled interviewers with an unvarying prepared speech on the boredom of film work versus the thrill of live appearances, the Big Drag of waiting for shot setups, waiting to screen dailies and the frustration he experienced over not being able to choose or re-do a particular take. The drag that really caused him problems at Fox was the one Zanuck feared Johnnie would turn up wearing. He was nitroglycerine, not gold, at the box office. One wrong move by Johnnie and no one would be left to mop up the smithereens.

It was a season of disappointment. On December 17, Johnnie checked into Cedars of Lebanon and underwent surgery to remove the infectious toothpick particle. Marilyn spent the night with him there. Queried by the press about their plans, Marilyn hesitated. "We're just good friends," she said.[39]

"*Just let* me get my hands on enough velvet and chromium," Latin Quarter operator Lou Walters once said, "and I will build nightclubs like the world has never seen before, luxury like the Roman emperors never dreamed of. And I will give all this, and an eight-course steak dinner, too, for a reasonable price."[1]

Walters did exactly that. Having perfected the formula with two other Latin Quarters, first in Boston and then Miami, the New York facility began wowing Gotham in 1942 with the lure of Parisian-styled entertainment and dozens of the most sizzling vixens in the East.

Johnnie's twenty-eighth birthday was marked there during his debut engagement in January 1955. Despite New York City's annual migration to Miami, his run was another SRO frenzy. Only the Lachrymal Lochinvar could get 'em out in such numbers during the dead of winter. His defiant abandon still fractured the Cafe set; with three years of stardom behind him, it became apparent to the trade that despite volleys of poisonous controversy, Johnnie Ray "had legs." With rock & roll simmering on pop music's outskirts, Johnnie represented both an unsettling harbinger and familiar reference point.

Mitch Miller knew it. On the 23rd, Johnnie recorded blues shouter Joe Turner's "Flip, Flop & Fly." A timely notion (Bill Haley's sanitized 1954 cover of Turner's "Shake, Rattle & Roll" had sold several hundred thousand copies), Miller's prescience was fine in theory but withered in practice under a phalanx of screaming brass. An obnoxiously square record, it sounded as if they took the charts from Johnnie's "Alexander's Ragtime Band" and turned them upside down. While a noble gesture of renewal for Johnnie's black and tan affections, it came off more as an affectation. This, surely, would not raise hackles at the F.C.C. Neither would it raise temperatures at record hops.

Johnnie had precious little time to worry about the unstable tenor of pop music or public rating of his hip quotient. Bernie's bookings for 1955 would take him even farther around the world than Johnnie's most extravagant childhood fantasy visions. He returned to Australia in March. Just as in his debut there the previous September, he played stadiums and arenas seating 10-20,000, despite the fact that his first visit was a skin-of-the-teeth, near-disaster affair.

His Australian tours were put together by Lee Gordon, an eccentric 34-year-old American impresario, who also booked Sinatra and, later, Elvis Presley. Gordon had arrived in Sydney two years before. "All I knew about Lee was that he was a bit of a whiz kid in electronic retail sales," said Alan Heffernan, a partner in Gordon's Big Show production company.

"His organization in America would ring housewives all over the country and invite them to take part in a simple competition with a money prize. Of course, no one ever lost, even if it meant giving lots of clues. But the $20 checks they won could only be used at Lee's stores for the purchase of gramophones or washing machines, or something like that. He had a number of schemes, but that one in particular moved the American Senate to change the law."[2]

Expatriated by choice to Sydney after legislation dried up his mainstay scam, Gordon's first venture in music promotion was an all-star jazz revue featuring Artie Shaw and Ella Fitzgerald. When Gordon broke even on the tour, his Big Show Company was born. On the heels of this prestige event (the first time such a package of American musicians was featured in Australia), GAC gave him the go-ahead to bring Johnnie down. Both Gordon and Heffernan knew it was a gamble; even with a considerable reputation preceding him, neither promoter anticipated such a shaky start. In fact, the way things had initially shaped up it seemed like Johnnie's 1954 visit would be his last.

The day before Johnnie arrived for his Sydney debut (leaving behind Marilyn, and her hopes for a reconciliation, at the Warwick) Heffernan was horrified to learn that advance sales came to less than one hundred pounds worth of tickets. "I went and saw Lee," Heffernan said, "who was at his apartment, lying on a leopard skin rug wearing a pair of skimpy black undies, and said 'This is no good. We've got to get out of here. You go to Africa and I'll go to South America.'

"Well, Lee wasn't perturbed at all. He said to get the printer on the phone. He ordered three million leaflets offering a two-for-one ticket promotion and had them dropped from airplanes over Sydney, Brisbane and Melbourne. There was a hell of a row and headlines in the newspapers, and the city council was furious." Even with this radical stroke of cheapskate appeal, ticket sales remained slack. Johnnie was delighted by the tumult and Gordon's casual, unorthodox style. Here was a mix of both Mr. Emotion and Mr. Commotion, and both Bernie and Johnnie dug him.

Johnnie knew they would pull it off. Despite empty seats at the Sydney opener, "Johnnie was sensational—one of the best I've ever seen at the stadium," Heffernan said. "It was built for boxing fights and in a sense, those early audiences wanted blood. Johnnie gave and gave and they loved him. At the end of each number he would collapse, and we would rush out and give him what everyone thought was a sip of water, but was really vodka."

The next day, scalpers were getting as much as fifty pounds for a single ticket. Although Gordon nearly lost his shirt with the "two-fers" still circulating, Johnnie's 1954 Australian bow was a sensation. There was no question that he should return as soon as possible; Australia became a regular addition to his itinerary. Fans there more than compensated for their slow start the first time around.

Johnnie returned to Sydney for his second Australian tour on March 6, 1955. There were 10,000 fans waiting for him. For an hour and a half, the airport was a battle zone. Inside the terminal they stripped off his jacket and left his shirt in tatters. "The adulation was great fun, but I was always worried about people getting hurt," Johnnie said. "The other problem was if my hearing aid was knocked it felt like red hot needles going through my head."[3] Police finally managed to wedge him behind a ticket counter, but waves of fans clamored and howled for the Cry Guy.[4]

The insanity of this reception set the tone for his visit. The days and nights were lived to the tune of a constant siren harmony, the swoon and bellow of a nation who, having recently accepted civilization as an unavoidable (it was only 87 years since the last convict transport ship landed), found themselves plunged giddily back into a state of primal instinct and spontaneity. Johnnie's impact resonated even more profoundly than in Britain; naturally, he developed an affection for the place as intense as the Australian fans proved to hold for him.

There was no lack of Johnnie Ray; in the twenty days he was there, he gave forty-two performances. The Australian tax men, having missed their taste of Johnnie's money from his September 1954 visit, took great interest in all this, and Johnnie was forced to cough up $19,750.00 before they would allow him to leave the country. When Lee Gordon was questioned about Johnnie's earnings, he refused to answer, saying only that Frank Sinatra had paid out $12,000 in taxes on a January 1955 gross of $25,000—almost fifty percent (it follows that Johnnie got $10,000 per show).[5]

The tax net which snagged Johnnie before he could depart Australia was nothing compared to the send-off he received from its citizens. By the time eight policeman formed a flying wedge around Johnnie, a crowd of 500 semi-hysterical hard core fans had shredded his clothing and composure. The wire photo from that day's riot at Sydney airport was the first since his Detroit mug shot where stark fear was evident upon Johnnie's face. The riots were becoming less and less of a kick. Once on board the aircraft, Johnnie, who was flying to Britain, told the press corps, "I belong here, and will be back as soon as I can." He also cryptically added, "I'm going to retire from stage life much sooner than anyone expects."[6]

This was not the first time he told reporters he was thinking of giving it all up. Earlier in the year, he told a Los Angeles reporter, "I'm sick of singing in cafes. It bugs me. You know something? Around New Year's I got so disgusted, I was ready to retire." The interviewer asked why. "Have you," he quietly replied, "ever faced an audience at 2:15 on New Year's morning in a Statler Hotel?"[7]

Dorothy Kilgallen ran a frosty item from the same visit: "Johnnie Ray must be one of the most confused fellows in all Hollywood. During a recent singing engagement there, he spent most of his time in his bungalow at the Garden of Allah crying his eyes out and being just downright miserable. Wouldn't see pals or take phone calls from anyone. He finally admitted he hated nightclub work and wanted only to sing at teenage benefits because it gave him a chance to be with kids his own age. Teenagers, his own age?"[8]

Johnnie may have blamed his career, but he was growing up and hating it. He apparently bellyached the entire time he was in town; he told another reporter, "I was sitting in the Coconut Grove recently. I looked around and said to myself 'Well, you've got it all, but what have you got? Here you are, still sitting alone in a nightclub on a Sunday afternoon.'"[9]

*   *   *

Johnnie could not afford the luxury of self-indulgence and so flew into Glasgow, with his first date set for April 5. There was no peace for him, it seemed, in any of the world's four corners. At the sold-out opening, police had to be called to "disperse teenster mobs at the stage door."[10] If the Australian fans seemed vulgar and earthy, they were nothing compared to the hordes of ga-ga Glaswegians.

When he opened at the Palladium on April 25, London's adoration of the Prince of Wails was more lusty than ever. Johnnie's performance was "extremely exciting . . . evoking ecstatic squeals and hysterical fervor" from the crowd. Outside, "youngsters smashed the stage door barriers and police were called to control the crowds."[11]

Strange, high times. Among those in the audience were Noel Coward and American starlet Terry Moore, best known as the love interest in Willis O'Brien's 1949 King Kong homage "Mighty Joe Young." That night, she was cast to romance Johnnie, whose headline-making split and subsequent non-elopement with Marilyn cried out for public image re-enforcement in the UK.

Johnnie dined with Terry Moore after the bobbies cleared his way. Noel Coward's diary accurately summed up the evening: "On Monday, Johnnie Ray's first night. Squealing teenagers and mass hysteria, quite nauseating, but he gave a remarkable performance both on stage and later at the Embassy, where he fondled Terry Moore for the cameras. Poor boy."[12]

Wire services flashed the dis-information world wide. "Of course, I'm very fond of her," Johnnie purred to reporters. "But I feel that any comment on our relationship should come from the lady."[13] Moore wasn't talking. Like the tragic and noble Mighty Joe Young, Johnnie was another beautiful monster, a compelling figure whose ability to both frighten and evoke sympathy worked against him as surely as it had the giant gorilla.

If they would not let him retire, he would do as he damn well pleased. During a late night revel at London's swank Dorchester Hotel, Johnnie and several brothers-of-the-bottle were passing the early morning hours by drunkenly capering, naked, up and down the hushed corridors and stairwells. Johnnie found himself separated from his pals and began pounding on the door of what he assumed was his suite. No response. Singing to himself, he kept on pounding.

"My husband called me the next day and said 'Guess who arrived at my door with no clothes on last night?'" actress Jan Sterling recalled. "'Who?' I asked, and he said 'Johnnie Ray!'"

Sterling was married to actor Paul Douglas, a respected New York stage actor. Douglas was a rough-hewn character with a reputation as an outspoken liberal. "It was about that same time," Sterling said, "that he was called a 'Red Tool,' on the floor of Congress, because he was appearing in a play in the South and had said that 'The South is a place of shit, sow-belly and segregation.'"

"Paul said that Johnnie was singing something, and that he was on the wrong floor, so he just sent him downstairs," Sterling continued. "And the next day a chambermaid told him 'there was one with nothing on, one with an eiderdown on, and one with nothing but Johnnie Ray on him!'"[14]

The couple, who had both attended Marion Davies' show-stopper of a wedding reception, laughed about the indiscretion and thought nothing more of it. Johnnie probably did not even remember any of it. He was to be emphatically reminded of it before the year was out.

Johnnie loved London. By 1955, his established social set there consisted of blonde bombshells Diana Dors and June Wilkinson. while perhaps his closest male friend was Lourie Younger, a blue-blooded black sheep rake of Scot descent with the requisitely ferocious thirst for booze. Johnnie also socialized with Noel Coward, a friendship that grew over the years in London, New York and at Firefly, Coward's Jamaican retreat.

Johnnie drew great respect in Britain, and would give several command performances for the Royal Family. His careless attitude apparently charmed them as much as his emotionalism moved them. There was little delicacy in his socializing with the peerage; to Johnnie, none of their titles had the glamour of show business. Tempest Storm was more his idea of royalty.

Johnnie returned to New York, and the Latin Quarter stage in June. He burned the house down. "Johnnie Ray can sometime be a revelation," a reviewer noted. "He has the evangelistic fervor of Billy Graham, the know-how of an old time troubadour and the tortured ritual of a boy with devils . . . the adult cafe goers support him with bobbysox fervor."[15]

It was true. When Lou Walters gave his daughter's hand in marriage to Bob Katz on June 21st, Johnnie was hired to entertain. The bride, of course, was television star Barbara (working at the time as producer on "Ask the Camera," a live fifteen-minute kiddie program on WNBT), and the Plaza's Terrace Room was loaded with flowers, booze and food, reportedly $20,000 worth, the black tie cream of high society and entertainers like Milton Berle.[16]

"Hey, hey Johnnie Ray," as every disk jock i.d.'d him, had gone from the "strong misgivings" of 1952 to become almost totally accepted by New York society. Although considered a guilty pleasure by some, as in Dorothy Kilgallen's case, a "revelation" to others like Yul Brynner, Tallulah Bankhead, Ethel Merman and Jackie Gleason, and a vulgar buffoon to some who ran with Sinatra, he remained apart from them all.

The humiliating postures forced upon him underscored the fact that his inspiration was originally drawn from his conscious choice to flout convention. This acceptance, such as it was, offered nothing to stay his inner anxieties, first manifested by the persistent and quite tangible effect his muted adolescence had upon him, now further complicated by life in the spotlight's demand of restraint.

Johnnie had it all, but felt as if he had nothing. Romance was strictly on the QT or wholly public. His music no longer offered the sanctuary it once had. Although he rarely questioned Mitch Miller's direction, Johnnie's records were increasingly unsatisfactory (the most recent session, on June 12, yielded the shrill fake gospel "I've Got So Many Million Years").

There were two Johnnies now, and between the travel, riots, booze and pills by the fistful (the days of Cy's sugar placebos were long gone), it was often difficult to tell which persona was expected to appear at any given time. The public Johnnie Ray was defined for fans in a 1955 souvenir program:

> Johnnie Ray is five feet, eleven and a half inches tall, has hazel eyes and weighs one hundred fifty five pounds. Greatest ambition is to be a movie actor in every sense of the word.
>
> His pet extravagance—money.
>
> Pet economy—never wears cufflinks while singing; wears well concealed paper clips, because he works so enthusiastically that the links break, or fall off, or both. *(Johnnie no longer used paper clips; he commissioned a New York jeweler to design and craft a special octagonal shaped design which withstood his most frantic gesturing.)*
>
> Is not superstitious, but there are always two pennies in his left pocket, a token of good luck from his personal manager, Bernie Lang and his business manager Cy Kertman.
>
> Is very unorganized, a poor letter writer and phones his folks every week in lieu of writing.
>
> Enjoys the rugged things in nature, mountains and trees.
>
> His travels have made him interested in history. In driving from place to place, he stops at every marker and at every Chamber of Commerce to get any pamphlets about the historic aspects of the vicinity. *(He rarely drove from date to date; almost invariably flew. He was an inveterate shutter-bug; Copa girl Beck Steiner Gordon recalled Johnnie saying "I want*

to see Manhattan by day," in April of 1952. They met the next day, and Johnnie, clad in a powder blue leisure suit, with several cameras dangling from his neck, snapped and filmed every landmark on the island. "It was so funny," she said. "This huge star, the toast of New York . . . he was just like a big kid.")[17]

Pet aversion—going to the dentist.

Hobby—writing short stories. Is thinking of writing a TV show for himself. *(By 1955, Johnnie never wrote anything; this was a veiled plug for his "semi-autobiographical" GE Theater drama, "The Big Shot.")*

His biggest thrill—as a kid, he wrote asking for autographed pictures of Tallulah Bankhead and Lucille Ball and got them. He later had his picture taken with Tallulah Bankhead and Ethel Merman and met Lucille Ball. *(He drank, naked, with Bankhead; swapped dirty jokes with Merman.)*

Says his only claim to fame ancestor-wise is his great-great-great grandfather, George Gay, who built the first brick house West of the Rockies. Gay's second wife is the Blackfoot Indian from whom Johnnie is descended. *(Poor Hazel.)*

His best studies at school were dramatics and speech.

Collects records by Frank Sinatra, Perry Como, Billy May and Ray Anthony. *(Collected records by Billie Holiday, Edith Piaf and Judy Garland, and was capable of impressively accurate impersonations of each.)*

Has written both the words and music of all 154 songs he's composed.

Loves Movie premieres.

Has released 15 discs and a Johnnie Ray long player, the latter the first time in recording history Columbia has put out an album without a name, just Johnnie's picture.

Is sentimental about birthdays and anniversaries. *(Was sentimental about everything.)*

Has a cocker spaniel named Mike. *(Had a Doberman Pincer named Sabrina.)*

His favorite girl singers are Kay Starr, Doris Day, Ethel Merman and Betty Grable. *(Also Little Misses Cornshucks, Sharecropper, Mabel Scott, and Lady Day.)*

Likes every kind of music, classical, swing. *(Would not have known classical music from John Philip Sousa.)*

Loves amusement parks.

Favorite audiences—servicemen. *(No comment.)*[18]

The most accurate characterization of Johnnie, one common to all who knew him, was Copa Girl Gordon's: "just like a big kid." Life was play, the world his playground and any object became a plaything in his hands, even his hearing aid. "He used it as a toy," Bill Franklin said. "He would take his hearing aid off and pass it around at parties. But first he'd turn the volume to a frenzy point, plug it into someone's ear and get his jollies because it was up so loud they'd go through the fucking roof. I saw him do that a lot."[19]

He also used it as a tool; if an argument reached the point where Johnnie wanted to end it, he would smile ear-to-ear, fish the battery power-pack from his pocket, raise it and, with a broad pantomime flourish sure to enrage whoever was in disagreement with him, snap it off and return to whatever routine activity he pleased. End of discussion.

This was not calculated to escalate contention but to end it. He did, as Jack Devaney pointed out, consciously avoid dissension at every turn, an often deleterious practice quite in psychological vogue at that time. For Johnnie, it was a natural response. His staunch refusal to confront a problem laid an impenetrable emotional bedrock which enabled him to conduct life as pleasurably as he could.

Despite his tendency to bury vexation, Johnnie's characteristic nature remained as sunny and carefree as the barefoot country lad of Summer Stock comedy. As demonstrably affectionate to pals as he was stone-faced and tight-lipped with detractors, Johnnie Ray was a fiercely loyal and generous friend. Always eager to learn, fascinated by details of routine lives of those outside the trade, Johnnie retained much of his native Willamette Valley naivete; his undeniable charm was due, in large part, to a wide-eyed, utter lack of sophistication.

This incongruous air of bright innocence was enhanced all the more by the fact it had completely eluded darkening. The grim hand-to-mouth days at Ohio's hooker hang-outs and burley houses and the considerable misfortunes which success had plunged him into could have embittered the most charitable of souls. But Johnnie had been dodging woe full-time since his sudden of loss of hearing 13 years earlier.

Johnnie's temper was even and slow to flare, but when he flew into a rage, those around him prepared for the worst. His eyes assumed a sudden ferocity that in itself was bone-chilling, and Johnnie would rail, quite violently, until victory was his. Mostly high-handed dramatics, the "blood, guts and thunder" he was so masterful at delivering would erupt with gale force. Those in his entourage knew how to handle it.

Drummer Herman Kapp, who replaced Sammy Fede in 1955, was once dining with Johnnie, Bernie and Cy. The subject of an important interview, set for early the next morning, was broached. Johnnie, usually attentive and responsible in such matters, flatly refused to be disturbed for such an imposition on his rest. Bernie quietly stressed its importance. Johnnie became fiery and ended the argument with a blistering repudiation of Bernie, the press, his schedule—the whole enchilada. He crescendoed with "And I'm *not* going to do it because I am a star, God damn it, a very *big star*." Silence. Kapp spoke up, very softly. "Twinkle, twinkle," said he. Everyone fell out laughing and Johnnie went along with the schedule.[20]

The backhills boy in Johnnie felt more and more as if he were negotiating a maze. He thrilled at the unknown prospects ahead but half the time he felt completely lost, thwarted, confused. Johnnie rarely had a sense of personal direction; the result was a dizzying spin exacerbated by the knowledge that many were out to cripple, if not completely destroy him.

In August 1955, Johnnie was in Las Vegas appearing at the Desert Inn, when his and Bernie's worst fears were realized. Scandal magazine *Lowdown* (The Facts They Dare Not Tell You!) appeared with an enlargement of Johnnie's 1951 Detroit arrest record plastered across the cover. "*Lowdown* Demands Michigan Governor Pardon Johnnie Ray!" it howled. This was disaster.

Thinly veiled with a "forgive and forget" angle, the magazine recounted the entire horrible mess in a story that ran an agonizing eight pages. It reproduced his mugshots, gave a minute-by-minute account of that evening and published Officer Demmers' testimony. The venomously supportive editorial slant neatly side-stepped slander and featured conciliatory statements like "after all, he hasn't been convicted of murdering anyone . . . " while pleading for a pardon for Johnnie.[21]

"Moe Dalitz made one phone call," Johnnie said, "and you couldn't find a single copy of the rag in Las Vegas - or anywhere in Nevada." This may have saved the engagement, but not even Dalitz could reverse the damage it caused in the eyes of the public. Johnnie was hammering out the rhythm of "Cry" on very thin ice.[22]

*   *   *

When he returned to Britain in October, some of the popular bloom was off his blackened rose; he was now subject to the same dime-store psychologizing there that he had to endure at home. In Newcastle, he was publicly blasted by a city councillor over the fact that he required a police escort.

"Obviously a publicity stunt," sniffed Councillor Arthur Grey. "I am disgusted that eight members of the police force should be used for this purpose." Stung to riposte, a senior officer of the constabulary told the press, "We were not protecting Johnnie Ray. We were controlling the one thousand strong crowd of irresponsible teenagers following him. If Councillor Grey owned a shop near the theater and the crowd crashed through his window trying to get at Ray, he would soon want to know where the police were."[23]

Two weeks later, BBC television's "Brain Trust" program was devoted entirely to an examination of "the annoying Johnnie Ray phenomenon." One guest, psychologist Dr. John Bronowski, explained the frenzy by pointing out that "Johnnie Ray has a peculiar trick of looking at girls as if he was making love to them individually." Sunday Express editor John Gordon allowed as to how Johnnie's "delirium of quivers and contortions gives audiences quite a thrilling emotional experience," then got at the heart of Britain's sudden disenchantment.

"Outside of the theater," Gordon railed, "his exhibitionism is becoming a public nuisance. The police, tired of this nonsense, have warned him that if there is any more of it, he will be arrested."[24] The nuisance level never reached a point where Johnnie was clapped in irons. When he learned that Billy Graham was running one of his tent revival shows in London, Johnnie tried to belay further such discussion by offering to sing for the Reverend. He managed only more shock; Graham, who welcomed performers like Roy Rogers and Dale Evans, was in no hurry to take him up on the kind offer.

The "Brain Trust" blast, at any rate, aired just days before he gave his first command performance for the Royal Family, at The Victoria London Palace. Johnnie was presented to Queen Elizabeth. He stifled his natural urge to curtsey, and realized he had failed to brush up on his protocol. He wound up calling Her Royal Highness simply "ma'am," inadvertently hitting upon the correct form of address.[25]

Johnnie was forgiven—Britain had a much more troublesome pop music phenomenon to worry about: Bill Haley. By the end of the month, "Rock Around the Clock" was the number one record, and Haley's fans, the troglodyte Teddy Boys, were smashing up not just stage door barriers, but the interior of the Palladium. Johnnie's tribe of ecstatic love children suddenly seemed vastly preferable.

He went on to Paris and an engagement at the Moulin Rouge. Not since the days of Le Petomane had a performer inflamed Parisians so. The critics, still miffed and self-conscious from their recent tenure as boot-licking collaborators, felt compelled to belittle any import and turned in uniformly downbeat reviews. Nonetheless, he played to near capacity houses and Variety said "results overall were more than satisfactory."[26]

While Johnnie staggered through the Montmartre seeking thrills in the early bright, newsstands back in the U.S. were selling the new issue of *Confidential* magazine. More trouble; page 22 featured an eye-catching double spread photo montage of Johnnie, arms extended, serenading an image of tuxedo-clad, dour-pussed Paul Douglas. It was headlined "Knock, Knock! Who's There? . . . Why Did Johnnie Ray Try To break Down Paul Douglas' Door?"

Scandal hack Francis Dudley did a superlative job inflating the previous Spring's gaffe: "The tipsy nude staggered to the door of Room 417 and began beating a tattoo on it with his fists while wailing demands to be let inside . . . he was up to an old trick of his that even merrie olde England won't tolerate. He was manhunting.

"Even the liquefied Ray recognized the occupant. It was husky and he-mannish—very he-mannish—Paul Douglas . . . there were a couple of resounding smacks as strong hand met bare flesh and Ray came flying out . . . to land in a heap in the corridor."

Dudley laid it on. "The caper was old history to veteran observers of the weirdies in show business . . ." and ran the Detroit accosting and soliciting charge by for good measure, then concluded: "Every now then—as Paul Douglas discovered—the girl in Johnnie Ray just has to come out."[27]

While the story was based in fact, those "resounding smacks of strong hand on bare flesh" were fiction. "All Paul told me," Jan Sterling said, "was that he made Johnnie get back downstairs to his room." She laughed, then added "'The Demon,' as I sometime called him, was the kind that if he was suddenly woken up—by anybody—he'd just have to say 'Get the fuck down those stairs!' And if somebody had stayed there, he might have pushed him, but I just don't know anything about that.

"At the time, we both thought it was very funny. And those scandal magazines printed so many stories that you didn't pay them any attention or deal with it as anything serious." Johnnie's way of thinking was completely opposite. He took it very seriously.

After a whirlwind tour of Italy he returned for another run at the Latin Quarter. On opening night, teenage fan Tito Adami (who was so Ray-crazy that he bleached his hair and often wore a fake hearing aid) came down from Brooklyn to join the inevitable clutch of teens waiting for their idol's arrival.

"I had a copy of *Confidential*, the Paul Douglas one. There was a big picture of Johnnie in it, so I bought the thing," Adami recalled. "So, anyway, there was a whole bunch of girls there in that big hall outside the Latin Quarter entrance, I had the magazine and we were lookin' at it. When I saw Johnnie comin', I took the magazine and put it in back of me.

"He was talkin' to the girls and all that, and then he asked me what I had behind me. I said, 'Aww, nothin'. Just a magazine.' 'Well, let me see it,' he said, so I showed it to him. He looked at it and said 'Oh, my God,' and just ran up the stairs. I don't even remember if he took the magazine or left it, he ran off so fast."[28]

Johnnie saw black. Billie Rosenfield, now Mrs. Seymour Heller, came in with her husband (who was riding high with his hottest attraction Liberace). Bernie flew to her. "'Thank god you're here,' Bernie said to me," recalled Billie. "'Johnnie's terribly upset, he's refusing to go on. Please, go talk to him—he'll listen to you.'" It was a long, long way from their lunchtime song sessions at Sunset and Vine. But Bernie was right; he did listen to her, and went on.

Over the next three months *Uncensored, Anything Goes, On The QT* all ran taunting, venomous hatchet jobs on him ("The Secret Agony Of," "Why the Babes Still Cry For," "Why Johnny Ray Likes To Go In Drag"). Even Bernie's attempts at damage control backfired. When Johnnie was prevailed upon to announce his engagement to British actress Sylvia Drew during the previous October's UK tour, no one in the trade paid much mind; silly, standard flack.

The scandal magazines jumped on every such incident and milked them mercilessly: "His name may be *linked* with the girls but they definitely do not make up *all* of his fans. One of Ray's big secrets is that he's got something for the boys too." Each piece was, by now, usually almost word-for-word re-hashes of those which preceded them. The most painful reality of the scandal magazine's attacks was that this terrible consistency could be attributed only to one factor: they told the truth. Johnnie had to concede that, describing Confidential's stories on him as "A few facts and a lot of fabricated stuff." But even when misspelling his name, they quoted him accurately.[29]

Johnnie had sat atop the world, seen it kneel in supplication and heard it praise him with a passion as intense as now used when damning him. He was backed into a corner. The panic, isolation and pain he had sang so convincingly of in "Paths of Paradise," and "Mountains in the Moonlight" were insignificant compared with the thrust of the scandal blade. They plunged into him again and again, delighted, it seemed, to drive it ever deeper.

What could he do—sue them? Fat chance. It was all true. That was the terrible reality of most of these publications at the time. It was neither conjecture nor slander, but solid, on-the-record fact. Johnnie reached for his drink.

All this took an ever deepening toll, heightened by the fact that Johnnie was never anywhere by himself. He had no self left, except for what remained of his soul as evoked under the spotlight. It was almost as if his career placed him back into the same state of disconnected inertia he experienced after losing his hearing.

"The loneliness, the isolation of the business got to me," Johnnie said. "People don't realize but I was denied what you might call my early manhood. I was a kid those first years of my success—my life consisted of bodyguards, police, security all the time, people tearing at my clothes.

But, really, the only time I had alone, to myself, was when I was on stage. That's an awful way to live."[30]

What few genuine friendships he did have, with Betty Kean, Sophie Tucker, Stan Freeman, Brynner, Merman, the people he loved and who genuinely loved him, were predicated entirely by the trade's demands. All were slaves to the itinerary. Johnnie's life completely lacked any sustained emotional warmth. He got it from Elma, but that was mostly over a long distance telephone line.

His self, reduced to something he came in contact with only when working, now seemed to be evaporating under the lights. Even the empathic bond between performer and audience, a nourishing source of pride he depended on as much as he did the booze, was being eroded by the scandal rags and the knowledge that riot was the most likely outcome of an unbridled Ray performance.

Achievement of international fame was the only skein of esteem and purpose left in an otherwise unraveling personality. His best friend was his accountant. Johnnie was smothering and starving, all at once.

With no one to confide in, to explain the void his life was spiraling into, Johnnie was turning into a ghost, a transparent half-man capable only of routine, conditioned to the plush cell which became the Cry Guy's home.

Not long before his twenty-ninth birthday, Johnnie was in the studio. The session yielded a handful of undistinguished pop toss-offs, "Goodbye, Au Revoir, Adios," "Because I Love You," another ersatz gospel number "Walk Along With Kings," and a version of Fats Waller's show biz anthem "Ain't Misbehavin'."

For Johnnie, the latter was an opportunity of definition. He sang the final verse as he always did in performance, taking sweeping liberties with Waller's meter and lyric, tailoring it to a Pure John fit:

"Like Jack Horner,
in a corner . . .
Nowhere!
What do I care?
Believe me little darlin',
I ain't a tom cat . . .

... dig radio
lookin' for a *soulmate* ...
Go, Go, Go!"

It was hip, inside stuff, the stuff that made him a winner in the black and tans. It was as close to true rock and roll as ever he got, laid down with a plangent edge that oozed helplessness. A soulmate for Johnnie Ray was a mighty tall order. He did not anticipate finding one.

It was all a drag, one big mess.

14

Johnnie's career continued to lurch, grind, spin and dip. Along the way, he sat down with Los Angeles Mirror reporter Paul Coates, ordered another beer and let his hair down to cry the success story blues. "Hate to drink, but if I don't get half stiff every night, I can't sleep," Johnnie said. "I got a thing—I can't be alone. It's a real drag for me, gets me way out nervous. I lie in my hotel room and stare at those four walls and I get so jumpy, I feel like I'm going to climb them.

"When I finish work at night, I can't walk out of the joint alone. I got to find somebody to keep me company. If I'm alone, I feel all bugged up. I don't know what's the matter with me . . . If I'm alone, I can't relax.

"I haven't got any friends, man, and that's what I really want. It's the travel—it's no life living in every hotel room across the country. You hit a town and just when you make friends with some guy, or some chick, your agent hands you an airline reservation." He looked around the bar. "Man, I hate to think of when this joint closes tonight. I hate to think of going back to that hotel room."[1]

A lot of this was undoubtedly the bottle talking, but even considering his tendency to jive the press, there was real pain buried in his spiel; he claimed to have suffered from insomnia since age 17, and all who knew and travelled with him agree that he was up until dawn most every night, and not by choice. What little sleep he did get was almost invariably troubled by a recurring nightmare that stayed with him his entire life—one of unspecified peril from which he awoke, drenched in sweat, and calling out for his father. Johnnie was drifting. He was unhappy. And he was alone.

Suddenly, 1956—and the rise of rock and roll—was upon Johnnie. The eruption of this trade-staggering new pop sound came so swiftly that the Cry Guy was virtually unaware of it. For most of that Winter and Spring, Johnnie opened new territories: Lee Gordon, with Bernie's ardent blessings, booked Johnnie in South America, the Philippines and South Africa. He made such a deep impression on the Afrikaaners that Variety reported, "Johnnie Ray whammed Johannesburg," where he was "better received than any other visitor except the British Royal Family."[2]

Bernie mostly remained at his Broadway office. Since breaking the price barrier and challenging the mob, most of the adventure had gone out of managing Johnnie, as well as much of the personal warmth that existed between the two during their hectic ascension together. It was business now, routine, old hat. Johnnie was more meal ticket than friend. But Johnnie had brothership, between Kappy, as everyone knew drummer Herman Kapp and Jack Devaney (who had replaced a road-weary Cy Kertman). Touring still meant a few good times, perhaps not always smooth, but never mediocre, particularly on his days off. But those were rare (and their infrequency soon wore Jack Devaney down; within a year he called it quits and moved to Hollywood).

Back home, things were moving fast in pop music, faster then Johnnie realized. He had not come up with a hit since "Alexander's

Ragtime Band" over a year before. Mitch Miller wanted to see gold. In February, they had another abortive session, cutting a wild uptempo bump-and-grinder "Ooh, Ah, Oh, (This is Love)" and a country ballad "Why Does Your Daddy Have To Go?" Neither was released (considering the former's opening line, "It makes me laugh, it makes me sigh, it makes me gay and it makes me cry . . . " the decision was no surprise).[3]

Before he came up with a solution, Johnnie left the country again: back to England, back to Australia and on to Tokyo. Lee Gordon, who had done no wrong thus far, lost something in translation with promoter "Tats" Nagasaki. While Johnnie was warned to expect a low-key response from the Japanese, his reception was one of dumb founded, sullen silence. "Ray Really Weeps After Tokyo Flop" Variety headlined an item on his April 1st opening.[4]

He canceled two matinee shows set for the next day. Somebody had goofed—every poster and placard that went up prior to his arrival announced Johnnie Ray, Famous American Prize Fighter. The perplexed crowds at his opening were dyed-in-wool, samurai-type boxing fans. The date had been appropriate—April fucking Fool's Day, Johnnie said to himself. After some hectic last minute airwave promotion, the situation was rectified and the rest of his dates went off flawlessly.[5]

When he flew back to New York, the awaiting press corps clamored with an intensity which surprised even Johnnie. They all wanted to know the same thing, kept yelling the same question. He didn't know what they were talking about. "What do you think of Elvis Presley? What do you think of Elvis Presley?" His reply stunned them. "What's an Elvis Presley?" Johnnie asked.

"Big mistake," he said later. "But I'd been out of the country and had no idea of what was going on there, because he hit so fast. Of course the press jumped on it, and tried to make out like it was sour grapes on my part. And after I found out, all I could think was 'That poor son of a bitch. I just hope he knows what he's getting into.'"[6]

From New York, Johnnie went directly into the Desert Inn. At the New Frontier directly across the Strip, the headliner was "Elvis Presley— the Atomic Powered Singer, with Freddy Martin's Orchestra." The billing smacked of Johnnie's handle "The Atomic Ray." It was, of course, the only viable marquee analog for use in presenting an unconventional teenster heart throb to Las Vegas swingers.

Johnnie wasted no time going to see Elvis work. "I went in there," he recalled, "and at first I couldn't even tell which one was Elvis, because they all had guitars. It was pretty obvious that he was doing it by rote, something that about 300 other black guys had done before him." He was unimpressed. "Really, it struck me like something that college kids would do for laughs."[7]

That impression was shared by just about everyone in Las Vegas. Overnight, the billing was changed to "Freddy Martin's Orchestra, also Elvis Presley." Number one record regardless, Vegas was in no way ready for the Memphis Flash.

But Elvis attended Johnnie's show numerous times. "He came over to the Desert Inn to see me quite a few times," Johnnie said. "He came backstage to visit and we became friends." Photographs of their first meeting are extraordinary. They seem deep in conversation, yet are clearly sizing each other up. Two moody young rebels, one, slight and fair, near exhaustion from the whips and scorns of outraged morality, the other, dark and sprawling, scarcely realizing what battles awaited him.

At the D.I., Elvis studied Johnnie with the same intent eye he had trained upon the gospel quartets who fascinated him as a teenager. In a sense, any 21-year-old Southerner with that inevitable hillbilly/gospel musical background who combined Johnnie Ray's exuberant physical style with the slick, careless sexuality of Dean Martin (whom Elvis idolized) might have arrived at the same style and presentation as Presley.

Elvis, like any who attended that particular engagement, was doubtless flabbergasted by the climactic production which capped Johnnie's show. Choreographer Donn Arden, inspired by Johnnie's customary Jubilee closer, cooked up "The Deluge," a production number that featured Johnnie singing "Noah" while chorines in animal costumes can-canned up a ramp and into a huge Ark set piece. "A real eyebrow lifter," noted one reviewer. "The question of good taste is ventured."[8]

Considering his subsequent work as Graceland's interior decorator, Elvis probably dug it. Ray's influence on Presley was strong; Elvis' stance onstage—shoulders back, arms loose, hips thrust forward, the sweeping gestures—was entirely Johnnie's. When he got out of the Army, he immediately recorded "Such A Night." In the 1970's, his act prominently featured Johnnie's trademark stunt—leaning over the footlights to kiss femme ringsiders, and he would later acknowledge Johnnie as an encouraging influence.

From the D.I., Johnnie went back to work for Lou Walters. The Latin Quarter, just a few blocks from the Broadway apartment Johnnie had rented for the last several years, became his New York mainstay. Rock and roll notwithstanding, his opening proved to skeptics that here was no "flash in the platter novelty, but a magnetic performer whose almost hypnotic effect on the audience won him a thunderous reception."9

Between shows the next night, Johnnie rushed back to his West 55th Street pad, where a CBS television crew was set up to broadcast a "Person To Person" interview with Edward R. Murrow. Johnnie was modest, genuinely humble with Murrow. His opalescent, smoky murmur was a singular counterpoint to Murrow's trademark laconic but clipped enunciation. Despite the severe case of nerves television appearances always caused (exacerbated by Twentieth Century Fox's rejection), Johnnie seemed almost relaxed.

But when Murrow asked "How did you . . . develop . . . your famous . . . ah . . . cry-ing rou-tine?" Johnnie winced. Rather than cite performers like Cornshucks, Billy Daniels or Billy Ward, he replied that he had "learned from watching the great performers, people like Jimmy Durante and Sophie Tucker." When Murrow inquired if he ever planned to make his home in Oregon again, Johnnie blanched visibly. Even beneath the customary thick layer of pancake make-up, color seemed to drain from his face. He stumbled for a moment, then haltingly explained "After all the travelling and theatrical work I've done, Ed . . . I really can't imagine myself going back," hastening to add that he regularly flew his family in for various engagements around the country.

It was a successful appearance, marred only by one spectacular goof. Conducting a tour of his modestly appointed apartment, as "Person To Person" guests invariably did, Murrow asked about a leopard skin which lay at Johnnie's feet. "I see . . . ah . . . that rug there, Johnnie . . . it must be something you picked up . . . in South Africa."

"Why, yes, Ed, that's right," Johnnie purred. "It's one of those tiger rugs."

Of course.

Such fame, such success, such wealth, such talent. Such a rube.

While stage fright was never a problem for Johnnie in the early years of his career, he tended to clench up before the camera, although his natural trouper instinct masked it almost entirely. When a Jimmy Durante show called upon him to join in a top-hat-and-tails dance routine with the Schnozzola, Liberace, Peter Lawford, and slick veteran taxi-dancer George Raft, Johnnie looked as if he were about to faint—the show was broadcast live from the D.I.'s Painted Desert Room; still, at least he came off looking better than Lawford.

And he did a lot of television, starting with the Como and Sullivan shows, going on to make numerous appearances on the Jimmy Durante, Martha Raye and Jackie Gleason shows, Arthur Murray's Dance Party, Patti Page's The Big Record, just about every national variety program being aired. These programs were hard pressed to decide how best to stage—and soften—Johnnie's appearances; alone, under a spotlight, he was too inflammatory. They tried everything: he sang gospel on a tent revival set; he was carried out on stage, borne by chorus boys grasping his ankles as he waved his arms and bellowed "Cry" from on high; he sang from a piano draped with show girls.

On the Jack Benny show, Johnnie performed an exaggerated "Cry" while Benny, in a steamy, hand-wringing send-up of bobby-soxer rapture, fell apart so convincingly that it was hard to tell where comedy ended and Johnnie's thrall began. Once, when the Great One was indisposed, Johnnie filled in as last-minute guest host for a Jackie Gleason Show featuring Peggy Lee, ventriloquist Jimmy Nelson and Art Carney (as Ed Norton, he broke into a comedic "Cry," "If your sweetheart / sends a letter / to your wife . . . " Johnnie cracked up. It looked almost natural).

His only small screen dramatic role was as up-and-coming crooner "Johnnie Pulaski" in a GE Theater drama "The Big Shot," a corny melodrama (his apparently Polish parents used inexplicably stagey Italian accents) that hinged on Pulaski's refusal to compromise for a big city talent agency. Johnnie handled the role quite gracefully, and a second version of "Paths of Paradise," with a much punchier vocal and minus the Four Lads, played throughout the show (as background music, as a demonstration record and sung by Johnnie twice on-camera), adding considerable heft to the otherwise fluffy proceedings.[10]

Johnnie was in constant demand for television appearances, an always nerve grating obligation, that also meant fewer and fewer nights off. There was always something new, a show he had not yet worked on. In the Spring of 1956, he was mystery guest on the enormously popular quiz show "What's My Line?" The blindfolded panel whose job it was to question and identify the guest consisted of Bennett Cerf, Arlene Francis, Fred Allen and Dorothy Kilgallen with moderator John Daly.

The limousine awaited. He got some fresh batteries, knocked back a stiff vodka, and went downstairs. It was a gentle dusk. Johnnie had no reason to suspect there was love in the air.

Even though Kilgallen's Voice of Broadway column tended to run condescending, occasionally snotty, items on Johnnie, she had privately considered him "endsville" since April 10, 1952. But the next morning, when her husband expressed strong critical sentiment on their WOR radio show "Breakfast with Dorothy & Dick" (the same discussion that, as reported in the Saturday Evening Post, "almost came to crockery throwing"), Kilgallen rarely spoke of Johnnie again. At home, anyway.

Outside their palatial townhouse, Dorothy surprised many with constantly recurring Johnnie-themed conversation. A friend from the CBS studio realized that Dorothy was "smitten, overwhelmed by the electricity of his new style." Her make-up man on "What's My Line?" wondered over the way she swooned about the singer when, to his recollection, she had never mentioned her husband.[11]

"What's My Line?" was serious fun to Kilgallen, who adored games. She regularly oversaw the play of a variety of cocktail hour word-play and guessing contests in her social life, and was passionately competitive about her "What's My Line?" success record. If another panelist nailed the mystery guest's identity, she often wept bitterly. Such was the case when Johnnie appeared.

When he masked his distinctive voice with gruff *sotto voce* responses to the panel's questions, Dorothy was stumped. When Arlene Francis asked "Are you the young man who made crying a national institution?" and Johnnie answered yes, Kilgallen's sporting blood simmered. She did somehow manage to keep tears in check during an introduction to Johnnie following the broadcast.

A scrupulously coiffed model of respectable high fashion style, her deportment and appearance bespoke the 400's traditional veil-and-white-gloves sensibility with an added twist of enviably tasteful, up-to-date chic. She exuded class, grace and noble distinction.

An attractive woman with a delicate, moon-pale complexion, lush dark brunette hair, a knock-out hour glass figure and not inconsiderable bustline, Dorothy was, viewed from the proper angle, quite a dish. Her sole physical flaw was a weakness in the chin line, a tiny crescent which receded quite abruptly between lower lip and jaw. But her bearing, vivacity, charming good humor and highly articulate speech made for a poised, altogether enviable image.

Misgivings over past *Voice of Broadway* barbs aside, Johnnie was impressed as hell by Kilgallen. She was, after all, one of the most powerful women in America, perhaps more feared than admired by many. The *Voice of Broadway* could make or break the career of most in the trade with a single well-armed negative item. That night at CBS, it was natural that, as Johnnie told Kilgallen biographer Lee Israel, "We decided to be nice to each other."[12]

Johnnie followed up on this *entree* rather judiciously. Later that month, Kilgallen's daughter Jill was celebrating her 16th birthday. As columnist Louis Sobol related it, "The girl and her friends were fans of Johnnie Ray . . . Dorothy phoned Johnnie's press agent and asked whether he could find it convenient to send over any of Johnnie's latest recordings. To her amazement and the unbounded joy of the girls and boys at the party, the 'errand boy,' arriving with an armful of the platters was Johnnie himself—and for more than an hour he entertained the youngsters."[13]

The five-story townhouse on East 68th Street, between fashionable Madison Avenue and Park, provided Johnnie a significant glimpse of real, high-toned New York *class*. Once he was welcomed inside on this gracious, semi-professional/quasi-social mission, it was much easier to step up their acquaintance. Johnnie, after the barrage of mud-slinging scandal broadsides, was eager to gain her approval and did not, at first, realize he had already reached exalted status.

On the surface their backgrounds seemed irreconcilably different. He, simple son of a hardscrabble farmer and mill-worker who grew up wandering through forests of trees and man-made jungles of reeking saloons, an unlikely celebrity whose fame now tormented as often as it gratified him, was—sublime artistry aside—still a coarse, undefined creature.

And she, daughter of a veteran Hearst reporter reared in a gracious social milieu, polished at exclusive boarding schools and universities, seasoned by almost six years of hard crime reporting (inured to the sight of corpses, grief and disaster) was literally and figuratively, the First Lady of Broadway columnists, and had enjoyed that glamorous high life since November 1938. And she had been married since 1940.[14]

Their primary common ground was, of course, music. Dorothy was a surprisingly hip chick with impeccable good taste in pop and jazz. Two of her closest friends, Bob and Jean Bach, were deep jazz buffs who had been tight with Duke Ellington since he first rose from the Cotton Club. She avidly followed all the latest developments, and Voice of Broadway was as likely to feature items on LaVern Baker or Mabel Mercer as often as it covered Doris Day or Ethel Merman.

The Broadway columnist's nightly rounds required both independence from, and frequently escorts other than, her husband. As a theatrical producer, radio actor and high profile raconteur, Dick Kollmar had his own Broadway reputation and action-packed nightlife schedule to attend to. Since Johnnie, Dorothy knew, was irresistibly lured by Broadway first nighters, and reveled shamelessly in the intoxicating premiere ritual, it was almost routine when he was invited to escort her to the New York premiere of "An Affair To Remember."

The swelling Vic Damone title song lulled the pair. The bittersweet on-screen romance of Cary Grant and Deborah Kerr moved both to tears ("I cried my silly eyes out," Johnnie said). There was an air of mutual intimacy in the darkened theater. Tears and romance—a more appropriate first date could not have been.

Johnnie suggested an equally ideal wind-up, and took her to a Count Basie gig (Basie and Johnnie had beeen friendly since their 1951 State Theater engagement). Dorothy, at the time, was not an energetic drinker, but together they inhaled a fifth of vodka. The booze slid down her throat as smooth as oil rolling off an oval of polished onyx, sweetened by the charge of a night out with The Man the Girls Strip.[15]

Johnnie also felt it. Once he recognized the warmth he was starved for, those long, narrow arms clasped Dorothy to him. Very shortly afterwards, they found themselves in bed—a cascade of violent release and deep passion. Johnnie always claimed that he provided Dorothy, at the age of 44, with her first orgasm.[16]

Suddenly headlong in hectic, desperate love they launched their own affair to remember. This romance was so unlikely, so public and so downright on-the-face-of-it inconceivable that Manhattan was agog.

The scorn hurled previously at Johnnie by *Voice of Broadway* was replaced by a barrage of nurturing publicity. No less frequent were surprise gifts, a series of deliveries from the likes of Cartier (a pair of diamond and sapphire encrusted cufflinks) and Steuben (crystal decanters engraved "Johnnie's Vodka" and "Just Gin").

Johnnie reciprocated with bunches of her favorite flower, the exotic lavender rose. "They were steel blue, and gorgeous. I think they were brought in from Holland," he recalled, "I could never understand why she loved them more than red or pink." The romance was of a rare nature, such as he had known only in sentimental love songs. Johnnie, in fact and in deed, was mad about Dorothy. "She was probably the most feminine woman I've ever known," he said. "And I always thought she was a pretty lady—the softest thing you ever touched."[17]

It seemed as if the formerly contentious relationship in her column and the vast gulf between their respective backgrounds had brought them together with a fated inevitability. "What John told me was that, at first, she thought he was just a hick," said Jimmy Campbell, the jazz drummer who got to know Dorothy when he became Johnnie's musical director (and close friend) several years into the affair. "That's what bothered her in the beginning, when she was writing those things in her column.

"Let's face it, he still was a hick, but one who burst all of a sudden into a big star, and who had absolutely no etiquette. So, she took him under her wing and put some polish on him. She taught him how to sit at these big functions and use the right forks, how to go to parties with the top people and not screw up. And she started to dress him—what did he know? He had come right off the farm, and that fact bothered him too.

"Kilgallen, I think, was the only woman that he really had deep feelings for—I know he had plenty of feelings about her because I was there. She represented a lot of things to him—she had the power of the press, she was educated, she really taught him." Campbell paused, reflecting on the two. "Maybe you could call her a mother figure."

He cracked a skewed grin, "Maybe you could call him a motherfucker! No, no—she was a lovely, lovely gal. She was great. She loved his singing and she loved him . . . they were almost somehow, like, tied together."[18]

The bond with which fate linked them was strong enough to withstand considerable exertion. Dorothy, after all, had two teenage children, Jill and Kerry, from her sixteen-year marriage to Dick Kollmar. Dick was not one to sit back as Mr. Kilgallen; apart from his duties on the "Breakfast With Dorothy & Dick", which had been broadcasting from their town-house, via live remote hook-up 5 days a week since April 1945, he also starred as "Boston Blackie," one of radio's most popular sleuths, and still dabbled in a variety of entrepreneurial theatrical and charity ventures.

He made his bones as Broadway producer in the mid-40's with a string of lavish musical shows, all featuring as many half-naked women as could possibly be worked into a production number. On discovering that topless women were permissible under New York law so long as they remained completely motionless, he rounded up every well endowed showgirl along the Eastern seaboard and installed them, like set pieces, in his musical sequences. A veteran playboy (it was Dick, Earl Wilson claimed, who originated the phrase "Hubba, Hubba") now degenerating into a paunchy *roue*, he was a widely recognized philanderer able by dint of his wife's fearsome clout to caper with impunity.[19]

Dorothy, of course, was aware of most all his transgressions and had been for years. As a true blue Roman Catholic, ignoring these was, for her, requisite. Her tolerance evolved into a skewed, mute understanding which now she took advantage of. Just as none risked Dorothy's sting by tattling on Dickie, neither would any openly bruit about her and Johnnie's frolics.

Johnnie and Dorothy were thus able to paint the town red without fear. They began slowly, but soon covered the entire burg with thick lay-ers of crimson, sloshed by the bucketful from Greenwich Village to Harlem.

Johnnie's life suddenly gained the context and security it had lacked. With Dorothy at his side, the threat of scandal and opprobrium melted away, as did her own long-stifled yearnings. Together, they walked on air. Even more surprising, to her friends, they walked in Central Park. Dorothy actually went so far as to don slacks for these rambles, a supreme concession. No stranger to the best-dressed lists (she admitted to owning 138 pairs of shoes), her staunch high fashion/little lady wardrobe aesthet-ic was as well known as it was influential.[20]

His anxieties and fear, the early bright panic which had increasing-ly cursed Johnnie's hours, dissipated. The affair's sense of liberation evinced a powerful response in each. It brought changes—sexual, behav-ioral, psychological—as profound as any of the extremes either one had so far experienced.

* * *

Johnnie's life was marked by an almost cyclical pattern of epic ascents inescapably followed by disastrous plunges. Even on the rise, he felt as if in suspended free fall. The sequential convergence of fortune with disaster built a distorted reality, where an uneasily resigned anticipation of inevitable woe prevailed.

His emotional equity, shifting sexual whims, moods and tempers marked the same tidal ebb and flow; balance and order became transitory concepts, reliant almost exclusively on intuition. But Johnnie's perception was gauged more and more by the isolating, fantasy-based instruments of fame and celebrity: Star Psychology.

Star Psychology is a complex, skewed process peculiar to celebrity. It takes precedent over common sense and grants personal whim and irrational impulse a completely free hand. It knows better; the logical reaction to any given situation often becomes illogical, flat-out untenable. The obvious and straight-forward, filtered through a self-absorbed lens, is redefined and acted upon. It is a man-made instinct, informed not by racial memory and evolved reaction, but by tinsel-draped accolades and spotlights. Once accepted, it supplies answers to any question.

This psychology can dismiss, explain away, supersede or transcend any obstacle, no matter how deleterious the ego-fueled momentous course may actually follow. Previously foreseeable consequences became invisible. Johnnie had nurtured his Star Psychology since childhood, and these engines drove him atop pianos, face down on nightclub floors and to the top of Billboard's pop charts. These engines drove him to roller skate in drunk and disorderly charges, to pound upon the doors of strange hotel suites. Given his way of thinking, all of these were perfectly natural.

Such obscured perception is common, in some degree, to all who receive the fruits of fame, power and recognition. Old hat to Dorothy Kilgallen, Johnnie's use of it was unquestioningly accepted. What was new to her—Johnnie's revelatory brand of personal disimprisonment—affected Dorothy on a much more startling, primal level than his Star Psychology's typically flagrant disregard of societal rules.

Her recognition and embrace of that primal emotion seemed like the pay-off for everything her life had unconsciously built toward but, as her public spouse and mother role demanded, veered away from. She took journalism—real reporting, not her column—very seriously; Kilgallen had covered every high profile criminal case from the Lindbergh baby to Dr. Sam Sheppard. Journalism was to her a solemn (verging on sacred) obligation, one of responsibility, truth and principle, a devout commitment that won her recognition as one of the world's best working newspaper writers.

But this ethic overlapped into Dorothy's personal life, which was always conducted under the same scrupulous journalistic code. Limited further by a religious faith that demanded she ignore an unfaithful husband, it began to sour. By 1956, it was positively rancid. The soft whisper from life's other side now rang loud and clear to her. Johnnie's throaty encouragements to swing, to ball—to *celebrate*—created a resonant harmony. A slow, delicious corruption of her divisive, rigidly structured self began. The process was long overdue.

It was Johnnie's music that revealed all this to her. A powerful, throbbing message from life's other side, it spoke to an instinct that existed far beyond the restricted borderline of the tough-minded, high principled newspaperwoman/wife/mother. The message was exhilarating, leading her to realize the error of combining all her roles into one. When Dorothy let her hair down, the reversal was positive. She remained a first-rate journalist, but also became a round-heeled libertine of the highest order.

When Johnnie became her lover, the climaxes shared were explosively, incalculably nurturing. It was an ecstacy which shattered the psychic walls Dorothy had laboriously erected in an attempt to mask her own beautiful, running dog self—the very same moon howling, careless primitive Johnnie had released long before, and built his career upon. Together, Johnnie and Dorothy crashed out of reality and into their personal dimension. Given the Star Psychology's fantastically presumptuous, narrow-channeled thought process, they indulged themselves in a display of splendid excess.

In Dorothy, this was first manifested with lavish gifts and vigorous preening and gentrification of her new endsville love. Johnnie, for his part, enthusiastically administered a crash course in the Bacchanal. Each partook deeply of the other's sensibility, and entered worlds so foreign they may have well been on Mars.

But they were at P.J. Clarke's, El Morocco, the Plaza, the Stork Club—a world that belonged to Dorothy in a way that transcended the dry, formal respect Johnnie received. He was unquestionably part of the domain, but its atmosphere was strange, still unnatural to him. While accepted therein, he was a portentous alien.

Dorothy was that domain's unquestioned shaman and arbiter, High Sheriff of manners, physician of morals. All Cafe Society was under her thrall, a sphere of apparently limitless influence reaching far beyond mere Gotham society to the sulphurous depths of the underworld and the highest offices of government. She was all-powerful. When she partnered with Johnnie, all eyes looked away, all lips buttoned up; to do otherwise spelled disaster.

Johnnie and Dorothy. Dorothy and Johnnie. They created social shock waves as intense and electric as their marathon sex sessions. Charged, volatile, a shock from the beginning, it only became more complicated. This was a decisive alliance, as unlikely as it was inevitable, a scandal of epic scope that was nonetheless completely secure, inviolately armored against accusation.

Johnnie was sitting pretty. He had, at last, found his soul mate. With Dorothy beside him, he was shielded from any and all public attacks. His enemies' schemes and the trade's politicized duress could not touch him. Despite the scandalous nature of this illicit alliance, it drove up his wavering respectability. Perceived less as the unstable freak of 1952, he achieved a tenuous context in which to operate. Even more surprising, through Dorothy's tutelage, he slowly gained a recognizable aura of dignity.

The fact that Johnnie's public sanctity came from such an illegitimate partnership mattered very little. New York teemed with former n'eer-do-wells risen to fame, wealth and social prominence. The Stork Club's Sherman Billingsley was a former bootlegger and speakeasy operator. All knew Jules Podell and Jack Entratter had attained their exalted status through the ministrations of a notoriously violent and amoral criminal organization. It was in fact quite rare for a player to enter this glittering arena wide eyed and innocent.

When stand-up Bostonian Lou Walters arrived, he had heard all about how the town ran, but dismissed it as hogwash. Soon after work on the Latin Quarter got underway, three of The Boys paid a call on Walters.

They told him exactly from which companies he would be purchasing all his kitchen equipment, fixtures, linen, glassware, liquor and food. Walters laughed it off.

Promptly visited by a dour city inspector bearing five single-spaced pages of on-site electrical and building code violations, he realized there was, indeed, much more to all this talk than anticipated. "Mr. Walters," his electrician, a Broadway veteran, advised, "I think you better make a deal with these people."[21]

Rules must be followed. That was how they played it in Gotham. But Dorothy Kilgallen was in a position to change the rules anytime it suited her—everyone from the Mayor on down to Frank Costello (who occasionally joined her table at P.J. Clarke's) knew it. No longer would Johnnie have to fret about his cabaret card being invalidated. He could come and go, rant and riot, caper nude down Broadway during the evening rush hour if he pleased, completely without fear of reprisal.[22]

*　　*　　*

Dorothy was virtually untouchable, but was not without her fair share of enemies. She and Johnnie shared a prominent mutual nemesis: Frank Sinatra. Although Dorothy and Frankie had been major league chummy throughout his war-time glory days, something emphatically soured between them in the late forties.

Frequently questioned as to this rancor's source, she would never go on the record, publicly or privately, as to the specifics of their falling out. She hinted vaguely about having once refused a favor Frank begged of her; when Mike Wallace interviewed her for his P.M. East show, the rift came up. Dorothy said she herself was still at a loss to understand why and recalled how she once asked a friend of Sinatra's about it. "'You see,' the friend replied, 'Frank just doesn't like anybody to say no.'" Dorothy looked steadily at Wallace, adding only, "You take it from there." For his part, Sinatra told everyone that Kilgallen, after making a serious pass, was livid over his rejection.[23]

Whatever the reason, this private rift soon became, via the Voice of Broadway, an ugly public feud. When Frank's star began its humiliating descent, she only escalated the attack. Learning that he was making unkind statements about her to mutual friends, emotion ran high.

Dorothy chose to print his New York address. He moved. She printed his new address.

Worse, she ran snide items about his passion for Ava Gardner before, during and long after their marriage fell apart. He had a tombstone engraved with Dorothy's name delivered to her office. The battle came to a head when the New York Journal-American ran Dorothy's "Frank Sinatra Story" in February 1956. A blistering front page series that reviewed all of his many gaffes, feuds, vulgarities, assaults, failures and shady associates, she also publicly revealed his several suicide attempts.[24]

Frank took the gloves off.

At his next Copa engagement, Sinatra previewed a monologue which stayed in his act for the next nine years, all centered on Kilgallen and what an ugly broad she was. Midway through his show, in the hush between songs, he reached for his glass of Jack Daniels. "Dotty Kilgallen couldn't be here tonight," he said. "She's out shopping for a new chin." He took a drink, made a broad gesture and pleaded with the stunned audience, "C'mon, let's all chip in and buy Dorothy a new chin." The crowd tittered. He again lifted the glass, trumpeting "This is a toast to all my enemies." He spat a mouthful of whisky onto the floor and screeched "This one is for Dorothy Kilgallen!"[25]

Sinatra attacked her constantly with a withering, venal intensity. In the process he favored the American lexicon with a permanent entry when he coined, in Dorothy's honor, the phrase 'Chinless Wonder.' "You're being too rough," friends cautioned him. "I'm not being rough enough," he grimly answered.[26]

On stage at the Sands, he held up his car keys, squinted and asked "Doesn't that look like Dorothy Kilgallen's profile?" One fine day at the Stork Club, it was said that Sinatra noticed Dorothy, wearing a pair of sunglasses, sitting across from him. He arose, marched over and dropped a dollar bill in her coffee cup, announcing "I always figured she was blind." If true, it is at least to Frank's credit that he was not timid in doling out the abuse.[27]

Many were appalled. Louis Sobol, the columnist from whom Dorothy inherited *Voice of Broadway* (and a staunch F.S. supporter of long standing) lashed out at Sinatra: "His several recent derogatory remarks, directed at one of our fellow columnists—tossed off right on the floor of the Copa during his act—are not to be condoned. Regardless of what differences exist between Sinatra and the columnist, they should not be the subject of airing on a nightclub floor. They are in bad taste—and many of his most ardent admirers have expressed their shocked disapproval."[28]

Johnnie was more blunt: "The people that made fun of her—that was just plain sick." Sinatra's impotent rage was not wasted on his audience. "I saw him at the Sands," Igor Cassini said. "He was really quite vicious. But people laughed." TV talk show host Jack Paar also began insulting Dorothy ("Sad Creature," she said of Paar). At CBS "What's My Line?" began receiving viewer mail demanding the removal "of the Chinless Wonder."[29]

Dorothy refused to acknowledge any of this unless asked directly, but it became impossible to ignore. Attending a Broadway premiere, as Dorothy stepped out of her limousine, a disheveled bag lady pushed up against the police line and pierced the milling crowd's noise with a shrieked greeting: "Hiya Chinless!"

It was as close as anyone could come to damaging her, but in order to do so Frank made himself look like a jerk. The knowledge that Frank detested both Johnnie and Dorothy, yet was powerless to stir up any further stink only sweetened their passionate, open secret affair.

Once Johnnie entered her life, she dismissed the whole Sinatra magilla. They laughed about it. Dorothy needed Johnnie, hungered desperately for his touch. They tumbled into bed and screwed through the night at Johnnie's apartment; her car and driver waited at the curb outside, hour after hour. Her weekly limousine bill ran into hundreds of dollars. No price, however astronomical, would have been too high.[30]

Johnnie's life may have settled into a comfortable groove, but his record career was beginning to show signs of rigor mortis; his last release to hit the charts was "Johnnie's Coming Home," an overblown pop shuffle that barely managed to reach #100—for a week. Not acceptable. Shortly after he and Kilgallen came together, Mitch Miller scheduled a session for late June.

Miller had the song which he knew would put Johnnie back on top of the charts, "Just Walkin' In the Rain," originally recorded by The Prisonaires, a black vocal group who were all doing time at the Tennessee

State Penitentiary, and released on Sam Phillips' Sun label. Joe Johnson of Columbia's country division brought it to Miller's attention shortly after Gene Autry cut it in early 1954, saying it was a perfect tune for the Cry Guy.

Mitch had been after Johnnie to record it since May of 1954, when he flew to Hollywood only to find the disconsolate weeper was on a hard mope locked inside his suite at the Garden of Allah. They went into Radio Recorders', but after one miserable take the Beard, recognizing Johnnie was unable to turn in a creditable vocal, told him to forget it and go home.

But on June 29th, 1956, the Beard was bound and determined to make a hit record. Johnnie had cursorily familiarized himself with the songs chosen for the date; with new material, he always wanted a fresh approach. One, "Look Homeward Angel," was a melodramatic number that turned out to be one of the best things he had done for months.

Session leader Ray Conniff cooked up one of his thrumming, rhythm guitar heavy bolero arrangements. Johnnie poured his heart out and the resulting disk was exceptional. The sound is so eerily similar to Roy Orbison '60s hits "Running Scared" and "Crying," that those Nashville cats must have used it as a virtual blueprint—*sans* Miler's trademark French horn. The other songs recorded on that date were "In the Candlelight," a neutered throwback to Johnnie's spare 1952 sound, the prophetically titled "Weaker Than Wise" and "If I Had You," which was never released.

Having successfully gotten three titles out of the way, the musicians, back-up singers and Johnnie were already wearing down and began to joke and jive. Miller appreciated the levity, but considered this song crucial for Johnnie. A studio whistler came in to supply "Just Walkin' In the Rain's" plaintive intro, which led to further goofing off.

Their gags took an oral turn, so the Beard, always an earthy sort of cat to begin with, walked up to the microphone and rubbed his goatee against it. "He said, 'I want you to pretend this a woman's pussy,'" Johnnie recalled. "Of course, Mitch was never known for being tactful, and I was embarrassed when he said that in front of all the girl singers.

"I was tired and almost refused to do the song. I said, 'Mitch, I'm tired. Let's skip this piece of crap.' He said to me, 'John, this could be a song that'll do it for you. Try it. Give it your best.' So we did it in two takes, because it was easy, there was nothing to it." They were, in a sense, both right. It really is a piece of crap: trite, simplistic, sub-Ink Spots stuff. Johnnie gave it an appropriately on-the-money, straight pop delivery, and Mitch had the last laugh.[1]

Released a month later, it debuted on Billboard's pop chart September 1st and although it peaked at #2 (stiff competition from Elvis' "Love Me Tender," and Jim Lowe's "Green Door" kept it from #1), "Just Walkin in the Rain" sold a million copies. Johnnie's first RIAA certified gold record in years, he was back on top, at the height of rock and roll's first national commercial blush. He was immensely gratified. "Just Walkin' In the Rain" spent 28 weeks on the charts. Typically, Johnnie did not learn the song was a hit until returning from an overseas tour, he picked up a copy of Variety at the airport and was stunned to see his name topping the pop chart. Nobody told him anything.

Shortly after hanging his new gold disk on the wall, Johnnie cut two duets with Frankie Laine, who had turned his nose up at Johnnie's songs seven years earlier in Hollywood. In October, they made a propulsive record of Sister Rosetta Tharpe's hard rocking gospel song "Up Above My Head (I Hear Music in the Air)", with another brassy Mitch Miller train-wreck "Good Evening Friends" on the flip.

Johnnie was on a roll, making good records after a depressing slump, having sex, getting groomed and digging all of it. When he appeared on "Frankie Laine Time," on the 19th, he looked relaxed, happy, nearly natural. He and Laine did some bits together and sang "Up Above My Head." The spectacle of the Singer with the Steel Tonsils and the Nabob of Sob, working up a storm that threatened to pop cathode tubes all over the country, was a gasser. It was these two, after all, who first kicked open the doors for R&B and rock & roll, and both were still riding high and happy, turning on and (Pow!) swinging heedlessly while pop music, as a whole, slowly passed them by.

In November, Johnnie cut "You Don't Owe Me a Thing," a follow-up single to "Walkin'," that again featured the whistler but drew out a much better vocal performance from Johnnie. Even Kappy got in on the date, one of the only times he recorded with his boss. Johnnie stretched on this one, taking an idiosyncratic, playful approach, a unique sort of bubblegum jazz reading that was an altogether superior piece of song styling. Backed with a moody ballad "No Wedding Today," replete with ironic church chimes and a heartbroken throb in his voice, "You Don't

Owe Me a Thing" (released after "Walkin'" ran its course) went to #10 and stayed on the pop chart for 12 weeks.[2]

At the same session, they cut an extraordinary version of Leroy Carr's 1928 "How Long Blues." With clanking harpsichord rhythm, an incongruous notion that worked perfectly, and Johnnie keening a spooky, off-mike falsetto vocal riff throughout, he chewed through the lyric with emphatic, masterful skill. This was the music Johnnie was born to sing, and his re-definition of the blues standard was a breath-taking demonstration of the rare musical instinct developed in the black and tans.

With his commercial success and personal satisfaction reaching another zenith, Johnnie was free to operate as he pleased. The felicity visited upon him carried over to Mitch Miller, who let him choose the titles for his first 12-inch long-player. Three days after the "How Long Blues" date, Johnnie went back in to record "The Big Beat," a misleadingly titled album of rhythm & blues songs that stands alongside his best work from 1952.

He was singing better than he had in years. Free to deploy all of his sinuous, black-influenced blues phrasing, it was a return to wild, high and delirious Johnnie of the Flame Showbar. His voice thrives on the lyrics, dropping from scalding heat to frosty chill throughout a superbly assembled set of personal favorites. "The Big Beat" album is marked by an aesthetic sense of logic and completion, arranged and orchestrated with a taste and sympathy that, while still a bit too uptown professional, makes it a triumph from start to finish.

The titles provide a glimpse of Johnnie's personal taste and proved once again that when it came to the blues, as Jimmy Witherspoon said, "He didn't clown or bullshit—he did it with dignity." It opens with "Pretty Eyed Baby," which he learned from Ivory Joe Hunter, a Ray influence of long standing, offers three from the Basie song book, "I'm Going To Move To the Outskirts of Town," "I Sent For You Yesterday," and "Everyday I Have the Blues," the Memphis Slim blues standard which Johnnie first heard Joe Williams singing at Club DeLisa (Williams' 1952 Checker recording, with Basie, was what put the singer on the map).

Johnnie's deep, deft reading of "Trouble In Mind" displays how intimate a familiarity he had with the old-time Blues Jungle's tangled track, and his fervent penchant for now obscure blues women rings loud and clear. He covered Faye Adams' "Shake a Hand" (released on New York

nnie's 1951 mugshot and rapsheet as they appeared in "The Lowdown" scandal rag.

(L to R) Elma, Johnnie, H
and Elmer celebrating with
friends in Oregon.

(L to R) Elma, Hazel,
Johnnie, June Allyson
and Tyrone Power live it
up at Ciro's, fall 1952.

Ciro's
1952

One step ahead of
the fans, Albany,
New York, 1952.

Scenes from the Ray Tilt-a-Whirl (clockwise from top left): stage door, Oriental Theater, Chicago; bobbysox disheveled, location unknown; ducking out of a riot in Sydney; torn up in London.

The women in his life (clockwise from top left): Ethel Merman coaching Johnnie in a "There's No Business Like Show Business" production still; cozied up with Sophie Tucker; with Jane Kean, savoring his conquest of the Copacabana.

rothy Kilgallen and Johnnie between smooches at the Waldorf-Astoria, c. 1960.

Best man Johnnie with Judy Garland and Mick Deans on their wedding day, London, 1969.

Johnnie faces the Queen Mum after his disastrous 1977 Silver Jubilee appearance at the Palladium.

th drummer Herman Kapp and fan club members, Washington, D.C., 1960.

igh and dry: Johnnie as Bo
a "Bus Stop" publicity still.

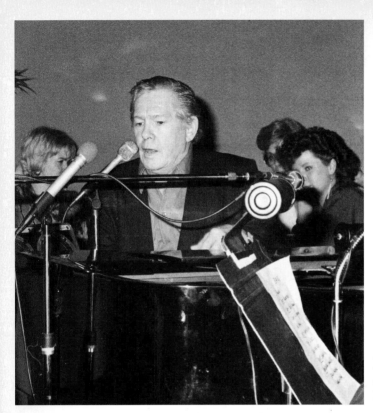

Looking lost at Vine
Street Bar & Grill,
Hollywood, 1984.

Laughing on the outside,
crying on the inside:
a late publicity shot.

independent label Herald in 1953, Adams' topped the R&B charts for 9 straight weeks; Little Richard cut it around the same time as Johnnie, LaVern Baker also had a strong seller on it in 1960; Elvis closed in on it in 1975),[3] and resurrected "I Want To Be Loved (But Only By You,)" written and introduced by proto-R&B queen Savannah Churchill on another Big Apple indie, Beacon.[4]

Most illuminating of all is Johnnie's sublimely forlorn, atmosphere-laden "Lotus Blossom." This is hip, inside stuff, one of the rarest and more exotic prizes Johnnie carried away from the black and tans. An obscure old reefer song, it was necessarily re-titled to fit both its meter and obvious commercial-release standards by piano pounder Julia Lee & her Boyfriends in 1947. "'Lotus Blossom?' Oh, that's an old, old song," Jimmy Witherspoon said. "It was really called 'Sweet Marijuana.' I still got that in my book, but I do a different arrangement on it than she did."

Johnnie was never a reefer aficionado, but the exotic melody and moody lyric are models of indigo desolation ("You alone can bring my lover back to me / even though I know it's just a fantasy / and then knock me clear out / sweet lotus blossom / please do . . .") which suited his style perfectly.

For the first time in several years, everything seemed to be going his way. Life was kind to Johnnie now, a perfumed, glistening and attentive lover who pledged support and affection. He tried not to think about such good fortune.

*   *   *

While Dorothy's grooming softened much of Johnnie's abrasively ingenuous behavior, it never penetrated to the degree many of her friends might have wished. The romance was a source of confusion to the high-toned social circle who gravitated towards her. When she, Johnnie and two of Dorothy and Dick's oldest friends, Hubie and Lillian Boscowitz, spent an evening on the town it was a tense situation. On one such occasion, they dropped in at the African Room, a Third Avenue joint whose name alone gave the conservative socialites a sick feeling.

Once inside, Mr. B. remarked,
"It smells terrible in here."
"I don't smell anything," Johnnie said.

"If you'd take that thing out of your ear and stick it in your nose," Boscowitz said, "You'd smell it."

Johnnie disturbed them terribly. "Very frankly, we didn't get Mr. Ray's message in any way, shape or form," Boscowitz, a wealthy industrialist, said. "It had to mean that we weren't going to see as much of her."

Lillian Boscowitz shared her husband's disdain. "He wasn't even scintillating conversationally . . . but she was mad about him," she said. "She didn't want to waste any time away from him when she had the opportunity to be with him. When she was with Johnnie Ray, she was extremely happy. She was exuberant."[5]

Quite. Dorothy, in fact, absorbed more of Johnnie's careless paganism then he did her poise. Together they had eyes only for each other. The rest of the world went out of focus and became nothing more than a backdrop for indulgence of their spontaneous passion. "Maybe we weren't the most discreet people in the world," said Johnnie, "but we were having the most fun. At certain times people got uptight, but that was their problem. I was never reaching for her boobs. Where does it say we're supposed to be saints?"[6]

Their relationship, whether locked away in Johnnie's bedroom or sharing a table at the Colony or the Plaza, was extremely physical. One evening at El Morocco, Johnnie was seen to remove Dorothy's shoe and kiss her foot. P.J. Clarke's owner, Dan Lavezzo, recalled many an evening when they "necked in the corner with the whole world watching." They made out like teenagers—aggressively. "The *groping* of each other and the *kissing* and the *necking*! Two tables away from me. This is no hearsay—I observed it myself at El Morocco and the Stork," television columnist Jack O'Brian recalled with earnest distaste. "It turned out that while she criticized other people, *Miss* Kilgallen was not too blameless in her own life."[7]

"Of course, the big gossip in New York was the Dorothy Kilgallen affair," Jane Kean said (a friend of Dorothy and Dick's, her first break on the Great White Way was in Kollmar's 1943 musical "Early To Bed"), "And it was a very, very heavy love affair on her part—she was really crazy about him."

When Johnnie turned 30 in 1957, Dorothy spent days arranging a "Progressive Party," with reservations for dozens of guests at seven different clubs and restaurants. The group included Yul Brynner, Jane and Betty Kean, Betty's husband Lou Parker, and Broadway couples like Gig Young and Elizabeth Montgomery, all shuttled from spot to spot in a chartered bus complete with wet bar.

"She had the bus decorated, and everyone was served cocktails between stops. The first course was served at the Colony, the second at Le Pavillon, and then the St. Regis, only the best," Kean recalled. "And at every spot, there were place cards that she had gone over and arranged that day, so you would be sitting next to a different person at every place we went to. And the last stop was at El Morocco, where everybody danced. That's a lot of work—you've got to be pretty crazy about someone to do that."

The delicacy of carrying on the affair was a complex matter of masquerade and reliance on high society's basically hypocritical amoralism and strictly nominal discretion. The only aspect of the subterfuge that bothered Dorothy was reconciling it with her faith's restrictive dogma. No problem, with Johnnie in on it. "We came to terms with the Catholic problem," he said. "Once we decided to have some kind of commitment, it resolved itself, though it didn't resolve itself in terms of her mother finding out."[8]

Her desire transcended everything, even threat of burning eternally in hell. Dick had shied away from performing his husbandly duties for years, resulting in a pent-up yearning which Dorothy released with stupendous, and increasingly careless, ardor. "God, she was starved for affection," Johnnie said. "Sometimes I didn't know how to handle it." While Dorothy's inviolate stature as Broadway potentate rendered both generally secure from accusation and exposure, there were myriad considerations and logistics which the pair flouted with increasing boldness.[9]

At first they carried it out with a classic smokescreen. "I was the Beard on numerous occasion," said Jane Kean. "Johnnie and I used to go to a lot of openings together, black tie first nighters at the Roxy theater, Radio City, and he was once quoted in the papers as saying 'the only two women I've ever loved are my wife and Jane Kean.' So we were already linked together. I used to go with them to El Morocco, the Stork—it was great fun. Of course, I'd be left alone at the table while they were dancing."

Johnnie and Dorothy, unless attending an event which the press corp, would be photographing, soon abandoned such camouflage almost entirely. Of course, Johnnie's widely held reputation as a strictly gay fellow allowed them an even wider margin. They were out together as often as possible.

Both adored "Gypsy" and saw the show so many times that one night each was handed the conductor's baton and allowed to take turns leading the orchestra. Johnnie saw "The King & I" front row center so often that he and Brynner developed a series of hand signals which Brynner would flash him during his deathbed scene, pertaining to everything from their after-hours plans to football scores.[10]

It was a mad, mad, mad time for each and they floated along on a tide of booze. "In the early days, when I first met Johnnie at the Copa, it was beer, beer all the time," Jane Kean said, "and then he got into the hard liquor. They were both drinking very heavily. And I don't remember Dorothy as being a drinker before that, I really don't think she was, but it started during that whole crazy period.

"We'd go to Trader Vic's and they'd have Scorpions, that drink served with a gardenia in it. Between the two of them, the gardenias would be lined up on the table, enough of them to make a lei around her neck— and that's very potent stuff. Johnnie was never into dope, to my knowledge, but drinking, yes. He drank an awful lot."

*　　*　　*

In 1957, Johnnie was contracted to make quarterly appearances at the Latin Quarter and alternate runs at Las Vegas' Desert Inn and Sands. Other domestic engagements that winter and spring were set for Newport, Kentucky's Beverly Hills Club (a mob enclave), San Francisco's Village, and at Sinatra buddy Paul "Skinny" D'Amato's 500 Club in Atlantic City (another hotbed of Mafiosi). Each averaged a minimum of two weeks, more often lasted four, and generally required the spindly weeper to perform two shows a night, 5 or 6 nights a week.

In July he flew to England to tape a television special for Val Parnell, did a string of dates in Blackpool, went on to play Rome, on to Germany for another television special and dates at U.S. military bases, then on to France for more U.S. service installation work. He headlined a gala at Monte Carlo's Sporting Club on August 16th, then opened in Ostend, then went off for more work in Britain.

Late August found him back in the U.S., to appear at the Michigan State Fair starting on the 25th. On September 9, he opened at the Kentucky State Fair, then flew directly to Australia for his fourth tour there. He closed in Melbourne, and opened in Honolulu the next night. He closed in Honolulu and opened a two-week stand at Hollywood's Coconut Grove on September 25 (he also taped two Ed Sullivan shows while there). He closed in Hollywood and opened in Las Vegas, working 4 weeks at the D.I., then flew up to Canada for another 4 weeks at Montreal's El Morocco, returned to the United States to open a four-week engagement at Philadelphia's Latin Casino and smashed on into 1958 with a five-week run at Brooklyn's Town & Country.

He grossed $400,000 from these dates, but the percentage drained by expenses and commissions was nothing compared to the toll taken on his health and temperament. Figure, too, on the hangovers, nightmares and lack of sleep, and the reality of Johnnie's day-to-day life gleams with a bloody, momentous desperation. There was nothing out of the ordinary in this slice of the Cry Guy's itinerary; he had maintained the same pace for the last five years running.[11]

This consistently ceaseless schedule had not allowed for any over-hauling of Johnnie's act; it was virtually unchanged. The last injection had been in 1954, when his "Live at the Palladium" album required new charts and titles (and arranger Joe Reisman, "who wrote great lush saxophone parts," as Bernie said, had done a fine job) but Johnnie's set list, staging and between song patter remained the same. Change was overdue.

Now, having scored several top ten hits, it finally arrived. Using Reisman again, they refurbished the entire act early in 1957. Johnnie was equipped with a chest mike, which freed him completely from the mike stand's visual anchor and allowed him to work and wail anywhere mood prompted. It featured "a shrewdly devised book that brings more of the ballads into the stint than formerly," Variety reckoned. "New act is obvi-ously designed for the smart hotel and tv route. Typical of the re-staging is his workover of "Look Homeward Angel" early on to establish the qui-eter more subdued approach."[12]

The refinement was not of a sort to cast Johnnie as a typical croon-er—he still worked like a 3-D kaleidoscope, tossing torso, sprawled atop the piano, pounding, gasping, wailing with all the rabid zeal of 1952. Visually, at any rate.

The very nature of the business had to a degree refined Johnnie, more than Dorothy's tutelage ever would. When a particular move or ges-ture suited a specific lyric, it was catalogued and retained, and his performance became a manicured and manifestly streamlined theatrical assault. Corn was a tear drop away; although standardized, he avoided seeming routine, and never sank to the point of trading on a false, rote hysteria.

If anything, as a May 1957 review of his debut appearance at New York's high-toned Waldorf-Astoria saw it, "Johnnie Ray seems a much happier man these days. Seemingly with good reason, since he's riding high again with disks and has attained the status of working the Empire Room." This was a step up, and another apparent spontaneous triumph.

The manner in which Johnnie graduated to this prestigious spot was a typical Broadway back-alley scheme. He was contracted to play these dates at the Latin Quarter, but "a flap over television appearances" had led GAC to put him in the Waldorf. Publicly, at any rate.[13]

In reality, it was a Lou Walters caper. Since late 1956, Walters had been preparing to pull out of his partnership with long-time cohort Elias Lowe. His first move was to announce that he would divest himself of interests in the Miami Latin Quarter, a shock for Lowe that turned to a slap when Walters also said he would erect his new Cafe de Paris on the site of Miami's old Copa City. He was laying groundwork for a master plan that did not include Lowe or the Latin Quarter. Despite the fact that the New York Latin Quarter was annually grossing five million dollars, Walters decided he could do better elsewhere.[14]

His New York warning shot to Lowe was this scotching of top draw Johnnie's L.Q. run, via a bogus brouhaha that turned the singer over to the Waldorf-Astoria. The Empire Room's E. Claudius Philippe was one of New York society's big guns, a Frenchman of perceived nobility and social grace who had established his name in 1951 with the April In Paris Ball, a lavish annual charity fete. He also oversaw august food and wine societies, Les Amis des Escoffier, a gathering of two hundred top chefs, and the Lucullus Circle, which hosted such high-octane capitalist gourmands as David Rockefeller, Duncan Hines, Bernard Gimbel and Alfred Knopf.[15]

Philippe of the Waldorf, as the 400 had titled him, was also a close friend of Walters. They had much in common, their habits, tastes, dress, a similar physical appearance, temperament and common vendors and business resources, with one significant difference. In reality, most of Philippe's fortune was corrupt, acquired through a series of food and service supplier kickbacks and tax evasion, and within six months, he would be exposed, charged, convicted and fined substantially for this activity.[16]

Walters' manipulation of this scheme was typical of what many contemporaries despaired in him at this point. His heedless decision to break from Lowe was purely empirical, based on whimsical instinct and pride in his track record, but ignored the tenor of the day—television's offering of the same acts he paid to appear, the undermining of pop music's recognized base by radical firebrands like Elvis—elements which spelled disaster to many nightclub operators. As it turned out, Walter's L.Q. split was catastrophically timed.

At this point, though, the Waldorf caper went off superbly, orchestrated to the point where "Philippe broke precedent by joining Johnnie Ray on the floor and telling the crowd how pleased he was with the singer." The stuffed shirts "split their mitts" over Johnnie all over again; Philippe's last-minute talent coup was a graceful success; Elias Lowe, without a headliner, was numb; Walters felt he had an implacable upper hand, and forged ahead. Johnnie, with invariably good reviews, simply continued to "beat on, heat and all, with considerable vim."[17]

Life on the road was as wild as ever. In Rome, at a pool side party where guests were encouraged to dive for bobbing bottles of champagne, Johnnie was said to have erupted with a streak of Tallulah Bankhead-esque nudity. Madly exhorting other guests to join him, he allegedly went so far as to have "pantsed" an Italian count and turned the whole affair into a skinny-dipping session ("I can't swear it was Johnnie who did this indignity to me," the outraged count said. "But all I know is he certainly loves diving. He was underwater most of the evening.")[18]

In England, he was said to have been up all night, "rollicking with a rolex," shooting cheesecake candids of British model and tv siren Norma Sikes, also known as Sabrina, better known as "The Playing Card Queen" and "London's Most Scandalous Nudie," and several other lurid monikers. "Johnnie Ray can hug harder than any man I know," said she. "He hugged me plenty and I didn't scream once!"[19]

He was considerably more serious at a Frankfurt press conference a week later. When asked about Elvis Presley, at the time being denounced from radio station control booths, Southern Baptist pulpits and gubernatorial manses all over America with a vehemence that outstripped the accusatory howls from indignant citizens Johnnie had already taken, he answered with obvious relish. "I'm inclined to sympathize with Presley in the controversy he's stirred up," Johnnie said. "He's accused of inciting juvenile delinquents. You can't tie a delinquent kid to a hit record by Presley.

"Charges against him are unfounded, unfair, bigoted." He was speaking directly to the trade, giving a speech he should have made about himself four years earlier. "People resent his success. Well, he'll be around a lot longer than most of them think, and his records have stimulated a controversy that's helped the whole record industry. We have Elvis to thank."

Did he, a reporter asked, think Elvis was influenced by Johnnie's own "tortured, twisting style" of singing? "A lot of people ask that," he said. "He might have been influenced, but then every performer has a lot of influences. I was influenced by Kay Starr and Billie Holiday. You could say that Bing Crosby was influenced by Russ Columbo and Perry Como." Realizing he was at the heart of the matter, this linear progression which the trade itself was only beginning to recognize, Johnnie's next remark was a revelation which pop music fans still refuse to accept.

"There is nothing new," he said. "Only a new way of doing it." Having gotten this off his chest, Johnnie rolled on, and continued to demonstrate his own flair for controversy.[20]

In Paris, he was keeping company with Genvieve Khotinoff, yet another busty blond model linked to King Farouk and Nicky Hilton, who was smarting after an abortive fling with Marlon Brando. This was, to Kilgallen's chagrin, no flack man's damage control stunt, and they were seen "making the rounds of hot spots, cuddling and cooing." Barely out of her teens, Khotinoff was a spitfire, and at Paris' Club de Paris, got so hot under her brassiere that she launched a bottle of Mumm's at Johnnie's head. Fortunately, "an adroit Frenchman, more concerned with salvaging the vintage wine than Johnnie's skull, caught it in mid-air and Genvieve burst into tears and apologized to Ray."[21]

Back in the U.S. to appear at the Michigan State Fair (with Jack Devaney's replacement, Lourie Younger, Johnnie's thirsty British play-mate, acting as road manager), he found himself where it had all begun— and nearly ended—Detroit. There were plenty of old friends to roar with, new ones to tangle up alongside, and trouble to get into. Invited to a party thrown by one of Motor City's social lights, he attended clad in Younger's kilts.

Staggering drunk shortly after they had arrived, Johnnie wandered downstairs to an empty bar/lounge and collapsed in a stupor. Singer Thelma Carpenter, who knew Johnnie from his days at the Flame (as a black variety artist who favored show tunes, she was never booked there—they considered her "too white,") happened by and glanced in. Carpenter was appalled by what she saw: Johnnie was spread out like a free lunch, surrounded by several tuxedo clad closet queens actively engaged in satisfying their hands-on curiosity over what a man wore under his kilts.

"These sons of bitches were trying to take advantage of Johnnie, because he was in such bad condition," she recalled. "He drank a lot and he was completely out of it, you know? And because of that trouble he had gotten into right before his record made it big, everybody in Detroit had been makin' jokes and talkin' trash about him ever since.

"And these motherfuckers—pardon my french—were all around him, getting ready to . . . well, you know what I mean. So, I went in there and yelled and screamed my head off, to get these guys away from him, which they did. And I went and told the host, who threw those bastards out of there and found the boy who had come there with Johnnie. We got a taxi and sent them home."[22]

They were making jokes and talking trash about Johnnie in every city in the nation. When he arrived at the Desert Inn, Tempest Storm was headlining "The Minsky Revue" at the Dunes. He wasted no time re-uniting with this paragon of red-headed wham.

"When I was starring at the Dunes, I had been going around with a Saudi Arabian prince, and Vince Edwards came to take me to dinner, then Nat Cole took me out, and all of a sudden here comes Johnnie Ray! And the pit boss called me over and said 'Boy, I tell you, you must have scraped the bottom of the barrel,'" Storm said.

"'What do you mean by that?' I asked him. 'It's the bottom of the barrel,' he said, 'When you go out with Johnnie Ray.' So, I told him, 'He's my friend, I don't know what you're talking about. He's a nice guy, an upbeat, classy guy and he has respect for women.' And that was the end of it."

Their first meeting in 1952 was not without sexual tension, and Johnnie, his taste for female flesh heightened by a kick-start arousal which Dorothy's intense response ignited, was trying to make up for lost time with Storm. "We went out and did the town, went to a lot of places together. Johnnie wanted to get involved—deeply involved," she said. "He said that he loved me dearly and wanted to be with me. I asked him what happened with his marriage, and all he would say was that it was a disaster but wouldn't go into any detail."

When she failed to tumble, he took a different tack. "I guess since nothing sexual happened between us, he denied all the stories about him in Confidential and Whisper," recalled Storm (who said she was "heartbroken" when he wed. "I thought 'I could have been that woman standing beside him at the altar—maybe all those rumors aren't true.'")

"He figured that if he denied everything and made me believe it wasn't true, eventually I'd say, 'Hey, you're right.' But there were so many rumors, and my friends talkin' to me about him that I did sort of 'put on the brakes.' I figured that if a person was undecided about which way to go, I didn't want to be involved. But it never did affect our friendship. He was a very sweet guy. Maybe too good and too sweet for his own good." Storm was one of a very few in Las Vegas with respect for Johnnie; the only others were those who got a share of his b.o. receipts.

Columbia set up for live recording at the D.I., capturing his new set on a LP released in early 1958. Many were relieved at the low-key mood of the "smart new act." As one reviewer pointed out, "wisely, he's dropped the femme kissing routine because last time many husbands and boyfriends took a dim view of the demonstration, especially when he left some of his make-up on faces and furs."[23]

The "Live in Las Vegas" album was heavy with standards ("Should I," "As Time Goes By," "Ain't Misbehavin'") and throwaway turns on recent hits. He delivered a couple of standout performances: a haunted reading of Jerome Kern's "Yesterdays" and a sublimely soft, gasping "Don't Worry 'Bout Me" that imparts a startling depth of candle-singed intimacy.

Despite his outspoken support for Elvis, something very few joined him in, Johnnie was definitely not aiming for recognition as a rock and roll prototype—who would after Elvis' leaden egg at the New Frontier? Nonetheless, Johnnie's undeniable role as such was being recognized by the trade as rock and roll's dominance of the field mounted. It was another paradoxical twist in the public's perception of Johnnie.

Variety began to regularly cite him as rock and roll's forerunner that autumn. Prior to arriving at the D.I., they reviewed his Coconut Grove

Wednesday night opener, where "the crowd was sparse but the applause was large. He should have made it with this crowd, *despite* the fact that he's one of the pioneers of the belter brigade and younger performers who have caught the public's fancy with the steaming beat and the rocking roll." Johnnie's act was not all that toned down: "On 'Such a Night,' he writhes, contorts and almost prostrates himself."[24]

At Brooklyn's Town & Country two months later, Variety came right out with it: "Indeed there are times when his tunesmithing shows lines indicating that he fathered the rock and roll movement, with the latter breed of singers expanding on an original and clean model propounded by Ray. He remains a performer of great potency, strong enough to hit repeated calls for an encore."[25] The issue of whether his hand shaped rock and roll was as ambivalent as his sexuality. When Edward R. Murrow asked his opinion of it a year before, Johnnie hesitated before replying "Well, frankly, Ed, I can take it or leave it." A crookedly mischievous grin spread across his face.[26]

The part Johnnie played in clearing the way for rock and roll was highly significant, in the United States and Britain. By breaking a word into separate syllables, giving each a distinct and individually phrased shape, he completely redefined vocal style; that, and his radical presentation, introduced the skeletal frame all American rock and rollers built upon—a fact acknowledged by everyone from the trade papers to Alan Freed, 1950s top cat arbiter of hip.

However, Johnnie's shattering impact on pop music's status quo has been nearly obliterated by the industry's aggressively self-serving revision. A broad pattern of distortion, its results were a narrow, authorized reality—what few recognized originators and influences still left on the contemporary accepted record present a truncated version of history.

The latter-day hysteria of Little Richard's howls for recognition and acknowledgement is a prime example of how key players have been routinely cast into the boneyard. No other performer, black or white, put his ass on the line the way Little Richard did, just as none could rival his inflammatory music and tumultuous society-shredding image. Yet by 1980, he was all but forgotten; only by acting the high-profile, hollering fool could he force his name back onto the popular honor roll.

This revisionist campaign was born through the paranoid reaction which rock and roll, a clear and terrible danger in 1957, stirred up in those unable to embrace it: flacks, song publishers, corporate strongmen—the Trade. Their fear was understandable. Rock and roll touched off a revolution, affecting morals, behavior, sexuality, values and racial attitudes with a swift impact Western Civilization had never before seen.

As a popular, wholly bi-racial phenomenon, rock and roll profoundly recreated social values all over America. It did so through a heady primitivism and lyrics which seemed to be written in letters of fire, blood and semen all over the country. One way or another it had to be met, head-on, and defused before disaster shook the trade apart entirely.

The process was slow, but once began, they constantly refined and perfected it, orchestrated to reach a degree of control never before exercised over any field of popular music. The reverberating effect this industry revisionism had was so pervasive and effective that only those who experienced it first hand or were part of the trade during rock and roll's first blush are able to give a clear account of what occurred.

"Because of marketing and the whole change in the business, there has also been a complete change of history about what really went down in the music business," Tony Bennett said. "Johnnie Ray was completely different from anything else before him.

"I have very strong feelings about it, and who knows why the marketing people changed the story, but now they only say it was Bill Haley & the Comets who was the big early influence, before Elvis Presley. I've got to explain it this way—they have a different story now. What I'm trying to say is that I consider Johnnie Ray to be the father of rock and roll, especially in Britain: the Beatles, Elton John all those people followed him. But now they never mention Johnnie Ray, and I don't understand it—because *I was there* Charlie, you know?"

In 1953, when Sam Phillips paced his Memphis Sun Studio's floor and told secretary Marion Keisker, "If I could only find a white man who sang like a negro, I'd make a million dollars," he meant, quite simply "another Johnnie Ray"—albeit a heterosexual model of same. The shock of Johnnie Ray was so intense that even four decades later he is still too way out, too dangerous, too *free* to accept.

Just as Johnnie himself was too wild, extreme and free to presume that such a derivative and limited art form as rock and roll was his child. The plain fact of the matter is that he was its father, but refused to acknowledge the sorry bastard.

16

Johnnie was so fired up and cocksure careless in his Kilgallen-bolstered self-assurance that, as the year drew to a close, taking philosophic stock, he realized his picture of himself was nearer to an ideal than ever before. Anticipation of his approaching birthday reached dizzying heights of ambitious gratification. His chosen gift would trump even Dorothy's Progressive Party of last January.

Johnnie's wealth was something he rarely thought about in concrete terms. His attitude toward money remained the same as in the days when he and Marilyn, as Mr.

& Mrs. Ray, were living on a weekly allowance of $80.00.[1] Expenses were Sol Lazarow's concern; primarily, his earnings were spent on booze, party favors and lavish gifts. His heaviest outlay came when the mood struck (as it did fairly often) to purchase a dozen or so first class round-trip airline tickets and arrange to import members of his European party crew to assist him in squeezing the cider from Big Apple niteries.

But Johnnie knew his wealth could be used for something more deeply satisfying. Money, he realized, was good for something that, within a few days' time, could eradicate the scars and blisters that flaked and festered across his psyche and return him to the pristine state of wholeness, grace and joy stolen during childhood.

Johnnie was going to buy back his hearing.

Secretly, he entered an undisclosed New York hospital on January 9, 1958, and spent his birthday in surgery. The press was called in the following day. Propped up in bed, with a huge bandage wrapped around his head and a doting, doe-eyed nurse melting beside him, Johnnie smiled for the photographers but did not answer questions.[2]

The operation was a flop. Doctors brainstormed, then suggested an immediate second go at it, Johnnie agreed. He went back for another attempt on the 12th.

On the 14th, in a special report headlined "Johnnie Ray Ear Miracle Thrills New York," Earl Wilson ballyhooed "the great good news that Johnnie Ray can hear after a second operation has Broadway again believing in miracles." By the second paragraph this cheery tone dwindled to more sober observations like "at least partly a success . . . it appears he is going to be able to hear."[3]

The basis of this story lay in the fact that Johnnie had detected a gust of wind vibrating the window pane next to his bed when Wilson called upon him. Earl was doing him a favor with the miracle angle.

While the first operation had been a failure, the second was a disaster. The surgery completely eradicated what remained of his left ear's hearing and also diminished that in his right ear by almost 60 percent. Happy birthday.

"Johnnie was very angry. He told me that at the time there was talk of a lawsuit against the surgeon, but nothing ever came of it," Bill Franklin said. "And all that publicity was put out so no one could accuse him of using the truth as a ploy for sympathy. That operation was a huge disappointment to him, and is also why he had to begin wearing his hearing aid in the right ear." They kept the miracle flack going for a month, up until he returned to the stage.[4]

Kilgallen's Voice of Broadway featured the climax:

> "Johnnie Ray passed his Big Test with flying colors—came onstage at Philadelphia's Latin Casino without his hearing aid and performed with all his old vitality and exuberance.
>
> The audience quickly realized the drama of the moment when he turned and sent a grinning 'I can hear you!' signal to the band, and by the time he came to the lyric 'Do your best and always remember that dark clouds pass in time,' there were tears in the eyes of many ringsiders."[5]

No doubt. The bitter poignance of Johnnie's feigned exult was agonizing. The painful necessity of this charade was the result of his fear of being seen as a cry-baby hungry for coddling. This refusal to court sympathy carried over to his private life—very few of Johnnie's friends were even aware of what had occurred. His childhood fear of being seen as a "weird kid" never diminished.

Accepted with the grim determination of an inveterate trouper, Johnnie went out and shopped for the most powerful hearing aid available. The fact that those which delivered the best amplification were also the heaviest and ungainly models meant nothing to him. True to his characteristic code, Johnnie walked away from strife and trouble into the bright artificial sunlight of his ingrained, deliberate construction of resiliency. He moved on.

After he closed in Philadelphia, Johnnie returned to New York for the ABC network debut of "Dick Clark's Saturday Night Show" on February 15. Johnnie appeared, along with another Danny Kessler discovery, Chuck Willis (hot with "The Stroll"), the Royal Teens ("Short Shorts"), Connie Francis, Pat Boone and Jerry Lee Lewis. The Ferriday, Louisiana piano pounder climaxed his performances with a move copped from Johnnie—the viciously swift backwards kick to the piano bench (a fact not lost on Dick Clark; interviewing Lewis's fan club prexy, Clark, to the young girl's horror, inadvertently substituted Johnnie's name for Jerry Lee's. Realizing the depth of this gaffe, Clark hastily added "I know you're going to hate me forever.").[6]

More astonishing than Johnnie's stoicism and swift return to the stage was the indisputable fact that his musical ear and ability were totally unaffected. Two months after his trip to the butcher, Johnnie was in the studio with jazz genius Billy Taylor. A pianist whose lulling, understated style would seem completely opposed to Johnnie's "blood, guts and thunder" they were set nonetheless to record an entire album together. The resulting disk, "'Til Morning," is one of his finest Columbia long-players.

A set of standards and ballads, they recorded a dozen songs in two days, on March 3rd and 6th. Taylor provided ideally tasteful and unobtrusive support, and his moody, languid piano improvised through as many choruses as inspiration required. No two and half minute pop ditties here, rather, this was a jazz session in the truest sense—flowing, loose, spontaneous, emotional. Johnnie was completely down with Taylor; his vocals are more relaxed, attuned to the mood and full of color.

Familiar material like the Ellington hit "I'm Beginning To See The Light," the Gershwins' "They Can't Take That Away From Me," Henderson, DeSylva and Brown's "It All Depends On You," Sammy Cahn's "Teach Me Tonight," Johnny Mercer's "Too Marvelous For Words," was romanced by Johnnie. He undressed the lyrics one by one, lay beside and caressed them tenderly.

His re-definition of Cahn, Weston and Stordahl's "Day by Day" is a lush gossamer passion piece, charged with a rich sense of romantic fealty and marvel that buries Sinatra's 1949 recording. The 1935 Tin Pan Alley chestnut "Hands Across The Table" is equally extraordinary—the subtlety and restraint, the quiet wonder in his voice is the last thing anyone (except Dorothy) would expect from him.

Johnnie was a balladeer of rare quality, gifted with keen insight and ideally languorous timing. Measuring the sumptuous economy of his singing against his increased deafness and lifelong protestations of the difficulty he had keeping time in his head reveals the purity of his instinct. At a time when his musical faculties were at their most unstable and damaged, Johnnie rose to give a superlative performance; his gift ran far deeper than anyone credited him for, to a depth that, with his disability, was near inconceivable.

That was always one of his greatest weaknesses—too damn much talent for the narrow funnel through which Columbia pop stars had to be squeezed. Even with the atrophy of his songwriting, corrosive effects of chasing commercial success via dozens of unlistenable bubblegum-crap songs and the ceaseless road work's erosion of stamina, Johnnie, against considerable odds and terminal drunkenness, manifested consistent artistic growth and increased interpretive prowess. "'Til Morning" was a trophy of vindication, proof that he had nothing left to prove to the public, proof that he was a master in his chosen field—proof that he was not a "weird kid."

Of course, Dorothy's attentions were all directed towards nurturing his inspiration, providing much of the fire and direction (stopping just short of telephoning Billy Taylor and personally arranging the date) that enabled Johnnie to conquer such vexing circumstance and turn out this gem. Up in the "Cloop," her fifth-floor bedroom *cum* hideaway sanctuary, she must have worn out several copies of the album.

The irony of his turning to jazz as rock and roll was tearing New York apart is a prime example of Johnnie's one step beyond timing. In May, Johnnie was back in the Latin Quarter. Several short blocks away Lou Walters had just opened his big gamble, the Cafe de Paris. He poured every cent he had into it; stripper Sherry Britten dived into a jumbo champagne glass, chorines floated over the floor on garlanded swings.

It was a disaster from the start. Technical problems plagued the joint, Britten's champagne glass began to leak just before opening; many suspected it was sabotage carried out at behest of his former partner Elias Lowe. Worse, days into the grand opening engagement, headliner Betty Hutton suddenly bowed out. Walters replaced her with Jerry Lee Lewis, fresh from the infamous British non-tour that ended in disgrace and scandal after Fleet Street went ape over his marriage to 13-year-old Myra Gale.

It went beyond disaster at Cafe de Paris. The Killer found himself playing to a near empty house on his opening and all but destroyed a grand piano. It became obvious that Walters was sunk; Jerry Lee didn't even bother to show up the next night. Neither did anyone else.[7]

* * *

Johnnie's life had shifted to achieve a social framework and center previously denied him. That center was his high toned new address: 163 East 63rd Street. At the corner of 3rd Avenue, his apartment ran through the entire fourth floor, over 2,000 square feet—huge by New York standards, and dozens of large windows opening onto 63rd street made it seem even larger. In comparison to this grandeur, his modest bachelor flat at 55th and Broadway seemed like a two-dollar flop house.

Howard Rothberg's decoration scheme was all soothing, autumnal green, earth, orange and salmon tones. The living room was loaded with antiques, Kilgallen-approved paintings, a hi-fi set, stacks of albums (Dinah Washington, Billie Holiday and Edith Piaf were heard constantly), with a scattering of furniture, including a long sofa covered with plush salmon velvet and a white grand piano. A spacious dining area opened into the living room, but with its large oak table and massive, candle-burning crystal chandelier (another gift from Dorothy) it maintained a formal, gracious appearance. Uptown, baby, very toney.

Of its three bedrooms, Johnnie took the master, left one for guests and converted the other into a den. Here an equally ostentatious leather couch sat before a huge RCA color television, with another hi-fi, and as a concession to Johnnie's rural background, a rather unique conversation piece item consisting of a tall polished-oak pole supporting a crystal globe full of crab apples.

The den boasted Johnnie's pride and joy, his gallery wall, dozens of eight by ten photographs in black frames bordered with strips of different vivid colors. Guests spent hours staring at the images—Johnnie with Queen Elizabeth, Johnnie with Elvis, Johnnie with Billie Holiday, with Sophie Tucker, with Ethel Merman. An equal number of fondly inscribed photos from friends and admirers like Noel Coward, Marilyn Monroe, and Carol Channing shared the wall. It was a dizzying collection.[8]

High class accoutrement aside, it was a party pad, one that swung full-tilt almost all the time, whether Johnnie was in town or working in Aruba. Lourie Younger, whose guest visa had lapsed and could no longer accompany Johnnie overseas, was always broke (despite claims he was heir to Scotland's Younger Brewery fortune) and stayed on to oversee things when Johnnie was on the road. Where else could he go?

The 63rd Street party was a constant, a given. Lourie became the majordomo/concierge/bartender; he kept the ice buckets full and bottles uncorked whenever necessary, which was often. Johnnie could return from a recording date on East 30th Street or 6 weeks in Australia and find a full-scale brawl of lit-up celebrities and beautiful young men. He never gave any of this a second thought. He dug it.

Kilgallen, the Keans, Yul Brynner, Merman, Sophie Tucker all dropped by regularly. Lilo, star of "Can-Can," the toast of Broadway, became a regular. When Lucille Ball was appearing in "Wild Cat" on Broadway, she too, often made the scene. There was the endless parade of waspy male models, and business associates, like Sol Lazarow, who would tip in for a drink and a few laughs. Bernie rarely made an appearance, but his wife Gloria, often visited.[9]

Johnnie became fast friends with Christopher George, making his acquaintance after the strapping actor wowed New York's gay community with a topless appearance in a deodorant commercial. Johnnie adored George, and they enjoyed an enduring and non-sexual relationship for years. Whenever he and then wife Georgia George showed up, Johnnie was at his most relaxed and attentive. The purely social whirl was in many ways new to Johnnie, and entertaining guests in his home became a major kick.

Essentially, it was an open house and Johnnie always warmed up before any guests arrived. The routine was well established and Lourie rigorously maintained the drunken mood which prevailed. Shortly after Johnnie rose, between 2 and 3 p.m., Lourie would scurry over with a sloshing tumbler of iced vodka, crowing "It's time!" He would pass the drink to Johnnie with a nurturing "just like mother used to make," to which Johnnie invariably replied "Thanks, mom."[10]

They were stoned by 5, when guests began to drift in and the pace began to upshift. Hub-bub was routine; Johnnie would not have had it any other way. A frequent visitor to 63rd Street described the scene there as "Strange. The times I spent at Johnnie's parties were . . . pretty bizarre. Quite often he wasn't even there. He'd have gone into the bedroom, or gone out, but it just went on without him. You'd have 20 or 30 people who didn't know each other, and there was no one to introduce anybody to anybody else."[11]

The guests were well-behaved, few of them were strangers to their nominal host and rarely included hustlers or sticky-fingered types. His pet Doberman Pincer Sabrina went a long way towards quashing any dark-lensed intent any outsider might have considered. "I remember when I first met Sabrina," Stan Freeman said. "Someone told me 'watch out, she's very protective of Johnnie.' And she was—once we were walking down the street and she actually lunged at a couple of fans who tried to approach him."

As a host, Johnnie was liberal to a fault. He would entertain at the keyboard, or more often, ask Stan Freeman to handle piano duties. If the proceedings began to bore him, Johnnie never broke it up, preferring to check out by locking himself in the master bedroom. If a particular guest struck him as obnoxious, he would mix up a "JR Special," a technique he described to Jim Low, another regular guest. "If a person bugs me, when they ask for a drink, I'll pour them a goddamn drink that'll knock their socks straight—they drink it, they're out on their ass, I put 'em to bed and forget about 'em," Johnnie said with a devil's relish.[12]

63rd Street's mainstay ritual was the Sunday evening "What's My Line?" party. Everyone gathered to watch Kilgallen, who joined them shortly after the program finished. They drank, joked, talked endlessly about Johnnie, his career, his records. He was the sun around which everything revolved, and some of the waspish young men who hung out there resented anything that obscured them from his light. Meaning Dorothy.

"It was just part of the Sunday routine," one of them sniffed, "that she drug him out of the living room into the den, in which there happened to be a long leather couch. We would sit in the living room and listen to all the activity that was going on in the den . . . It was lust out of control . . . You could hear it. We used to go over to the keyhole and look into the room. It became a joke among us."[13]

Johnnie's theme song at his parties became "Baubles, Bangles and Beads," which he would entreat Stan Freeman to play—endlessly. "I used to go nuts," Freeman said, "because Johnnie loved that song so much he asked me to play it constantly." After improvising on the melody for three quarters of an hour, he would finally stop only to find Johnnie at his side, begging him to continue.

The song, from "Kismet," was like Johnnie: bittersweet, minor-keyed, gentle, wistful, evocative. "'Baubles, Bangles and Beads,' that really was one of Johnnie's favorites," Marlin Swing, a frequent visitor, said. "And Stan is such a genius he could make the hairs on the back of your neck stand up the way he played that."[14]

Johnnie had met Swing at CBS that year when hosting his short-lived "Johnnie Ray Show," on the radio network. He would spin records, perform and have guests like Errol Garner and Sarah Vaughn. When Bernie, at producer Allen Ludden's suggestion, hired Swing to write additional material for the show it began a life long friendship. A classically trained musician, Swing's eyes were opened to the potency of pop through Johnnie. After he travelled to New Orleans to see Johnnie perform at the Roosevelt Hotel's Blue Room, things were never quite the same for Swing again.

"I became fairly close to him when we were doing the show," Swing said, "And of course he had been friends with Dorothy Kilgallen since before I met him. One night the phone rang and it was Dorothy—I thought 'Oh my goodness!' I'd never met her but I was enamored of her power and position, and she and her husband being 'Mr. & Mrs. New York,' at all the first nighters, so I was very pleased to talk to her. She asked 'Would you mind if I came over to the studio?' And of course, I said, 'No,' and she came over and we just hit it off right away."

The thrill was nothing compared to his first visit at her townhouse. "We were at the studio and after rehearsal Johnnie said, 'I'm going over to Dorothy's, do you want come with me?' We go over and were let in by James, the butler. I know it sounds phony, but his name was James. So we walked into this huge marble reception hall, with a staircase leading up to an elevator. We got in and I remember very clearly, I said "Pheeeeew," and shook my hand like this." (The universal "Some Dump, eh?' pantomime)

"We got up to the Black Room and there was Dorothy. The Black Room was the showpiece, it was the width of the entire house, the walls were painted flat black, with a kelly green rug, a white ceiling and red furniture. On one wall was a huge painting of a revolutionary war scene, in fact, one of Johnny Mercer's relatives was in it, which Dorothy pointed out to me. It was very elegant, a gorgeous room. Beautiful. So, we were talking and Dorothy said 'I'd like you to see the drawing room,' and she called James and said 'Would you light the drawing room for us?'

"It was a beautiful Victorian room, and the reason it needed to be lighted was because there was no electric light, only hundreds of candles, in candelabras and sconces in the walls. So James lighted it and we went down. In the elevator, Johnnie said 'You know, when we were coming up here, Marlin said Pheeew!' and waved his hand like I had. Oh, I was so embarrassed." Johnnie was as relieved by Swing's wonder (the same reaction Johnnie had on his first visit) as he was pleased over being able to embarrass him with it.

Dorothy became a friend to Swing. He soon found himself, like Jane Kean, a stand-by beard in their romance. "I became close to both of them, and since Johnnie and Dorothy were *very close*, I ultimately became the in-between excuse man. If she wanted to go somewhere, she'd tell Dick she was going with me. I would pick her up and take her over to Johnnie's, and then they would go wherever it was they were going, or sometimes I would go with them. I became the beard. Her husband respected and liked me and it all seemed perfectly all right."

Johnnie and Dorothy became increasingly bold. Another frequent beard was Stan Freeman. "Johnnie, of course, was gay, but he had this affair with Dorothy—it was real, I mean I know that," Freeman said. "I don't know what the attraction was, she was older than Johnnie, she was not an attractive lady. I don't know if he was trying to prove something to himself or whether it was because she was such a powerful lady. But obviously there was something going, and it lasted quite awhile.

"We'd go out together, sometimes just the three of us or if we were going to an event where we knew we'd be photographed, we'd bring along another woman, sometimes Jane Kean, or various other people. Dorothy always had a chauffeured limousine, and at the end of the night we'd drive up to Dorothy's house—I don't know where Kollmar was—but they would get out, and Johnnie would say 'Wait for me.' Then they'd go up into the house and I'd sit there for an hour, until he was through and then he'd come out and take me home.

This chicanery was primarily wool to mask Kollmar's bloodshot eyes. The situation, however, was not that simple—Dorothy did her fair share of looking the other way, and ignoring Johnnie's "With Love From Your Little Man" ID bracelet was the least of her worries. Throughout their affair, Johnnie had several concurrent male lovers, a number of whom actually shared the 63rd Street apartment with him.

He still often welcomed his longtime paramour Stan Halpert, and later Hank Wesinger (who met Johnnie through Howard Rothberg in 1959), Stan and Dorothy's nominal rival. Dorothy's attitude remained surprisingly benign. The only aspect of her strained tolerance that bothered Johnnie was a running joke about Stan, who modelled as Steve, from which arose a series of wisecracks. "And Stan/Steve—or is it Steve/Stan?" Dorothy would say. "Dear me, I can never keep it straight." The gag annoyed him, but he was scarcely in a position to get huffy. Johnnie and Dorothy were true libertines with the moral capacity of two Bowery alley cats, and preferred to concentrate on preening and purring among themselves.[15]

When they hit the bars, it was with vigorous aptitude. They continued to celebrate each other's company with such deep, concerted effort that even their most accepting friends wondered at it. "I always felt that Dorothy was a good influence on Johnnie, yet there were times when I'd see them just smashed out of their heads," said Don Ovens, a Capitol flack man who was friends with both Marlin Swing and Johnnie.

"One time I came out of P.J. Clarke's, after Johnnie and Dorothy had been in and left," he recalled. "I was walking up Third Avenue, where there were a lot of antique and junk shops. At that hour, of course, they were all closed, and it was very dark. About five doors up from P.J.'s, I saw the two of them lying in a doorway. They had just fallen down and passed out. I recognized them immediately, so I got them up and hailed a cab. They were laughing and carrying on like it was very funny, 'Oh, we just decided to take a little nap.'

"That was the only time I saw them that bad off, and it was amazing because no matter what Dorothy was drinking the night before, the next morning, she was right at work. I used to take a lot of artists up there, who were booked as guests on 'Breakfast with Dorothy and Dick,' and she was always sharp as a tack."[16]

Johnnie and Dorothy pursued their boozy passion with unbelievable zest. Such resiliency could not last.

*   *   *

This increased degree of sociality and now constant gaggle of in-house friends was maintained to the highest degree by Johnnie. He began flying back into New York whenever he had a chance, even if only for 24 hours. After years of star spangled hurly burly and a phony social life solely based on the attraction of his fame, Johnnie genuinely thrived on 63rd Street's anchor.

He was elated by the remarkably odd and cherished extended family. Never mind that he called upon many to lie and masquerade as beards for him, or that they routinely peeped through his keyholes trying to catch . a glimpse of a fabled physical attribute; the sense of ongoing relations with a steady cast of friends was an emotional charge he was starved for.

Kilgallen, Marlin Swing, Chris George provided emotional links to a peace and tranquil contentment he felt had been denied by career. Instead of the ghost-self he recognized only under the spotlight, Johnnie now had an operative self, a natural, day-to-day persona. The renewal of his perception as a human, a civilian—rather than a freak commodity shielded by bouncers and red-faced cops—was nearly as intoxicating as his double vodkas and chloral hydrate "jelly beans." Taken altogether, Johnnie felt a wonderful, nurturing high.

So, he went back and forth, in and out of New York whenever the theater was dark. He returned not only for soul-renewal and sexual release but also to keep up interest in, and operation of, one of Bernie's more ambitious investment schemes. The days of Ray compacts, Teardrop suits and selling 30,000 dozen pairs of Ray bobbysox a week were far behind them. Royalties had dwindled to nothing, license deals were not renewed and Johnnie Ray Enterprises was disbanded.

Johnnie had been prevailed upon to lend his name to the most ludicrous venture yet, proposed by Bernie and Gloria Lang as sure-fire, the germ facility for what they assured him would become a regional, maybe even national chain. The first opened in mid-town Manhattan in 1958: Johnnie's Bowl 'N Bite combined two of America's favorite pastimes, eating and bowling, into a bizarre whole. His friends were at loss to appreciate the concept.

"The Bowl 'N Bite was on the East Side, somewhere in the middle fifties, and it was sort of a delicatessen. They served lox and bagels, things like that," said Stan Freeman. "I used to go there because I was a friend of Johnnie's, but you couldn't carry on a conversation because of all the noise from the bowling lanes. It lasted, I think, almost a year. It was supposed to be a chain but I don't think any others opened."

The place drove Dorothy absolutely mad. "What an operation! Can you imagine anything as devoid of class as 'Bowl 'N Bite'?" she would moan, eyes rolling. "Ye gods, he should be in a tuxedo at the Waldorf, greeting his guests and entertaining at a grand piano. But 'Johnnie's Bowl 'N Bite!'" It confirmed something Dorothy already suspected—that all was not right with Johnnie's management.[17]

She began to question other aspects of his professional life and presentation. She carped at his habit of doffing his jacket and loosening his tie after the opening number, derided his patent leather footwear, suggested changes in the staging and bemoaned his record covers artwork. After the Bowl 'N Bite closed, Dorothy became convinced that Bernie was inept. While Johnnie bristled at these observations, he should have reached the same conclusions.

He was still hot as hades in Britain, Australia, South Africa, Brazil and Argentina, and a solid draw at major cosmopolitan rooms like the Latin Quarter, New Orleans' Roosevelt Hotel's Blue Room and Hollywood's Moulin Rouge, but bookings elsewhere in the continental US were increasingly more Bowl 'N Bite than wine et dine in nature. The blush of success which "Just Walkin' In the Rain," and "You Don't Owe Me a Thing" brought was two years past—ancient history, long forgotten.

After 1957's string of dreadful record flops (grating bubblegum like "Pink Sweater Angel" and "Texas Tambourine," some of his all-time worst releases) and the public humiliation of the Bowl N' Bite, it was obvious to Dorothy that his prestige was in danger. They began to argue about it.

"Why are you so blind?" she shouted. "Can't you see what's happening to you?"

"Tough titty! I've got a contract. I've got a manager," he hollered back at her. "*He* tells me what to do."

Tension never hung in the air for long; it was dispelled between the sheets.[18]

Dorothy took action wherever possible; her faith in Johnnie as an artist was as unshakable as her love for him. When Betty Whyte, a friend affiliated with the International, a new Manhattan club, asked for a favorable mention in Voice of Broadway, Dorothy agreed—conditionally. They had to book Johnnie Ray. With some reluctance they did. At the time, Whyte had asked "Do you really think Johnnie is such a great talent?" Dorothy replied, "You have no idea of the depth and sensitivity of the boy." No one did. Depth and sensitivity were hardly the popular vogue. Johnnie's was often obscured, buried under brass and bubblegum.[19]

Johnnie had followed through with her encouragement to exploit these qualities via "'Til Morning," and done a highly creditable job. The next step was even more ambitious. Johnnie was set to record, on September 9, with Duke Ellington and his Orchestra. Ellington, Prince of depth and sensitivity, was feeling the pinch of rock and roll and bebop himself. Together, perhaps each could triumph.

A most exciting prospect, so much so that Johnnie arrived at the East 30th Street cathedral studio with a two-limo entourage. Johnnie and the Duke already knew each other (since escorting Elma to an Ellington date years earlier—a rather different experience than spinning "Take the A Train" on her portable out in the Oregon woods) and everyone involved was curious as to how the pairing would go.

Billy Strayhorn, Ellington's musical alter-ego was still scribbling out the charts when the party entered. The session began smoothly. But Johnnie, who had never worked with such a musically adventurous band, was unprepared for the free flowing length of Strayhorn's arrangement. The first number assayed was Ellington's "The Lonely Ones." Lyricist Don George recalled the session:

> Johnnie got up on the stand with his copy of the song. He was a pro, had rehearsed the songs and knew them well. Johnnie was singing and the band was playing . . . Johnnie was singing and the band was playing . . . Johnnie was singing and the band was playing . . . and they still hadn't come to the end of the arrangement. Johnnie stopped singing. looked around and held up his hand for silence. Duke hit a sustained chord on the piano. The music stopped, and everyone gave Johnnie his complete attention. He said, "Gentlemen," and paused. Raising his voice a number of decibels, he yelped, "What the fuck *is* this, an LP?"[20]

Everyone cracked up, and they finished without further incident. The results, "The Lonely Ones" and "To Know You Is To Love You" were merely fair; Don George had tailored the lyrics a bit too close to the restrictive Tin Pan Alley pop Johnnie needed to avoid, but there is an over-all slightly exotic air of Ellingtonian grace that Johnnie complements with the easy heat in his vocal. "The Lonely Ones" emerges as the superior effort, and both sides outshine by far the majority of Johnnie's latest efforts on disk.

After the session, Johnnie left for an engagement at Chicago's Chez Paree. Late in life, he would call it "an honor and great privilege to record with Duke Ellington." Ultimately, that was all it was. "We did that date with Ellington," Bernie said. "But they buried it." The songs were never released.[21]

* * *

Johnnie closed at the Chez Paree, and set off for an October tour of Britain. He was booked onto BOAC's maiden jet-liner flight out of New York, an atom age thrill. The occasion, like so many in Johnnie's life, seemed to call for a celebration. "We all went out to the airport with Johnnie, it was me, Betty and Lou, Dorothy, and some other people," Jane Kean said. "Because this was such a big deal, the very first jet flight. We were all concerned, asking ourselves 'oh, is this really safe?' But the atmosphere was like a cocktail party, we all drove out together, had drinks, and saw him off.

"Before he left, Johnnie asked me what kind of souvenir I'd like him to bring back, so I just said, 'oh, just something white and gold, something for the apartment,' because I had just moved into a beautiful new place on Central Park South. I thought he'd just get an ashtray or something.

"But when he came back, he brought me a full set of Wedgewood china, the white-and-gilt pattern, and he had carried it on the plane with him! When he came back from a tour of Brazil, he brought Dorothy a huge pink quartz ring, it was just beautiful. Johnnie was always doing things like that. He was very generous." Why not? Johnnie only thought about his money when he was ready to spend it, and he could shop for gifts at the most exotic bazaars and gracious shops on the globe.

After Britain, Johnnie returned to Brazil and Argentina, then made his debut in Santiago, Chile, a hectic two-day engagement during which he performed at the Astor Theater and Hotel Carrera, with an additional personal appearance at Radio Cooperative Vitalicia—hounded non-stop by rabid fans. It was just Johnnie and Kappy ("my musical director and friend,") on the road now, two little men toting all the band charts, and that damn set of Wedgewood.[22]

They struggled through endless roiling, sweaty mobs and innumerable difficult rehearsals with local orchestras. It was hard work—the flights alone were exhausting—and the drain was intensified by the fact that they carried no other road crew. Overhead and costs were an increasingly pressing concern for Johnnie. And an even bigger one for Bernie.

But there was another more pressing concern that Bernie should have been attentive to—Johnnie's health. The years of drunkenness, poor sleep ravaged by nightmares, pills, more pills, atrocious eating habits were running him down. He felt more and more dissipated more and more of the time, and ate more and more pills to counteract it. His annual physical had not turned up anything serious and Johnnie pushed on. What, he worry?

He closed out the year at a Philadelphia hotel, staring through a glaze at the shirt fronts and furs and burning up with thoughts of the party he was missing at Dorothy's. She and Dick hosted the only New Year's Eve affair that mattered in Gotham, costume parties legendary for their decor and entertainment. Just as at the Marion Davies reception, a series of rooms duplicated specific nightclub interiors, with entertainment in each by the likes of Judy Garland, Count Basie, Billy Butterfield, and one or two of the top hotel dance bands. The parties invariably ran through the night and past sunrise. Onstage in Philly, Johnnie was positively green with envy.[23]

Envy and jealousy were not unknown elements in Johnnie and Dorothy's relationship. Although ignoring Johnnie's various attachments with other men was as easy for Dorothy as slogging through the psychic dirt required to organize the ring of beards their relationship demanded, any other woman who came near him was in for the treatment. One night at the Waldorf, "She left the table for a moment and some pretty young girl usurped her chair and proceeded to tell Ray how good she thought he was," recalled an unnamed "friend" in a New York Post profile on Kilgallen. "Dorothy came back [and] flew at the girl [telling her] to 'Keep your hands off my escort and leave the table.' It was the only time I ever saw her lose her temper in public."[24]

That her emotion ran so high—and this was high dudgeon indeed for Dorothy—was hardly a surprise. The many tales of Sabrina, Genvieve and Tempest had not eluded her, but the bond between Johnnie and Dorothy always overrode these flare-ups.

Shortly before the record date with Ellington, Johnnie played an August engagement in Hollywood, at the former Earl Carroll Theater at Sunset and Gower, which promoter Jack Sennes had recently purchased from H.D. Hover. Sennes redecorated and retitled the huge room as Los Angeles' own Moulin Rouge. Among the well wishers who attended opening night was Jack Devaney, whose party included Bill Franklin, a young man who by night shared both Devaney's home and heart, while trying, by day, to make a name for himself as a motion picture flack.

Franklin, a dark-haired, handsome twenty-year-old with piercing blue eyes, knew all about Johnnie from Devaney but had never seen him perform. Like Dorothy seven years earlier, Franklin too was "smitten, overwhelmed by the electricity" of Johnnie's gasping, jaw-grinding style. Several nights later Devaney threw a party for the singer at his home on Laurel Canyon's Appian Way. Johnnie showed up drunk, got even drunker and wasted no time in making a pass at Franklin. By his Star Psychology lights, he saw no conflict in chasing after an old buddy's squeeze. Then again, neither did Franklin. It was a sneaky start for an alliance that turned out to be as decisive as that which Johnnie already enjoyed with Dorothy.

Dorothy had been bolstering Johnnie's self-esteem and polishing his image for four years. Her influence was pervasive, even affecting the most personal and guarded area in Johnnie's life—his

music. None of her direction was erroneous, and each suggestion and change supplied by her was right on target. Johnnie had always been ahead of popular taste and whim, and now he pulled further ahead, gently navigated by Kilgallen's instruments toward the only idiom flexible enough to comfortably accommodate him, jazz. He had worked with the best names in the field; it seemed a logical place to go.

But the 1959 model of Jazz was, for all its toplofty refutation of accepted order and regulation, an increasingly restricted field where in-house rules were paramount. One could invent one's own rules so long as they fit into the accepted framework of artistic evolution, but rules they must clearly be. Wrong for jazz, they were also wrong for Johnnie Ray.

The shattering replacement aesthetic provided first by bebop's Charlie Parker and then climactically deconstructed by John Coltrane toweringly prevailed, heightened further in Parker's case by death's glamorous hindsight. To play along, one must do as they did—replace emotional appeal with vulgar mechanics, strive for the most *outre* and unappealing squalls and eddies conceivable. Entertainment was out. Mouldy figges, man. Even Louis Armstrong was a square.

The rejection of entertainment by jazzmen (who loathed R&B honkers because they were so demonstrably earthy, humanistic and well loved) created a Give-the-People-What-They-Don't-Want ethic. Despite claims of artistic profundity by high-handed, brown-nosing critics, the jazz body politick was a musically bigoted, ultra-hincty jive routine. It ran from everything Johnnie thrived on and espoused: Love and Beauty, replacing it with the agonizingly turgid and psychotic-cerebral "Love Supreme" bag.

Johnnie was all about Love Supreme; not the mysterious squawks blown by nodding heads with hooded yellow eyes, but a Love Supreme as it could exist right then and there, if people would open up to it. Johnnie's love supreme coursed with hot blood, gleamed with late night perspiration. It was a hands on, groping, gasping musical celebration of emotional potentialities, drawn from the rhythm & blues realism and heat of Big Maybelle and LaVern Baker, all of which jazz denied in favor of avant garde junk-blind falsity. Jazz was no place for Johnnie to attempt to settle in.

The only other field in which he could frolic, rock and roll, reduced celebration of love and beauty to insignificance. The love, mystery and beauty that Elvis had first threatened the world with in 1955 became a commodity, one shouted about endlessly but never explored. When public reaction first curdled on rock and roll, they quickly watered down the message into a simplistic, rote emotionalism, then replaced it altogether with an updated version of harmless Tin Pan Alley spooning, packaged as neatly and cheaply as a Tootsie Roll. The powerful erotic forces which had kick-started the entire sound in the first place were denied and forgotten. (No wonder Elvis included a searing "Such a Night" following his 1960 discharge and return to the studio. Like Johnnie, he was already anomalous.)

What was left for Johnnie Ray? He was cursed with a primal sophistication and sense of theatrical tradition that threatened both jazz and rock and roll. Johnnie Ray did not flout convention as a grandstanding form of entertainment nor race about the stage confronting and shattering taboos as a slick shtick—those were notions he simply never recognized. Even as a child, he discounted these rules long before they took root in his consciousness, a rejection as deep-seated and natural as Johnnie's musical drive.

That was why it seemed so threatening when, as he often described it, "Johnnie Ray went out of control and started making all these headlines in 1952." He was like some kind of frightening Atlantean, so far above, and such a stranger to established social mores that few dared acknowledge or confront the blood-churning wholeness of his artistic thrust.[1]

The hour had passed for Johnnie Ray. The recognition of his ability to incite emotional tempests and physical riot, "the great and sacred power" he vowed six years earlier never again to abuse, had cast him further into a mire of imbalance. The leniency shown audiences by choosing to muzzle and soften his presentation and message was the biggest mistake of his career. They still went after him, and Johnnie suffered artillery fire and bayonet stabs from an army of outraged squares in gray flannel. These attacks were delivered with an intensity that could not have increased even if he had carried out his firebrand antics to their extreme and logical conclusion—the mysterious "I'll do something more for them, I'm just not ready yet . . ." he menacingly hinted in 1952 interviews.

Johnnie's timing was always terminally anticipatory. He was out on the front line of the 1950s cultural and ideological war. A duty bound trouper, Johnnie was, in his heart, fearful. He even frightened himself, but stuck it out. By 1959, there was no choice but to dig in and go by the book. The nerve required to launch an offensive was more than he could muster. And that was the only move from which a positive result could have been achieved.

Johnnie's inability to suit word to action can be traced directly to the fact that he stood alone. Bereft of an artistic context or social framework, there was nothing behind him to shore up confidence or offer encouragement. More and more Johnnie felt "Panic all around me, the black of night surrounds me, like a child who's been left alone" (as he wrote in "Mountains in the Moonlight.") Rather than concede and serve the lunar influence, going out as a lupine blues shouter, Johnnie hung on, the frightened child awaiting his mother. And as it turned out, she was Dorothy Kilgallen.

Her influence re-enforced his esteem and seemed to validate his choice to stop pushing and hold tight. Her power managed to keep him lingering and tingling on the cusp of legitimacy, her nurturing clasp had led to a cessation of his anxieties and shored up what few shreds of determination lingered within. For all his missteps and concessions, Johnnie was as true to himself as he believed possible.

And he was having a hell of a lot of fun. Johnnie was balling the Gala-jack, making every night a big time—his ultimate show of personal conviction and dedication. But the constant exercise of this credo was catching up with him. The years of pill gobbling and his mounting tolerance to their effects took its toll by rendering Johnnie's control of his bladder quite unpredictable. His bedroom was now fitted with blackout curtains and rubber sheets, the requisite furnishings of one on the brink.

Lourie Younger, in for the long haul at 63rd street now, reflected the toll such hedonistic ritual was bound to take. A chronic dipsomaniac, barely able to maintain upright position, he poured booze down his gullet until oblivion destroyed consciousness.

Several months earlier, Johnnie had prevailed upon Dorothy to help Younger get his visa straightened out. She easily rectified his status with a well aimed telephone call or two; now she realized it had been a grave mistake. "I think Dorothy regretted that for the rest of her life," Marlin Swing said. Neither a pretty sight nor pleasant companion, Younger in Dorothy's view was downright creepy. She reached a point where she was no longer able to screw in the apartment if he was there. And for Lourie, even a trip to the corner bar was a major undertaking. He was always home.

Resulting from Johnnie's over-generous and accommodating nature, his homelife was becoming dark, twisted. Built around blind childlike simplicity, the swinging 63rd street scene precluded recognition of such tawdry and unnatural circumstance as keyhole peeping and strangers sleeping it off. By light of day and pain of hangover, it was easier to take another drink and forget it than rectify or improve the situation. Johnnie had precious little energy to waste on domestic concerns.

And he was never home for long; he rolled on and on and on, spending weeks in Texas's tonier hotel showrooms and nightclubs, a familiar smear of footlights, keyboards and audiences. At the Houston Hilton's Continental Room that February, he was at his mildest.

Opening with "Who's Sorry Now?" ("You're sad! I'm glad—you're bad!"), he eased into "Walkin' My Baby Back Home," loped off stage to "nuzzle a femme," then returned to the piano to accompany himself on "Just Walkin' in the Rain" and "All the Way." It was clear to reviewers of his opening that even with "the superb staging, including a spot that picks up only Ray's head and shoulders . . . the anguish is gone." The anguish was not gone—Johnnie was simply too weak to conjure it up for the typical K.O. his act revolved around.[2]

Johnnie closed in Houston and flew to Nashville. There, on March 9-10, he recorded an album of traditional Western songs and folk standards, released as "On The Trail." It was a poor commercial choice—especially at this crucial period in his cooling relations with Columbia. But Johnnie's emotion, as ever, took complete precedence over practical consideration. This was an affectionate and filial homage to Elmer from his son, the payback of artistic debt from one musician to another.

Songs heard throughout childhood, he rendered them with deliberate, gorgeous measure and soulful depth. Johnnie poured it on, making them sound more like "Little White Cloud" than the campfire staples every American grew up on. Familiar titles like "Home on the Range" and "Red River Valley" were transformed by a delicacy and restraint the material was rarely favored with.

Bradley's Barn was a far cry from the vaulted ceilings and uptown guitar mafia of Mitch Miller. Here, Johnnie worked with Boudelaux Bryant and a close-knit team of dyed in the wool redneck musicians, completely foreign to him. He remained as natural and as in command there as he had been with Billy Taylor. Johnnie was still proving what a great interpreter he was, even completely divorced from his black influence—this is a white man's record in every cultural and artistic sense.

The salty, hell-for-leather, often obscene lyrics of true 19th century cowboy song bore little resemblance to its commercial descendent. Western song as we know it was, for the most part, codified, updated and recreated in Depression era Hollywood by the Sons of the Pioneers and

Gene Autry. But this modern synthesis relied almost entirely on lyrics that, like Johnnie's own, painted lush, idyllic pictures of a dreamy paradise where wind-strummed sage and lazy sunsets were wondrous events delineated with almost mystic reverence.

Most revolved around the same nature-obsessed aesthetic, closely linked to themes of destiny and mortal insignificance lost in a beautiful but dangerous wilderness. Death is a recurring mainstay, viewed from a plaintive, resigned, almost atavistic perspective that Johnnie felt profound empathy with. His readings are superlative, charged with a gentle, contemplative passion quite unlike anything else he had recorded.

As impossible as it was to picture Johnnie Ray on horseback, Colt .44 sidearm strapped around his 28-inch waist, he made it all seem perfectly natural—so much so that the album's only venture into Tin Pan Alley, a requisite version of Mercer's "I'm an Old Cowhand," comes off as jarring and vulgar. The Nashville cats uptown hokum did not help matters, but Johnnie could never credibly manage the line "I know all the songs that the cowpokes know 'cause I learned them all on the radio," because he really learned them by lamp light in the barn and around the campfire, beneath those deep starry western skies.

While most of the album oozes Nashville Sound syrup, several, ("Springtime in the Rockies," "Home on the Range") are stripped down to a bare bones accompaniment—guitar, string bass and chorus. They are sublimely wistful, tender and elegiac. Behind the sense of marvel and wonder lies a gently inevitable sense of mortality, doomed but peaceful acceptance, a resignation to death that is striking.

Johnnie's re-working of "Bury Me Not on the Lone Prairie" is the most extraordinary; originally the plea of a moribund penitent craving the churchyard's consecrated ground, Johnnie reverses it. He sings "Bury Me *Out* on the Lone Prairie," eschewing fear of Judgment Day in favor of resting out where the coyotes howl, winds blow free and neither man nor beast shall be held accountable.

There is warmth and fascination to this unorthodox revision, a pagan yearning for eternity in a remote wilderness that evokes Johnnie's sense of spirit and personal ideology, the free soul untrammeled by conventional religious teaching of fear and self-compromise to avoid divine retribution. A message to Elmer (and, in a sense, a razz to Hazel) it tells of his son's only viable return to the rural homeland.

When he finished recording, the mood left him. Screw the lone prairie. He flew immediately to Britain, his seventh national tour in as many years. There had been numerous additional short hops to England as well; "We used to go over on weekends and do 'Sunday Night at the Palladium' all the time," Bernie Lang said. "It was a television variety show, like the Ed Sullivan Show of Britain." He was there so frequently that Johnnie considered London his second home.

At London's Palace Theater, Johnnie made "the usual impact on his teenage audience. Squeals of delight at every song, posies flung upon the stage, mobbing at the stage door. He still fills the stage with frantic energy. But it is done with more discipline and even members of the audience who dig him, coolly admit his showmanship."

A good review, by and large, yet there was a disturbing observation: "There are many empty seats in the house." Discipline was odd enough— but empty seats? Johnnie never paid much mind to reviews ("Critics," he always said, "are just doing their jobs.") but did not want anyone to point out a half-full house. Like Jack Horner, in a corner—Nowhere. What did he care? Dorothy's love was what he was dreaming of.[3]

When returned to Australia for his fifth tour, he was everywhere, including the top of the charts. His own composition "I'll Never Fall In Love Again," originally cut with Mitch Miller early in 1952 but never released, was remade as a routine pop lament in 1959 and promptly went to number one in Australia. Despite that success, money was so tight that only he and Kappy made the trip.

Opening the bill were two Australian rock and roll acts Johnny Rebb & the Rebels, followed by the nation's top wild man, Johnny O'Keefe. He hit the stage clad in Teddy Boy drapes and howled frantically pitched-up bastardizations of American R&B hits, always at jarringly rapid tempo. Johnny and Johnnie hit it off right away and spent a lot of time boozing together.

"Johnny and I were great buddies," Ray said. "After the show, we would often spend time together and unwind, having a couple of beers." *Quite* unwound. One night at a Rushcutters Bay hotel, he decided not only to buy drinks for the house, but to serve them as well. He jumped over the bar and commenced pouring booze. The landlady apparently took umbrage at being abruptly elbowed aside and struck a blow for Australian propriety. She dumped a tub of run-off draught beer slops over

Johnnie's head. O'Keefe fell on the floor laughing. "There were lots of times I went behind the bar, but I don't recall that incident," Johnnie told an Australian journalist. "I was a bit of a heavy drinker in those days."[4]

Despite his chart success Down Under, it was clear that Johnnie had better duplicate it at home. If he did not score with some substantial sellers in a hurry, he would find himself in the same circumstances under which he first met Frank Sinatra in 1952. How could anyone create a hit record on command? Not even Mitch had the answer to that. Johnnie kept on; he clambered on and off the aircraft, did what was expected of him and rarely let it be known that he felt wasted, ill, *wrong*.

These equator-crossing flights around the globe were no picnic. Johnnie counteracted the punishment with the best medicine he knew: booze. Double vodkas, and plenty of them. "During the hey-day, John was like a string bean, popping pills to stay awake and drinking up a storm, vodka tonics," Jim Low said, shaking his head in wonder at his chum's capacity. "We'd sit there between shows, and he might have ten vodkas. God Almighty! I would've fallen on my face, but he'd go out and perform, and you'd never know it. He was a hell of a drinker."

Johnnie was often a sloppy drunk, and occasionally a belligerent one. "Johnnie was a party boy, and he did drink a lot," said Hank Wesinger, who shared the 63rd Street apartment starting in the early 1960's. "And when he did drink a lot, there was very little conversation—it just rattled on. I didn't listen.

"I've had some very rough experiences with Johnnie and his drinking. In public, he was sometimes appalling. I've seen him get out of control on airplanes, to the point where I had to carry him off—which I was not thrilled about. But I never knew him to be embarrassed or remorseful about a fucking thing in his life . . .

"When I was living with him, my whole life revolved around the drinking and drunkenness. He used to get obnoxious with me once in awhile, and I never approved of that—it's not that I don't drink—it's just that he was obviously killing himself. I used to scream at him not to do it, and sometimes actually had fist fights with him over all this shit . . . he had so much to offer the world, to people and his friends—and to lose friends like that over a fucking bottle of booze is pretty stupid. But that's what he did.   "Then again, all the people around him wanted to party all the time. Johnnie *was* party time, he went out and bought all the booze and everybody had a good time—but that I did not approve of."[5]

When he was on a good deep drunk, Johnnie regularly dropped glasses, cigarettes, plowed into door jambs, and fell down stairways. His body was often a catalog of bruises and scrapes. Many report seeing him make his way down the halls at 63rd Street not simply by placing one foot in front of another but by bouncing off the walls like a pinball caroming off spring-laden bumpers.

To Johnnie, all was joyous, natural, *right*: the softly lit twinkle twinkle of his dear, mad, baubles, bangles and beads. To sober observers it was a horrifying display. A scarecrow-man lost on a near-insensate permanent high, a startling euphoria that seemed toxic and desperate in nature.

It was. Nightly. But Johnnie, die-hard trouper, never missed a date, never screwed up. If something went wrong in the act, he dealt with it directly—exactly the opposite of how personal vexations were handled. Johnnie could not ignore the critics' trend of assessing him as having lost the anguish, and, even worse, the charge that he had grown tame. He and Kappy cooked up an entire new song list, rushing to have it ready for his return to the Latin Quarter in June.

During a previous May 1958 L.Q. engagement, Billboard had commented: "Noticeable among the missing were the tunes from his latest Columbia release, 'Lonely For A Letter' and 'Endlessly.'" Strange move for a pop singer. But why should he plug them? The songs were, like so many of his recent disks, embarrassing bubblegum crap. If the "Sultan of Sob" was to remain a "solid self salesman," he could ill afford to palm off either bobby sox doggerel or the same act performed at least four times on the Latin Quarter stage. His showmanship was all that mattered.[6]

"The former weeper is essaying a new set of songs," Variety said of his Latin Quarter opening, "Tunes incidentally, that he doesn't seem to have fully worked in. However, as he got acclimated . . . his effectiveness increased considerably. By closing, he had the crowd under full control.

"Ray is still the frantic performer who seems to feel the songs he's singing and virtually acts out every one. In these numbers he shows a little strangeness."[7]

Johnnie could not help coming across as seasoned pro, but he was not going to abandon his top calling card—strangeness. Rarely any less physical and wild onstage, he wrenched and hammered it out with all the high-impact empathy and thunder he could draw upon. In that sense, Johnnie was relentless.

Equally as relentless was his boozing. His appearance began to reflect it, his countenance vacillating between sickly wan and florid bloat. Still rail thin in body, his face was a visual record of his romance with intoxicants. Whether swollen or pinched, the itinerary remained constant. Neither Johnnie nor Bernie were demonstrably concerned over it; Mr. Emotion never discussed his abysmal condition and Mr. Commotion was past caring.

Johnnie's cyclical fortune was preparing to shift. The run of good favor was done. His record career dipped ever nearer toward oblivion's mud. When the tide turned on Johnnie's streak of luck it did so with a resounding, concerted and brutal finality that made the surgical destruction of his hearing seem like a picnic.

*　　*　　*

Two years had passed since Johnnie graced the pages of any scandal rag. The last one appeared in September 1957, Inside magazine's charming "Tears, Fears & Too Many Beers." But in November 1959 two of them ran features on Johnnie, Uncensored's "Why Johnnie Ray Couldn't Stay Married" and The Lowdown's "How Johnnie Ray Regained His Manhood." Neither offered anything new, but together they sounded an ominous harmony.

Johnnie spent most of September at New Orleans' Roosevelt Hotel, then returned to New York for a record date with Mitch Miller on October 8. They cut "An Ordinary Couple," a most ironic selection from "The Sound Of Music." Johnnie's performance was a sleepwalk. The song wound up as flipside on the "Springtime In the Rockies" single, a miscegenate coupling typical of Columbia's shattered and inconsistent marketing of his records. Johnnie left for a five-week engagement at the Desert Inn.

He closed and returned to New York. Even with Thanksgiving's approach, Johnnie was only at home for days before he and Kappy split once more. There was a band he had been hearing raves about, led by a young Lionel Hampton alumnus named Quincy Jones. Johnnie wanted to check them out, perhaps discuss using them on some upcoming jobs and hook up with arranger Joe Reisman to fine tune the act.

It was also a handy excuse to live it up at the Detroit nightspot where the band was appearing—the Flame Showbar. Johnnie and Kappy arrived in Detroit on November 20, checked into the Statler-Hilton, then hightailed it out to the corner of Garfield and Canfield.

The Showbar's pink neon bubbles and crimson tongues of flame shimmied and winked as beguilingly as he recalled; Johnnie was imbued with nostalgia. He regaled Kappy with affectionate tales of the wild times and brilliant performers who made such an impression on him. After a few hours and more than a few rounds of drinks they repaired, with several old Showbar chums in tow, to the Brass Rail, a musician's hang-out on nearby West Adams street, where they were to meet Joe Reisman and get the new charts for use in Tahoe.

Reisman came in, handed over the goods and called for a drink. Johnnie was relaxed, happy, completely at ease in the surroundings. A bit drunk, too. His re-living of the Flame era carried over to his bar order— Johnnie drank beer exclusively that night, eager to demonstrate he had not changed all that much. Around 1:30 a.m. three men drifted in. All took separate seats.

Presently, Johnnie felt a tap on his shoulder. He turned to face a tall young man who said he was a travelling salesman named Gene and a big fan of the Cry Guy's. He produced a handkerchief and asked Johnnie for an autograph. Happy to oblige, Johnnie inscribed the hankie as he always did, "To Gene, Glad to know you. Your best buddy always, Johnnie Ray." He bought the stranger a drink and returned to jawing with Kappy, Reisman and his other pals.

The joint closed and the party broke up. He and Kappy wished their drinking buddies good night and drifted, in the manner of the turned out barfly, out to hail a cab. All that beer had backed up in Johnnie's unreliable bladder; he bid Kappy wait, stepped into the dark and started to piss. Gene suddenly reappeared. Johnnie, standing there with his dick in hand on a Detroit street, should have recognized them: Cop Eyes.

He did not.

He shook himself dry, zipped up, clapped his arm around Gene's shoulder and invited him for a nightcap. "Detroit Police! You're under arrest," someone barked. Gene's two accomplices sprang out of the shadows and informed Johnnie the charge was accosting and soliciting. His fury was mute. "I have nothing to say," Johnnie announced as they bundled him into a car.

In the Detroit lockup, all he could think of was the next morning's headlines, being typeset as fast as his bail was being made.

They ran, and how: Johnnie Ray Accused On Morals Charges; Vice Squad Police Nab; Seized On Morals Charge; Vice Squad Picks Up; Is Jailed In Morals Case; Arrested On Vice Charge; Arraigned In Vice Case—a bushel of poisonous items on the front pages of every paper from the Los Angeles Mirror News to the New York Post. Fleet Street roared with it.

Following summary arraignment, Johnnie went home. It was no party at 63rd Street.Dorothy was awaiting him and he fell into her arms. She refused to consider the implications of his arrest, and even offered to testify as a character witness but Halsey Cowan nixed it.

"Johnnie was very upset, very angry, and said that he had been set up," Marlin Swing said. "The police were out to get him, and this handkerchief signed 'Your Best Buddy Always' was their 'evidence' that he had solicited. It was harassment, I think. He was a famous pop star and they *were* out to get him.

"You have to bring yourself back to 1959 to understand this thing. You could read into it that, at the time, people thought he sounded black, and that he was too nice to black people—that could be a possible reason. They thought he was a black lover, and they wanted to get him."

"I think the cops set him up," a friend said. "They hit him with it deliberately because they knew which way Johnnie swung." This was the general consensus; another recalled what Johnnie later said of it: "He told me about that Detroit arrest. Those guys were looking to make a name for themselves and thought they were going to get promoted, so they set him up, man. They set him up." (Not all his friends were satisfied by the scenario. Hank Wesinger still is not sure: "I have my own opinion on that. I know Johnnie too well to comment on it.")[8]

Mitch Miller, ever the earthy pragmatist, said, "How many of us have drank a lot of beer, been out on the street at 2 or 3 in the morning and had to urinate? You go behind a bush or a car and you do it. Well, he did it in Detroit one night and these police were lying in wait and arrested him."

Not unfamiliar with Johnnie's history, Miller traces it back to 1951. "It all started, for whatever reason, at the Flame, see? It was a black and tan, which was bad enough. And in those days, with the homophobic thing, these cops decided he was gay. Johnnie was his own worst enemy in the sense that a lot of things in his personal behavior—which is nothing compared to what people do today, *nothing*—were wrong at that time: he would have a bunch of beers and put his arm around you. I would swear on my children that Johnnie wasn't gay, but so what if he was? You don't try and entrap him just because you thought he was."

The prospects were grim. Even with the fishy circumstances of the bust, his 1951 prior loomed threateningly. If convicted on this charge, Johnnie could forget about ever working in New York City again. His cabaret card would be yanked, branding him as an officially recognized pariah throughout the trade. Having Inside and Lowdown's stories on newsstands only cast further gloom over the atmosphere. It was a convergence of disaster worse than any suffered since his days as Charlie Morrison's son-in-law.

But Johnnie had an ace in the hole which Detroit Vice obviously did not consider—Dorothy Kilgallen. As Marlin Swing said, "That was a very powerful woman—people don't have any idea of the contacts and power she had. Just as an example of it, I remember sitting in her office, we had just come back from an opening and she had to finish writing her column because it was always picked up and had to be down at the paper by two a.m.

"The phone rang, and it was very late, 1:30, almost two in the morning. It was Sorenson calling from the White House [Theodore Sorenson, special counsel to the president—no small potatoes]. They were talking and I heard Dorothy say, 'Oh say hello to him, too.' Jack Kennedy had walked into the room, asked who he was talking to and when he learned it was Dorothy said 'Say hi for me.'

"Dorothy had *contacts*."

She wasted no time in learning the particulars of Johnnie's case and telephoned the judge who would preside over it. "I was with her when she called the judge," Swing said. "And she put pressure on him—made sure it would be expedited and that Johnnie got fair treatment. Dorothy had favors she could call in from people all over the world. She made sure that Johnnie was exonerated."

Kilgallen was not content to merely operate behind the scenes on Johnnie's behalf. "That time he got into a situation with those plain-clothes cops in Detroit," Jane Kean recalled, "right when all that bad publicity was going on, Dorothy marched him down the aisle on open-ing night of some big Broadway show, to vouch for him—to show that she still believed in him."

Johnnie and Halsey Cowan returned to Detroit for conferences with Bernard Fisher and Sidney "Chickie" Sherman, the local attorneys hired to present his defense. The trial got underway on December 1st, before Judge Davenport and an all-female, mostly matronly, jury. The court room was jammed. For 90 minutes, Chickie argued the case with such passion that several simpatico observers openly wept. Fisher took the high road, citing use of enticement to secure the charge, claiming it was the result of a longstanding Detroit Police Department vendetta against his client. He pointed out that the maximum penalty of ninety days jail time and a $100 fine were nothing compared to the damaging effect a conviction would have on Johnnie's career.

To the prosecution, it was cut-and-dried. Look at his record, his guilty plea. Gene appeared; called to the stand, he testified that he was patrolman Eugene Caviston and that on November 21st Johnnie Ray had invited him to his room at the Statler-Hilton Hotel for a nightcap and as they were leaving the Brass Rail bar, Ray made an indecent proposal. Court adjourned.

The following day, a sleek, pensive and dignified Johnnie took the stand. He denied the charge. "All I know is that this man," he gestured at Caviston, "came up and asked me for my autograph. I gave it to him and asked him to join us for a drink, and I don't think there's anything inde-cent about that. When we got ready to leave, he was still hanging on, so I asked him to come along for a nightcap at my hotel."

Under cross examination, the June 1951 guilty plea was thrown in his face. "I was unknown and penniless then," Johnnie said. "I was repre-sented by a court appointed attorney who simply told me the best thing to do was plead guilty. So I pleaded guilty." That being said, neither side had anything left to present. Dotty's pal Judge Davenport instructed the jury "that police officers, in the course of their duty, may make themselves available to apprehend wrongdoers but must not assist in or encourage an individual in an act that is against the law." He sent them to start deliberations. Outside, Johnnie looked confident. He ran a comb through his hair and told reporters, "I have nothing to hide."

The jury came in with a verdict just 50 minutes later. Not Guilty. Johnnie, in the prisoner's box, was so relieved that he went into a dead faint and slipped like a limp glad rag doll onto the floor. Jury forewoman Rose V. Draginda rushed to his side. "Oh, the poor boy!" she cried, cradling Johnnie's head in her lap. He came to, looked around and began weeping. He composed himself and told the press he considered Detroit his "city of destiny."[9]

As Johnnie was leaving the courthouse, he felt another tap on his shoulder. "Remember me?" It was Francis Demmers, the cop who had brought him in the first time around. "No," Johnnie lied, "I'm afraid I don't." Demmers hissed an ultimatum which rattled Johnnie badly.

"He was told never to come back. They said, 'Okay, this is it. We don't ever want to see your ass here again.'" Bill Franklin said. "And even years later, we never played Detroit. He wouldn't—and we had offers. We played across the river in Windsor, Canada, but he would never set foot in Detroit. He was terrified of it.

"And he was very pissed off about it, how he was entrapped. He always told the story of how when he was arrested it was on page one but when he was acquitted they buried it on page 83. Johnnie was very bitter about that, and he carried the anger over it through the years."[10]

But Johnnie was officially clean. With Dorothy's help, he got some of his own back. "Those cats who set me up?" he gleefully told friends. "They're out walking a beat in the middle of nowhere! At midnight!"[11]

He entertained a variety of sinister notions regarding the second arrest. Police vendetta was a given, unquestionably an element, but the sudden twin scandal magazine jobs spun his panicked perception elsewhere. Later in life, Johnnie told numerous friends he believed the frame up was carried out at the behest of Frank Sinatra, but there is nothing to either corroborate or prove the claim.

Johnnie's angry conjecture was merely that, a way to lash out and ease the pain of a severely damaging episode. This arrest frosted many of the Mob Boys' long standing affection for Johnnie— fruits they did not dig. Of the myriad implications and snags the arrest caused, this was perhaps the most debilitating to his career. He also had the public to worry about.

Braced for the worst, Johnnie's delayed engagement at Harrah's opened on December 10, 1959. It was a critical moment; he felt like Gene Krupa returning to the bandstand after his reefer rap, expecting disdainful jeers from a cold, half-empty house. Johnnie prayed as intently as he had before taking the Copacabana stage for the first time. He walked out. They applauded. Johnnie did not shy away from the permeating sexual crackle of vanquished scandal. Instead, he gave them a soft and smoldering message:

"Don't save your kisses,
just pass them around,
You'll find my reason
is logically sound,
who's going to know
that you passed them around . . .
one hundred years from today?"

The crowd cheered.

"If publicity re: the Detroit incident will have any adverse effect on the marquee value of Johnnie Ray's name, it's not obvious at the South Shore Room," Variety reported, "The opening night audience gave him an ovation that should have assured him he was well received . . .

"With the physical gyrations subdued, he gives the audience what they want to hear: a lot of Johnnie Ray, in fine voice and with the exaggerated, stylized movement of the lower jaw. Despite indications between titles that he had a bad case of nerves . . . by the end he was in full control."[12]

It might have looked that way from the audience, but Johnnie was actually as out of control as he had ever been.

By the time Johnnie got home it was 1960. He would soon turn thirty-three. All he wanted was to get with Dorothy and celebrate. They celebrated his birthday, celebrated his acquittal, celebrated their love—celebrated every damn thing worthy of a toast.

On February 16, Johnnie went into the studio and recorded "Before You," a slice of schmaltz, and "I'll Make You Mine," a propulsively rocking hoodoo raver. Driven by a ringing, metallic electric guitar and a ju-ju/fetish slanted lyric straight out of the Screamin' Jay Hawkins school, Mitch had chosen a hard-nosed, uniquely

American rock and roll style, one subsequently obliterated by the British Invasion. It was also Johnnie's obliteration—his final Columbia session. With those two titles in the can, he was wiped off the roster.

While Johnnie's marquee value remained solid, in the record market he was just so much deadwood, a tainted albatross on Columbia's neck. Though hardly a surprise, the label's decision to drop him came as a blow. Johnnie genuinely admired and respected Mitch Miller, who in turn held great affection and respect, artistically and personally, for him. "Johnnie was a fantastic talent, with a great musical mind and I loved him like one of my own children," Mitch said.

This mutual regard produced huge hits, but carried no weight with the label's corporate rulers. Securing another record deal was less worrisome than the prospect of recording without Miller. Despite innumerable miscalls and travesties Johnnie experienced under the Beard, he bitterly regretted losing the continuity and understanding between them.

Johnnie realized he was back on the tightrope, solo, working without a net. He was scared. Decca Records almost immediately offered him a short-term contract, with options to be determined after the release of a single. Johnnie signed. But shortly after the Decca studio date began, he blacked out and collapsed.

Marlin Swing was there. "Johnnie always wanted to record because he knew that was the only way to bring him back," he said. "I don't know why, but the proper material was never presented to him. But he passed out at that session, had a seizure or something and they wanted to scrap the entire session."

After a short delay he came around and finished the songs. Despite a flawless vocal, Decca was not encouraged by the vision of Johnnie, scrawny limbs akimbo, face down on the studio floor. The single's plug side,"Lookout Chattanooga," a Southern pop ramble of surprising quality, was an exuberant frolic delivered with loose polish and sass. Backed with "After My Laughter Came Tears," an undistinguished country ballad, it failed to "bring him back."

It was a long way back for Johnnie. His final appearance in a scandal rag coincided with the record's release. Hush-Hush's May issue carried the most lurid and lengthy story of them all. While it revealed nothing save what was on the public record, the eagerly venomous scandal style had high impact.

The title alone ("Why Detroit Isn't Home Sweet Homo For Johnnie Ray!") sank the yellow hatchet deep into Johnnie's skull. No slander or libelous assertions were necessary. Fantasy never could top the scandal hack's impressive weaving of fact and gutter jargon:

> "A fag or a gag? That is the question.
> Is Johnnie Ray 'a prodigious pervert' with such feeble control over his wayward passions that he will go on a 'manhunt' at the mere drop of a scented hankie?"[1]

The option in his Decca contract went unexercised. Johnnie, undaunted, continued circling the globe.

His resilience was beyond imagination; in the face of his continually weakening physique Johnnie never did anything except what was expected of him, grimacing through pain and exhaustion. He lost weight but ignored it. He felt exhaustion as never before and ignored that. When he began coughing up blood, he flipped and rushed to his doctor. Johnnie's resilience was astonishing—he had tuberculosis, and, as it turned out, had been infected with it for quite a long time. Johnnie was sure he was dying of cancer; informed it was only TB, he cried "Thank God!"[2]

An infectious disease considered fatal until the introduction of antitubercular antibiotics a few years earlier, under normal circumstances Johnnie would be in little danger. But the ceaseless grinding roadwork and booze-steeped lifestyle had reduced him to a painfully weak wretch, one who had worked straight up until the last possible moment.

When the legendary country singer Jimmie Rodgers had tuberculosis, they set up a special cot in the recording studio so he could rest between takes. When the legendary pop singer Johnnie Ray had tuberculosis, he opened and closed numberless engagements in Cleveland, Glasgow, Perth, Rio, Houston, Johannesburg.

The prime difference being, of course, that Johnnie Ray was managed by Bernie Lang.

Johnnie checked into Mount Sinai Hospital and began his recuperation. It was the closest he had come to a holiday in almost ten years. Dorothy visited daily and kept the mood upbeat. She regularly smuggled in bottles of liquor. As Hank Wesinger pointed out, "Would you search Dorothy Kilgallen?"

One afternoon the pair got absolutely wasted and, on a whim, sailed an empty fifth of vodka out the window of Johnnie's room. It shattered—missing a nurse, crossing the courtyard below, by inches. When the staff went to investigate, they found Dorothy in bed with the patient. She was not taking his temperature. Kilgallen was banned from Mount Sinai. His other friends, Rothberg, Swing, Wesinger, Halpert, Younger raised such a racket that they too were often censured by staffers there.[3]

Johnnie found himself with time on his hands—a most unnatural circumstance. The chance to review his career was welcome, but the vantage point from which he looked back left much to be desired. He was proud of so much he had achieved; his records, the good ones, were even better then Johnnie himself would concede.

There were moments he created on disk that are altogether stunning. Records like "Love Me," light hearted jive put over with a swinging, bluesy, black-medicine-show feel; Alec Wilder's "Don't Say Love Has Ended," a stirring, moody plea Johnnie gave thrilling life to; "Glad Rag Doll's" exceptional vocal, another slice of his playful bubblegum jazz style. Despite clipped, exaggerated enunciation, each word had volumes of ironic, sly mockery jammed into it.

"Glad Rag Doll" was masterfully idiosyncratic interpretation, as powerful and unorthodox as his writing style. Time's passage seemed to weaken and dissipate both of these extraordinary gifts. As Johnnie said, "The critical writing was between ages 16 and 22. I couldn't keep it in. It just flowed out and I wrote everything down." His themes went from the young aspirant's starry-eyed pop fluff to profound, almost inspired examinations of self, spirituality and natural order.

Such philosophizing was no easy commercial sell. It was not insignificant that, as he recalled, "the only time I got feisty about pushing my own music was with my song 'Paths of Paradise.' I had that whole GE Theater show built around it." Johnnie pushed hard, convincing Mitch to go all the way for this song: "We re-recorded it for 'The Big Shot,' and it sold a quarter of a million copies." Those brisk sales came during the winter of 1954-55, when people still feasted on Johnnie's language. But when they got scared and began to lose their taste for it, so too did Johnnie.

If he remained that "feisty" his career and perhaps, his health would have benefitted. But Johnnie frightened himself as badly as everyone else and he let it slip away. The result was a load of garbage. "A lot of the songs I did at Columbia were dogs," he said. "They were like bad news that you hoped people would forget about—real bombs." This prompted an even more damaging result. "I had to eat all that bad press. When the critics got on my case, it was not fun. I took it all very seriously and very personally." All of these led to the most damaging self-abuse of all, sailing on an ocean of booze which threatened to pull him under.[4]

Yet even after the glut of mortifying commercial experiments he had been forced into after rock and roll hit, Johnnie and Mitch managed to come up with some prideful senders; among these were his singular "Soliloquy of a Fool," a song Ray Conniff tailored perfectly to Johnnie's blood, guts and thunder approach. Now he was no longer even making records; Decca buried "Lookout Chattanooga." It was forgotten even before release. Maybe now he could get that long dreamt of contract at Capitol. Fat chance.

Johnnie, bemused but drained, tried to fight off any shred of recalled disappointment but it was a pitched battle. The greatest pain was over his failure in motion pictures. Zanuck had built him up to a point of exalted golden expectation, but the film mogul's flight from Fox and abandonment of Johnnie had produced a numbing, dreadful bruise that was still tender five years after the fact.

Back at 63rd Street, Hank Wesinger and Dorothy were boiling the infection out of Johnnie's clothing. Lourie sat by, slowly yellowing from booze. At 1650 Broadway Bernie was still operating; after several weeks, Johnnie was deemed fit to return to work. He played out of town dates, the Adirondacks and Catskills, but was so weak he had to go back into the hospital. It became a pattern that soured on Johnnie quickly. "God damn it," he often snarled that year, "I'm either on stage or in a hospital."[5]

To Bernie, the attraction's poor health was just another p.r. angle. "There have been times when Johnnie may not have been feeling well," Mr. Commotion said not long before Johnnie contracted tuberculosis, "but once he gets onstage, it is the greatest tonic he could have. At every performance, he gives to the utmost of his ability, even though at times, unbeknown to anybody else, he may have been painfully suffering."[6]

Elma was appalled by this attitude. Like Dorothy, she increasingly viewed Bernie with outrage. In truth Bernie was no worse or any more ruthless than any other personal manager. It was acknowledged throughout the trade that p.m.'s always pocketed more of their client's money than they were due, always booked them as often as possible and used every sneaky trick conceivable to drive up their earning power.

Exploitation demanded a mercenary. Explain that to an attraction's family sometime and see how far you get. "Bernie would send Johnnie, who was a very sick man, out to work. He would go onstage and then go back to the hospital for treatment," Elma said. "I once wrote Bernie and told him 'You are an inhuman son of a bitch,' and someone, I believe it was Kappy said, 'If Bernie didn't have Johnnie, what would he do?' Ha! Christ, I hoped he'd kill himself—he nearly killed Johnnie for his percentages."

When at last he had taken the medication long enough to rout the disease into dormancy, Johnnie prepared to officially re-enter the trade. It was November 1960, a year since both his private and professional lives had started imploding.

The venue chosen for this auspicious return was Basin Street East, a tiny New York City jazz joint; it was there, a year before, that Peggy Lee had made her fabled career-resurrecting engagement, a triumphant record-breaker which brought the club almost as much attention as it did Lee's floundering career. The bill for Johnnie's return was an impressive one; The George Shearing Quintet as opener, followed by a set from the Quincy Jones Orchestra, who would also accompany Johnnie. The four week engagement opened on November 3, election night. This time Johnnie paid close attention to the critics.

The Variety review's lead gave him the heebie jeebies: "Johnnie Ray, compared to the new flock of teenage idols, is already in the 'Elder Statesmen' category though still a young man. This date in fact represents a 'comeback' for Ray after a year's lay off due to a bout with Tuberculosis, from which he's completely recovered.

"Ray returns with an excellent book, stand out arrangements by Joe Reisman, superlative backing by the Quincy Jones Orchestra, and in a spot that has been pulling big b.o. consistently from the hipper elements of cafe society."

Ah, that's more like it. Johnnie smiled and lit a cigarette.

"He opens with 'Alright, Okay, You Win.' The hour long show offers the usual oldies and standards, including 'Such A Night' and '100 Years from Today.' Ray's special twist is the intensity with which he projects his material. By current rock and roll standards, Ray can be considered restrained, but he still charges his songs with a fervor and excitement. Ray, in fact, can be considered the prototype of the current disk singers who subordinate finesse to raw feeling."[7]

As well received as it was constructed, the Basin Street East run went a long way towards re-establishing him as a legitimate, serious voice; Jones' artful mix of hard bop extremism and deep swing rhythms gave an ideal presentation. Dorothy and Johnnie were ecstatic; during the engagement, Nick Lapole, one of Kilgallen's editors, attended and was told they awaited him in the dressing room. When he opened the door and saw them locked in embrace, Lapole quietly shut it and resumed his seat on the nightclub floor. They were far too happy to be interrupted.[8]

* * *

Meantime, Bernie had secured his boy a recording contract, another one-shot with an option deal for Archie Bleyer's Cadence, an independent reputed to be a mob-backed outfit. He cut "In the Heart Of a Fool," an oversweet Mel Tillis ballad, coupled with Johnnie's own "Let's Forget It Now," ("before we both get burned . . . "), a throbbing, corny ballad. His vocal is sock-o, full of mournful melodrama but a badly recorded bargain basement string section douses what few sparks are struck. The 45 made as small a noise as Decca's "Lookout Chattanooga" and slipped, along with the unexercised option, into oblivion.

In early 1961, Johnnie signed with Liberty Records, the Hollywood-based label which had big success in the 1950's with the great song stylist Dinah Washington, Martin Denny's Exotica series and the pop-rockabilly of Eddie Cochran. Johnnie was set to record in Hollywood with producer Belford Hendricks and Clyde Otis, who were responsible for Dinah Washington's best work at Liberty.

They recorded "Johnnie Ray" an album of standards that Johnnie delivered with a gentle elegance and subtlety of emotion that was even more restrained and deliberately crafted than his vocals on "'Til Morning." Hendricks let Johnnie do as he pleased, resulting in some beautiful music, particularly his smoldering, blue reading of Alec Wilder's "I'll Be Around."

While he was in Hollywood making the album, Johnnie got a call from Jim Low, who had just moved to San Diego. Low was assigned to the crew of an atomic submarine, and invited him to drive down and look the vessel over. The prospect fascinated Johnnie. He called Hazel and Elmer, flew them down and went to meet Low. They spent an entire afternoon aboard the craft, even lunched with the captain. Johnnie asked questions about everything he saw—life outside the trade was an intoxicating mystery and he plunged into it at every chance, revelling in the minutiae and routine of normalcy.

At Liberty, of course, he was also coerced into a re-make of "Cry," which did not exactly thrill. Hendricks was just following standard procedure—any company that snagged a major hitmaker had them re-do the biggie. Johnnie never thought he would regret "Cry," but now found himself cursed by it.

"Why won't they take me as a serious singer?" he railed. "Why do they have to go back to all that Cry-baby shit? I've grown, time has passed. I sing different songs now, but it's always the same thing. Why don't they just lay off that Cry bullshit?"[9]

Dorothy agreed. She was delighted at his description of the songs he recorded for Liberty, but horrified when the album arrived on her desk—the front cover was a stark black and white head shot of Johnnie, hand upon brow, face contorted in an expression of desperate anxiety. "It makes you look like something out of Charles Addams!" she told him. Johnnie could not dispute that, but his characteristic preference to never argue, even over control of his image, prevailed.[10]

That silence did not propel, benefit or secure his creativity. Johnnie never again recorded one of his own compositions, unless it was a new version of "Little White Cloud." But he had begun writing again, just for himself. "The best songs that I have written," he said, "nobody will ever hear. I might sit down and play them at 3 or 4 in the morning at my house, but that's it."[11]

Johnnie began to separate himself from the Johnnie who appeared on stage. In that fashion, he could protect himself and avoid the hurtful subjugation of personality he experienced as a young pop star, and make sure he did not assume the rote, cut-and-dried Cry-baby persona this phase of his career relentlessly demanded. "There are two Johnnie Rays," he often said. "and they don't resemble each other at all. The one that walks out onstage is somebody else—it's not me."[12]

Of course, there was scant difference between the two, but it was either allow the undertow of public life to tear him apart or initiate the split himself, while remaining as close to being master of each as he could manage. Concentrating on that problem, Johnnie never considered the effects his own habits were having on him.

He consciously worked for this division, fashioning a private life as J.R., the sunny, feckless kid from Oregon. Only under the spotlight's heat did Johnnie Ray, torso-tossing demon, materialize—no matter what his condition. "I can go on stage in pain and while I'm on, that is eliminated from my mind for the duration of the performance. It's like a form of self-hypnosis." A self-hypnosis rooted in denial and ignorance. Johnnie's refusal to face dissent, blithely blind, only led him closer and closer to the brink.[13]

Neither did he consider or analyze his career and its course, which also seemed to be steaming towards disaster. When Johnnie was laid up in the hospital for most of 1960, Bernie had, for the first time, begun representing other artists. He rounded up a variety of low-grade lounge chanters whom he booked by using his big-name attraction as leverage—like a carrot Lang dangled just beyond the reach of prestige-hungry talent brokers.

"Bernie was good, very good for Johnnie, until he started 'double dating.'" Marlin Swing explained. "He had solely represented Johnnie through the years of his 'Big Career' and then he started taking on other clients. So now it was: 'Two B's will get you an A,' where Bernie said, 'You book two of my B grade clients and I'll get you an A: Johnnie Ray.' And from that point on, Bernie was not good for Johnnie—he would book him anywhere if they would take his other clients. And Johnnie finally caught on to that."

The results of Bernie's new policy were demeaning, all the more so for the fact that Johnnie responded to it, inevitably, with his Hear No Evil, Speak No Evil, See No Evil ethic, and by turning to the bottle. Who could blame him? Sure, Bernie was opening new territories, sending Johnnie into spots he had never before worked. Spots he never should have worked.

It was May 1961 when the ludicrous nature of Bernie's direction sank in. Great shades of Ernie Paluso's and Ashtabula, Johnnie thought, I'm booked for ten days at Angelo's, the hot spot of Omaha, Nebraska—with a one dollar cover? He hit the stage with an ironic selection, "When

You're Smiling." Kappy winced and hit the drums as hard he could just to keep from blowing his stack. It was a nightmare of a debut.

"His engagement is well advertised and publicized, so what happens?" a Variety reviewer wrote, "Not even fifty people show up for opening night . . . in a plush nitery that easily houses four hundreed and fifty. You have to give Ray credit. He worked as though the house was packed. His biggest slips came in introducing celebs in the audience. The World-Herald's critic (Bob McMorris) was intro'ed as Bob Miller. Gloria DeHaven took a bow as 'Fran Warren.'"14

Johnnie was never one to stint on showmanship—or cocktails. He was plastered that night. And the next. When he walked out and saw four hundred empty seats it was a blow, a sucker punch, totally unanticipated, that hurt profoundly. His bout with TB did nothing to alter his intake of liquor or "medication," the endless supply of pills. Capsules, tablets, spansules were gobbled daily, the dosages increasing steadily as physical tolerance built up—and ten days in Omaha can drive your tolerance right through the roof.

In July 1961, Johnnie, accompanied by Bernie and Kappy, was in London for a six-week run at Talk of The Town, a posh and intimate West End nightclub. His drawing power was on the wane even in England, but Glyn Jones, his British agent, was a shrewd, fair and loyal man, and Talk of the Town rated as a class joint. Johnnie was relieved to put the Atlantic ocean safely between him and all those damn corn fields.

Johnnie poured it on there: "He approaches every song like a ritual, and some as a wrestler might apply a half nelson. But his act adds up to a very holding piece of showmanship which retains most of his trademarks, the gangling knees, the half-closed eyes, the flexible body and the offbeat arrangements and delights the audience." He packed the room nightly, despite the fact that "his faithful, squealing adolescent contingent is conspicuously absent."15

By day he was taping a television series, "Johnnie Ray Sings" working with drummer Jack Parnell's big band and warbler Shani Wallis. She sang only one number in each half hour episode, which meant Johnnie had to carry the entire show. He managed handily. He looked fit and his vocal delivery was sure and emphatic. But at the end of the night Johnnie was always staggering, sloppy drunk and pill-wasted. He needed something upon which to lean.

Then the phone rang in the apartment Johnnie had rented. It was Bill Franklin, afraid Johnnie might not remember him from that hot night in Hollywood almost three years earlier. Fat chance. Johnnie could not wait to get together, he reassured Franklin. He was leaving tickets at the door and counted on seeing him that night.

"I was travelling in Europe that summer with a friend of mine. I picked up a paper in London and saw that Johnnie was appearing at the Talk of the Town," Franklin said. "Through a series of phone calls, I finally got through to Bernie, said the magic words 'Jack Devaney,' and Bernie put me in touch with Johnnie. We went to the show that night and visited backstage with him. It was all very platonic, a 'gee, I'm glad to see you, let's be friends, I'm having a party, please come' kind of thing.

"So, that night, we went to a party at the place he was renting—with a lot of people there. And Johnnie had been very good onstage that night, but he was so drunk at the party," Franklin, who barely knew their host at the time, paused in his recollection. "Johnnie was in and out of bed with some guy, half naked, in this apartment full of people. He was really out of control, just literally bouncing off the walls, all that kind of stuff."

Johnnie's feral decadence struck Bill as more fascinating than frightening, but it was his blunt Oregonian charm and pigeon-toed little boy quality that got under Franklin's skin. "So, I saw him socially a few more times while I was in London," said Bill. "We had dinner together, and Johnnie said, over and over, 'If you're ever in New York, call me.' Then I went on my way around Europe, and eventually back to my p.r. job in Beverly Hills."[16]

While Johnnie's full-throttle bacchanal was only mildly daunting to Franklin, Kappy had seen more than enough. In early 1962, he gave notice that he was quitting. Johnnie, hardly able to blame him but saddened nonetheless, fell to searching for a replacement. Since the failed ear surgery his drummer was more important than ever. As Johnnie's musical director and onstage anchor, he was the only one able to get him back in time and tempo should he lose his way mid-song.

With Kappy's help they assembled a list of the best trap men in New York, and quickly boiled it down to one name—Jimmy Campbell. A tall, rangy Philadelphian with Lincoln-esque features cut from the same genetic fabric as Johnnie's, the drummer had an ideal background for this gig. Campbell had risen from a dues-paying journeyman knocking around the joints to the top of Downbeat's annual talent polls, an honor accorded him several times.

Campbell was in perpetual demand—worked the road with Woody Herman and Stan Kenton, recorded with saloon song diva Silvia Sims, sat in with various combos at Birdland and had crossed over to Broadway orchestra pits. His contract with "Bye Bye Birdie" would soon expire, and Campbell was looking for a bandstand gig.

"I got a call from Bernie Lang," Campbell said, "asking if I'd like to go work for Johnnie Ray. I first met him years ago at a party I threw at my place in New York, but he didn't remember it." (The 1952 reefer and fingerpainting shindig which Ray Anthony's band members took Johnnie to). Campbell told Bernie he would take the job.

"We were going to get together and practice," Jimmy continued, "The car pulls up, he opens the door and the first thing he says to me, 'Do you drink?'

"'Shit, yeah,' I said.

"'Okay, you're gonna be alright,' he said.

"I asked him, 'Is there any problem?'

"'Hell, no,' he says, 'Welcome to the club.'"[17]

It was the beginning of a close and very drunken friendship. "See, I was a perfect drinker—I could drink a lot, and he was a good, heavy drinker," Campbell said. "But he didn't get crazy, I can't ever recall that he lost control."[18]

Music, not liquor, was the real bond between Johnnie and Jimmy. "He had a jazz mind—he wanted to be a jazz singer, and he could play the piano, sometimes he would get a real jazz thing going on it. Musically, he was a very adventurous kind of person, and liked to try all kinds of different things, but the hearing was a handicap, as far as venturing away from a melody. He carried it off though.

"I would put my drums on a platform in front of the band instead of in back, and if he got confused with his hearing about where he was at, he would come stand on the platform and the vibrations would give him an idea of where the hell he was at. And he didn't get lost too often, either. It became pretty well ingrained."

But Johnnie was never in the same spot for long—he was all over the stage. "Once in awhile if he did get off, he'd turn around and I could tell he was lookin' at me—he'd put his foot out and I'd hit real hard for him and then he'd be right back on." Campbell's encouragement drew Johnnie's creativity out, seemed to loosen and free him from the book's constraints. "Some nights, he'd sit at the piano and play and I would follow him. One of his singing idols was Billie Holiday and he could mimic her absolutely perfectly.

"He'd sneak that impression in sometimes. It always just broke me up, and the people loved it. I said 'Do more of that,' but Bernie didn't want him to do that. He'd say, 'You're Johnnie Ray, not Billie Holiday.' And I'd say, 'Man, he loves it, come on, everybody likes it.'"

Campbell, picturing Bernie, shook his head. "Managers—they're a strange breed, man."

Through relentless stifling and exploitation, Johnnie's manager was inadvertently destroying his star. But the star was also destroying himself. Hank Wesinger had grown sick of sparring with a wild-eyed drunken lover and tired of competing with Dorothy for his attention. "Johnnie was like a big child, always had been. Up until he died, he never grew up. A big child . . . whose favorite expression was 'I'm a Star!'" Hank explained. "He was of the school of thought that 'Stars Can Do Whatever They Want.' That is how Johnnie did think—he got off on it." Wesinger made his exit from 63rd Street shortly before Campbell was hired. In short order, the drummer became a 63rd Street resident.

Jimmy Campbell arrived at a critical moment in the weeper's life and contributed more than he or anyone else close to Johnnie realized. In the wake of Hank's departure, Jimmy's laconic cool, the jazz cat's nihilistic beatitude, brought a new, welcome and illuminating carelessness to Johnnie's murky worldview.

He shared the apartment with Lourie and Marlin Swing. Dorothy, hoping to promote a more stable atmosphere, had avidly encouraged Marlin to move in during Johnnie's tubercular episode. It was an interesting mix; Swing's elegantly cerebral influence was counterpoint to Campbell's casual jazz, who-cares-anyway ethic. They all jammed in the living room; Marlin's Hammond B-3 organ sat beside Johnnie's baby grand. Music was constantly being played, much to the annoyance of their less nocturnal neighbors; Johnnie regularly spent hundreds of dollars for the delivery of floral peace offerings.

"There were so many rooms in the apartment, and Johnnie always kept one open for me," Campbell said. "In fact, he kept me on retainer, even when he wasn't working. That place was like Grand Central Station, there were always people coming and going—John had a lot of friends, and not all guys, either. It was always a mixed crowd, at least 15 people most of the time. But on Sundays, for 'What's My Line?', there'd only be 5 or 6 people. It all depended. There was no rhyme or reason to it, but we always had a good time, either way."

Dorothy always arrived within twenty minutes of the show's close—thirsty. "Every Sunday night, she came by the apartment for an hour or so and drink, drink, drink," Hank Wesinger recalled. After a few cocktails, Dorothy became a fount of jaw-dropping gossip; one Sunday evening, she regaled the company with tidbits on President Kennedy's prodigious extramarital activities. "Why don't you print it?" one of the more naive hangers on asked. "I couldn't possibly," she replied. "No one would."[19]

Johnnie was back at 63rd Street for Thanksgiving 1962, and in his most enthusiastic Big Daddy persona, hosted a family dinner. Marlin, Lourie, Hank Wesinger, Jimmy Campbell, with his red-haired swinger of an old lady Dee Dee, and Sol Lazarow, were joined by Stan Freeman, Jane and Betty Kean, Lou Parker (Betty's husband), and a parade of friends, among them Howard Rothberg, Chris and Georgia George, the usual crew of male models; even Dorothy managed to drop by.

Bill Franklin had just been relocated to his firm's New York office, and telephoned Johnnie that afternoon. "I'm so glad to hear from you," he said. "I'm having some people in tonight, can you come?" Franklin had dinner plans but wasted no time in beating a path over there as soon as he could. He, too, began spending as much time at 63rd street as he could manage.

"The apartment was very comfortable, very lived in and very . . . eclectic," Franklin said. "Which is a nice word for messy. Not really untidy, it was just full of all kinds of good stuff, books, tons of record albums. And lots of music going on, lots of people coming and going, famous people, not so famous people. It was a good time, and after that I started hanging out there a lot."

Life at 63rd Street continued ascending to new heights of social grace. Johnnie entertained a wide variety of show business characters. He was close to both the Hermiones—Baddeley and Gingold, deliciously eccentric battle axes who loved Johnnie as much, and perhaps more, than he adored them. His brash little boy persona intoxicated women, as Elma said, "from the youngest to the eldest—the eldest particularly."

Gingold and Johnnie spent hours together in a ritual of mutual admiration and inside gossip; she would enter, buss him enthusiastically and take a seat. Launching into whatever monologue the occasion called for, Gingold would peel off her opera length gloves with deliberately exaggerated care; it seemed to take five minutes to remove just one. She would then gracefully cast it upon his lap; as their banter continued Johnnie would put on her glove at the same leisurely snail's pace.

Johnnie absorbed Kilgallen's passion for word games and everyone played them constantly; a favorite was a song lyric guessing game where one player would supply no less than 2 and no more than 4 words from a particular lyric and defy the others to identify it. Marlin Swing, on one occasion, gave this clue: "All kinds of weather." It stumped everyone at first. When Kilgallen grasped it, she held her tongue. Johnnie was beside himself, rattling off titles in vain. Learning that Swing was quoting from "Little White Cloud," he flipped.

Dorothy, of course, provided the mother-stumper of all time, with the maddeningly brief clue "whose broad." The players ran through the litany of obvious choices. Johnnie immediately thought he had it: "South Pacific's 'There's Nothin' Like a Dame'?" Incorrect. "Guys & Dolls' 'Luck Be a Lady'?" Wrong. Johnnie, Marlin and Bill ran through dozens of saloon and torch titles and could not nail it.

Dorothy refused to reveal the title. She drew the play out into weeks of mystery. Johnnie, beside himself with anguished frustration, desperately begged for the answer. "Whose broad stripes . . . " she crooned. "The Star Spangled Banner!" Johnnie crowed in torrential relief. "He delighted in that," Franklin said. "He played a lot of games with Dorothy."

"They were like two little kids," Hank Wesinger said. "We used to rent cars and drive up to my parents' place in the country. They would go romping off and do their silly little things. When they went out and did things together in New York, she was very condescending to him, but she also helped him a lot—and she did flatter the shit out of him. Together, they were like two children. They were in love."

There was always an abundance of affection at 63rd Street. When Jimmy Campbell wed, the Cry Guy took control of the festivities. "I got married to a girl dancer I met during 'Bye Bye Birdie.' I was getting ready to move into this little apartment she had, before we found a bigger one for both of us," Campbell said. "It was just a small civil ceremony that day, and John was my best man.

"But we had to do the show that night, so he said, 'The party is at my house, come over after the show." We walked in that night and he had this pull-out couch that opened into a big bed, and it was set up in the living room with hundreds of tropical flowers, Hawaiian stuff. There were flowers and pineapples, all these leis and stuff spread over the bed. Crazy son of a bitch! That was our wedding night. We all stayed up 'til dawn and got plastered."

Just as Campbell drew out more of Johnnie's jazz heart, he in turn steeped the drummer in the heady glamour of Kilgallen's New York. "I thought Dorothy was great," he said. "There were a lot of laughs in that relationship. When Rudolf Nureyev first came to this country, he debuted with Margot Fonteyn in 'Swan Lake,' and it was a big opening night. Dorothy loved those things, and she wanted Johnnie to go, so we all went—my girl was Johnnie's 'date' and I was Dorothy's.

"We all got tuxed up, and gowned up, into the limo and off we went. We pulled up in front of the Metropolitan Opera House with all the cameras flashing, all the reporters were there. We got out of the car and it was just *flash flash flash*! I thought 'My God—I love this!' I think we probably didn't fool anyone, because everybody in the business knew Johnnie and Dorothy were swinging."

They were indeed swinging, and boozing harder than ever. What was already drastic became utterly reckless. One choice evening, a typical crowded two-limousine foray heading from bar to bar, climaxed spectacularly. Johnnie and Dorothy decided to go for drinks at the Left Bank. Its pianist was a marvelous young man able to play every title in the Cole Porter songbook; however, the Left Bank was owned and operated by Dick Kollmar.

At the time Kollmar also ran Paris in the Skies, a supper club across the river in New Jersey; Dorothy perhaps assumed he would be there. He was not. The rest of the party wisely begged off and headed back to 63rd street to keep the pad's momentum up. Johnnie and Dorothy strutted into the Left Bank, settled down and ordered up.

Presently, the necking routine began. Kollmar stood nearby at the bar pouring booze down his neck. This was too much, a bizarre self-destructive scenario no one close to Johnnie or the Kollmars was ever able to understand. After a few moments, not even the bartender could stand the tension. "Are you just going to stand here and let her humiliate you like that?" he hissed into Kollmar's ear. Dick responded by ordering another drink.

Hours later, long after Johnnie and Dorothy departed, Kollmar, by now well plastered, returned home. When he came across the pair still groping each other in the Black Room, he blew his top. Kollmar was a big man, one who had endured this monkey business for almost 6 years and when he strode into the room and began bellowing, it struck fear into Johnnie's heart.

"I'll kill you," he howled into Johnnie's hearing aid, "if I ever see you with my wife again." Johnnie managed to keep his cool. "That is entirely her decision," he replied, speech booze-thick but measured. Kollmar was unimpressed. "I want you out of here," he screamed, "and out of her life." Johnnie took his cue and prepared to withdraw. Dorothy close to tears, pleaded with Johnnie in a shaky voice, "I want to go with you now. Please take me with you. I don't want to be in this house anymore."

"I thought very fast," Johnnie told Kilgallen's biographer. "I knew that if she were to walk out—and she was ready—everything would collapse for her. I explained to her that she'd lose the column, the television, everything she worked a lifetime to achieve. She said she didn't care about any of it. And I thought about [her son] Kerry. I told her 'I'm gonna have to walk out and leave you here.'" She was shattered by his pronouncement.[20]

He returned to his apartment in a dazed condition, as Dorothy mumbled a promise to Kollmar that she would cease keeping company with Johnnie. The blow was so great she was nearly in shock. At 63rd Street, the awaiting revelers were stunned when Johnnie told them what happened, but reaction was divided. Some of the keyhole peepers, who had lusted after Johnnie a long and lonely season, urged him to end it once and for all. Dorothy's friends were concerned and scared over damaging fallout; incredibly, everyone seemed surprised it happened.

"I purposely didn't ask for any details of that night," Marlin Swing said. "All I know is that it was a triple lulu of an evening and what the results of it were—Dorothy was forbidden to see him, and that just wasn't going to happen. She was even forbidden to write his name in her column."

Several days later, Dorothy phoned Johnnie's apartment. He refused to speak to her—Kollmar really had gotten to him. When Johnnie still would not talk to her a week later, she began to call constantly, sobbing to whoever answered the phone, "He can't keep avoiding me, I won't live without him. If Johnnie doesn't come back to me, I'm going to kill myself."[21]

"Johnnie showed me a letter Dorothy sent him, written on her stationery, begging him, but I mean *begging* him to see her," recalled Jane Kean. "And Johnnie kept asking me, 'What should I do?' He did not want to cross paths with Kollmar again, because he could make it very embarrassing, publicly, for Johnnie."

Dorothy fell apart completely. Withdrawn in behavior, her speech that of a timorous little girl, she seemed increasingly disoriented; the Kollmars' bookkeeper, Anne Hamilton, began to fear Dorothy would fall down the stairs which led from her fifth-floor sanctuary.

When Hamilton came across Dorothy, shuffling and blank-eyed, and was asked by her to call for the limousine, as she was running late and had to get to CBS for "What's My Line?" which went out live on Sunday evenings, Hamilton had to act—it was a weekday. "It's okay, honey," she told Kilgallen. "You sit down here and I'll take care of everything."

Distraught, the bookkeeper ordered James to awaken Kollmar and "tell him that Mrs. Kollmar is going to hurt herself if he doesn't get a doctor here fast." She was checked into a hospital, and stayed there for a month. Kollmar later explained to Hamilton, that this episode was touched off by Dorothy's anemia, a longstanding condition, and that the doctors were amazed she was able to walk around at all. "The blood was pink," Hamilton said, "and the brain had been affected."[22]

Johnnie gave in and rushed, teary-eyed and breathless, to her side. Dorothy was released from the hospital in May, and they renewed the affair—on a strictly covert basis. "It was after that when I really became the go-between, and Dorothy began saying that she was out somewhere with me," said Marlin Swing, who frequently served as a reference source for any musical question that arose during a "Breakfast with Dorothy & Dick" broadcast. "They were always asking 'Marlin, who wrote this?', right over the air, so I'd call James with the answer and he'd write it down and slip it under the door of the room they broadcast from."

"So, if Dick ever called me at CBS in the morning, when he was off the air, I'd have the secretary say I wasn't in. Then I'd call Dorothy and say 'where were we last night?' and she'd say, 'Oh, at the Copacabana!' And he wasn't necessarily checking up on us, but I always wanted to make sure where 'we had been' the night before, in case he was, before I talked to him. Then I'd call Dick back to see what he wanted."

Johnnie and Dorothy began to meet out of town as much as possible. "Kilgallen had to go to Washington D.C. one weekend, and we weren't working, so Johnnie took me down there with him," Jimmy Campbell recalled. "We jumped on the plane. He and Dorothy connected, we all went out that night and then came back to our hotel. John said, 'I'll call you when I'm finished. You want to get a drink or something?' I said, 'Don't worry, John, I do very well by myself.'

"So, about four hours later, I get a call. He had just come back from taking her over to her hotel, and he said, 'I'm down in the bar, come on down and help me out here. Jesus christ, am I worn out!' And I said, 'Well very good John, you need the exercise.'" Campbell laughed at the memory, then fell silent.

"She loved him," he added.

Johnnie's characteristic perseverance never flagged. Faced with the slow descent of his prestige and name value, he nonetheless remained loyal to Bernie and went wherever the itinerary led. These

obligations, even as they became more humiliating, were all that kept him going. That, and the new flame in his heart. While Dorothy lay wretched and dissipated in her hospital room, Johnnie, after striking out in Hollywood and London, finally managed to get Bill Franklin into bed.

They fell for each other hard, initiating what became the most intense and long-lived relationship with another man

Johnnie ever undertook. The situation was strange. Slipping around behind Dorothy's back was not so extraordinary; but doing so as she recovered from a breakdown caused by Johnnie's refusal to commit was rather unsavory.

That he did it in an apartment shared with two other former lovers (both Lourie and Marlin had enjoyed periods of intimacy with him) was certainly off kilter. And the fact that all of them tacitly understood they would serve as beards once Dorothy returned, was the bizarre cherry on top of Johnnie's pagan confection of ego and lust.

That Johnnie expected such humbling fealty from these men can not be explained in "civilian" terms. This was megalomaniacal Star Psychology at its most manipulative, exploitive and presumptuous, but the compliance he unfailingly received was a result of Johnnie's rare, careless charm. Even in the depths of his most wretched drunkenness, Johnnie still had, in the eyes of these men, an irresistible goodness, a charm and innocence that cried out for succor.

He still managed to give the impression of an apple-cheeked, barefoot innocent out of Norman Rockwell, but he looked like a tuxedo-clad scarecrow, with waxy skin that assumed an increasingly moribund pallor. His painfully thin limbs and lanky frame were fragile, stretched out of proportion.

Steeped in the toxicity of a continual vodka and chloral hydrate diet, his typically disjointed, spidery gestures now jerked, writhed and twisted to new extremes. Johnnie at times looked positively ghoulish.

In the wake of his last arrest, the trades rarely followed or reviewed Johnnie; he had clearly become so strange it would be difficult to accurately put him down on paper. When they did cover him, though, there was no question of his ability. Variety's review of a 1962 appearance at Pittsburgh's Holiday House conceded that it was "an inspired performance . . . applause was deafening . . . a tomblike silence falls over the packed room as patrons strain to catch every note."[1]

At 63rd Street, Franklin quickly became a full-time fixture. After Dorothy straightened out Younger's legal status, he returned to accompanying Johnnie on the road. "Lourie still worked as everything: road manager, valet, dresser," Bill Franklin explained. "I had a little apartment of my own at the time, but when Johnnie went on the road, for short spurts, he'd take Lourie and Jimmy Campbell and I would stay on 63rd street. It was just me, Marlin, Sabrina and the maid who came in every day. Then that translated to Johnnie saying, 'Move in. Move in.' So, around Christmas of '62, I did.

"And then some conflict started between Lourie and me, because like everybody in Johnnie's life who was at all sensitive, I wanted to take care of him. Johnnie had that little boy quality, and you felt for him. Not just sympathy, you felt passion and just instinctively wanted to take care of this person.

"The conflict with Lourie was because I could see he was one of the big reasons Johnnie continued to drink—he was always right there with a glass saying 'It's Time!' Lourie was not a bad guy, but he was not good for Johnnie because he drank even more than Johnnie did. If he hadn't have been so young—he was in his thirties—there was no way he could've held up, or kept it up, and he looked like a boozer: his face was puffy, eyes bloodshot. He looked weird, he really did. Lourie was always drunk, and he was like the puppeteer there, who had both of them sloshing around very early in the day."

Franklin, hardly the first to recognize the unpleasant and increasingly destructive nature of Johnnie's life, was the first to consciously question it. "And Johnnie, with the bladder problem and the rubber sheets, he was a mess. I remember the first night I stayed there, I heard him get up in the middle of the night and start scooping water off the bed.

"I thought to myself 'Why? Why? Well, no wonder he's boozing all the time, he's around people who are drunk all the time.' I mean, Campbell was so bad that he shook all the time. I drank, too, partied a lot and enjoyed it, but not the way they did, first thing after getting up."

Yet the glamour and passion of Johnnie's mad lifestyle was seductive. "I was having a wonderful time, all the limos, things happening all the time. I met Dorothy—I couldn't believe that, 'Here I am with Dorothy Kilgallen!'" Franklin said. "And we became great friends, instinctively hit it off. She and I shared a lot of the same ideas about Johnnie, how he wasn't being handled right, and how things could be improved."

Lourie was not the only one who clashed with Franklin. "It wasn't bad living at 63rd street," Campbell said. "Huge apartment, a doorman, a cook, everything. Parties all the time, Dorothy coming by—lots of fun—until Bill Idiot-Head showed up. See, I watched this whole thing with Bill starting. I didn't like him when he first came in, just as a party guest. Bill was like an underhanded person, and I watched him worm his way into Johnnie's good graces. Pretty soon he was living in the apartment and I didn't like that at all. And if you ever said anything to Johnnie, he'd get mad at you. He was taken by Bill, he fell for all of it."

It was Franklin's concern for Johnnie's health and over-indulgence that Campbell, the perfect drinker, resented. That was precisely what Dorothy liked about Bill. Johnnie, as ever, straddled the fence and did his best to keep everyone happy. He had no interest whatsoever in cutting back on the booze or pills.

Franklin was in the right—Johnnie looked like a cadaverous husk on the verge of implosion. But despite Franklin's whispered entreaties and guidance, Johnnie kept on roaring.

When Bill was called back to Hollywood by his company in the Spring of '63 to publicize a John Wayne bomb "The Alamo," Campbell and Lourie gloated in boozy rapture. They should have heeded Franklin; neither had noticed the yellow cast Johnnie's skin began to assume. Between their own drunkenness, the soft party lights and Johnnie's non-stop schedule, who was looking?

*   *   *

Johnnie's output as a Liberty recording artist was limited to two albums and a rather extraordinary duet with Timi Yuro, the diminutive white chick who sang like a manic depressive Dinah Washington. Yuro enjoyed support from an adoring cult built up via juke boxes in gay bars across the country, and these same machines wore out countless copies of the single she and Johnnie cut together. It was an ideal pairing; although its commercial potential was strictly limited, in artistic terms, Johnnie and Timi complemented each other tremendously.

The vocal blend of these smoldering, emotionally driven styles had a rare, almost reverent quality. Both titles, "A Mother's Love" and "I Believe," featured lyrics rich with evocative natural images and a quasi-sacred slant that side-stepped just short of acknowledging religious faith ("A Mother's Love" was an emotion more powerful than religion; "I Believe" was about a mortal love more profound and beautiful than all of God's creations). They were so closely tailored to Johnnie's aesthetic that he could have written them himself. He sings wonderfully on the single, as gentle, tender and wistful as ever. Sales, however, were as low and for-lorn as the blues he should have been singing.

The fall-out of his Detroit bust was, even three years later, a stain that diminished his self-esteem and tainted Bernie's ability to break away from the Angelos of the trade. People fucked with Johnnie more than ever; sneers, whispers, wisecracks and pranks plagued him. "There are too many kooks and cranks out there, and you never know where they're going to come from. I had to learn to protect myself, not expose myself to these things," Johnnie said.

A prime example came when he was playing a series of Canadian dates not long after Franklin left in mid-1963. "In Montreal I got a telegram that said 'Very sorry to hear about your father.' I was about three minutes away from the overture and there wasn't anything I could do," Johnnie said, anger clear in his voice.

"I do not even remember doing the performance, but I got through it and rushed to a phone and called straight home to my dad. And he said 'What do you mean? We got forty new chickens today, that's all.' Some cruel person had done that. And to this day, I still have a phobia about telegrams."[2]

Johnnie closed and went on to Windsor, directly across the river from Detroit. The proximity to his "city of destiny" reached out with a high impact whammy, but this was no conspiratorial attack. Johnnie was turning a sickly jaundiced hue overall, stomach swollen, limbs, tongue and mind sluggish. He tried to bring himself around with a few drinks. He may as well have guzzled cyanide. His booze-marinated liver shut down entirely; he collapsed shortly after going on stage, an inert bag of poison, bones and yellow skin. Johnnie believed he was dying.

Johnnie was checked into a local hospital and flew home when his health stabilized. His severely cirrhotic condition was complicated further by the chlorals and ten years of ragged on-the-road malnourishment. Bernie panicked—how could he keep the commissions rolling in? TB was bad enough, but cirrhosis could end it all. Johnnie was released on strict orders to abstain and rest; the entourage began what more than a few believed was a death watch.

When Johnnie finally realized what was happening, the thought of returning home to Lourie and Jimmy's sodden influence terrified him—not only was he desperately ill but his body's chemical balance, so long reliant on prodigious maintenance doses of chloral and alcohol, screamed long and loud to be fed. It was torture without relief, but to give in would certainly kill him.

Death preyed upon his mind. His mood grew more frantic and bleak. "I've been an insomniac since I was 17. I used alcohol to put myself to sleep. It damn near killed me. In 1962, I realized it would either be me or alcohol. I contemplated suicide, but felt I'd fail, that I'd make a mess of it," Johnnie said in an unusually soul-baring interview. "I decided it was better to stick around and see how it all turns out."[3]

Subsequently, when reminded of the statement, Johnnie would hotly insist it was a mis-quote. In the New York Times? Even in retrospect, this period was too painful to acknowledge.[4]

Johnnie saw no way out, and knew there was no practical aid forthcoming from anyone in his immediate entourage. He begged them to call Bill Franklin out in California and have him rush to New York. Bill was unaware of what had happened, or that he was perceived as a threat by both Bernie and Jimmy Campbell. Johnnie's collapse was not reported outside Montreal; the trades never picked up the story (they were sick of Ray health crises).

Not until Franklin got a pleading call from Dorothy did he discover Johnnie's condition. "They're killing him here," Dorothy said. "He needs someone like you around who can make decisions for him." Although a career change was the furthest thing from his mind, Franklin soon found himself caught up in the center of a pitched struggle for control of a valuable commodity: the Prince of Wails.[5]

Bernie and Jimmy instinctively feared Franklin, a paranoia based on the knowledge that Kilgallen would no longer allow Younger to pull the strings, and in the wake of Hank Wesinger's exit, Johnnie was without the minder/lover he always relied upon. Everyone around Johnnie became bumbling, confused. That was why Hank split—it seemed as if idiocy was contagious at 63rd Street. Marlin Swing, the only other one with his head screwed on right, was wisely unprepared to saddle up as guiding light. Years of Johnnie's mad, celebratory hyper-realism and necessary "looking the other way" made it impossible for the rest of his circle to rationally view the dangerous circumstance that now threatened them all.

After Dorothy called him, Bill telephoned 63rd Street to find out what the situation was there. "I wanted to get to Johnnie," Franklin said.

"And I finally got Jimmy Campbell on the phone, and of course he was drunk. I had this horrible conversation with him, where he said 'Ah, you fucker, you asshole, you wanna know what? You ain't gonna see him. We don't like you around.' I was having real problems with Campbell, he had, in his mind, made up this story that I had already deserted Johnnie once by coming back to California which was bullshit—I had to, it was business."

Franklin requested a transfer to the firm's New York office and flew East as soon as he could. "Of course I went straight to 63rd Street, and Jimmy was there drinking, Lourie was there drinking, everybody was carrying on. Johnnie, of course, looked like shit, and he was just hanging out."

Franklin was appalled at Johnnie's condition. "It was like a dead body speaking to me. He was skin and bones, his eyes were rolled back. He looked like a pregnant woman, his belly had swollen up to 3 or 4 times its natural size, because all these fluids had backed up, his eyes were sunken and yellowish. He was a real mess, and he was still drinking and taking those pills—heavy downers."[6]

When Johnnie hit the deck that night in Windsor it was with decisive impact. Just as his career reached the murky bottom slime, so too did his health. Each reflected the other perfectly, a fateful show of how closely they were linked, and had been from the days of his childhood avowal of stardom. But Destiny exacted a devilish price for the decade of favor, enacting a clause in the deal which Johnnie was unaware of, specifying that physical well being decay at the same rate as fame.

Over the last three years, he watched this erosion growing swifter, felt prestige and health tumble away in small handfuls. That slow crumbling gave way to a sudden roaring avalanche and Johnnie, supine, jaundiced, writhed feebly in an attempt to keep from being swept away and buried. He felt like a cockroach flipped over on its back, kicking impotently, rocking from side to side with nauseating futility. He was stuck, as good as dead.

Johnnie refused to enter another hospital—after his ear surgery, who could blame him? Franklin ignored his mumbled protests and got on the telephone. "Dorothy agreed with me, and I talked to Sol," he said. "Somehow we got he and Bernie to agree to take him up to Montefiore Hospital, in the Bronx." The next day Bill rode the subway out. He ran into Dorothy outside Johnnie's room. "We cried together and talked for a long time," Franklin recalled, "because the prognosis for someone in that bad shape with cirrhosis is that death is imminent. He was in there for weeks. I began commuting out there on the subway every day. A couple of times I went out with Dorothy in her limo, but she still had to sneak around because of Dick."

"Chris George and I went up to Montefiore Hospital," Marlin Swing said. Both were stunned when they arrived at Johnnie's bedside. "We walked into the room and neither one of us recognized him. We saw an emaciated old man, a skinny little old man. I thought we were in the wrong room, so I walked out and looked at the door—his name was on it so we knew it had to be Johnnie. That's how bad the cirrhosis was."

Weeks passed. Johnnie was about three fluid ounces away from the grave when Franklin intervened, and he remained insensate, feeble minded. But the atavistic drive which carried him first to fame and then to death's doorstep still burned, a link to natural forces so deep-rooted that it alone was able to strike a spark of life within him. Bill Franklin observed a startling demonstration of this pagan-fascination's overwhelming hold on Johnnie's will power.

"He wasn't making much sense at that point—couldn't really remember when you were in the room and when you weren't. But Johnnie was so much into nature, it was like a sense of connection to the universe, it amazed me a lot of times. When he heard on television there was going to be a solar eclipse that day, as dull and doped up and nutty as he was, he suddenly rolled out of bed and mumbled 'C'mon, let's go over to the window.'

"I thought he'd really lost it. I remember I wrapped his hospital gown around my wrist, I didn't know if you could open those windows to jump, but suddenly he was lunging right towards it. I said, 'Johnnie, what are you doing?' and he said, 'let's watch the eclipse.' But he remembered how to see an eclipse with this rolling the paper up, and the pin and mirror, all this business. And he did this whole thing, which was quite involved and he was very intelligent about it—and then when the eclipse was over, he was bumbling again."

In a strange juxtaposition, as Johnnie lay in Montefiore, Dorothy and Bill did the town together. She was, of course, sizing up this latest entrant in the Ray romantic stable, but Franklin never realized it. "Dorothy started to ask me to escort her to the theater and things, when

Marlin couldn't make it. I'd worked in public relations, with lots of show business people," he said, "but I was never really star-struck until this. For about the first two hours when we were together all I could think was 'Jesus—here I am with *Dorothy Kilgallen!*' But then it came down to 'who are you really?'

"And Dorothy was great. I remember especially 'Funny Girl.' We went backstage and saw Streisand. They'd had a feud, she and Streisand, of some sort, but they sat down and started talking, and I remember Barbra saying, 'You know, I thought you were a real bitch, but you're a terrific girl!'"

Shortly, Dorothy came to the same conclusion about Bill Franklin.

*　　*　　*

The eclipse viewing was a significant turning point; Johnnie's subconscious drive was revived by the solar ritual and he began to improve. When it was announced he would soon be able to return home, Johnnie begged Bill to join him at 63rd Street. "And become another Lourie?" Franklin challenged him. "I've got enough money for everyone," the confrontation-hating star replied.[7]

But Franklin did move in, to assist in and oversee the recuperative process. He and Dorothy sat on either side of Johnnie's bed, feeding him nourishing food and advice on how to conduct his life in the future. A cook was hired, and as his appearance become more that of a young man rather than a tawny ghoul, Johnnie thought about himself with greater intensity and depth than ever before. It became clear that all the conflicts and worries so long ignored were the primary cause of this flirtation with the reaper.

He began to clean house. Between Dorothy and Bill's aggressive encouragement, it was easy for Johnnie to finally yank Lourie, like a stubborn rotten tooth, out of the liquor cabinet and into the streets of New York. The cases of booze and a hi-fi set that disappeared along with him were a small price to pay.

"Johnnie was sober and he finally saw what was all around him, which was a change, because before he'd been so drunk he didn't get it," Franklin said. "It was just time for Lourie to go, but I did have a lot to do with it. Johnnie was all for it. And then Marlin, who was a true friend, one of the most intellectual friends Johnnie had, also moved out. So it came to down to where it was just me, Johnnie, the daily maid and Jimmy Campbell." Lourie's ouster was a clear signal to the horde of Ray worshipping glamour boys who had decorated so many 63rd street parties: get lost.

Gone were the Louries of every stripe. Johnnie's entourage was strictly family now, no longer the booze-warmed holding tank for male models and footloose aspirants, but a home for genuine friends like Swing, George, Freeman, Wesinger, Lazarow, Kilgallen to visit, to socialize—to help Johnnie.

"Then, it was 'eating right,' which he hadn't done for years, and we established regular meal times, that was a real departure for Johnnie," said Franklin. Johnnie's preferred meals were simple dishes, exactly what you'd expect. He adored pork chops, meatloaf and mashed potatoes, and when he had the time, he prepared his specialty, chili.

But since leaving Hazel's table almost 15 years before, his diet was predicated by circumstance, hot dogs and spaghetti straight out of the can in the early days, and later, dining at impossibly late hours, or not at all. Usually by the time Johnnie realized he was hungry, hotel kitchens were closed for the night, or he was in a restaurant and so drunk that he merely picked at his order. Now Johnnie was getting the best food he had eaten since his soul food salad days in Detroit.

Franklin did everything possible to gratify and satisfy his patient. But there remained one area where Bill was unable to help-Johnnie's troubled sleep. "He had nightmares almost every night, and almost always the same one. He called out for his father, in a very loud, shrill, jarring voice, 'Dad! Daa-a-a-d! DAD!' And the speech was almost like that of someone with a hearing problem, very poorly modulated—the last 'd' was never quite there.

"Obviously, it went back to something in childhood, like everything does, but he could never explain it," Franklin explained. "And it went on for years and years, he had it at almost the same time, every night. I don't know what to make of it. He was closer to his father than to his mother. He loved Hazel but there were lots of times when he put her down, for the way that she, to use his term, 'castrated my father.' And he used to get mad and always say, 'Oooh! My mother is so evil!' There was something there, but I never could figure it out. And the nightmares continued."

Although he was off the booze, insomnia and his physical dependence precluded a reduction of his "jelly beans" intake, and he popped not yellow, not green, but red ones, the color denoting maximum strength. Yet even these did not bring relief from restlessness and nightmares—but they did keep him high and happy.

"During the recuperation, he was not drinking at all but he was taking lots of jelly beans, sleeping pills, and probably a lot of other pills I didn't even know about," said Franklin. "And it seemed he was taking the chloral earlier and earlier in the day. It took the place of booze, instead he was getting drunk on pills, and it's a different high. He would still lose control, a lot of times, fall down, all that stuff. But he did get healthier and healthier, and not long after he quit drinking, the rubber sheets went."

By the summer of 1964 Johnnie's health reached a near normal state, his physician, Dr. Louis Finger, pronounced that "probably the best thing for him was to return to work—only not a long string of dates, none of the constant grind." One evening at 63rd Street, Betty Kean announced she would be playing Cherie in a Bucks County summer stock production of "Bus Stop," and the director was still casting. It became a family affair. Johnnie took Bo, the lead, Jimmy Campbell played Virgil, and Franklin handled publicity.

Johnnie's dream of thespic glory still reverberated in his heart; both he and Jimmy had been studying acting under New York dramatist Josh Shelley. Several years earlier, Johnnie played Sky Masterson in a western-themed production of "Guys & Dolls," mounted in Dallas during the Texas State Fair. An unlikely bit of casting, the production was memorable for all the wrong reasons.

"He told me about one night, when he sang the line "if I were a bell, I'd be ringing,'" Jane Kean recalled. "The way the number was staged he had to lift the girl up in his arms. When he brought her back down, she accidentally hit him, or bumped into him, and knocked the batteries out of his hearing aid. He had to finish the song without being able to hear anything!"

The Cry Guy's "Blood, Guts and Thunder" experience notwithstanding, a theatrical production's gauntlet of lines, cues, and blocking were daunting to him. Jarring incidents such as that in Dallas did little to calm Johnnie's stage-wary nerves. "Betty Kean was the best. Johnnie loved her, and so did I," Franklin said. "I helped get Johnnie cast in it, and

Jimmy, too, who had a great look anyway, and with his mustache, he really looked a cowboy, so he was perfect. It really did become a family affair, because I knew that having people he was close to would put Johnnie at ease. "He'd never really done anything like that, except 'Guys and Dolls' and he wanted to do more. Betty was a riot, because she'd have vodka stashed three or four places onstage and ad lib lines like, 'Oh, it's so hot in here! I've got to have a glass of water.' But Johnnie wasn't drinking, because the cirrhosis really put the fear of God in him. And doing 'Bus Stop' was perfect, because it would keep him out of the saloons.

"Jimmy Campbell held up very well, but Johnnie was quite wooden at the opening," Franklin continued. "and then he got better and better. But when the reviews came out, they were not kind to Johnnie, and Betty was really worried. She called me and said 'Meet me at the Canal House.' We talked about it, and she said 'He can't see this. There is no way that he can ever see this.'

"I agreed and we plotted how to keep Johnnie away from the reviews, keep him away from anybody that might tell him about it, keep him away from the newsstands. There were two of them near the playhouse and Betty and I went and turned the newspaper around, stuff like that. We did everything we could because we knew he would just go off and then probably still go on stage and be even more horrible, and it would affect everybody in the show and be a total disaster.

"And we succeeded. He did see the reviews several days later, but by then he'd had enough applause and success with his performance that he could look at it differently and it worked out okay. Betty was wonderful—funny, boisterous, drunken, charming, warm. A great lady. She was like a mother to him."

So was Franklin; no one in his position had ever gone so far out of his way to shield Johnnie's delicate temperament, or do so much to try and keep him sober. Just as Bill encouraged Johnnie, Dorothy encouraged Bill to take advantage of his p.r. background and start working as Johnnie's publicist. He balked; Hollywood and Broadway were two different worlds.

"You could handle his press," Dorothy told him. "God knows he could use some help in that area." Kollmar's ban on any Ray items in Voice of Broadway was total—a far cry from the days when Johnnie himself had begged Dorothy to "cool it," so numerous were her rapturous mentions of him. The next day, she arrived with a new typewriter, stationery and a stack of press agents' submissions for Franklin to use as a guideline.

"Dorothy sat down and told me exactly what to do," he recalled. "She showed me how to plant items and how important it was to get out and pick up on what was buzzing around New York, and to give them one 'client' item and several 'non-client' items. 'Earl [Wilson] is very important—establish a relationship,' she told me, 'don't write to him. Telephone after 11:30.'" She told Bill the electric portable was his to keep; he asked her to bust the machine's cherry. "Dearest Bill," she clattered out, "Blessings on this typewriter and love from another typist . . . Dorothy."[8]

"And I did great," Franklin said. "In fact, I even got a phone call from Bernie congratulating me on all the wonderful items on Johnnie running in the columns. At this point, I didn't know anything about Johnnie's finances, I assumed he was secure. But there was great pressure from all the people around him—pressure to come up with money. After Dr. Finger said he could return to work, and "Bus Stop" closed, it was just a two-week run, we had a meeting with Sol.

"And Sol said, 'Johnnie, we've got you a date at the Plantation Club in Greensboro, North Carolina.' And because the p.r. firm I was with was going belly up, they offered me an opportunity, to go with him, all expenses paid, and I'd get $100.00 a week salary. Bernie said, 'Okay, you're his road manager.' I thought 'What's that?'"

The Plantation Club was a moderate class pleasure pit with a redneck tang to it. A BYO joint that sold five dollar set-ups (the bowl of ice always strategically placed next to the huge candles atop every table) with an emcee who mis-announced upcoming acts like "Mamie Van Durham." Johnnie was booked in for two weeks and would receive only $8,000 for the engagement; five years earlier, he was making more than that for one night's work.

Johnnie needed the money—lately the IRS had been beefing quite vociferously about payments, or lack thereof, of property taxes due on Hazel and Elmer's farm in Salem. The deed was in Johnnie's name but apparently Sol was under the impression his parents were dealing with the land and its taxes. Whatever the cause, the government was not satisfied, and Johnnie was appalled to learn that his parents were being put under pressure. He had to keep working.

The Greensboro engagement was a crash course for Franklin, personally and professionally. "I found very quickly what a road manager does—he does everything. You hold hands, do the lights, make the cues, count the money, handle the receipts, you do it all." It was also the first time Franklin met the hard core of Ray fans, a handful of women dedicated to a worshipful life, following the Prince of Wails from engagement to engagement.

"They were all in their thirties, and all in love with Johnnie," Franklin said. "There was Bonnie, from Connecticut, who had polio and was in a wheelchair, and Carol, a tall redhead from New Jersey, with an acerbic sense of humor but who was actually very loving, and Donna, who was from Montreal, and one more, Claire, from the East also, and Claire was the only one who was married. I thought 'How nice, they came all the way down to North Carolina to welcome him back!' I didn't realize they would be at practically every date! They would just take off from work and go. They showed up almost every day, either for the weekend or the whole run—they were *there*.

"These girls were okay. I liked them because they cared about him, and up until then I had met so many people who were not treating Johnnie right, or just boozed all the time. They were loyal and they watched after him. And he loved them. His attitude was 'They don't get in the way, they know their place and they are alright.' After shows they'd ask if they could visit, so I'd clear it with him first, and most of the time it was 'yes.' Some of the time it was 'no,' but whatever it was, that was fine with them. And they didn't drink, which was nice because of course Johnnie wasn't drinking. So we'd hang out together, have something to eat, and they'd also help me sort the music, count the charts. They were quite incredible."

Shortly into the run, he got his first taste of the star's gale force temper after a minor screwup with the lighting. Johnnie blew up, screaming profanities at the shocked young man. A true novice, Franklin began to give him the same treatment; Johnnie whipped out his hearing aid power pack, smiled evilly and switched it off.

"I just lost it when he did that," recalled Franklin. "I picked up a lamp and threw it across the room, and yelled at him never, ever to do that to me again. And he didn't, although I did see him do it with other people." At the time, Johnnie was shocked. But pleased. This was an altogether different bag, one he kind of dug.

It was not their last fight—Franklin learned the hard way. When Johnnie, who was absolutely obsessive about the spelling of his name, appeared on a local Greensboro television show, he told Bill, "Be sure and check the crawl." Franklin said he surely would, but thought to himself "What the fuck is 'the crawl?'"

He found out. "At the end of the show, they rolled the credits—the crawl—and sure enough his name was spelled with a 'y.' And he just lost it all over again. He was so adamant, so passionate about that. Every time his name was misspelled he would fly into this rage." Like they say in the trade, any change, addition or deviation from correct billing may result in cancellation. Not in Franklin's case.

Even with the tension and screw ups, Johnnie found the naivete and fresh enthusiasm Franklin brought with him a delight. "He even let me call him John," Franklin said. "Which he did not like, except from a very few people who were close to him, like Elma, Jim Low, Jimmy Campbell, and I was one of them. I started calling him John-John after the Kennedys, and he liked that because it was affectionate."

John-John and Willie. They were in love. After returning from North Carolina, Franklin assumed the road's mantle of responsibility full time, still for a hundred a week. Additional weekend dates in the Adirondacks and other out-of-town spots ensured everyone that Johnnie was safely able to return to work. With Franklin on the pay-roll and the Cry Guy back in fighting trim, the pair was sent to England in early 1964, on an eight-week tour of Britain. Bill was still worried about the singer's health. "They all said, 'Johnnie's ready. He's tough.' Which he was."

"It wasn't big time stuff," recalled Franklin. "It wasn't London, it was the Midlands and the North. Very hard work at what they called Workingmen's Clubs, which were huge places with gambling, very successful at the time, where the working bloke could go and slam his mug of beer on the table and see big name entertainment like Johnnie Ray, Eartha Kitt, people like that.

"I know the world needs coal miners, but this was an experience. A different kind of show business altogether! But they were a fabulous audience, gave him lots of standing ovations, a lot of cheering. Even though I really didn't like the type of venue, I could see that it was really like medicine for Johnnie, because he was being appreciated, and he was performing well—and still not drinking. It was really good for him."

In Manchester, Diana Dors came to visit Johnnie, the sole high point of what was becoming a grinding routine. He played the working-men's clubs week after week, until Johnnie himself got sick of it. "That fucking Bernie Lang," was a phrase frequently used by him, one which grew to become a chant, a mantra. "Once he was sober, he was putting Bernie down all the time," Franklin said. "And during this time I found out more and more about Bernie from Johnnie and that there was a money problem—which I just could not believe."

Even before his liver failed, Johnnie had sunk to the bottom. For the first time he began to contemplate his life and consider the possibility that he ought to confront the problems which hounded him. Johnnie quickly reached a conclusion—he was fed up with all of it.

"When I kicked out my entourage and went to England after doing 'Bus Stop,'" Johnnie said in a moment of rare candor, "I'd just about had it. I'd had it with the press, had it with the critics, had it with my manager, I'd had it with the IRS, and I'd had it with drinking. I could've drank myself to death ten times over, that's what Hank always used to tell me. But all those lousy days were behind me, and I was ready to check out."[9]

From England, they went to France for a series of dates at U.S. military bases. "'Gee, how glamorous,' I thought, 'we're going to be based in Paris!'" Franklin said. "Well, shit, we rarely saw Paris. We were in a car constantly travelling hundreds of miles to do a show. It was exhausting. I was younger than Johnnie and I didn't have to sing, and I still got tired. This was hard, hard work. I kept watching him and he seemed to be okay. But we did it and did it and did it, all these shows and all the time Johnnie kept mumbling 'That fucking Bernie Lang, Jesus Christ, look at the places they're booking me. That fucking Bernie Lang.' He was so down on Bernie."

At the tour's close in early 1965, he and Bill checked into the Dorchester Hotel and met with Glyn Jones. "Glyn was Johnnie's agent in Britain, and he was in charge of collecting the money from all these dates," Franklin said. "And he said he was going to send it to New York.

"'Why are you going to do that?' I said. 'It's Johnnie's money. Put it in his bank account here.'

"'Well, Johnnie doesn't have a bank account here, and this is what Sol asked me to do.'

"Then Johnnie said, "Bill's right. Why do I send it to them? Glyn, open an account for me here, at your bank.'"

Jones obliged. Franklin was dumb-struck by that bit of information and began to research the matter. "I saw all the people that were involved—accountants, musicians, managers, conductors—and I began to wonder what Johnnie was going to get out of this. And I started to figure, from the $5000 a week he was getting, after hotels, airfares, meals, all of this stuff, what would be left. I finally asked Glyn what Johnnie was going to come out with after a tour like this, and what he told me wasn't exactly terrific, less than ten thousand dollars.

"And I thought 'What's the point? The man is recovering from a serious illness, one that could've killed him. To come over here and do this and then just walk away with a few thousand dollars—why?' To me, it was totally illogical. And Bernie was getting a big chunk and Glyn was getting his percentage, but Glyn was a good man and he said 'That's just the way it always is.'

"I said 'Show me exactly where it goes and who gets what.' And he did. I went back to Johnnie and said 'Has anybody ever told you what you come out with when you do these tours?' He said 'No. I don't know. I just do it. They tell me where to go and I do it.' I sat down and showed him and he was just fucking shocked—he couldn't believe it. And then I showed what Bernie was going to get out of it—and I wasn't down on Bernie, I hardly even knew Bernie, I was just being logical. 'What am I going to do?' Johnnie said. 'How am I going to get out of this?'

"'Well, you're always bitching about Bernie,' I told him, 'and I know you've got a long term contract with him—break it.'" Johnnie did not see how he could. Franklin reminded him with the money in an English bank account, they were in a bargaining position, that Glyn would do as Johnnie wished, and they could negotiate an end to his contract with Bernie. Franklin suggested they repair to Southern Spain and take a break.

"Think about what you want to do with this situation, what you want to do with your life," he told Johnnie. "You're always thinking about everybody else—Fuck 'em. Think about yourself. A couple of years ago I was in Torremolinos, Spain. You've been tramping around in this rotten weather for weeks. It's sunny down there, we could get a house for fifty or sixty dollars a month, servants are dirt cheap. Let's do it, go down there and sit in the sun and decide what it is you want to do with your life."

Within days the question of where the funds were grew heated. "Sol, who always stuttered, had gotten very tough with Glyn, he kept saying 'We *n-n-n-need* to have the *m-m-m-money.*' And I thought 'Why do they need it so badly? They must have reserves.' And that's when I found out about everything, that Johnnie was basically here because he had to be, simply in order to be able to pay the rent!" explained Franklin. "And I began to have conversations with Sol, from London. And he leveled with me: 'This is the way it is.' But I still didn't believe it.

"'You've got to talk Johnnie into sending the money to New York,' Sol told me, 'because Bernie really needs the money.'

"'What do you mean 'Bernie needs the money?' So does Johnnie, from what you're telling me. What about him? He's the one over here working his ass off.'

"'Well, he's g-g-got to come home and play some d-d-dates anyway!'

"Then, I got very emotional over the phone, Glyn and Johnnie were there in the room with me. I said,

"'Fuck that! What for if he's not making any money? why should he bother? Fuck it. He's got money over here, so he's just going to stay here on vacation, take it easy and look out for his health. Let's just let Bernie go fuck himself. And you? You go fuck yourself, too.'"

Johnnie was beaming—Franklin had articulated precisely what he had so long ignored and run from. He grabbed the phone out of Bill's hand.

"I think it's a good idea, Sol," he said. "I think sitting in the sun and thinking about myself for awhile is a good idea. I've been on the road for years—I've been on the goddamn road forever! And if I'm not sick, I'm on stage singing. Bill's right about this. That's what I'm going to do." He gave the phone back to Bill.

"'B-b-but Bernie is b-b-broke.' Sol protested.

"'Sol, so is Johnnie!' Franklin snapped. 'I don't know about Bernie, but I'm here, with Johnnie, and I'm going to look after him.'"

That this epiphany had to be forced upon him is characteristic; as Johnnie explained it years later, "There's a lot of stupid innocence in me and I'm not proud of it. In a lot of ways I haven't managed to grow up very well—but when you realize that and know it, that's half of getting there. Bernie Lang fast-talked me into a management contract, and when I signed, it was probably the worst mistake of my career, and I paid for it in several ways. So, I quit. I fired my attorney, fired my manager, paid everybody off. I quit and went to Spain."[10]

Torremelinos was the sublime antithesis of everything Johnnie's life had previously centered around. The months spent there with Franklin were gentle, happy, deeply romantic and comforting. He adored the remote, untamed sensation it afforded; such rustic simplici-

ty was a rare luxury, a contentment that seemed to free him by renewing a childlike wonder long since dimmed by urban twilight.

Johnnie plunged into the simple life. He no longer dressed for dinner; going into town wearing blue jeans was a kick. Eager to fit in, he found a local young woman to teach him Spanish, no small undertaking for one with such a severe hearing problem. Johnnie went to her hut for weeks. "She was very sweet, and very patient with Johnnie. And of course, she fell madly in love with him," Franklin said. "The poor girl."

Johnnie relished his independence to the exclusion of all else. "I had *really* quit show business. I became so absorbed in that life, I didn't want to come back at all," he said. "And in Spain, I had enough money to live like a king." At the age of 38, Johnnie felt closer to normalcy than he had since living in Dallas. Much of his contentment was due to the fact that he was free of Bernie Lang's influence and demands, but an even greater portion of joy came from his romance with Bill.[1]

"We found a furnished, two-story house on a cliff overlooking the Mediterranean. It was really incredibly charming, there were two burros who lived underneath our balcony, and parrots everywhere," Franklin said. "This was Torremelinos before the big Costa del Sol boom, before all the condos. It was probably the happiest I've ever seen Johnnie. He was a pasty faced New Yorker, but he sat out in the sun and got color, we took long walks, met a lot of local people, and expatriates, Americans who were living there."

His sobriety lent everything a vivid, lively edge; "It was easy for him to give up drinking, because he was really scared that he was going to die if he didn't. Johnnie didn't want to die, and he found more and more reasons to want to live. Going back to just hanging out with himself, he found he could enjoy more than performing. He was simply being happy—being a person. Most of the Spaniards didn't even know who he was . . . he lost all sense of himself as Johnnie Ray the singing star, he was more like, 'I'm just Johnnie, I'm just hangin' out here.'"

Johnnie was in Spain to heal and forget—two prodigious undertakings. The cirrhosis he was whupping had been brought on by a thirst nothing less then epic; when Danny Kessler first went to Detroit to romance the singer for Okeh, Johnnie regularly had eight cases of beer sent up to his room. Jim Low's account of him tossing back ten vodkas between shows reveals what a frighteningly high volume of liquor Johnnie used.[2]

The barest possible minimum statistic one can calculate, using Low's ten drinks as daily average, is some three hundred drinks a month. That's three thousand, six hundred a year and a very low estimate of forty three thousand, two hundred drinks since he recorded Cry in October 1952. Obviously, his liver had been called upon to metabolize several hundred thousand ounces of alcohol, but probably was likely two or three times more than that amount.

That he was able to survive the booze defies comprehension. Figuring in the conditions under which he did this drinking (the physical exertion of performing, lack of sleep, atrocious diet) and the various pharmaceuticals he was using, it seems positively miraculous. Johnnie was as much a physical as he was an artistic phenomenon.

That he was still unable to sleep even after this average daily elbow bending and pill dropping regimen is an ugly insight to the myriad tensions, pressures, anxieties and mental snares that assailed him. Johnnie's life was an exercise in extremes, unimaginable emotional zeniths, the rise and plunge of glorious rapture and shattering torture. His anguish, like his capacity for intoxicants, was beyond comprehension.

It was not until Bill Franklin appeared that Johnnie was shown what seemed the genuine interest and dedication he hungered for.

What impressed Johnnie most about Bill, of course, was the boy's eagerness to subjugate and re-direct his entire life in order to serve and protect his. Although Bill was unable to grasp the violent depth of Ray's dissatisfaction, he tried. The very attempt itself bespoke an integrity and trustworthiness Johnnie rarely stumbled across. The relationship was both pure natural romance and a textbook case of dizzy star and eager sycophant feeding off each other.

Franklin's devout commitment armored Johnnie. In Spain, he felt a slow de-pressurization. He was nearer to achieving a civilian lifestyle and consciousness—a contentment he thought was, for him, impossible. But Johnnie was still controlled and driven by incomprehensible force that never really loosened its hold on him. That hold was something he could feel as much as sense, a power rattling his system. It was a primal, implacable dilemma, and the involvement of fame, power and wealth intensified Johnnie's frustration over his failure to confront and understand the power's source. All he could hope to do was corral and domesticate what seemed to be a limitless, terrifying drive.

At long painful last, that tension was behind him. Also behind him was the glory, the manic vermillion juice of being the world's top heartthrob. At the Marion Davies reception, the biggest stars in the world had toasted him with glass slippers full of champagne but that seemed like a half remembered dream. Lost. It was almost impossible to believe that had actually occurred. Johnnie had a universe full of magic to bury and forget. Amazingly, he was able to do so.[3]

Happy to be away from New York, happier still to be off the bandstand, the only thing Johnnie missed was his friends. The phone in their villa ran up hefty bills; Dorothy would lie on her bed up in the "Cloop" and await his call. Years before she had installed a private telephone line whose number was a closely guarded secret; when it rang, she knew it could only be Johnnie.   They spoke frequently, and at length. "Johnnie missed her," Franklin said. "There was some question of her visiting, she said she would come. We both invited her. But she never did." Kilgallen was quite busy at the time, working on the biggest story of her already major league journalism career.[4]

Although Dorothy rarely discussed on-going trials or the independent investigations of cases she was covering, she was passionate about one she concentrated on almost full time: the assassination of President John F. Kennedy and Jack Ruby's role in what seemed a broadening mystery. Dorothy was in and out of Dallas throughout early 1964 for Ruby's trial. When she told one of his attorneys, Joe Tonnahill (the other was Melvin Belli) that Ruby and she had a mutual friend, "some kind of singer" from San Francisco and wanted to personally deliver a message from this character to Ruby, Tonnahill agreed to ask the presiding judge to arrange a private interview with Oswald's killer.[5]

To Johnnie, it all seemed like a distant madness. As appalled by Kennedy's death as anyone, Dorothy's vague dispatches from the front intrigued and impressed, but never concerned or worried him. His health returned and bloomed under the Mediterranean sun. He became deeply tanned, blond hair lightened even more by the sun. He re-immersed himself in the barefoot boy persona. At first, it was a familiar role played to the hilt; he finally reached the point where he no longer rehearsed, but lived it, completely and naturally. His true character emerged—unconstrained, boisterous, spontaneous.

That was probably the greatest gift Franklin's plan of action rendered him. Johnnie's neurotic, relentless drive had no place on the beaches of Spain, and to feel that slipping away was a joy. The knowledge of self his freedom brought was a marvel. Unwound, with sand in hair and stars in eyes, Johnnie sincerely thought he was forgetting and forsaking all the bullshit and glitter of the trade.

But he could not. The urgent recognition of destiny that first stirred and tingled when Elmer took him to the movies kept tugging within. Johnnie was a showman, an entertainer, the Atomic Ray. He could not let it all slip away, even if he tried. Nothing short of death would quell his intense adoration of the applause and lights, and even after that world of cosmetic glamour had almost killed him, its roots still clasped him tight.

Stripped of obligation, freed from his puppeteer's tugging, Johnnie got more satisfaction from sitting around on his scrawny ass than he had guzzling Dom Perignon from a gallon size crystal Frederick of Hollywood pump. Bill Franklin was a novice to the Trade, but he was masterful at conjuring that which Johnnie led his life for: love and beauty. Together they scared up more than Johnnie had ever known.

As admirable and necessary as this was, Franklin was also overseeing a crucial business deal—the deep sixing of Bernie Lang. "Johnnie once told me that his life was not worth living unless he could get away from Bernie," Elma said. "And Bernie always said, I heard him say it myself, 'Johnnie, if we are not compatible, if this contract is not working, we'll just tear it up.' But when Johnnie did not like the way his career was going and told him so, Bernie said, 'Well, fine, but I still want my percentage of your earnings,' up until a specific date, which I don't recall.

"Bill Franklin probably saved my brother's life. At that time, he was very sick, very vulnerable. Bill helped bring him back to a wholesome attitude and frame of mind—to do battle and face life again. I love Bill for that and I always will. I don't like to indulge in hate, but I would look Bernie in the face and tell him: 'You are a worm. If you were a cockroach on the sidewalk I'd step on you and squish you.'"

While the idyll of Torremelinos was a dreamy period in Johnnie's tumultuous life, Franklin was in far over his head as Johnnie's manager. Due to a combination of inexperience and haste, the negotiations with Bernie were stacked in the manager's favor. To Johnnie, Bernie was a threatening boogie man; he was scared by the entire matter. Bill tried to stay cool throughout what became a complicated and protracted ordeal. Sol Lazarow (the only business associate whom Johnnie considered a true friend and remained on the payroll) was their go-between.

"I never talked directly to Bernie. I wrote a lot of letters to Sol, there were phone calls back and forth. Bernie got an attorney and Johnnie became very nervous. I told him 'There's nothing he can do, he can't touch you, so don't worry.' We first went to Spain in January and it wasn't until July that we succeeded in dissolving the contract with Bernie. It was done by mail, from grand New York to this tiny tumbledown post office in Torremelinos."

Bernie's payoff ultimately included not only cash, but a large portion of Johnnie's song publishing. "Part of the settlement with Bernie was something to do with the catalog and publishing," recalled Franklin. "Bernie did get a major chunk of the publishing money. I don't remember the breakdown." This was a disastrous concession. By Sol Lazarow's reckoning, "Little White Cloud" maintained a sales average of over 100,000 copies a year. (And Sol computed that figure in 1983; even if Bernie got only his established standard 25% of the catalog's earnings, he probably still receives two or three thousand dollars a year off that one title alone).[6]

Johnnie, ultimately, did not give a flying fuck; he was that happy to be out from under Mr. Commotion. He stayed firmly on the wagon, and roamed the beaches and hillsides of Spain with Franklin. They adopted a dog who broke loose from one of the semi-feral packs that wandered the countryside. They entertained their neighbors. "The house was full of people when Johnnie wanted it to be," Franklin said, "and empty when he wanted it empty. We had whatever we wanted to drink or eat, daily servants, a cook, it was wonderful."

It was a limited wonderful. They had been in Spain through Winter, Spring and a divine, long summer, but the money dwindled with each page off the calendar. Johnnie, certain his swollen coffers back in New York were compounding interest at a brisk pace, was nonplussed. Secure in that knowledge, he never asked Sol for specifics; neither did Franklin. They only saw financial statements from the English bank account Glyn had opened and by Torremelinos standards, he was still a far cry from hardship.

It was not financial hardship that got Johnnie to return to the stage—it was loyalty. That was a quality which Johnnie always respected and strove for, even when it went unrequited. A textbook as-good-as-his-word-Westerner in that sense, loyalty was one of the very ethics Johnnie relied on. "I stuck with Bernie out of loyalty," he said, "but he had no loyalty to me. I never had anybody to help me out." Back in New York, an old cohort badly needed Johnnie's loyalty. He was counting on it.[7]

Lou Walters, now 70, had yet to bounce back from the Cafe de Paris catastrophe of 1958. Walters' former Latin Quarter partner Elias Lowe had done everything he could to ensure the venture failed. "He was the meanest bastard that ever lived," press agent Irving Zussman said of Lowe's campaign against the Cafe de Paris. "He gave out orders to his liquor, food and linen suppliers—'If you deal with Lou Walters, you can't deal with me.' I imagine most of them followed what he said because the Latin Quarter was solid as a rock and the Cafe de Paris was a new venture."

When Walters was forced to throw in the sponge less than a month after opening the club, he did so in bankruptcy court to the tune of $500,000 in liabilities, then fled to Miami. While Johnnie, still under contract to Lowe, was laid up with tuberculosis in 1960, Walters was slapped with charges that he had failed to pay over $16,000 in city cabaret and gross business taxes. He was even jailed for a time. Released on bail, he failed to make a court appearance in November, resulting in a bench warrant for his arrest. Walters surrendered within several weeks and claimed that he simply could not afford travel expenses from Miami to New York.[8]

By mid-1965, dogged by FBI investigations stemming initially from his association with E. Claude Philippe (who daughter Barbara had dated after he paid his debt to society) and another spectacular failure, the Aqua Wonderland revue, a twenty-two-scene water spectacular staged in Miami's 6,500 seat Marine Stadium (a lavish production that needed sales of 3,000 tickets per show just to break even but averaged an attendance of 300), Walters was falling apart.

After he suffered a heart attack that Summer, Barbara Walters secretly prevailed upon Sonja Lowe to help her get Lou back into the Latin Quarter. Although Sonja had divorced Elias Lowe almost twenty years earlier, she was able to get him to agree. Walters was re-hired as the Latin Quarter's general manager, signing a contract that ran only six months. Lou Walters needed to operate, to prove himself the great showman again. Naturally, he called Johnnie Ray.[9]

Of course, Johnnie, who had been set in 1959 to defect to the Cafe de Paris as soon as his contract with Lowe ran out, and no stranger himself to IRS thumbscrews, agreed to appear. He felt obliged—Broadway

Loyalty ran too deep. Franklin negotiated the details and an engagement booked. "If I hadn't had a contract with Mr. Lou Walters at the Latin Quarter that September," Johnnie said, "I would not have come back." He had not been in the United States for 11 months but now resigned himself to awaken from his Spanish dream and return to the breach. In truth, he could not wait to paint his face with pancake-makeup.[10]

"When we started to talk to Lou Walters, Bernie was already completely out of the picture." Franklin recalled. "I told Johnnie, 'If you're going to go back, it's got be Johnnie Ray's triumphant return from Europe,' so I had Glyn book him on a couple of television shows, one in Barcelona and one in Madrid, 'Noche de Estrellas.' Johnnie was terrific, he really tore it up—did his hand clapping Jubilee gospel number and they couldn't tell what the hell he was singing about but they loved it."

Back in New York by August, they brain-stormed endlessly on how to stage this, ahem, comeback. ("I hate that word!" Johnnie jokingly screeched in his best Gloria Swanson as Norma Desmond voice, "It's a return!") The pair formalized their business relationship. "I suddenly became his manager," Bill said. "And went on a commission deal where I got ten percent if an agent booked him but if I booked anything directly, I got fifteen percent. That's the deal we stayed with until we ended our relationship."

Times had changed considerably since Johnnie's last headline date in New York. The Beatles had knocked everything in pop music off-kilter. Johnnie was unimpressed; the sympathy he felt for Elvis did not extend to the mop tops. Whenever their hordes of squealing fans appeared on television he would dismiss the phenomena, quietly saying "Oh, I did that."[11]

Like New York, Dorothy Kilgallen had also changed. Johnnie was shocked when they met face to face. Dorothy was obviously deteriorating—her face was puffy, her figure was shot. She had gained quite a bit of weight and seemed weak; her bearing and gait were stilted, her speech was no longer the tuneful silvery voice of Broadway but closer to labored, thick-tongued voice of the Bowery. Dorothy's passion and principles ran as high, true and clear as ever, but her mental clarity and standards of practice were also degenerating.

WOR had killed "Breakfast with Dorothy & Dick" while Dorothy was hospitalized in '63, when an embarrassingly incomprehensible and obviously smashed Dick took to the air. Dorothy herself had begun to broadcast under color of inebriation, and by the early sixties she often gave up trying to read her sponsors' ad copy, explaining "the type is too small."

The days when "she was right at work, sharp as a tack, no matter how much she'd drunk the night before," were behind her. She was involved in a humiliating libel suit. She was drunk, high, out of it. Even her fellow "What's My Line?" panelists were concerned she might fall apart before a national audience. Dorothy had changed, and not for the better.[12]

Johnnie's time, however, was dedicated to his return; the showman was back, and deliriously happy for it. While they had several new-to-U.S.-audiences arrangements brought from England (the best of which was Anthony Newley's "Who Can I Turn To?"), this crucial booking demanded a smart, sharp, up-to-date book. Franklin hired arranger Hale Rood, and all three began sorting through new song titles; Franklin made the most influential suggestions.

"We made a lot of changes. I added dramatic songs with the same feel as those which had made him famous," Franklin said. "But they were contemporary songs like 'What Kind of Fool am I?' and 'What Now My Love?' We tried that with a bossa nova beat at first; that didn't work, so we switched to a bolero arrangement and that was perfect for him. We felt Johnnie had to be a little 'Now,' so we did a medley of Jerome Kern's "Yesterdays" and the Beatles "Yesterday." That was great. And, of course we couldn't get rid of the old hits, but Hale did all new charts, because he had to be contemporary."

The biggest advantage Franklin brought to this re-tooling of Johnnie's presentation was his own musical ability. "I had a good ear, a fair singing voice and I could carry a tune, so I worked with Johnnie a lot on this new material, to help him learn and keep time." he said. "That was the hardest part of learning new material for him. I had lots of nicknames in that capacity, 'Mary Metronome,' was one of them. We had a lot of fun putting the act together."

Johnnie opened at the Latin Quarter on September 1, 1965. It was a smash—lines stretched down Broadway and he sold out the club almost every night for three weeks. Lou Walters was relieved; he would stay with Lowe and the club up until its closure four years later. The new material was perfect, Rood's arrangements ideal and Johnnie at the peak of his form. The press poured favor upon him like syrup cascading onto a waffle. He readily soaked it up.

Even the New Yorker, relieved by Johnnie's familiar presence during this period of social upheaval, cheered him on: "The big thing is a tremendous and tense song recital (good show! good show!) by Johnnie Ray, who represents the agony and the ecstacy of it all." The disconcerting era of discotheques, cherubic mop tops and Oswald's Mannlicher-Carcano had shaken the 400 to their core. Tension was the order of the day, and Johnnie's staged conquest of it was a nurturing, familiar balm.

The entire Fourth Estate embraced this prodigal's return. "Ray opens strong and continues to pour it on, turning a ballad like 'What Now My Love?' into an emotional striptease . . . he does for tense what Perry Como does for relaxation," said Variety. "The opening night crowd embraced his return with cheers, bravos and a dozen encores," Hy Gardner wrote in his nationally syndicated column. "Johnnie Ray displayed all his masterly showmanship," said the New York Journal American's Louis Sobol, "and was rewarded with tumultuous applause."

Another New York Journal American columnist trumpeted his thrilling virtues, reporting, "Johnnie Ray is such a smash in this current Broadway engagement that he's been signed for the Tropicana in Las Vegas starting October 5." The item ran in Kilgallen's Voice of Broadway on September 15, the first time she mentioned Johnnie in print for almost three years. "Dickie may not like it, but I'm just reporting the facts," she explained to Bill. "He can't deny that the boy is a smash." Dorothy was backstage at the Latin Quarter practically every night, but cautiously. She allowed herself to be seen on the floor only once during the run.[13]

Kilgallen was equally cautious about not telling Johnnie the details of something else that developed during his Spanish exile. A new romance. She had fallen for an aspiring songwriter and journalist from California, a young man named Ray Pataky, whose greatest success was having several of his tunes recorded by Jerry Vale (perhaps as a result of Dorothy's influence). It was a serious crush; significantly, she had already given Pataky the unlisted number of her private line up in the "Cloop."

They met two years earlier when Dorothy joined an all-expenses-paid 20th Century Fox European press junket aimed at reaping praise for three on-location productions ("The Sound of Music," "The Agony & the Ecstasy" and "Those Magnificent Men in Their Flying Machines"). On the junket's last night in London, Pataky and Kilgallen spent a rhapsodic night drinking together, climaxed by a stroll across Waterloo Bridge at dawn's early bright. Quite romantic.

In the summer of 1964, the pair was already trysting at the Regency Hotel, located seven convenient blocks from her townhouse. By the time Johnnie opened at the Latin Quarter, she and Pataky were thick as thieves, but nowhere near as close as Johnnie was with Bill Franklin.[14]

*   *   *

The strength of Johnnie's raving press was felt coast to coast; the Tropicana's Entertainment Director started calling from Las Vegas within a week of the Latin Quarter opening. In order to keep the ball rolling, Bill took out a full page ad in Variety ballyhooing the New York success and upcoming Vegas date, and officially identified himself as Johnnie's personal manager.

Topped by a bold white on black print headline "When Johnnie Comes Marching Home," with "Marching" X'd out and a hand-written "Smashing" scrawled above, it showed the new, mad, mod Johnnie Ray. Gone were the black tie and pomade; clad in a bulky knit cowl neck sweater, and grinning from under a shock of tousled hair that was no longer slicked back but cascaded boyishly almost into his eyes. Johnnie appeared vital, face full, eyes bright and sharp, a picture of ruddy health.[15]

Maintaining that health was both Johnnie and Bill's primary concern. When they returned to 63rd Street, Johnnie found it disquieting. After the simplicity and Quixotic romance of Spain, even riding in the elevator bothered him. The muggy heat and rain of a September in New York was stifling, and Winter's approach was a dismal prospect. By the time Johnnie hit the Latin Quarter, he and Bill were already discussing a move West.

Franklin, after all, was a Southern California native and Johnnie a born West Coast man. During this same period, many of his friends were also moving out to Los Angeles. Jack Devaney was the first, Betty Kean had just moved; it almost seemed like a migration the entire trade was undertaking, eagerly becoming "bi-coastal."

Johnnie encouraged Jimmy Campbell to join this Westward movement. Campbell and Johnnie were happy to be re-united; he and his wife had separated and the drummer was in a rut. Even though the boss was not drinking, Johnnie and Jimmy thrived on each other's company. "Jimmy was very good for Johnnie on the bandstand, and he wanted to use him at the Tropicana," said Bill. "When we got back to New York he was just finishing 'Hello Dolly,' and he was still drinking. Jimmy was a sweetheart, but such a heavy boozer it was unbelievable. I remember lots of scenes with him just drooling all over the place."

Campbell was ready to get out of town; after Hollywood ice queen Ginger Rogers replaced Carol Channing, all the fun went out of the gig. "Channing was marvelous," said Jimmy. "Never forgot anyone's name, always had something nice to say, but Ginger Rogers was a pain in the ass—Miss Movie Star, and a bit long in the tooth to be pullin' that shit. I was gettin' very perturbed, and was thoroughly tired of 'Dolly.' As soon as John got back from Spain, he went back to work and asked me 'how would you like to go to Las Vegas?' At that point, it seemed like a beautiful idea."

Johnnie and Bill were preparing to get out of town permanently, although Johnnie, at first, could not grasp the logistics. "He liked the idea of moving to California a lot, but he said 'I've got a lease here—how can I move? How can I do it?' Everything seemed so difficult for him to think about, because he was so used to be directed, with everything. I said, 'It's easy. You just do it!'"

The apartment had stood empty for months (Sabrina, Johnnie's Doberman had been given away before they split for England in 1964). They packed everything, took down all of Johnnie's gallery wall photos, his half dozen gold records ("Cry," "Little White Cloud," "Please Mr. Sun," "Walkin My Baby Back Home," "Somebody Stole My Gal," "With These Hands,"), the commemorative brass plaques from all those record breakers at the Palladium. They boxed up his huge collection of records, took down the chandelier, all the paintings and antiques, crated the baby grand, and arranged for shipment to a Bekin's storage warehouse in Los Angeles.

Franklin flew out to Las Vegas alone. "I got out there first because I wanted to rent a place instead of staying at the Tropicana," he explained. "I was thinking of his health, trying to get good food into him. Because if you live at the hotel, you lead that life—you're up late enough as it is, but in the hotel the casino's your front room and you're up all fucking night. I wanted to get away from that."

In New York, Johnnie rattled around 63rd street like a ghost. It was a drag. Without Bill's watchful eyes upon him, Johnnie, ever the naughty boy, had to break the rules. "He called me up and said 'Come by and see me after the show,'" Jimmy Campbell said. "'We'll have some drinks together.' John started drinkin' a little bit then, not too bad." An indulgence whose appeal lay in its danger, Johnnie awoke so scared by an unfamiliar hangover and gruesome memories of Montefiore Hospital that he swore off all over again. By the first of October, Johnnie officially closed the door on that fabled apartment for the last time. It was a pivotal and uncertain moment; Johnnie had neither golden prospects nor melancholy regrets. "The only contract I have is with Tropicana," he told an interviewer the following week. "Just before I came here I fulfilled an engagement at the Latin Quarter, but I want out of New York."[16]

Johnnie, with Campbell out front on his custom-made rolling drum riser and Si Zentner's big band behind them, was a sensation at the Tropicana. The two-week engagement Bill had booked was extended for an additional twelve nights. Another post-Bernie Lang success, but with one minor flaw—Johnnie was appearing not in the main showroom, but in the Blue Room lounge.

The room was by no means a dump. Neither was it a Latin Quarter. It seemed, at least, a cornerstone on which to build the career back up. In their rented hideaway, a mini-manse on Las Vegas' Bonanza Road, Franklin was on the phone every day with booking agents, entertainment directors, talk show talent brokers and, most importantly, realtors out in California.

Even more important to Johnnie, though, was the news that Dorothy was coming to Las Vegas. She was taking advantage of another Joseph E. Levine press junket, to ballyhoo "The Oscar" timed to coincide with "Oscar" soundtrack contributor Tony Bennett's opening at the Riviera. Although Kilgallen had long considered such affairs inherently unethical, the grim fact that her and Dick's finances had been squandered away almost entirely by 1965 reversed this attitude. She realized the junkets were not only fine, *gratis* surrogate vacations, but after that dreamy dawn on Waterloo Bridge with Ray Pataky, a key to unimpinged and unobserved romance. And she badly needed to feel Johnnie's sensationally proportioned romance within her.[17]

He had not seen her since closing night at the Latin Quarter almost a week before, but her scarcity was understandable: Dorothy was in high gear working on the Kennedy assassination, an investigation that demanded more and more of her time. To Johnnie, it all seemed quite mysterious. She mentioned a planned trip to New Orleans for further research into Lee Harvey Oswald's background and connections there (a daunting contradiction of his pro-Cuba street corner politics and incongruous associations with right-wing conservatives and the Carlos Marcello crime family). And she was also regularly stepping out with Ray Pataky, an affair Johnnie was as yet unaware of.

Nonetheless, Dorothy was still quite mad about Johnnie. She stayed in touch with him as regularly as possible. Often telephoning at a hopelessly late hour, now almost always using her pitiful child voice. Alone up in the Cloop, her conversations were growing stranger and more fragmented. They usually ended with a murmured "I took a good-bye," her pet name for Seconal, signalling that the drug was quickly shutting down consciousness. Johnnie who was always high on "jelly beans," never perceived her "good-byes" as much of a problem. Franklin was concerned by it.[18]

"Dorothy became the 'Little girl lost, nobody-loves-me' kind of person on the phone," said Bill, who answered many of these calls. "Her voice totally changed into a pleading little girl's. Toward the end, it became more and more prevalent. To me, I sensed that it was definitely the drugs taking over. I remember a couple of times when she said 'I woke up and couldn't remember if I took the pill or not, so I took another one,' that same story we've all heard so many times."

The little girl routine manifested itself even before Dick caught them necking in the Black Room. It had always bugged Johnnie; she usually slipped into it when he tried to beg off and call it a night. "I've had it, honey. I'm goin' home to bed, this boy's *tired*," he would announce with cheery diplomacy. "But why can't I go with you?" she implored over and over in her wispy, wheedling baby voice. But so much had changed, and his annoyance over it was long forgotten—he loved Kilgallen deeply and eagerly awaited her.[19]

Since Johnnie was scheduled to submit to an interview for the Los Angeles Times when Dorothy's flight arrived, Bill drove out to meet her. He bore a gift—the most vulgar souvenir he was able to find. "I picked out the most outrageously awful, hideously Vegas coin purse, made of mesh gold and put it into a Tiffany box." Dorothy was mightily tickled.

He escorted her to the Riviera and waited while she changed into a shimmering stunner of a black formal, a scattering of pearls swept up in her coif—and Bill's tacky metal-mesh bag clutched in one hand. "Everything I need is right here in this extraordinary purse," she announced. "We had a lot of laughs over that, Dorothy was so funny." Franklin recalled, "And she took it out with her, beautifully dressed, all the time she was there."[20]

They rushed over to the Tropicana to meet Johnnie. It was a rich, emotional, happy evening. Between performances, they went back to the Riviera for Bennett's show, made a stop at Levine's schmooze-and-booze press party, then returned to the Trop.

"She was so happy that night." Johnnie said. "As far as I was concerned, nothing had changed. The only reason she came out was to see me. The Levine party was a pretext. She wasn't much on junkets."[21]

Dorothy surprised Johnnie when her conversation turned to Kennedy, Oswald and Ruby. Her policy of not discussing an ongoing case until the matter was settled, when she regaled friends with every juicy morsel, seemed to go out the window (covering Sam Sheppard's murder trial, Dorothy, in chambers with the presiding judge, was appalled when his honor flatly pronounced Sheppard "guilty as hell." Clearly grounds for a mistrial—opening arguments had not yet been heard—she said nothing. Only after Sheppard's conviction did Dorothy mention the comment).[22]

Something had loosened her tongue. "She talked about the Kennedy assassination endlessly," Bill said. "Dorothy was very disturbed by the whole thing, was sure there was some kind of conspiracy. She said she was close to breaking the whole thing open, and also that she felt threatened, life-threatened, as a result of her work."

Dorothy, one of a very few legitimate journalists aggressively challenging the Warren Commission's findings, was no less outspoken in print. She had already infuriated and perplexed the FBI by printing Jack Ruby's verbatim testimony to the Commission—long before any of the material was to be released. Her latest coverage had been downright inflammatory:

> Those close to the scene realize that if the widow of Lee Harvey Oswald (now married to another chap) ever gave out the "whole story" of her life with President Kennedy's alleged assassin, it would split open the front pages of newspapers all over the world. Even if Marina explained why her late husband looked so different in an official police photo and the widely printed full length picture featured on the cover of Life Magazine, it would cause a sensation. This story isn't going to die as long as there's a real reporter alive—and there are a lot of them.[23]

*   *   *

Dorothy spent four days in Las Vegas. Between her boundless passion and limited time, Bill felt even more uncomfortable than he had as part of a trio in New York. "We all saw a lot of each other, and there were times when Johnnie and she went out alone. She would come out to the house one night, Johnnie would go to her hotel the next," he said. "I kind of felt in the middle there . . . a lot in the middle. That had happened a lot with her anyway, but it seemed she was feeling like maybe Johnnie didn't love her like she thought he should."

Bill mentioned his discomfort, and, he said, "Johnnie got on his high horse, saying 'Well, fuck her! Who does she think she is?'" Franklin probably wished he had kept his mouth shut; he wound up as telephone conduit, relaying heated messages between Johnnie and Dorothy, who refused to speak directly. The weird game lasted only several hours; all converged amicably in the Blue Room and then went out to do the town.

"We had close times in Las Vegas, and spent some beautiful nights together, but there was some dissension between Dorothy and Johnnie," Franklin continued. "I think I know what caused it—all the independence he re-discovered in Spain came out. After years with Bernie and all those people telling him what to do, he wasn't taking any bullshit anymore, and he became rebellious towards a lot of things that he had taken for granted. Johnnie still loved her, he loved her dearly, but there was a place for that love."

Emotion ran high between them. When the high of Johnnie's self-reliant independence blurred into his impulsive Star Psychology, it got weirder. "They were having spats. Late one night, we were taking her to the Riviera," recalled Bill. "She and Johnnie were in the back seat, and she gave him her room key, which she'd done a lot in the past. But then she said something he didn't like, so Johnnie opened the window, threw the key out onto the Strip and screamed 'Anybody want to fuck Dorothy Kilgallen? Here's her room key!'"

With the Tropicana engagement drawing to a close, Franklin escalated his hunt for another gig. "The Blue Room was very successful, Johnnie was great, Jimmy Campbell was great,

but other entertainment directors in Nevada were not too receptive," he said. "I wasn't successful in getting Johnnie a job to jump right into after the Tropicana. I was talking to a lot of different agents in my capacity as 'manager,' but I didn't turn up any worthwhile offers.

"Frankly, I couldn't find one agent, who I considered strong enough, that wanted him. We had left New York for good, and there we were out in the middle of the desert, just going with it . . . looking for free-lance stuff. For me, the main thing, because I was so fond of this man, was keeping him healthy," Bill stressed. "And he was healthy, he was looking great, doing great, and no drinking."

The trio resolved to move to Los Angeles. This meant finding a suitable home for Johnnie. "While we were in Vegas, I took a weekend and came to L.A., which is my hometown and I knew quite well," Franklin said. "I looked at houses to rent, and finally found one on St. Ives Drive, a big house up in the hills. People said that Vic Damone had lived there, it had a wonderful view, lots of room, so I took it."

With Bill off scouting prospects, Johnnie and Campbell were left alone together—which meant no one was around to save Johnnie from temptation. Except himself. Jimmy Campbell, the "perfect drinker," gave the matter no thought. He had been bunked in their Bonanza Road rental's servant quarters. "It was a nice little apartment up above the garage," Campbell recalled. "I stayed in there to get away from Bill Franklin." No such worries now. As soon as Franklin split, Johnnie inspected Campbell's liquor stash, moved him into the main house and initiated a bender.

"We'd usually finish up in the Blue Room about two in the morning, then go back home, watch some TV, and drink," Jimmy said. "I had a little car, a '64 Mustang I'd bought when I was still with 'Hello, Dolly,' that I drove out from New York. One night after the show, we were just drivin' around. Got near Vero Pass and John says, 'Hey, let's really get away from town—why don't we go to the dam and have a drink?'

"So we drove out to the dam, stopped at a little bar up there, called the Gold Strike Inn. It's a big casino and motel now, but back then it was just a joint. A few slot machines, an old upright piano, and hardly anybody else in the place except the bar man. We'd already been drinkin' from the day before, and somewhere around five a.m., John decides he wants to play the piano. He sits down, starts playin' and the bartender, naturally, was very impressed.

"About seven in the morning, we're still in the joint, John is singin' away and we were really gettin' out there now. And a bus full of tourists pulls up, all these people suddenly walk in and now he starts to sing for them! Does all his tunes for them, they're fallin' down, he's signin' autographs. I was just breaking up, and John loved it—he was just singin' and signin', signin' and singin'. It was great." Campbell laughed at the memory.

Johnnie seemed to court disaster and enjoyment with the same hand. Fortunately, Bill never learned of the all-nighter; he would have gone completely berserk. They were even luckier—freewheeling home at nine in the morning, just as Campbell turned onto Bonanza Road a police cruiser, siren blaring, pulled the Mustang over.

"I thought "oh, shit! What did I do?' The guy wanted our ID's," Campbell recalled. "But then he looked at John, recognized him and asked 'Aren't you Johnnie Ray?' Checked the ID and then he got real impressed. Turned out, there was a stolen car report for a '64 Mustang, same color as mine. I had some pretty good chops in those days, could hold my booze pretty good, but inwardly I thought 'Thank God.' I'd be fine as long I was sittin' down, but if he asked me to walk the line, forget it. Finally got home, boom! that's it, man, went inside and crashed."

Johnnie awoke at dusk, painfully hung over and cursing his stupidity. With a jolt of terror he remembered the police siren's wail. That was one damn *close* call. Realizing the stunt's peril both health and career wise, and how readily he jumped into the situation, Johnnie felt a familiar bemused disgust, the hot blush of hangdog shame so typical of his last few years as a drunk.

Having narrowly eluded dire consequence, his thoughts were whipped up into a twister of adrenalized paranoia and self-recrimination. His self-described "stupid innocence" combined with a dread of what Willie would do if he found out terrified Johnnie. He dutifully clambered back onto the wagon.

The Tropicana run closed on November 3. A none-the-wiser Franklin returned to Bonanza Road and herded Johnnie onto a Los Angeles-bound flight. Below the aircraft, Campbell's Mustang burned through the desert; he arrived at the address Bill specified shortly after their cab from the airport. Jimmy, a native Philadelphian, was impressed by the California version of opulence.

"Franklin rented Vic Damone's old place in West Hollywood," he said. "Beautiful house, way up in the hills, with I don't know how many windows, decks running around two sides of the house. You could walk out the sliding doors and look down onto Los Angeles, really fantastic. Great party house."

They threw one immediately. A number of Franklin's sleek, tanned West Coast pals came up, along with several of Johnnie's nearest and dearest: Jack Devaney, a gracious gentleman, happily attended, as did Jim Low, Betty Kean and Lou Parker. Elma was there, too. She re-married in 1962 and lived in the San Fernando Valley, which was, as she reminded Johnnie, "just over the hill," a phrase of home-spun reassurance. Johnnie immediately felt right at home.

He flounced about and entertained with an impersonation of Damone's wife Pier Angeli in "Sodom and Gommorah" ("Where I come from, there is no evil. Everything that brings pleasure is *goood*") and recalled that he and Dorothy had first held hands while Damone crooned "An Affair To Remember". He feigned distress at the possibility of being once again chased up and down the Sunset Strip by Marilyn Morrison (in fact, she began calling soon thereafter).

Later, Johnnie sat at the piano and sang "I'll Get By." It was a lovely occasion. No regrets over leaving 63rd street ever arose. Seeing his closest friends again, reassured they were "freeway-close" neighbors all, Johnnie exhaled.

The only drawback on St. Ives Drive was its wall-to-wall carpeting, recently dyed a garish orange. They quickly discovered it was done on the cheap—the color absorbed into almost everything that touched it, transforming a white sock into something resembling an emergency room swab. Remedies were discussed, jokes cracked, and white slacks ruined. Once they got some dates and went on the road, they would arrange to have a new, insoluble carpet laid.[1]

Franklin went into high gear on his hunt for bookings. He spent almost every day going from agency to agency, establishing contacts, building rapport and fielding offers. For most of that first week in Hollywood, Johnnie hung around with Campbell, gobbling jelly beans, reading the trades, watching TV, telephoning friends, waiting for Bill to return, going out to dinner. On the afternoon of November 8, he arose at his usual 2 p.m. Brain-cloudy from last night's chloral and craving coffee, he checked in with Jimmy. How about maybe we wheel on down into town and get a bite to eat? Shit, yeah, John. Sounds good. There was a joint on the Sunset Strip both men favored.

They had to hurry though—Johnnie wanted to get back in time to watch television identity quiz show "To Tell the Truth." The mystery was to determine which of three masked guests was "The *real* Joan Crawford."

Her red herrings were Arlene Francis and Dorothy Kilgallen; Dorothy mentioned taping the show during a telephone conversation just before Johnnie left Las Vegas. To Dorothy's surprise, she and Crawford had hit it off together and even went drinking after the show.[2]

"We had lunch on the Sunset Strip," Jimmy Campbell recalled. "And John picked up a newspaper, opened it up and there was the headline: 'Dorothy Kilgallen Dies In Her Sleep.' Jesus Christ—he almost fainted on the spot.

"He said 'Wait a minute now . . .' and started crying like a baby. He cried for real. She was a good lady, man. Good to him, good to me, good to all of us." Campbell's voice tapered to near silence with the recollection. "We got back up to the house, we're both crying now, and John says 'Give me a drink.' We got drunk. They were close, man, really tight. She was one of the best friends he had.

"After he got done crying about it, he got pissed off," Campbell said. "John didn't believe she died of natural causes. He said, 'I ain't gonna tell you everything that I know about what Dorothy knows, but I don't believe that she just laid down and went to sleep like that.' He didn't tell me the whole story, though. Never would. I asked him that day and he just said 'It's dangerous to know what Dorothy knows.'"

*   *   *

The circumstances and details surrounding Kilgallen's death are clouded. Accounts by witnesses as well as police, coroners and medical examiners are fraught with error and conflict on a number of specific and significant points. The cause and time of death, at what hour and by whom the body was discovered are simple questions still obscured by myriad contradictory on-site reports.

The body was found, not in the "Cloop," where she habitually slept, but a third-floor bedroom. Spotlit by a reading lamp, head propped on a pillow, clad in a blue robe, Dorothy's false eyelashes and extensive coat of thickly layered from-cleavage-to-crown makeup had not been removed. A novel by Robert Ruark (whose scathing 1952 New Republic essay on Johnnie Ray had "invited him to step outside and fight like a man."), lay where it had slipped at her side, but Dorothy's reading glasses were still in her purse.[3]

The Kollmar townhouse had seen a great deal of activity that morning, well before the announced discovery of her body. Shortly after 3 p.m., when the 19th Precinct station was officially notified of the death, CBS also learned the news. Eager to break the story, they asked Marlin Swing to telephone the house to confirm the truth. He agreed; a woman answered.

"May I speak to Miss Kilgallen?" Swing asked.

"She's not here at the moment," the unknown voice replied. "May I have her call you back?" CBS went with the 19th Precinct source and announced the death.[4]

The initial reports, quoting her father, attributed Dorothy's death to a heart attack. Two days later, the New York Times cited a Medical Examiner's report that laid the cause to "the effects of a combination of alcohol and barbiturates." Five days later the city issued a death certificate, stating cause of death as "acute ethanol and barbiturate intoxication," standard M.E. speak for "booze and pills." But it was amended by a rather extraordinary designation: "Circumstances undetermined."[5]

This was a phrase rarely used—New York City's official pathological and forensic services, even in the case of Hudson River floaters and unidentifiable Bowery indigents, are famed for the rigor and infallible application of every possible method to determine a true and correct accounting. That such a phrase was entered onto the record, yet neither explained nor resolved, is baffling. A weak framework upon which to erect a case for foul play, but one fact did lend an air of dark mystery to her unexpected death.

Every scrap of material Dorothy had amassed on the Kennedy assassination had disappeared. The fruit of an eighteen-month investigatory work load, it was described by contemporaries as a bulging sheaf of documents, notes, research, interview transcriptions, contacts, photographs and clippings. She had personally guarded the material, kept it either by her side or under lock and key.

Dorothy suspected that Oswald had not acted alone, but as part of a sinister cabal. Hers was one of the first voices crying conspiracy. Unlike most of the crackpots and paranoids who swiftly joined the chorus, Dorothy's suspicions were grounded in apparent fact and backed up by intense research.

Her coverage of the case, before and after the Warren Report, was the most aggressive and in-depth being done. Kilgallen not only anticipated many of the theories since endlessly propounded, she was able to explore and attempt to verify specifics at a time when the trail was still fresh. Dorothy's political and underworld contacts were unrivaled within the Fourth Estate; if any reporter had the capability to follow a chain of conspiratorial evidence to its end, it was Dorothy.

She went to Dallas in February 1964 to cover Jack Ruby's trial, already talking conspiracy. On her first morning there, Dorothy told a young reporter assigned to navigate her around town, "I don't see why Dallas should feel guilty for what one man, or even three or five in a conspiracy have done." Clearly, Dorothy was privy to something that raised suspicion. She began digging for something, anything, to illuminate her controversial beliefs.[6]

Ruby mouthpiece Joe Tonahill showed Dorothy his January 1964 request (a 10-page letter sent to J. Edgar Hoover, Attorney General Robert Kennedy and the entire Warren Commission panel) for copies of all material which the Commission had compiled on the assassination, to use in Ruby's defense. At first denied, within weeks Tonahill received summarized testimony from 1500 FBI witness interviews pertinent to Ruby's case, but included nothing on Oswald or the assassination itself.

The lawyer still wanted more on Dealey Plaza. Assistant Attorney General Herbert Miller informed Tonahill the Justice Department did not see why he needed it. On February 21, Tonahill's story, headlined "Defense Got Secret Data" comprised Dorothy's first in a series of assassination exclusives. She dramatically seized upon Herbert Miller's stated refusal to hand over the goods on the assassin:

"'Information concerning Oswald's assassination of the President will not be available as it does not appear to be 'relevant.' Say that again, slowly."

She built to a heated extrapolation:

"Why is Oswald kept in the shadows, as dim a figure as they can make him, while the defense tries to rescue his alleged

killer with the help of information from the FBI? Who was
Oswald, anyway?"[7]

The very day this appeared, Jack Ruby began asking to meet with
Kilgallen. During a recess, she spoke with him briefly, and used their con-
versation for another exclusive the following day: "Nervous Ruby Feels
Breaking Point Near." It offered little, other than relating that she left
Dallas "wondering what I really believed about this man." Many ques-
tions. No answers.[8]

She was in and out of Big D several times during the trial; sometime prior to Ruby's March 14 conviction and death sentence, Dorothy's
"mutual friend, some kind of singer from San Francisco" ploy got her the
interview. They spent eight minutes alone together in a small court clerk's
office. Melvin Belli told Kilgallen's biographer that "Dorothy Kilgallen did
have several interviews with Jack Ruby . . . Jack would talk to anyone and
by this time I had resigned myself to it, and didn't try to stop him. Most
of what he said, anyhow, was gibberish . . . He saw in her a very prestigious person who could get him an 'audience' with almost anyone."[9]

The notes carried away from the Ruby interview were the germ of
her realization about the truth of Kennedy's assassination. Yet she printed
nothing that revealed, nor hinted privately to anyone, what the exclusive
interview yielded. Dorothy apparently preferred to continue her research,
and use the results in a long-planned book "Murder One," a retrospective
of her most sensational trial coverage. Contracted by Random House in
1961 at the suggestion of editor and "What's My Line?" panelist Bennett
Cerf, he had been trying to get her to complete the manuscript for the last
three years.[10]

In print, Dorothy continued to insist "the whole truth has not been
told." Intriguing, but decidedly insubstantial. She continued digging
throughout that Spring and Summer—while also digging Ray Pataky and
her favorite night spots.[11]

In mid-August, she came up with a breakthrough; Howard
Rothberg recalled a social meeting with Dorothy, toting a copy of Life
magazine with the controversial cover photo of a gun-brandishing
Oswald. A fat sheaf of papers bulged between the magazine covers; when
he asked what they were, she breezily answered, "Oh, just the Warren
Commission Report."[12]

The Warren Report was not released until late September, but Dorothy somehow obtained 102 pages—Jack Ruby's testimony, in its entirety. She ran all of it in a three-part series starting on August 18, 1964. It was a plum scoop, but Ruby's testimony shed no light on anything except his confused mental state. The FBI immediately began an investigation to learn how she got hold of it. Agents interviewed her at home on August 21, demanding the name of Dorothy's source. She refused to answer, saying only that the transcript in her possession was limited to Ruby's testimony, and that it had been responsibly and legally obtained.

Dissatisfied, the FBI was soon back at her door. Dorothy, conceded the source was a man, "a friend of long standing," and blithely announced the feds had gotten more out of her "than the Journal American editorial staff had." When they continued to press for a name, Dorothy told them, "I would rather die than reveal my source." (She specified it was a man only to clear a female typist Dorothy had learned was the FBI's prime suspect.)[13]

Dorothy ran story after story based on inconsistencies and hinted at her own posited conclusions. The most sensational installment of her leaked Warren exclusive appeared on September 3. Under the headline "Pre-Assassination Mystery—Warren Told Strange Trio Got Together":

"A man who loved President Kennedy.

A man highly critical of President Kennedy.

A policeman who was killed immediately after President Kennedy's assassination.

"These incongruous three allegedly met in Jack Ruby's Dallas Carousel Club eight nights before the president's murder, according to previously secret and unpublished testimony given the Warren Commission."[14]

The "incongruous three" were reported to be Ruby, Bernard Weissmann, the man responsible for November 22, 1963's notorious black-bordered anti-Kennedy newspaper ad and doomed police Officer J.D. Tippit. The piece read like a stunner, but concluded nothing.

That secret strip joint meeting was a hard act to follow, but Dorothy, after meeting with the New York attorney representing Marguerite Oswald (Lee Harvey's mother), who had introduced that subject to the Warren Commission, kept up a volley of controversy and speculation.

Marguerite Oswald's lawyer was closely assisting Dorothy's invevestigation; he assured her she was correct in assuming that the lines of her home and the Journal American office's telephones were wiretapped. They began to meet late at night, in dimly lit bars or under street lights and assigned each other code names for use in covert phone contact. She became "Parker" and he "Robinson."[15]

The Warren Report's conclusion, that Oswald alone was responsible, was unacceptable, not only to "Parker" and "Robinson," but millions of other outraged citizens. Days after it was released in September 1964, she spelled out what so many believed:

> "It's a mite too fishy that a chap kills the President of the United States, escapes from that bother, kills a policeman, eventually is apprehended in a movie theater under circumstances that defy every law of police procedure and subsequently is murdered under extraordinary circumstances."[16]

Her stylishly glib tone was employed to mask the raw emotion and outrage Kennedy's death brought to a certain generation of Americans. Such a light touch was, in truth, well suited to the occasion. Her investigation had begun as purely objective, dedicated journalism; by the time she ran her "This story isn't going to die as long as there's a real reporter left" piece a year later (focusing neither on any solid facts nor privileged communication with Ruby, but vague assertions regarding Oswald's widow, Marina) Dorothy's reports had become a self-serving, opportunistic game that exploited a national refusal to accept the truth.

Americans did everything possible to avoid conceding the decay of a mythic, self-perpetuated innocence common to that era. Dorothy, like countless others, was suckered by the conspiracy kooks.

Say that again, slowly.

"Who was Oswald, anyway?" A psychopath, the classic assassin—another Wilkes Booth, another Guiteau, whose action was complicated by a remarkable confluence of emotion, paranoia, coincidence and good luck (he got away) followed by bad (he was stopped by Tippitt). That the Feds, in collusion with the Mafia, organized it and called upon Ruby to silence their patsy, is a scenario quite a bit more fishy.

Journalism was, after all, her career. By 1965, it was no longer so much an avocation as a profession. Dorothy and Dick were running out of money, having squandered a fortune being concurrently sapped by bad investments and hefty legal fees. She had long since blown the advance for "Murder One," but was unable to start work on the manuscript. Dorothy also faced a million dollar libel suit; when her attorney Edgar Hatfield tried to collect a portion of a $20,000 bill, she fired him. And the New York Journal American was also in desperate shape, on the verge of imminent collapse. They needed to sell a lot of newspapers.[19]

Dorothy not only faced financial hardship, she was drunk virtually all the time. By 1965, staggering into her CBS dressing room, arms at her side, palms flattened against the wall, Dorothy often looked like she feared the building might collapse should her hands move, all the while repeatedly asking her makeup artist 'How do I look? Do I look alright?' Shortly after Ruby's conviction, she fractured her left shoulder—whether the result of a fall or CIA intimidation remains unclear. Dorothy was hospitalized twice more that Spring, for considerable periods of time. Detoxification, a doctor later told her son Kerry.[20]

Why three visits? Because, as a friend of the Kollmars said, Dick brought in "pills and liquor that damn near killed her.[21] Apart from her shambling gait and thick speech, Dorothy's jaw sometimes locked, a strange condition she never discussed. Her health was falling apart as rapidly as her financial state.[22]

She took advantage of press junkets as pretext, specifically a free flight to Zurich, where she underwent "cell-therapy," a popular at the time but gruesome and FDA-banned practice based on the injection of animal embryo cells. This miraculous rejuvenative technique was similar to the infamous 1920's "goat gland" craze which sent people flocking over the Mexican border; Dorothy was making a last-ditch attempt at survival.[23]

Her "Assassination Exclusive" series was, essentially, Dorothy's proposed salvation of herself, Dick and the Journal American. In truth, they offered little more than a skewed reincarnation of classic Hearst yellow journalism. After divining that Ruby was a kook who had killed on impulse alone, and that much of Mark Lane's theorizing was based on hysteria, an emotional irrationality loaded with appeal to a confused and saddened America, Dorothy probably realized it was all a game—a horrifying revelation. But she was in for the long haul and, even though it meant playing out the charade before her most intimate friends, she had to shoot a winning match.

She chalked her cue, and gave each shot just enough of a disorient- ing spin to strike at the heart of assassination anxieties plaguing American society. Clutching at straws while appearing as if she was tearing out hand- fuls of truth by the root, she consciously engineered the most sensational phase of her career.

Mark Lane had used Dorothy the same way she used public senti- ment over Kennedy; both claimed to put great stock in the notion the Life cover shot of Oswald was a government scam. The most persuasive argu- ment cited a visible paste-up line on the chin and a claimed disparity between that chin and Oswald's chin as captured on the Dallas mugshots Dorothy obtained.

The fact that this theory has long since been discarded pales beside the gingerly nature of Lane's handling of Dorothy. In their numerous dis- cussions on which sinister hand doctored the photo, and how to prove it, Mark Lane would not use the word chin in her presence. He admitted to Kilgallen's biographer that "I never mentioned it to her either, for rather obvious reasons." Less crucial evidence of national import than it is evi- dence of a self-serving advancing manipulation.[24]

Dorothy assumed mythic proportions early in life. With the end in sight, she shrewdly constructed a flawless myth, one which in turn would perpetuate her legend even further. Telling the FBI she would "rather die," telling Johnnie and Bill she "felt threatened," even her "as long as there is a real reporter left" line were all part of the set-up. Death was at hand; Dorothy had known it since being hospitalized after Dick confronted her and Johnnie in the Black Room. The myth was seamlessly prepared, and the American public gorged on it.

The entire lamentable JFK conspiracy experience was based on a fearful inability to openly admit that Lee Oswald reflected the Kennedy supporter's essential self-image: a free thinking, outspoken socio-political romanticist, a provocative idealist—the populist rebel, unafraid by dint of his rights as an American, to soapbox less-than-popular views. He was the consummate underdog flipside of Kennedy's monied New England poise.

In the time between November 22, 1963 and Ruby's conviction, Oswald's gift for arguing political pro's and con's became painfully familiar to the public, through tapes of Oswald's New Orleans radio Cuba debate and television news footage from his defector episode. Whether defending his Soviet residency or crying Fair Play for Cuba, Oswald's public tone and attitude were very similar to that which his victim had used to attain prominence.

That air of noble tolerance, sharpened by a condescending exasperation, tempered with patience, equity and well-modulated self-righteousness was, when delivered by JFK, intoxicating. Coming from Oswald, it was repugnant. Thus, Oswald's claim he was a "patsy" carried more weight than any other aspect of the case. Desperate nonsense, but America was desperate to hear it.

There are really only two significant loose ends in the questionable circumstance of Dorothy's death: her Kennedy file's whereabouts and exactly what involvement Dick had in the chronological hurly burly of domestic and secretarial staff, doctors, hair dressers, cops, medical examiners, house guests and telephone calls on the morning of November 8.

Like Johnnie, most of Dorothy's friends believe that she was overdosed, smuggled lifeless into the house and propped up in bed by an assassin who then made off with the explosive material. But such an organized assassin would have been thorough enough to take her up to the "Cloop" and professional enough to remove her false eyelashes. Considering the FBI's interest (after the little matter of 102 leaked pages of confidential information) the likelihood that it was scooped up that morning directly by one of their agents or delivered through the hands of NYPD is quite distinct. Kilgallen's FBI file, however, contains nothing pertaining to her death or FBI involvement, that day or at any subsequent time.

Dick apparently slept through the early stages of confusion, was awakened, fell into a paroxysm of grief, telephoned the second doctor, took some pills and began drinking. That James or Dick himself instinctively stashed Dorothy's Kennedy file is more probable than the FBI's snatching it; such an action would be the obvious and appropriate one for a spouse to take, with anything as sensitive and valuable as the file. Those who propound murder as the cause of Dorothy's end never consider, nor do any of them question Dick's vociferous refusal to allow an autopsy. A great deal of the mystery and contradiction surrounding her death and the body's discovery clearly originated within the household.

The Journal American printed two different versions of the body's discovery, the first reported a maid had found her at noon, the second indicated her hairdresser at 12:30. There was a second doctor, apparently called by Dick, who showed up well past noon and claimed he was the one to pronounce death.[25]

And there was an empty Seconal vial which some witnesses describe, others do not, and is omitted from all of the inordinately spotty official documentation.[26] Kollmar's attempt to avert a routine autopsy certainly implies an understanding and need for a degree of control more in keeping with tenets of the Roman Catholic faith than a man whose wife had just been murdered. Both her parents were still living; a suicide, even the appearance or inference of one, would have been more than they could have accepted.

Under circumstances which many insist are clear indicators of a murder, all Kollmar wanted was that Dorothy be left in peace. Dick never publicly acknowledged the melodramatic speculation which swept New York. If he did make off with the Kennedy file, it was with an intent to publish, as intended, in "Murder One" (which appeared in 1967 as Dorothy's posthumous swan song—*sans* Ruby).

The file was probably destroyed. By Dick Kollmar. Especially after scrutiny revealed it contained nothing more than interviews with confused Dallas residents, some Mark Lane fantasies, and Dorothy's notes from eight minutes spent listening to Jack Ruby blubber. With her Kennedy file gone, the eternal sanctity of Dorothy's myth was ensured. Kollmar took his own life six years later. In the same room Dorothy died.

*   *   *

Believing that she was murdered made it easier for everyone to accept, especially Johnnie, whose anger over her loss never diminished. But the drama of conspiracy and hired assassins was an outlet for him to vent his emotion and grief. Her passing officially ended the glamorous era of Broadway culture.

Of course, by 1965, the glory of Costello's Copa, Winchell's Stork, Dorothy's P.J.'s had already declined to such an extent, they were virtually invisible. Bill Franklin believed that Dorothy's witnessing of her devalued culture's fall had more to do with her steady decline—and her death—than either the CIA or forgetting how many drinks and "Good-Bye's" she had taken.

"Most all of the interests in Dorothy's life, all the things she loved, were on the wane. That was one of the reasons she clung to Johnnie so much," Franklin said. "She had done it *all*, met the Queen of England, met the entire world, and what did she have? I mean, as far as Dorothy herself, went: a life of fear and conflict. I loved her but, really, that's true.

"What she had up in the Cloop was wonderful, in one sense, she could get away from it all, that was her little domain. But from another point of view, a lot of the times she crawled up there, she was frightened and depressed, and probably thought 'What am I doing? Why am I going on with this charade?' *That* is what happened to her. That is what fame does to you."

On Tuesday, November 9, as her body reposed at the Abbey Funeral home, a massive power failure plunged the entire East Coast into blackness. Joan Crawford looked out a New York hotel suite window, rattled the ice in her cocktail and said, "What a wonderful tribute to Dorothy!"[27]

In Los Angeles, teen singing idol Tommy Sands, awaiting his wife Nancy, was with his father-in-law when the sad news reached them. Frank Sinatra barely paused. "Well, I guess now I'll have to change my entire act," he said.[28]

When Dorothy was accorded funeral rites at St. Vincent Ferrer Roman Catholic Church, a mob of 2,500 New Yorkers descended upon Lexington and 66th Street. Johnnie watched television coverage of the hectic scene, his tears soaking into Vic Damone's orange carpet.[29]

"John went berserk when Dorothy died," Jim Low said. "That just tore him apart. I'll never forget it. He was always very high on her, thought the world of her." The loss was a brutal, devastating blow that smashed Johnnie's life apart.

"They loved each other deeply," Elma said of their relationship, "with integrity and utter respect for privacy. I didn't care how they did it or how they expressed it. I only wanted them to love each other . . . I'll let it stand at that." Unlike his sister, Johnnie could not let go.

"Dorothy was the love of his life," a friend said. "No question. I don't know how many times we talked about Kilgallen and the JFK thing. He was very adamant about it. 'I *know*, man, what the facts are,' he'd say. Once he brought it up, if you asked him about it, all he'd say was 'You don't want to know. I've been told to keep my mouth shut.' Well, what the hell does that mean?" The murder/conspiracy tale was his only relief and method to cope with the anger of losing her.[1]

Franklin knew a more practical way: work. Fortunately, an Australian tour was booked shortly after Kilgallen's death and the trio plunged into it. The invariably packed houses did much to blanket Johnnie's morbid sense of loss; in time, he realized there was no other choice but to try and live down Dorothy's memory.

Ethel Merman was also appearing in Sydney, and had taken a drubbing from the local critics. Johnnie rushed to her hotel to both assuage and bask in her favor. Merman was angry but pragmatic over the reviews. "I don't know what the hell they want!" she trumpeted, "They wanted Ethel Merman, I gave 'em Ethel Merman. That's all I can do." Johnnie heartily agreed; in fact, as Franklin said, "He picked up that bit of dialogue, and that attitude, and used it constantly."

Johnnie, like Merman, found himself perceived more as an anachronism than ever. Nothing new in that, but initially it was his radicalism which brought it on; now it was the baggage of years gone by which settled like dust upon him. The fallout of overexposure, compounded by his sinful reputation, made it increasingly difficult to present and exploit Johnnie Ray. Franklin began a campaign to both update and tone down his act.

"At this point, it was very difficult for a lot of these performers, like Ethel, Judy Garland and Johnnie to keep from becoming parodies of themselves," Franklin explained. "And it was happening to Johnnie. In my years with him I tried and succeeded in toning him down—you had to do it or he became a caricature, especially on television.

"It was easy for him to do it the old fashioned way and absolutely revert back to the Johnnie Ray of the Fifties—working every fucking corner of the stage, flailing his arms, jerking around. He was determined that there would not be one person in the theater who was not going to get *JOHNNIE RAY!* He was gonna give 'em *JOHNNIE RAY!*

"I finally told him, 'John, they're going to fucking laugh at you.' And he got on his high horse and said 'Well, I'm Johnnie Ray, and this is what I do.' It was hard for him to do at first, only because it was easier to do it like he always had. But he worked with me on it."

Franklin took a shrewdly diplomatic course, flattery. Johnnie was always a sucker for that. "You do not run on the stage. You walk, gracefully. You're a gentleman—a mature gentleman with great talent," he told Johnnie. "You are a star and when you get up there, you're going to control the arms. And he did, and it was fine." Franklin's direction echoed back to Johnnie's TV drama "The Big Shot." (When Johnnie's character fought to retain his "natural style," the cigar-chomping manager barked, "You mean the prize fighter bit is for real? Waving the arms and all that?")

Despite the ironic fact that Johnnie's "old fashioned" style was becoming more and more prevalent through the frantic capering of rock and roll acts like the Rolling Stones, Franklin was correct to soften and smooth out the act—Johnnie's audience had not expanded, only aged. Loyal as they were, change, as much as an opportunity to hear him "Cry" again, kept them coming back.

Coming home to the U.S. was a nightmare—while Johnnie toured Down Under, the St. Ives Drive house had been burgled. The lost property (which was insubstantial—clothes, jewelry—a great deal of Johnnie's belongings were still in storage) was not as bad as their landlady's insulting attitude. Since she lived in a home just below theirs, an irate Franklin called upon her to ask what had been going on.

"I know that Mr. Ray has been in trouble with the law before," she snarled. "How do I know that what you're saying is true?" Her icy bark, on top of the pain of mourning Dorothy, that damn cheap orange-dyed carpet and her reference to Detroit shook Franklin. He insisted Johnnie spend that first night at a friend's. The air of conspiracy and fear on St. Ives became overwhelming, and they decided to move out. Johnnie was delighted by Franklin's next choice—a Malibu beach house. By the spring of 1966, they settled in for a life characterized by barefoot walks along the beach, fizzing colas and gorgeous sunsets.

Life in the casual, star-studded Malibu Colony was perfect, but bookings began to run more and more toward the low end. Franklin, in order to get Johnnie's price, five grand a week, often accepted engagements in suburban watering holes whose eagerness for name prestige was based on an inherent lack of class. Soon, he even went back to working strip joints. But Johnnie plugged on.

He was still a naive and unlettered country boy, albeit one who regularly bantered with sophisticates like Hermione Gingold, Tallulah Bankhead and Noel Coward. Johnnie and Noel admired each other; "Noel loved Johnnie," said Hank Wesinger, another friend of Coward's. "They loved each other, had great respect for each other." Both made it a point to get together whenever possible, resulting in scandal rag Top Secret's August 1957 smear "What Happened When Johnnie Ray Was Noel Coward's House Guest," which declared that "Cafe Society is chuckling over the strange friendship between the low-brow crooner and the high-brow playwright."[2]

When Johnnie visited Coward's Jamaican retreat, Firefly, his meager vocabulary collided with the host's eloquence. One evening, Johnnie and Noel were perched on a piano bench together, spontaneously improvising a song, trading line for line.

Coward sang, "Your love gives me the impetus to . . . "

Johnnie stopped cold, and interrupted him in mid-phrase.

"'Impetus?'" he yelped, "What the fuck is an 'impetus'?" Coward paused, fixed his gaze upon Johnnie and laughed so hard he fell off the bench. The next time Johnnie heard from him, Coward asked, "Johnnie, do you have the impetus to join us for dinner this evening?" Johnnie broke up. It became a running gag; he always replied, "Well, Noel, I'm not sure—let me check the level on my impetus meter."[3]

Such moments, and such friendships, were really the most important part of Johnnie's life. Through Coward, the Keans, Freeman, Jim Low and Elma, he received an emotional transfusion of light and affection that kept his vision from darkening. He thrived on repartee and jokes with his friends, and sought to spend as much time as possible roaring with laughter.

Johnnie's laugh, in fact, was one of such sustained, vehement delight that he had become notorious up and down Broadway. The star of one particular musical comedy which Johnnie frequently attended, front row center, found his braying so bothersome that she finally begged him to consider taking a seat farther away from the stage. Johnnie laughed louder than ever at that.[4]

*   *   *

Personal Manager Franklin at last came through. Booking Johnnie was no picnic, but hunting for a record deal was murder. The pop marketplace in 1966 was more transitory and inconsistent than ever. But now it looked as if Johnnie would get the shot he deserved. Bill had approached a label whose A&R director Jimmy Bowen was not only enthusiastic, he had a country and rock and roll background (playing in Buddy "Party Doll" Knox's band) not dissimilar to Johnnie's.

Bowen discussed it with producer Lee Hazelwood, who felt he could get a contemporary best from the Cry Guy. They promptly signed him (under the same developmental terms Decca offered, a single with options deal). Variety reported it in a brief item headlined "Reprise Ropes Ray."[5]

Hazelwood, a young hipster, had made his bones recording a million dollars' worth of twang with rock and roll guitarist Duane Eddy in Arizona during the late 1950's. Such a big noise coming out of the desert made the industry sit up and take notice. A certifiable genius in the studio, Hazelwood was also a songwriter and performer of considerable talent. He represented the best of a new breed and the label had such confidence in his ability, they gave him one of the very first independent production contracts. It allowed him a free hand to do what he pleased and turn in completed masters without prior corporate approval of artist or material.

Bowen and Hazelwood were young, eager and not too well versed in the trade's catalog of vendetta and rivalry. Reprise was, of course, owned by Frank Sinatra, who founded the label specifically for himself after leaving Capitol Records in the early Sixties. Sinatra wooed Hollywood record man Morris Ostin away from MGM-Verve (Frank, gesturing at the landmark Capitol tower, told him, "I helped build that. Now I'm going to build one of my own"), installing Ostin as the label's Veep; Reprise also took Dean Martin on board as soon as his Capitol contract was up.[6]

The label introduced and perfected a new brand of 1960's pop— typified by Martin's hits—brash, brassy, *now*, with playful arrangements, strong rhythms and on-the-beat vocals. Under Mo Ostin, Reprise let fly throughout the '60s with an unorthodox, free-wheeling range of pop performers, from the Dreamy Napolitano to (after Sinatra turned the company over to Warner Brothers) the likes of Tiny Tim.

Hazelwood was also recording Nancy Sinatra in 1966, resulting in her international 1967 hit "These Boots Were Made For Walkin'" and her famous duet album with Frank. This was a pairing which produced "Somethin' Stupid" and "Some Velvet Morning," an extraordinarily haunting pop record of world-weary anguish and almost surreal opulence ("Some velvet morning . . . when I'm straight . . . "). If anyone could present Johnnie Ray with sympathy, class and the contemporary edge he so badly needed, Hazelwood was the one.

Johnnie was overjoyed at the prospect, his first time in a studio in over three years, and proud of Bill for snagging the deal. "I remember John talking about the deal with Reprise," Jim Low said. "He was excited about going back in and cutting records. He couldn't wait to get moving again." The big day came; he and Bill drove to Hollywood's fabled Gold Star Studio late on a September afternoon.

"Johnnie was not drinking, and he was really concentrating on trying to do something musically," Franklin recalled. "And Lee Hazelwood's technique was to bring you into the studio to rehearse you and set everything up, and then everybody, engineers, musicians, back-up singers, I mean everybody, would break and go to a restaurant, get a huge table— and drink!

"And this particular night we went to, I think it was Nickodell, and Lee got drunk, to the point where he was slurring. And then we went back to record. This is the way Lee did it, and it just did not work for Johnnie—that whole scene really turned him off. In spite of that, Johnnie did some good work on the session."

The collaboration of Hazelwood and Ray represented a convergence of talent with great potential; despite an uncomfortable situation, Johnnie gave the three songs his best shot. The proposed single was scheduled for a November release. As the date neared, Franklin called Reprise president Mo Ostin.

"I had negotiated the deal with Mo, but really it was still Sinatra's label," Bill recalled. "And I forget exactly what transpired, but I called Mo and he just said, 'It's not going to happen.' I asked why and he said, 'Well, we gave it another listen and we just don't think it's the quality we were thinking of.' It was good work, it was supposed to be released and suddenly it was trashed."

Franklin dreaded telling Johnnie the news but did so immediately. Johnnie tensed. Except for the sound of waves lapping at the shore, the beach house was silent. Finally, Johnnie spoke. "It's Sinatra," he said.

Franklin, at first, did not understand. "Johnnie told me that Frank never forgot when Ava ignored him and wanted to be with Johnnie at the Copa—that's basically what it was. He said Frank never forgot and that Frank, who was in control of Reprise, continued to try and sabotage Johnnie's career whenever he could."

"John had some people, some very high up people in the theatrical business, down on him, from the very beginning," Jim Low said. "When he was going great guns, fine, but later they screwed him. I heard John talk about that, I mean, they put the word out—instead of being a headliner in Las Vegas, he would be in the lounge. Frank Sinatra did that to him. Frank Sinatra hated his guts. Sinatra always thought, for some reason or another, that John had put the make on Ava but John always swore that he never had."

The Reprise caper was one of the most baffling episodes in Johnnie's career and in researching this book. Letters sent to Lee Hazelwood requesting an interview went unacknowledged. Mo Ostin, through Warner executive Bob Merlis, said he "had nothing to do with Johnnie Ray," and did not have "anything to say" about the deal. Ostin suggested contacting Jimmy Bowen, "who was A&R director and had signed Johnnie Ray." Bowen, too, recalled nothing about Johnnie signing with, or recording for Reprise; he recommended asking Mo Ostin for the details.[7]

The notion of a Johnnie and Hazelwood collaboration was one of intoxicating potential, and became a sought-after Grail in my research. The crusade finally yielded a dub of three unmastered Johnnie Ray tracks ("Step Aside," "I Still Love You (By the Way)," "Every Night Lulu") preserved in the Warner catalog without any additional composer credit, session, or personnel information. All turned out to be a crushing disappointment.

"I Still Love You (By the Way)," a ballad given a typical Reprise countrypolitan arrangement (similar to those Bowen used on Dean Martin) features a decent vocal but is, all in all, a flat, un-engaging tune. The other two titles, brash, romping uptempo fluff, are so ill-suited to Johnnie they are sad to hear; while suited perfectly to the juvenile and vul-

gar pop tastes of 1966, the material was so contrary to his style they qual-
ify as unlistenable. While there is no clear evidence that Sinatra personally kiboshed the deal, Johnnie had no apparent reason to believe otherwise.
After breaking the news to him, Franklin went to bed early. The next
morning, not long after Johnnie finally crawled between the sheets,
Franklin awoke and walked into the living room. "There were some logs
still burning in the fireplace," he said, "and one of Frank's album covers
was on the hearth—smoldering. Johnnie had sat up, burning his Sinatra
albums."

*   *   *

Johnnie and Bill went out on the road, jumping all over the country, and
returned to tour England in late 1966. As pop music veered off into sugar-
coated and inane new directions, bubblegum rock versus pop slop, a hollow musical legacy born of the Beatles' cunning solipsisms, Johnnie continued to root around in the bloody bowels of his libidinous R&B kick.
He still disemboweled pop convention and celebrated worldly lust; next to
the cheery mop tops of 1966, Johnnie's Real Gone black and tan ritual
seemed as desperate and amoral as Gilles de Rais squatting to examine the
warm entrails of a freshly butchered child.

A television special "An Evening with Johnnie Ray," taped
December 28, 1966 at Chicago's WGN captured him working before a
live audience on a simulated supper club set.

Clad in a tux whose narrow cut accentuated his already painfully
wan figure, hair plastered across forehead in a moddish style that lent a
distinct Frankenstein-like impression, he really did, as Kay Starr once
described him, look like a ghost, or a man whose spirit and appearance
had been twisted by time spent in a concentration camp or haunted
house. Mike in hand, he sang three or four straight ballads with grace and
dignity. Johnnie then stalked to a nearby piano, affixed the microphone to
an awaiting stand and launched into "Such a Night."

The mild opener was a setup; his performance suddenly upshifted
into an extremely wild and exaggerated conflagration. Punctuated by riv-
eting shrieks and torso-tossing acrobatics, he tore through it with a feral
abandon made all the more frightening by the legitimate, conservative surroundings. He slammed the piano lid, twisted, vibrated, screeched, threw

himself to the floor. Johnnie seemed more anomalous, threatening and destructive than ever.

Johnnie left Chicago to open a two-week engagement at Houston's Shamrock club on New Year's eve; he turned forty that January. The Reprise fiasco seemed more than enough to deal with; but there was even worse news for Johnnie to face. He closed at the Shamrock, and kept jumping from club to club. "There were a lot of dates in Cleveland, places like that," Franklin said. "It really became such a . . . sameness. The pay was always in the same range, four or five thousand dollars a week, which was a loss, really, after expenses."[8]

As Bill became more deeply involved with Johnnie's career, he also learned, through Sol Lazarow, the actual state of Johnnie's fortune. Or what remained of it. The figures were not encouraging. Franklin began to pressure Sol for a complete statement of what the Cry Guy's coffers held.

"I told Sol that Johnnie had to know what the financial picture was," he said. "Johnnie had some idea that things were not what he assumed, because of what had happened in England, but that had nothing to do with all the money he'd made in the past. At that point, even I didn't know about all of it, until Sol told me it was zero."

Franklin was stunned. "Then I said, 'Sol, he's got to know. I can't keep this inside me any longer, I can't deal with it, without Johnnie knowing. He's a grown man. He has a right to know.' But Sol would always skirt the issue until finally I insisted. We drove in from Malibu, to Sunset and Vine. It was getting dark when we sat down in his office. I remember how he started the meeting: 'I have un-p-p-pleasant news for you, John.' And when he told him, of course, Johnnie didn't believe it. He said, 'How can this be? All these years, all of these tours, all my records and I don't have any money?'

"Sol said, 'Th-that's right.'

"'Well, whose fault is it?'

"'It's n-n-nobody's fault, it's just the w-way it is. You've spent a lot of m-money, a lot of things have happened and th-there is just nothing left. Z-z-zero.'

"The meeting went on for a long time but that's all it was about, the fact there was no money left. And Sol was a good man, he really cared, very deeply, about Johnnie," Franklin stressed. "I've seen him cry, when things didn't go right for Johnnie. He indicated that there were problems with the IRS and back taxes owed. At some point while we were on the road, the IRS had visited the Malibu house and left cards in the mailbox, and they had taken a bundle of his money. The IRS was a part of the problem, but the real problem was that there just wasn't any money."

Dazed by the revelation that he was flat broke, Johnnie stumbled outside. On the corner of Sunset and Vine, he felt much the same as when pounding that same pavement in 1949—desperate. Johnnie had no choice but to cut Jimmy Campbell loose. They parted ways shortly after Sol spilled the beans, and Campbell, embittered and angry, blamed Bill Franklin for both his own firing and Johnnie's financial ruin. Jimmy went grumbling back to Las Vegas, and settled there permanently.

Within weeks of Campbell's departure, they left for another Australian tour; Bill carried all the money Johnnie had in the world. Typically, Johnnie insisted they split it fifty-fifty. The grand total of Johnnie Ray's wealth was fifteen dollars.

*   *   *

Ironically, just as he hit the skids, Johnnie began to enjoy the bittersweet experience of being sought out and lauded by reigning pop stars. In Australia, Bill got a telephone call from Tom Jones' manager, inviting them to come and meet the singer. "He said, 'Oh, you've got to come meet Tom, because all he does is sing and fuck,'" recalled Franklin. "That was his reputation at the time and the way he was for real—always in the sack with some young lady. Tom was a very nice man, and he was in awe of Johnnie, told him something like 'I can't tell how much your records meant to me, you are a very important voice in my life,' all very respectful and sincere."

On their next tour of Britain, Johnnie and Bill came face to face with one of rock's top dogs. "When the Beatles first came out, Johnnie said 'Oh, I give 'em six months,' said all the things everybody else did, but he got over it," said Bill. "Then we had a very interesting encounter in London. Johnnie and I were in a club, and Paul McCartney walked in. He saw Johnnie, came over and introduced himself."

"This was at a little nightclub in London, called the White Elephant," Johnnie said. "I was amazed because he wouldn't talk to me. I said, 'I'm glad to meet you, Paul,' and he sort of shuffled his feet and ran out the door." The mop top, confronting a childhood icon, was tongue tied. Franklin recalled that "Paul was very nervous—he was pawing the ground with his foot and said some very nice, complimentary things. Johnnie liked that, it made him feel great."[9]

But Johnnie's gratification over these episodes of homage was short-lived. His artistic sympathies lay elsewhere; Johnnie imputed much more substance to performers like Durante and Merman, the fading legends of American popular theater, than he did to the shaggy, sweaty heroes of the '60s. "We went backstage to visit the Last of the Red Hot Mamas, Sophie Tucker," Franklin said. "She was in her dressing room putting the powder on, looking into the mirror, one of those scenes, and she said, 'Johnnie, you and I have paid our dues, but these kids today, they all come up so fast.' Johnnie quoted her endlessly on that, he loved the fact that she had said that. He felt the same way. There were some ill feelings during that whole Beatles era, when records hit so fast. I always thought it was a little ironic because he did the same thing with "Cry," but he didn't see it that way."

There were several differences, most important being the fact that "Cry" was the first of these hits, the one disk whose hectic ascendence shattered pop music's norm and opened the way for every unconventional singer to follow. A breakthrough achievement that nearly killed him, Johnnie's blossoming recognition as a vastly influential pioneer came as he struggled to survive by means of a meager hand-to-mouth existence.

Now, Johnnie more often found himself in the dressing room of a Sacramento strip joint reminiscent of Cy's Bar in Cuyahoga Falls circa 1950. When faced by these fawning millionaires half his age, all of whom had built their fortune and fame upon Johnnie's foundation, and now flocking to heap passionate tribute upon him, all he saw was Sophie Tucker's haggard glamour and all he felt was a profound sense of loss.

*   *   *

"Johnnie was screwed up so goddamn bad by Bernie and the IRS, that it was unreal," said Jim Low, who spent a lot of time with Johnnie in Malibu. "He hit bottom when they were living in Malibu, it was very hard for him to make ends meet, and the IRS was still taking everything he earned. John didn't know doodly shit about business, money or anything like that—he just left everything up to Bernie and Bernie just put the screws to him. As I understood it, he wasn't making the tax payments that he was supposed to, and the IRS came in and put a clamp on everything. They got a fortune. He didn't have a dollar to his name.

"So he was taking any offer he got, no matter what it was, I mean Jesus, he'd take anything. And it hurt to see that." Low paused and added with a pride born in the forests of the rugged Northwest, "I don't think I ever heard Johnnie complain. I can't recall him ever doing that—he just absolutely did not complain."

In September 1967, Johnnie landed a role in "Rogue's Gallery," a Paramount film being produced by A.C. Lyles, starring Roger Smith and directed by Leonard Horn. It was a mod version of the hard-boiled P.I. plot, loaded with celebrity cameos by warhorse veterans like radio ventriloquist Edgar Bergen. Franklin drove Johnnie to the set. Roger Smith was very friendly, told them he was a fan and that his wife Ann Margaret did a boffo Cry Guy impression he had to see. Johnnie's excitement over his return to the big screen quickly faded. Playing a police detective, his one scene included an establishing shot that called upon him to drive into the frame.[10]

The prospect of getting behind the wheel, stone-cold sober, disturbed Johnnie. He careened and jerked through numerous takes; they showed him how to put the car into gear several times. After he finally managed a usable take, they completed his brief dialogue and lensed a close-up. Horn had to discard the shot. As Franklin explained, "The fear and tension were so evident in Johnnie's face that the close-up could not be used."

"I was down at Malibu when he first started talking about that movie," Jim Low recalled. "I thought it was going to be a hell of a thing. Then I found what the hell it was—he had a very small part playing a policeman, and that it was just a terrible, terrible 'B' picture. That was really the bottom for him. I guess he made a few bucks off it, but not a lot. The whole thing was terrible.

"When you really like someone, you hate to see them put in that kind of position. That movie, Jesus, I'll never forget it. When I saw it, I cried. Afterwards, I asked John about it, you know, 'Jesus Christ, John, why did you do it?' He just said, 'Jim, when you've got the IRS on you, if you're offered something, you take it—because you want them off your back.'"

Low had watched Johnnie go between highs and depressions all of their lives, and still marveled over his friend's ability to maintain himself throughout such a run of ill fortune. He saw Franklin as being a major boost to Johnnie throughout the IRS ordeal, but also said "Elma, God bless her, she helped him an awful lot through that period. And I don't mean with money, she and [her husband] David didn't have a hell of a lot either, but she and John were very, very, close. That's what he needed, just her being there, and being available to him anytime."

Elma credits Franklin as being Johnnie's savior; if nothing else, Johnnie had their love to keep him warm, healthy, *whole*, or at least, reasonably sane. Chloral hydrate was still the only high at Johnnie's disposal; it kept his emotional stability dosed up to muster—without the exacerbation and aggression booze could bring to the surface. Johnnie, for all his naivete and ingenuousness, had nonetheless developed a thick hide. Rather than deplete and sap his resolve, the mid-'60s successive waves of bad news and trouble toughened him even further. Like Sol often said, "J-J-Johnnie can b-b-bounce back f-f-from anything. He's t-tough."

Life did not ease or soften for him; later that year, Elmer, well into his seventies, surrendered to a peaceful and natural death. Johnnie mourned him but refused to plunge into a vortex of loss. He and Bill knew the real tragedy lay in his wife's surviving him. Hazel broke down, utterly forlorn, unable to comprehend how her own life would or even could be led without Elmer. "It started that day, at the funeral," Franklin recalled. "She just kept saying 'What'll I do? How can I live without Elmer?'"

Within a year, her emotional collapse triggered a mental cave-in. Realizing Hazel was unable to manage alone on the Salem farm Johnnie had bought for them, he agreed with Sol that it ought to be sold (the money received for the land was, of course, already long since owed and accruing penalties).

Hazel was moved to a nearby retirement home. She degenerated rapidly; whether caused by Alzheimer's or grief's chilling touch, Hazel's mind failed. The next time Johnnie visited his mother, she did not know him. It was a regrettable and painful end.

Johnnie kept working. In December 1967, Bill managed to get Johnnie his first national television guest shot in several years, on the ABC variety show "The Hollywood Palace." A Los Angeles Times columnist ran a brief interview with Johnnie, asking where he had been hiding out. "It's a long story," Johnnie said. "Filled with mistakes like bad judgment and misplaced loyalties." Asked what singers he admired, Johnnie turned belly up: "I still like Sinatra for his electricity," he said, but tempered the acknowledgment by adding, "He hasn't the voice of an Andy Williams or Tony Bennett." The show went smoothly. He was asked to sing "Cry."[11]

Next, Franklin managed to get Johnnie a 1968 appearance on "The Andy Williams Show." Taping was a breeze; Johnnie was asked to sing "Cry." Johnnie, who had always been a sucker for smooth pop voices like Como and Haymes, dug Andy Williams the most. The two singers became pals.

The friendship blossomed further when both worked concurrent engagements at the Sahara Tahoe; Williams, of course, headlined the showroom while Johnnie toiled 'til the early bright in a lounge. They hung out frequently; Johnnie loved to hear about Williams' 1940's salad days broadcasting at Cincinnati superstation WLW, where not only Andy, George Gobel and Doris Day launched their careers, it was also a springboard for country music greats like Merle Travis, the Delmore brothers and Grandpa Jones.

Williams was such a fan of Johnnie's that before long, he offered him a recording deal with his Barnaby Production company. They went into a Hollywood studio in mid-1968 and cut several tracks but, just as with Reprise, something soured before any of them could be released. Johnnie, naturally excited at the chance to record, took it as an honor that an artist of Williams' stature, wholesome image and popularity had shown the confidence to take on such a project; even years after the fact, the stain of scandal was still visible to many in the trade. His acquittal in Detroit, "buried on page 83 of all the papers," had not penetrated the popular consciousness anywhere near as deeply as the arrest itself had.

Williams' partners at Barnaby were apparently among those who missed the items reporting Johnnie's exoneration; Bill's "Mary Metronome" routine in the studio perhaps led to a few raised eyebrows (Johnnie, after a series of disappointments, now preferred to work both television and recording dates with Franklin conducting him). The project was quietly shelved. "Andy was so gung-ho on Johnnie. But I had many conversations with him after the session," Bill said. "We went to lunch, dinner, we'd talk, but he always just skirted around it.

"He never really gave me a reason, a 'this is why not.' At the end, his cop-out, if it was a cop-out, was something about 'how Barnaby was going in a different direction,' or 'they didn't want to put the money into recording,' something like that. There was a genuine friendship between the three of us, and I think that's why he would never give me a straight answer."

"Straight" being the operative watchword and concept in Williams' career and image, cooler heads doubtless prevailed upon the crooner's offer to Johnnie. It was artistry and talent versus the issues of image and commerce. The choice was clear. No one wanted a frantic torso tosser muddying up the purity of "Moon River."

Johnnie did not take the news well. "He was terribly disappointed," said Franklin. "And there had been so many disappointments already, sometimes I would make up a story to ease the pain, but this time, I couldn't. But this wasn't like the stuff with Sinatra at Reprise, and he still loved Andy Williams, anyway, forever."

There was another abortive recording session, done purely on speculation, at the behest of a young San Fernando Valley-based pop tunesmith named Jack Newman. They recorded four songs, including Newman's "I Think It's Going To Rain Today." After several months of trying to shop the material to every label from high and mighty majors down to the lowliest independents, Newman also had to throw in the towel. "Jack was never able to get it going. Another disappointment, and that one even surprised me," Franklin recalled.

Newman came away from the deal with a bushel of frustration and one hell of a demo with which to pitch his songs (Jack Jones subsequently cut "I Think It's Going To Rain Today" on 1969's "L.A. Breakdown" album).

*   *   *

Although Johnnie tried to remove the sting of each successive disappointment, it was impossible. Disappointment turned to frustration which led to an anxiety that quickly metastasized into cold, bleak fear. It was difficult for Johnnie to realize that the majority of these record dates were poisoned not by substandard vocal performances but as a result of being tarred with the scandal brush. Either way, he was a failure.

So much time had passed since his last public keel-hauling, that Johnnie reckoned every faulty screwup which obstructed his career was erected by his own thoughtless hand. His lifelong inability to grasp the slightest shred of business acumen blinded him to the fact that commerce never saw potential in a publicly exposed homosexual. In this regard, Johnnie's particular brand of Star Psychology worked against him—bad business automatically equated, in his trouper's mind, to bad performances.

Bill Franklin, so personally close to Johnnie, had yet to grasp and recognize how the Psychology drove Johnnie, and was thus unable to steer him away from this deluded self-punishment. Throughout his career, Johnnie had never given a bad performance. But after the erosion of self-confidence which Reprise set him up for, Barnaby inadvertently furthered and the Newman project emphasized, Johnnie found himself back at the bottom—an aspirant. Worse, a has-been with unslaked aspirations.

Seeds of doubt and recrimination lay fertile and gradually taking root within his artistic soul; when Johnnie subsequently began to punish himself, he did so in a most effective way—by turning in bad performances. But at this point in sober late 1968, he and Bill wisely fled to a land where they not only respected Johnnie but took him seriously.

Back to England, of course.

Franklin had scheduled a full itinerary for this British siege. Johnnie was already booked for several months' worth of concerts, television and recording work, but Franklin kept an eye out for additional jobs. Based in London, Bill hoped that Johnnie could re-capture the thread of career momentum, self-respect and artistic continuity which so recently slipped from his grasp.

Johnnie would soon turn forty-two. He looked better than he had for years. The wan and cadaverous mien had filled out enough to bespeak robust health, and his newfound onstage restraint lent additional dignity. Most nurturing of all was the British public's undiminished adoration.

The trip was a relief. Johnnie escaped America's failure to respond just in time, and now secure in the bosom of England's favor, was able to concentrate on Bill. Johnnie was devoted to him, and revelled in their common romantic stability as much as he did an audience's cheers.

For him, Thanksgiving was no longer anything but an occasion of deeply personal celebration—their anniversary. The six years they had shared together, although more tumultuous and tragic than any in Johnnie's life, were perceived by him a season of invaluable quality. Johnnie knew if they had not been spent with Bill at his side, they would have been marked by Elma placing flowers on his grave.

Bill was likewise as passionate in his feelings for Johnnie, and had worked vociferously against draining their meager fortune, to bolster, care for and bring him joy. It was an intense way of life, much of it carried out in the public eye, complicated further by masking a frugal hand-to-mouth reality with the outward presentation of gilded celebrity. Johnnie didn't give a damn what anyone thought of him, as long as his poverty remained a secret. And Franklin also planned to reverse that situation with a heavy workload, the best possible way of life for Johnnie.

"We were going to be there a long time, almost six months; we had a lot of stuff to do," recalled Franklin. "We had checked into a hotel, and I said 'This is stupid—let's rent a house.' I found a mews house, a very, very charming little two-bedroom place. Mews houses were originally built for servants, they were all at the end of long rectangular lots, glorified alleys, really, that led down from a main house.

"They were very much in demand at the time, but I found one on Pavilion Road, in Chelsea. It was great—swinging London, Carnaby Street and all that, and Johnnie was great—he looked wonderful, ruby red lips, tanned and fit, he walked, exercised, it was just a wonderful period for him—and being off the booze, he became so young . . . so we moved into the house, and he just loved it."

Franklin had another recording deal worked out, and they got down to business not long after arriving. They were working with Tony MacAuley, who was fresh off "Build Me Up Buttercup," a hot blue-eyed Motown style pop smash which MacAuley had written, arranged and produced. But Johnnie, in the wake of his recent three strikes in the studio, felt "panic all around him," and tumbled into its pitfall. Never a simple task for Johnnie to feel comfortable with new material, fear thwarted him.

"I've never been very big on rehearsing new material too much," Johnnie said. "Because I don't want to become overly familiar and lose spontaneity in the studio . . . so, as a result, I'm not too good on memorizing new material either, which is a polite way of saying I'm not very bright."[1]

The first studio date was marred not by a lack of spontaneity, but by a non-performance from the vocalist. "I sat next to Tony in the booth, and this man could not believe that Johnnie was not singing the notes," Franklin said. "I don't mean Johnnie was flat, or off key—he just didn't absorb the song. It was partly his hearing, and partly fear. It was like something in the brain just didn't want to take it in.

"And Tony couldn't believe that Johnnie wasn't cutting it. I told him, 'You've got to go out and tell him what you need. Tell him the type of sound and feel, describe to him what you want.' And he said 'The man has had a million bloody hits—I'm not going to tell him how to sing!' I said, 'You're not getting it—you have to do that. And if you tell him, he will do it.' So he started telling him, but none of the stuff was released."

On top of everything else which dogged Johnnie, his unfamiliarity with contemporary recording techniques and the essential difference in methodology was daunting. It was the hey-day of layered 24-track projects, involving numerous different sessions and overdubs, a protracted aural jigsaw puzzle assembled in dribs and drabs over a long period of time. Johnnie was an old-school record man, cut it live and nail it in as few takes as possible—loose, spontaneous, free. Those days were already long gone.

Franklin had attentively done his best to re-define Johnnie's perspective on the issue. "I always approached it from the other side, telling him 'You have to look at it as an advantage, especially with your hearing. With the headphones on, we can turn the tracks up to a frenzy—and you don't have to worry about making mistakes. If you do we can go back and do it bar by bar,' which we did a lot of times. And that was okay, he pretty much agreed with me on that." It failed to bolster his performance in London, however.

MacAuley was not going to let the opportunity to record Johnnie Ray slip by as a result of intimidating studio hardware. He shrewdly counteracted Johnnie's lack of confidence by replicating the milieu and scope of that lost era. "At the next date, it was all ballads, so we walked into this huge studio, and I was just blown away," Bill said. "When Johnnie saw forty musicians sitting there, with tons of strings, waiting for him to do this as a live recording, he just smiled and said 'Oh, yeah!'

"He warmed up immediately, really enjoyed it, because it took him back to the old days. The first song was a ballad called "It's True," and Johnnie nailed it in one take. It was extraordinary—all the musicians stood up and applauded him. And that record came out, just in England, but it was released."

Johnnie felt back in control, and set out for road dates with few misgivings to plague him; workingmen's clubs, social clubs, theaters, community arts centers, he smashed from one job to another with tearful, shuddering aplomb. They were back in London by late December. When Bill had mapped out this British sojourn's particulars earlier in the year, he discovered all the best spots had long since booked their New Year's Eve talent. As none of the offers subsequently made Johnnie were acceptable, they had some time off before his next string of appearances.

There was no question as to how they would celebrate. The pair tuxed up and taxied over to Talk of the Town, where one of Johnnie's greatest idols and show business friends was appearing, none other than Miss Judy Garland. Franklin, inured to the thrill of celebrity socializing after being exposed through Johnnie to every major star in the trade, from Jimmy Durante to Bobby Darin, was beside himself with excitement.

Johnnie had first met Garland while tearing up the Sunset Strip with Marilyn Morrison, but had not become chummy with her until his New York days with Dorothy. He also spent vast amounts of time in Gotham hanging out with Liza Minnelli (so much so that Johnnie himself told the press "I was her housecat"). Judy and Johnnie were as close to seeming like family as any of their globe-circling, downer-gobbling ilk could be.[2]

Judy Garland was, at the time, quite near the end of her badly frayed rope. Having fled an IRS bill that made Johnnie's seem like a troublesome pittance, she was living in Britain as a virtual exile—the Feds would probably clap her in irons the instant she set foot back on American soil.

Garland was in so deep that she had been lucky to get to Talk of the Town at all. "I had written a song for Judy to use there, called 'I Belong

To London.' It was the last song she ever sang," Stan Freeman said. "I remember going to her place, and there were IRS agents who would not let her leave the room until she came up with something." She arrived in London penniless.

"This was a great thrill for me," Franklin bubbled. "I was a Garland addict, grew up on her movies; I loved this woman. And I'd only seen her live once, years before, so this was a grand treat—opening night, with Johnnie on one side of me, Ginger Rogers on the other. It was super. She opened with 'I Belong To London,' which she told me later that she never paid Stan for. Her voice was rough but she was *there*. It was a triumph for her, despite her scratchy voice.

"We went backstage after the show, and when I met her, I just shuffled my feet. Most celebrities didn't impress me, but I had placed her on a special pedestal. The dressing room was full of people, and it thinned and then suddenly it was just the four us. She was with Mickey Deans, who was acting as her companion/road manager/whatever.

"Johnnie and Judy hadn't seen each other for quite awhile, so we made plans for the next night. She was at Talk of the Town for a month, so all during that run, we were between dates and started to hang out a lot, go to her show, or just drop by at the end, and then the four of us would go out to dinner afterwards."

Garland, never having received the type of urgent wake-up call which Johnnie got in Windsor, had one foot in the grave but was too stoned to notice. Variety called it "a troubled success." A London Sunday Times review captured the essence of her derelict grandeur:

> "No logic, no analysis, no judgment in the world can completely explain the phenomenon of Judy Garland's performance at the Talk of the Town. She walks the rim of the volcano each second. Miraculously, she keeps her balance. It is a triumph of the utmost improbability."[3]

One particular evening, Judy spotted Johnnie in the house and called him onstage. They sang an off the cuff duet on "'Til the Clouds Roll By," the Garland chestnut which Johnnie included on his Liberty album. The Londoners went berserk—it was too much, too mad, too marvelous for words. Johnnie was as thrilled as any of them.

Mid-way through Garland's engagement, Johnnie and Bill prepared to leave for a weekend booking. "We had been seeing a lot of each other, but Johnnie and I had to go to Scotland to play these dates, and Judy and Mickey, who loved this little mews house, stayed there while we were gone," Franklin continued. "That weekend, Glyn Jones, who handled publicity for Talk of the Town, came to pick her up there. Judy, of course, was always late and Glyn's job was to get her to the performance on time.

"She was in particularly rocky shape this night, and when he did get her to the club she was over an hour late. She was slurring, she couldn't stand up—this was the night so widely reported in the press, because the audience threw bread and everything else at her and shouted at her to get the fuck off the stage. Big news at the time."

It was January 23rd; Garland was to be onstage at 11 p.m., but she shambled out at 12:20 a.m., promptly lost her tenuous footing and tumbled into the volcano. As soon the spotlight hit her, revealing a spindly, quavering ghoul, the crowd turned ugly. An empty cigarette package was flung in her direction, followed by more of the same, followed by the fabled flight of breadsticks, then cocktail glasses, all accompanied by garrulous cat calls and a bellow of profanities.

She froze, barely able to squeak out her distress. "Oh, dear," said Garland. A man leapt up onstage shouting "If you can't turn up on time, why turn up at all?" She burst into tears and plodded off into the wings.[4]

It was a humiliating fiasco that capped several years of steadily worsening public embarrassment; Garland was fortunate that night in one regard—Mickey Deans was not in the house. Had he been, the affair would have quickly exploded into a knuckle-splitting brawl and her ghastly and aghast press coverage far more damaging. Mickey Deans was a shark, a thirty-five-year-old loser who would soon make himself Garland's fifth husband.

Born Michael De Vinko in Garfield, New Jersey, he had knocked around playing piano in East Coast lounges and then inveigled himself, during a moment of administrative upheaval, into the plum doorman position at Arthur, the New York discotheque which heralded the end of Kilgallen's era and paved the way for Studio 54, the 1970's haven for society cocaine sniffers. Sybil Burton had opened the disco, shortly after Liz nabbed her Dick, getting dozens of pop and movie stars to invest a modest $1000.00 each in the venture.[5]

Arthur quickly assumed an exalted position among Gotham niteries; the columns were peppered with items about its habitues' indiscre-
tions, and only the most fab of the fabulous drank and danced there. It
was at Arthur that Deans first zeroed in on Garland, as she sat at the bar
in a barbiturate haze watching the ice melt in her cocktail. Most of her
intimates had long since forsaken the narcotic-swamped star, and she
badly needed a leaning post.[6]

Deans was an opportunistic, alcoholic rake in a sideburned mod
disguise, who affected an inconsistent English accent which he managed
to brush up by accompanying Garland on her flight from the IRS to
London. A key insight to his character is provided by Deans in his 1972
exploitation paperback Garland bio "Weep No More My Lady," relating
how he got a pet dog to keep him and Judy company.

> Brandy was a brown and black Alsatian dog who was origi-
> nally a vicious police trained guard dog at Talk of the Town.
> The first night we saw him, he was wearing a muzzle and was
> on a strong chain leash. I asked his keeper if I might pet him.
> "You'll lose your hand," the man warned me. He was wrong.
> It was instant love between us."[7]

Naturally. The dog immediately recognized Mickey as a kindred
spirit.

When Judy's engagement closed, she and Mickey necessarily
remained in London. Judy was so taken by the mews house which Johnnie
and Bill shared that she asked Franklin to see if he could scare up a similar one for her and Mickey to rent. He found one within a few days, on
Cadogan Lane, near Sloane Square. As the foursome continued to make
the rounds of London together, exploitation of two such high octane
celebrities was inevitable. Just as inevitable was Deans' scheme to sink his
hooks as deeply as possible into his doped-up meal ticket.

A notion, born from the impromptu duet they had muddled
through at Talk of the Town, developed into a proposal that the pair
appear together on a European tour. After much discussion, it was agreed
that Johnnie would open, Judy would join him for a duet or two, and then
close the show. Boffo. Once they settled upon it, Johnnie and Judy wanted to work up some material, alone.

"They hadn't been in the mews house very long when the idea for Johnnie and Judy to work together came up, which was the genesis of those concerts." Franklin said. "The two of them wanted to have some time together at the piano, so Mickey said, 'let's the two of us go out then,' which we did, leaving them at the piano there on Cadogan Lane.

"Mickey liked to get real bombed, he was taking pills, and also giving her pills, and he loved to drink Drambuie mixed with Scotch—ugh—and he got very bombed that night. So we finally went back to Cadogan Lane and Mickey was just . . twitching, like the old Jimmy Campbell twitch, only on both sides of his face. We walked into the living room and there was Johnnie and Judy, still at the piano, and Mickey just immediately went after her ass.

"He was screaming 'You fuckin' bitch, you're nothin! You'll never work again, I'm sick of this—fuck you!' and he reached out, he was actually going to hit her, so I got between them and I remember thinking 'What am I doing here? What's going on?' and Brandy, the guard dog was barking—it was horrible. And Mickey said, 'I'm gettin' the fuck out of here. You can do whatever you want.' And he left, slammed the door.

"Well, Judy was terrified. She said 'What am I going to do? My god, he's saying this to me, I moved into this house, I have no money, I'm here in fucking England . . . what am I going to do? Where am I going to go?' So, I said, 'Well, come to our house. You can stay there.' Johnnie had to leave almost immediately, for dates in the North. I stayed behind in London, and it was just Judy and me at the house, for weeks. Oh, what an experience that was—it was incredible. I learned so much from her, but she was also becoming a parody of herself, which is sad, especially since she thought she was getting away with it. Judy would get on the phone and say 'Hello, this is Judy Gaar-laand, G-A-R-L-A- oh, why, yes, that's right. *Judy Garland.*'

"As wasted and worn out as she was, Judy was amazing. And we had a great time together for those few weeks," Franklin emphasized. "She had such an incredible sense of humor—she was very similar to Johnnie in that sense, which is why they got along well."

Deans had returned to New York. Despite his violent rejection of Garland, he spent the next ten days hustling money for a proposed film "A Day in the Life of Judy Garland." During Mickey's absence, Franklin booked four European dates for Johnnie and Judy. When Deans got wind of it, he flew back to London, reconciled with Garland and the pair returned to Cadogan Lane.[8]

Deans immediately proposed; she accepted. The entire Garland/Deans exile, courtship and nuptial seemed marked with a quicksand inevitability which drew her towards ignominy and death. Throughout her European exile, Johnnie and Bill provided the sole illumination and sense of connection to legitimate show business. But before Johnnie provided Garland's final swan song, he was called upon to serve as Deans' best man.

The civil ceremony was performed at the Chelsea Registry office at noon on March 15, 1969, followed by a reception at Quaglino's in the West End. Garland, in a chiffon mini-dress festooned with ostrich feathers and her eyes darkened by a thick Maybelline crust, looked more like an extinct form of prehistoric bird than a living legend of stage and screen. That afternoon's reception was almost as humiliating as her Talk of the Town fiasco; of the several dozen friends invited to celebrate, only Glyn Jones and Bumbles Dawson, an old chum of Garland's, showed up.

The entire affair was fraught with symbolism. Their wedding cake, courtesy of Talk of the Town, was frozen solid and could not be cut. A crippled fan of Garland was treated to her idol's rendition of "You'll Never Walk Alone."[9] "There was a big reception, lots of people were invited and nobody came," Bill recalled. "Judy was drunk and horrible, all that stuff. It was sad. They flew off to Paris for a honeymoon and we were all going to meet in Stockholm for the beginning of the tour." Despite the ugly vicissitudes and weirdness of Mickey Deans, Johnnie felt blessed at such an opportunity.

The day before the first show, Variety, spoon-fed news of this starry venture by Bill Franklin, announced the pairing: "Garland and Ray Bow New Act in Sweden." Datelined London, the item reported:

> "Double star act debuts tomorrow in Stockholm, with four
> dates in Sweden and Denmark. Idea was Miss Garland's, a
> sudden inspiration when Ray went on stage during her act at
> Talk of the Town here and the pair improvised a singing stint.
> Negotiations are proceeding for dates in France, Italy, Spain,
> Switzerland and, maybe, South Africa. Some of the concerts
> may be taped for future LP's."[10]

It seemed as if these two battered careers were getting an international jump-start of sure-fire proportions. But the next time Garland made Variety, it was among the obituaries.

*   *   *

On March 19, Johnnie met Judy at the airport in Stockholm with a bouquet of flowers; a Swedish film crew captured the moment. Judy slowly emerged from the plane, barely able to negotiate the steps leading down to the tarmac. She clutched the handrail and looked as if she might tumble headlong at any instant.

Having depleted her amphetamine supply in Paris, Mickey substituted another stimulant in place of the Ritalin she had long relied on. The change in her body's dependent chemical balance was disastrous; Garland hallucinated frequently. The amateurish documentary footage shot of the tour, released as "The Last Performance," at one point captures Johnnie presenting a gift to her; she is unable to get the wrapping off. In another sequence, she and Johnnie, surrounded by sycophants, are at the piano, attempting a version of "Am I Blue?" [11]

Johnnie is attentive and accommodating; she fixes a piercing, hungry and unbroken gaze upon him—as if frightened to look elsewhere. "We haven't had much rehearsal," Judy says. "But we were a hit in Cadogan Lane . . . " Franklin hovers uneasily in the background; Mickey runs constant verbal interference in his faux blue blood accent. The atmosphere is one of doom.

Film of the performances themselves is altogether gruesome. Johnnie closes his set with "Who Can I Turn To?" and Garland totters out onstage. Each step a minuscule progress, her eyes constantly upon the floor, as if terrified she will trip over a microphone cord. After several agonizingly long minutes while Johnnie searches for a mike stand to use while he accompanies her ("Mickey, is there a microphone stand back there? They took mine!" he yells into the wings), Garland the while mumbling a breathy string of indecipherable comments punctuated with soft hysterical giggling.

Finally, they duet on "'Til the Clouds Roll By." They sounded like two maudlin drunks at last call in a waterfront gin mill; it is a mess, a sloppy, flat, grating, harsh and utterly careless non-performance. Left to her devices, Garland appears to degenerate even further. Spindly, grotesquely deliberate and tenuous in her movements, she appears undead. That she could perform at all was remarkable, considering the chemical war her central nervous system was waging upon itself.

The next three dates were no better, each show was more grotesque and desperate than the previous ones; had the tour played an English-speaking nation, the notices she received after her disaster at Talk of the Town would seem like raves. They somehow managed to finish it, and any plans for subsequent dates evaporated. The entire episode with Mr. and Mrs. Deans was tremendously upsetting and incalculably depressing for both Johnnie and Bill. It had a deep effect on the psyche of each and when news of Garland's death reached them in June, their relationship had already begun to come apart.

*   *   *

Johnnie and Bill returned home in April. Franklin was shaken by the experience with Garland; after everything he had already been through with Johnnie, Bill thought he actually understood what fame and the trade could do to an individual. But the wrenchingly painful time spent beside Judy and Mickey had forced him to stare over the rim of the volcano and into its roiling molten pitfalls. Franklin recognized fame's perversity and lust for destruction; realizing the force was so close to Johnnie had imbued him with a numbed dread.

On the way back, they stopped in New York for several days. There, Johnnie took his annual physical exam from longtime medicine man, Dr. Louis Finger. Immensely pleased at Johnnie's health and impressed by his robust appearance, Finger made a fatal error. "I really shouldn't say this, Johnnie, especially with your medical history," the doctor informed him, "but you're doing so well that I think it would probably be alright for you to enjoy an occasional glass of wine—just one, and only now and then."

Johnnie buzzed with appreciation for Finger's confidence. Franklin blanched. "I thought, "Oh fuck! *This* is trouble." Back in Malibu, Johnnie wasted no time in breaking out a bottle of Mateus Rose, a sickly sweet pink Portuguese wine. He liked it fine.

Franklin tried not to scream at him. As if it would have made any difference; Johnnie was back on the sauce. Starting with "an occasional glass," he quickly graduated to an occasional bottle. Soon, Bill was coming across bottles stashed way back in the fridge, obscured by heads of lettuce.

The return to Malibu also signaled a return to the stuffy nightclubs of middle America and the long hours demanded by Nevada's lounges. At home and on the road, empties began to stack up with a disturbing regularity. Johnnie knew only what he had been told throughout his career, by Maurice King, by Bernie, by Sol, by Dorothy. He had heard it so many different ways and so many times: Johnnie's tough. Johnnie can dish it out and Johnnie take it. Johnnie can bounce back from anything. Why doubt it?

While Johnnie pretended his liver was healed, Franklin tried to ignore the gnawing misgivings which had returned with him from Europe. Ray's career rose and fell with maddening cyclical regularity. Johnnie had also been sapped by the Garland tour, and the result was an increased degree of unreasoning fear; his self-confidence plummeted. Johnnie found that any engagement's opening night brought on his greatest anxiety.

"It was just like that first recording session in London—only now it was in his performance," Bill said. "There was an extreme lack of confidence, a tremendous amount of fear in just about every aspect of his life. And this fear, I think, had a lot to do with the disappointment of not remaining the *BIG* Johnnie Ray, of having to come down from that. The result was more disapointment, all this stuff just didn't work out." The fact that both press and trade insiders invariably gauged a performer's worth on the opener's quality meant Johnnie worked with a calamitous weak point.

Although he had frequently appeared in Reno and Tahoe lounges throughout the late 60's, Las Vegas bookings remained an elusive and irritating omission from the schedule. The city was no longer the Vegas of Moe Dalitz and Jack Entratter; it was Howard Hughes' town now. The mad millionaire had been buying every casino he could since 1967, starting with the Desert Inn, and continued on, fencing with the State Gaming Board, narrowly avoiding charges of monopoly and conflict of interest by accusing his rival, ultra-entrepreneur Kirk Kerkorian, of the same offenses. Johnnie's chance to re-establish himself in Las Vegas was a key to renewing his prestige, and ideally, driving up his price.

Franklin eventually found a simpatico Entertainment Director, Bill Miller. A veteran Gotham showman, Miller had previously run the fabled Riviera, a huge class nitery just across the Hudson with a stunning view of New York's skyline and a killer-diller gimmick—the ceiling could be cranked back to reveal the Summertime night sky.

"Bill Miller was a nice man, an old-time operator," recalled Franklin. "Johnnie had always been nice and polite to those guys and they remembered that, so I met with Miller and he said, 'Yeah, I'll try him.' Bill had other dates coming up in several weeks, well, really, he had openings for years in advance. I'd also been talking to other people in Nevada, and the climate in Vegas seemed very good for Johnnie at this particular time.

"And all Johnnie had to do was go on and do twenty minutes of shit he'd been doing forever, but the same thing happened. He just got too afraid, nothing could calm him down, and he just didn't cut it. He came out and tripped over the mike cord. It was embarrassing. People laughed. And Bill Miller just stood there in shock. He blew so many opportunities with that one performance. It was very damaging, in the sense that it damaged his ability to rise above the stature where people pictured him at that time."

Miller let Johnnie complete two weeks in the Flamingo lounge; despite the fact that the following night's performance was flawless, those first night heebie-jeebies plagued Johnnie's reputation. Although Franklin had felt the Las Vegas "climate was good," few of the gamblers availed themselves of an opportunity to let their hair down and cry with the Prince of Wails. Even old friends were distressed by the sight of Johnnie working the lounges.

"I was working at the Aladdin, and intended to go see the show," Tempest Storm said. "He was in a very small, open lounge. They say 'you're in charge of your own destiny,' but I don't believe it—I think people were down on him, entertainment directors, that 'Executive Wall' you have to cross.

"But I walked in and there were only about three people sitting there. It was just heartbreaking to see that. I thought it was so sad." Tempest, shocked, hovered for a moment. The red-headed exotic slipped out of the lounge before Johnnie realized she had come in. "That was the last time I saw Johnnie," Storm sighed.

Bill was not the type to place blame for this failure solely on Johnnie, and continued to hunt for an agent with the power and sympathy, experience and contacts to break through the "Executive Wall" and reinvigorate Johnnie's low stature. He finally found one, Milton Deutsch, another cigar-chomping Broadway veteran. Based in Los Angeles, Deutsch's Coast Artists also represented Frankie Laine and Billy Eckstine. The same breed of Pop music dinosaurs as Johnnie, through Deutsch's salty ministrations, they enjoyed the higher profile and price which eluded the Cry Guy.[11]

Johnnie signed with Coast Artists in July 1969, and Deutsch began sending him out to work engagements all over the country; while not exactly prestige dates, he was not working in strip joints, either. With a handful of chlorals melting into his bellyful of Mateus and a Coast Artists itinerary at his elbow, Johnnie felt as if his life was maintaining an acceptable degree of balance. The majority of this content stemmed almost entirely from Bill's affectionate, encouraging presence. The upcoming Thanksgiving would mark the romance's seventh year; Johnnie was grateful for the past and eager to delve into the future—but only with Willie at his side.

Bill tried to stifle his own growing discontent while still doing everything he could to keep Johnnie's health on the straight and narrow. An actress he knew

swore by a garlic and herb preparation concocted in Tijuana by a young woman, Doctor Francis Rosetti de Esparza. Bill and Johnnie began to make regular pilgrimages there, bringing back vials of the extract. "I'd been told it helped people with this kind of nervous trauma Johnnie had," said Bill. "And he took this stuff for a couple of years—very fresh and garlicky tasting—and it did help, for awhile." But only for awhile; Johnnie had guzzled a vial before tripping over the mike cord that night at the Flamingo.

Being the only one able to determine his life and quality of performance was an increasingly uncomfortable role for Johnnie—he needed more direction than ever. In most every aspect of his life, he was unable or unwilling to govern himself.

After signing with Milton Deutsch, Johnnie worked even more, and as Franklin said, "The money was better, but the financial problem still existed. When you get that far behind, it's very hard to catch up. And his royalty checks were pretty low, but then only a few of his own songs had been really successful.

"There were a lot of dates, a lot of work, Australian and Far Eastern tours—a lot of life during this period, but I don't know how significant any of it was, except that he kept afloat and his health was okay. He wasn't back on to hard liquor yet—I would've known that. But the culmination of our living together and the big change, both personally and professionally, happened as a result of the Garland tour."

Bill had been seriously questioning himself, and his role in Johnnie's life and future since Garland's June 1969 death. Distressed, emotionally battered, Franklin did not share Johnnie's silent capacity to absorb anguish. When Bill realized he could not mute nor deny the portentous fallout with which Judy's ghastly decay had infected them both, he slowly began an emotional withdrawal.

Try as he might to shake it off, the gulf seemed only to widen. Bill spent hours stalking the Malibu shoreline, vainly trying to find a convincing antidote. Johnnie did not make it any easier for him. Even before the Mateus bottles began stacking up, Johnnie's behavior, the ingrained silliness of Star Psychology, had become maddening. The Cry Guy, whether being interviewed or chatting at a party, worked from a stock of established spiels that he delivered with mind-numbing regularity.

Just as every song introduction and onstage statement had to be scripted and rehearsed, so too did his conversation. A practice Johnnie first developed as armor against prying reporters and perfected offstage to stave off embarrassment in the presence of social etiquette hawks, the technique had become second nature. His unvaried deployment of each soliloquy drove Franklin farther up the wall with every performance.

Candor to the press, Johnnie had learned early on, was like waiving one's constitutional right to silence during a police interrogation—anything he said could be, and was, used against him. The result was a series of what Franklin called "The dialogue tapes. They were things that sounded good to him and sounded good to other people, that he had tried and tested over the years. There were press tapes and party tapes. It got to the point where I had these pat lines numbered in my mind—we'd be at a party, Johnnie would start in and I'd think, 'Oh, God, it's 28-A!'"

Later interviews are liberally peppered with these defensive press routines; when queried about his performance's wild physicality and its effects on an audience, Johnnie would never give a straight answer. He would trot out a droning mainstay of the repertoire: "I don't consider myself a singer. I'm an entertainer. Being a teenage idol I knew would not last, and I realized that I had to learn my craft or forget about a career in show business."[1]

"The 'I realized I had to learn my craft' dialogue, that was a press tape." Franklin said. "Oh, I loved that one! One of his favorite party lines was 'I always have to size up a stage because if I don't size it up perfectly, it could cost me a turn, you know.' After knowing the real him, they were so phony to me.

"In and out of interviews, it was all scripted," Bill said. "He had to do the act, the personal act, for a lot of reasons—the blanket toss, the loss of hearing, the loss of fame, the booze, the drugs, the tuberculosis, the cirrhosis . . . It was very difficult for him to be natural, and he could only handle a situation this way.

"It was the same as on stage, where every word had to be scripted, because if he got away from them, he'd say weird, off-the-wall things. He was stuck with them—whether he was on television or over drinks or at dinner—he repeated them over and over."

Of all the routines Johnnie cooked up, the one employed to evade questions about the most painful failure of his life and career, why he never made another movie after "There's No Business Like Show Business," was perhaps the most pathetic of all:

"Making movies just proved to be something I didn't anticipate," he told an interviewer in the mid-1980s. "That is a very lazy way to make a living, the most boring way in the world to make a living, because by that time I'd had my taste of a live audience."[2]

Or: "I became very disillusioned about making films. It's a very lazy, very dull way to make a living . . . I had become accustomed to live audiences."[3]

Or: "It was take one, take two, take three, it kept going and going, and it got very boring. By the time I got to 20th Century Fox, I had had my taste of a live audience, which I realized by now was my calling, my first love."[4]

His bitter disappointment over being abandoned by Zanuck was so overwhelming that he lied even to intimates; Bill Franklin was told by Johnnie that it was Bernie's fault, that his Fox contract was for a single picture (it was, of course, a seven-year contract at $100,000 a picture). Johnnie's shame was so great he could not face the truth.

Bill was ashamed at his festering dissatisfaction but felt it spreading through his heart. He wanted to believe that, damn it, he could cure Johnnie of the shame and failure which caused him to endlessly repeat his store of lies. But Johnnie, of course, had been tendered a timely prescription by Dr. Finger—alcohol. By mid-1971, Johnnie was re-acquainting himself with distilled spirits.

He swiftly resumed his tendency for alcoholic acrobatics, making a return to the rubber-legged routine which prevailed when Bill first began to hang around 63rd Street. That was Last Straw insanity. Franklin wanted out.

"I decided I wanted to live by myself," he said. "I knew I couldn't handle Johnnie anymore, because I wasn't getting anywhere. When you care for somebody and do everything you can, and you don't get anything back . . . except so many bouts with cirrhosis, and booze, and him falling down. It got to the point where I realized 'he's not getting it, so I've got to get out of here!'"

Franklin eased into the announcement. "There were some harsh words," Bill said. "But I wanted a change, and this was it. I told him 'I've got to do this.'" Once Johnnie calmed down, he assumed the stoic role learned from Elmer, and said little of his desperation and fear over losing Bill. The measure of it was colossal, too immense for him to articulate. The result of Bill's withdrawal was more significant than either realized. Their conversation was forced from emotion to logistics. It was decided that Johnnie would take a home in Hollywood; without Franklin as constant minder/driver, he required a central location.

Franklin rented him a house in the hills where Hollywood Boulevard completes its winding western course, located on Queens Road (an ironic stone's throw from Jack Devaney's Appian Way home where Johnnie had first pursued Willie). "That address was something he could never get over," Bill said. "He always said 'I never thought I'd be living at the corner of Hollywood Boulevard and Queens Road!'" Franklin took an apartment nearby in West Hollywood, and the pair continued to spend a great deal of time together.

Johnnie had a friend, Chuck Jones (not the animator), move into the Queens Road home, to keep him company and make sure his stack did not blow too hard or often; Johnnie then re-launched his career as a full-blown boozer. His new kick was a particularly delusional one, centering on the type of cocktail which he considered "kid stuff, those fruity drinks—they're all just like soda pop." He was referring to Daiquiris, the potent rum drink he viewed as a mild whistle moistener.[5]

Hank Wesinger paid a visit at the Queens Road house. "To see anybody drinking to that extent is bad, but when Johnnie went back to drinking, it was cruel," Hank said. "When you watch a man go into the kitchen and make Daiquiris in a Waring blender and then drink them out of it, it's hard." It was more than hard. Estranged from Bill, he was miserable.

When Milton Deutsch got Johnnie back into the Vegas lounges in 1971, Bill and Sol went up for his opening. A night before his run started, the trio went to the International Hotel, where Elvis Presley was working his third engagement since returning to live performance. Despite SRO madness, a ringside table awaited the Ray party. Johnnie was excited. He dug Elvis, though he did consider him, musically, as a bit of a square in the sense of their common R&B background, and how each interpreted it. Johnnie had lived with, mastered and thoroughly understood the frivolous, theatrical nature of post-war R&B, where Elvis took it as seriously as he did Gospel.

Hot off his Top Ten record hit "Suspicious Minds," this was Presley at his magnificent peak, and the show bowled everyone over. Midway through the performance, he gestured for the audience's attention. "Elvis Presley gave Johnnie one of the most incredible introductions from the stage that I've ever heard—and I've heard a lot of people introduce him," recalled Bill.

"The gist of it, and I'm paraphrasing, of course, was 'There's a man in the audience tonight who, when I was in high school, had the top three records in the whole world all at once. He was a great influence on me— he made me believe in myself, made me go ahead and become what I am . . . ladies and gentlemen, I'd like you all to give a warm welcome to Mr. Johnnie Ray.'"

Head-spinning stuff. After the show, one of the Memphis Mafia herded them through a series of secret doors and service corridors to Elvis' dressing room. "There was a little conversation between Elvis and Johnnie about the old days in Vegas, 'Oh, when we were working across the street from each other . . . '" Bill said. "Johnnie thanked him for the introduction and Elvis said 'You deserve it. I really meant what I said—you know how much I've always liked you, and respected you.' He was very warm, very friendly."

Johnnie was amazed at the size of Presley's entourage. "I asked him about that," Johnnie said. "Why he had so many people with him. Elvis just sort of rolled his eyes, and said 'Well, that's the way it is.'"[6] Elvis needed the Memphis Mafia as much as Johnnie missed having his own private army of glorified fans; this was a classic show biz exchange that revealed the rather tender nature of these two figures meeting. The protocol of high and low, still linked together in ways no one save themselves could understand—despite the gulf of time, style and success between them. It was a gratifying but painful experience for Johnnie.

This brush with recognition worked on Johnnie in several ways; he went back and forth from Cloud 9 contentment to bleak depression with wilder, more unpredictable speed. The tidal pull between the two extremes assumed a higher-pitched, faster-acting cyclical pattern—hastened by the stimulating properties of "kid stuff" cocktails. Without Bill's constancy and faithful care, Johnnie's only other leaning post was his own celebrity. He courted it desperately.

"When I was conducting for him in Las Vegas," recalled Stan Freeman, "Johnnie seemed a little upset because people didn't recognize him. We'd go out to a drugstore, and he would stand in the doorway, sort of waiting for people to ask for his autograph. He was very conscious of the fact that a lot of people didn't know who he was anymore and, I think, very upset by that fact."

Johnnie kept himself out on this duty until he was exhausted. Freeman, concerned at Johnnie's absence, went looking for him. "It was four in the morning, hardly anyone in the casino, and there's Johnnie, out of it, face down on a gambling table, sound asleep."

There was an even more painful episode during this engagement. "Maurice King was in Las Vegas conducting for Gladys Knight," Franklin recalled. "I was up there too, and Johnnie and Maurice had a big re-union. We went out for dinner and things. For two or three days and nights, it was all very warm and wonderful. They were so close, from the early years, and Maurice was a wonderful man. The conversation got around to new material for Johnnie and I mentioned how I'd always thought he should do a country & western medley. 'I Can't Stop Loving You,' 'Born To Lose,' those were natural songs for him, material that he loved to do.

"Maurice got all excited about it, he said 'Okay! I'll do the charts for you, it'll be fabulous.' We had sessions at the piano, we all contributed ideas and we sketched it out. Gladys Knight was closing and Maurice said 'I'm going back to Detroit, you'll hear from me next week. The charts will be in the mail.' I was very excited about it because the material was so right, so perfect, for Johnnie. And to have Maurice King do the arrangements, I knew Johnnie would be excited to go onstage with this.

"We never heard from him again. That just blew me away and it really disappointed Johnnie. I tried to find Maurice, got a phone number, left messages, but never got a return call. That was a big mystery to me."

Johnnie was crushed. Frustration and faded notoriety filled his heart to the bursting point. Mixed with the pain of Bill's retreat, it simmered and fermented. Johnnie held it down—as long as he was working, he could choke it back, masking all the dread with his trouper's face. But Johnnie was falling apart. By the time he returned to Queens Road, he was sick with it, desperately looking for someone to fault, to place the terrible blame of his failure upon. He targeted himself.

*   *   *

Hollywood's summer heat pervaded the house. Outside, the crickets kept up a relentless clicking rhythm. Through Johnnie's hearing aid they distorted to sound like a scratched record, an awful ceaseless metronomic pattern. Scratched records were all that survived of his glory. One was playing inside his head. "Panic all around me . . . the black of night surrounds me . . ." He looked around, realizing he was upstairs in his bedroom. Was he alone? No, Chuck was around somewhere. Johnnie lifted the heavy Waring blender and inhaled daiquiri slush. Since falling off the wagon, no glass was large enough to slake his thirst.

The full moon shone through a window, illuminating what he craved to obliterate. A familiar, dreadful inertia enshrouded Johnnie, the suffocating reality of failure, of his evaporating fame. He still felt the jostle and surge, ghostly remnants of twenty years past, when his fans were drawn by the tens of thousands, clamoring after the Cry Guy. Johnnie clutched and scrambled after the memory just as they had clawed at him. The recalled whiff of arousal and love turned to the hollow bitterness Johnnie was learning to fear more each time it descended upon him.

Tepid lime rum slid down his throat; convulsive gloom chased it. Johnnie could not shake the bleak inertia. His heart shivered beneath it. A fugitive from glory, he refused to accept his fading place within the trade. As his fame diminished it seemed his soul slipped away with it. He thought with shame of the way he had stood in Las Vegas shop doors waiting for a fan to recognize him.

He thought of the warmth and dignity of Elvis's on-stage introduction before an SRO crowd at the International . . . last week? Last month? Gratified by Presley's public acknowledgment at the time, under the leering California moon, the memory soured, twisted and stabbed.

He was stumbling down the hall. Where did that blender go? He caught sight of his gold records on the entry way wall below. Johnnie's fall down the staircase was a carpet-chewing, tumble-down grind; no worse than usual. No damage done. Even his attempts at self-destruction were self-parody these days. When his legs changed from twisted rubber back to flesh and bone, he arose and found himself staring into a mirror. A violent surge of loathing and impotence overtook Johnnie. Instinctively, his hands came up, fingertips arcing inward. He pressed the manicured nails deep into his face and slowly pulled them down, from cheek bone to jawline. Curlicues of skin peeled off and accrued under his nails, leaving paths of blood. The blood was warm on his face. It felt like a nightclub pin spot.

Surprised by the warmth, he repeated the action lengthwise across his forehead. Johnnie's face bore sixteen crimson oozing scratches. War paint for his losing battle against fame, the fight for glory he had waged since childhood. Johnnie examined the ravaged monster in the glass before him. Blood began to fill his eyes, a curtain ringing down on the Million Dollar Teardrop's command performance. He found that he could not even cry. Why should he? No one was listening.

Johnnie began to scream. He kept it up until he passed out.

Chuck Jones called Bill the next day and tactfully suggested he drop by to see Johnnie. "There had always been a lot of falling down," Bill said. "The very first night I went to 63rd street, he had walked right into a door jamb and split his head open, but when I saw him a day or two after Chuck called . . . this . . . it was wild. I said 'What happened? This is just a little bit Frankenstein!'

"He had scratches all over his face, in sets of four, and I looked at them and they weren't deep enough to require stitches. He had just clawed down his face, it had peeled and then scabbed over. And he would not admit to it—he said that he had tripped and fallen, but you don't get that from a fall. Chuck told me what really happened—that he had thrown himself down the stairs, looked into a mirror, dug into his face with his fingernails, and just screamed until he lost it. He would do this physically destructive stuff a lot. It was the booze."

Franklin's matter-of-fact acceptance of this perverse, bloody behavior as seemingly routine is hardly a cold-blooded dismissal. By now intimately acquainted with the dire nature of Star Psychology's forceful hold on Johnnie, he had no choice but to view it as a significant part of Johnnie's nature. It was a terminal condition, something that could not be understood on normal, "civilian" terms, but nonetheless had to be lived with'—there is no cure for fame. Nor is there a more serious condition than fame denied and forgotten. It is a weird spiritual inertia, something unique and terrible, which both drives and chains the 'Star.'

"Inertia might be a good word for what these people experience," Bill said. "There's a line that any performer like Judy or Johnnie crosses, mentally, and something takes over. I don't think it has to do as much with career disappointments as it does with life in general. It's about not being in a place where they feel they should be, and it can't be explained in ordinary or laymen terms, but they cross over it and just go nutsy.

"They're on a stage with thousands of people going absolutely crazy and then they leave the stage, but how do you replace that adulation?

That's part of it—but it's same in their private lives, suppose they want to have an affair, or just have sex, and if they're not, well, why isn't that happening? It's about life, and there's no real answer for them. And with all the fears, all the shit in their head that makes them think they can get away with anything: 'Look what I've been through already.'

"It's almost like a belief in immortality—'I always bounce back.' And these fears and this belief in immortality somehow co-exist, they're voices or flashes inside the brain, and they've done it all for so long they think they can get away with anything, that they're fooling everybody, but they're not. It's anger, fear, resentment. There's very little clarity.

"And Johnnie just always expected me to understand: 'This is me.' But it was beyond explanation or understanding . . . Johnnie was a very complex being."

Driven constantly by this intricate and strange force, Johnnie merely slathered make-up over the wounds, and beat on, heat, scabs, shame and all, just as he always had:

"And now, ladies and gentleman, we'd like to do a couple of songs for your approval, they've done very well for us and we sincerely hope they haven't worn out their welcome mat . . ." He picked out a few introductory bars, brow creased, took a breath and sang, for perhaps the millionth time,

"I went walkin' . . .
down by the river . . .
feeling very sad inside . . ."

*   *   *

Even as Bill and Johnnie drifted farther apart personally, on professional terms, Bill did everything he could to ensure Johnnie's engagements were a success. After his contract with Deutsch's agency lapsed in 1972, Johnnie signed with Jack Parker Attractions, who dispatched him on extensive midwestern supper club tours. Australia and Britain remained gratifying constants.[7]

"He always maintained that same popularity in Europe and overseas," Jane Kean said. "I was in Australia doing a play in Sydney, this was in the 1970's, and he was playing one of the Sporting Clubs, membership clubs with gambling, well, just slot machines, and it was a huge, three tiered place that was jam-packed when we went to see him. Johnnie was always electrifying, not raw, but untamed, sort of, in the way he worked, and he was just as big there as he was that opening night at the Copa. They're more loyal, and he was always in demand, over there, for dates, nightclub engagements."

That overseas demand was a saving grace. No matter how foul and depressing nightclub work became in the United States, Johnnie was guaranteed annual maintenance doses of adoration. This pattern emphasized further the cyclical flip-flop of turbulent emotion that increasingly dominated Johnnie's life. He surfed the dark eddies and golden high tides alike with uncompromised vigor; the occasional wipe-out was unavoidable. Johnnie grew to recognize that as a fact, and key to survival.

Appearing at New York's Rainbow Roof in April 1972, he described the pattern to a reviewer, "You've caught me at a bad time—I'm in between decisions. I've been dribbled like a basket ball, up and down . . . travelling the world without roots for eighteen years." But Johnnie would not give up: "There's a whole generation who don't know who Johnnie Ray is, but I'm going to reach these kids. I'd like to have a new hit, but I've learned not to get my hopes up."[8]

The effort was intensely draining. Johnnie added contemporary songs to the set, titles by no-talent hacks like Kris Kristoffersen and Buffy Saint Marie, to little avail. Their lyrics sounded ridiculous coming from him; only when Johnnie returned to "Cry" did audiences turn on— "stomping and cheering for two minutes." As a result, critics tarred him with the nostalgia brush, a painful dismissal.[9]

His publicly avowed efforts to reach people never amounted to anything serious. If only he had re-worked his act by adding new Johnnie Ray compositions, the gap may have been easier to broach. But Johnnie no longer had the spiritual wherewithal. "You've got to be motivated, you've got to have a reason to write a song. I can't do it," he told a friend.

"I think he lost interest," that pal, Jeff Gazall, said. "A lot of the time he'd sit and play the piano until three or four in the morning, and he'd really get going, but he needed someone there to get him to do that. But he never got around to writing any music, it was just a lack of motivation. He had to have a reason to write—he had to be in love to write music."[10]

His dependence on Bill and mournful pining over losing him did not subside but, as time passed, Johnnie's war-horse resilience served him well. Despite suffering in ways few could begin to comprehend, the snuffing out of his artistic flame, Johnnie never lost his prevailing character, the liberated soul who called for Love and Beauty above all else.

"He was very youthful and exuberant, very warm and friendly always, very boyish," Jane Kean said. "Johnnie always was kind of a farmboy at heart and no matter what, he always maintained that same quality of naivete. Just homespun, never sophisticated. It was hard to dislike Johnnie, because he had that farmboy innocence. You had to like him. Johnnie was very loving."

These aspects of his personality were as true and ran as deep as the fears and anxieties that fame instilled in Johnnie. Franklin knew it and recognized also that the conflict which threatened his career—the opener's heebie-jeebies—could be outwitted and made to work for, rather than against Johnnie. He realized the best way was to fool Johnnie into a good performance, just as Betty Kean had when the reviews of "Bus Stop" appeared—by trickery.

Johnnie had not played a prestige date in Los Angeles for several years but was scheduled, in April 1973, to play the plush Westside Room in Century City. The opener was flawless; Stan Freeman conducted, he was introduced by June Allyson, and Johnnie killed the audience.[11]

But the show they reviewed was actually his second night— Franklin had deluded Johnnie into thinking his opener was the night before. He gave the usual halting, weak performance before a papered house of fans and warm-bodies. No press, no celebrities, no one from the trades. Sol attended and was shocked at how terrible Johnnie was. He blamed it on the material and, mostly, Bill.

"Th-th-this is all your f-f-fault, B-B-Bill," he sputtered. "The show is all wr-wr-wrong for J-Johnnie." Franklin refused to listen, telling him only, "Sol, you don't understand—it doesn't matter. Just come back tomorrow night." He did, and was all smiles as the curtain rang down. "Y-Y-You were r-r-r-right!" Sol beamed. The chicanery was ideal. Johnnie read and re-read the glowing notices in the trades the next morning. He felt like the king of everything.

For the next several years, he maintained a steady footing and even quality in his appearances; many of these were brief twenty-minute sets given as part of nostalgia packages that criss-crossed the nation; these were the brain child of Roy Radin (the obese and greedy entrepreneur who was subsequently murdered and dumped in the Mojave Desert). Johnnie rode on a bus with old friends like Helen O'Connell, Kay Starr and Donald O'Connor, often appearing in high school gyms and civic centers in towns like Irving, Texas or Waukesha, Wisconsin.

It was almost like his days with the Star Light Club in Portland. "Those were great for Johnnie, because he loved all those people and he could basically just phone in his show," Franklin said. "He really enjoyed those, but trying to get Radin to pay off was always a pain." Enjoyment of his work was crucial to Johnnie, and it continued to charge him.

Not long after the Westside Room engagement, Johnnie, on Bill's advice, bought a house. Paying rent was, he agreed, tiresome and wasteful. Despite Sol's misgivings over coughing up the down payment, Johnnie became, in short order, the proud owner of a large, gracious home located at 1654 Marmont Avenue, up in the hills, not far from the Sunset Strip.

He hung his gallery of celebrity photos on a wall along the main corridor which divided the house. The spacious, sunken living room boasted his collection of gold records and engraved brass plaques from his Palladium record breakers, the baby grand piano, and a bronze bust of himself, with floor to ceiling windows that looked out over Hollywood. An adjacent bathroom featured a larger-than-life blow-up of him, Marilyn Monroe, Dan Dailey, Ethel Merman, Donald O'Connor and Mitzi Gaynor lined up for the production number which climaxed "There's No Business Like Show Business." Johnnie had his first real, rooted-down home since leaving 63rd Street. All seemed jake with the angels.

Yet he slipped back into the trench; in late 1973, Johnnie entertained a houseful of guests. He got drunk. After everyone left, he fell down and ripped open his scalp on the corner of a coffee table. He toweled the blood off and called Bill. "He was really slurring," Franklin said. "I asked 'Are you okay? I'm worried about you—are you taking too many pills, drinking too much? What's going on?' He said, 'No, no. I've just got a little bit of a sore face, it's kind of hurting me. But it's nothing, I just scratched myself a little bit.'"

A day later, his cleaning lady showed up for work and was terrified at the picture he presented. She telephoned Bill, who rushed over only to discover Johnnie, nonchalantly watching television, with a thick paste of pancake covering the wound. Franklin inspected the cut—it was deep, running from his forehead well past the hairline and over his skull.

"To his eyes, the makeup disguised it, but it was raised and tufted and looked really painful. I looked at it really carefully and asked him:

"'When did this happen?'

"'Oh, It's nothin'. I just fell down. It won't show onstage. This makeup covers it—it'll be fine.'

"'You've really hurt yourself. When did this happen?'

"'Two nights ago.'

"'We're going to Cedars emergency, and we're going now.'

"'Oh, you're making a big deal out of nothing.'

"'Just get your ass in the car,' I said."

At Cedars, the doctor on duty was appalled. "Are you guys into Christian Science or something?" he asked. Johnnie was hospitalized for three days while waiting to see if an infection had developed. Fortunately, it was clean and he was sent home, healthy, but with a permanent scar.

Johnnie had chosen a special day to "accidentally" crack his head open. Thanksgiving.

*   *   *

In 1974, Johnnie was booked to appear at the London Palladium, his first time there in eighteen years. He headlined a bill that featured Billy Daniels, the Ink Spots and Frances Faye. Johnnie's conductor at the Palladium was Jerry Blaine, an accomplished pianist and booze-guzzling party hound whose capacity rivalled the boss's. Naturally, the pair were great friends. Even with that extra sense of security, the Cry Guy was jumpy. On his first night, August 3, Johnnie was white knuckle nervous—but nowhere near as wound up as Bill, who accompanied them on the trip. If Johnnie screwed up this opener, the long-term effects would be serious.

Johnnie made his entrance. The crowd exploded with cheers. He looked into the house and saw a banner unfurling from one of the boxes: "Welcome Home, Johnnie." His British fan club must have paid dearly for the seats, but the expense was well worth it—more so than they realized. "Johnnie saw that banner and he relaxed immediately," Bill said. "I could see it in his face. That was all he needed."

When he finished the set, the sold-out house leapt to its feet and gave Johnnie a standing ovation which lasted for fifteen minutes. Never before had any performer been so vociferously applauded at the

Palladium, not Danny Kaye, Lena Horne—not even Johnnie. It was an historic occasion, and reported as such, with due solemnity and surprise, in newspapers and trade journals across Europe. The London Times called it "Memorable." Even the New York Times reported this extraordinary event, noting that "Observers said they could not remember such a reception for another performer."[12]

The triumph was sweetened further by SRO's every night of his two-week engagement; when the Palladium announced his run would be held over for an additional four weeks, it was another first. No one had ever been granted such an extension by the venue, and he continued to sell out every night (and twice on Saturday) for the six weeks he was there. The lines of fans stretched for hundreds of yards. Johnnie was deliriously happy.

The high sustained him for a long stretch of one nighters in Britain and back in the United States. Together, he and Jerry roared down the road. Johnnie was on tour when, shortly before Christmas, his home on Marmont was gutted by fire. "He was still out of town," Franklin said. "And had a friend staying there. He was okay, a little weird, but you had to be in order to hang out with Johnnie.

"I got a call from the neighbor across the street, saying there was a fire. It had started in the hallway area and engulfed his bedroom and another bedroom, and spread into the living room—pretty much the whole house. The kitchen and some other parts were okay, but there was smoke damage, water damage, but the fire went through the roof.

"It destroyed a lot of the pictures on the gallery wall and melted his gold records. I asked the investigator from the fire department how it started and he said 'See these pictures here? If a long nail was used to hang one and if it pierced the conduit, that would cause it.'"

Johnnie was enraged when he got Bill's telephone call. "Why do these things happen to me?" he railed, placing the blame on his house guest. He returned and moved into an apartment on Larrabee Street in West Hollywood while the home was rebuilt. In the wake of the disaster, Johnnie seemed almost liberated. Life in the heart of the city seemed to agree with him. He bought a bicycle and relished pedaling from shop to shop picking up odds and ends for the apartment.

Don Ovens had recently opened Celebrity Records, a Tin Pan Alley nostalgia store on Santa Monica Boulevard not far from Larrabee Street.

Though he had known Johnnie since 1952 and often visited at 63rd Street in the late fifties and early sixties, the pair became fast friends during this period. "He loved coming into the store, just to visit," Ovens said. "I served coffee in the morning and wine in the afternoon. A lot of people hung out there, Charles Nelson Reilly, George Maharis, Steve and Eydie would drop by, Barry Manilow practically lived there.

"And it became Johnnie's second home. When he wasn't working, he was in there all the time, just visiting. That was when we became closer and closer. He'd go tootin' around town on his bike, to the pharmacy to get his prescriptions filled, to the hardware store, go from shop to shop, put everything in the basket and then come over to my record store."

Johnnie tested Ovens' friendship there one afternoon. "At parties up at his house, if he didn't like the conversation, he'd turn his hearing aid off, I'd seen him do that before," Don recalled. "I was talking to him in the store and I saw him turn the sound off and I said 'Johnnie, I saw that! Don't ever do that to me again!' And he laughed, he thought it was very funny, because I'd caught him. He was very much a little boy, he was." Johnnie had gotten precisely the reaction he wanted from Ovens—one whose prideful outrage bespoke care and candor, evoked by a typical display of his childish petulance.

The time spent in his apartment, taken with West Hollywood's small town neighborhood atmosphere seemed to regress him to his youth in Dallas. "A lot of the time, Johnnie was a little kid," Ovens said. "I think the funniest thing I ever saw him do was the first time he rode his bike to my store—he came through the door so fast that his feet were off the pedals, he just flew into the store, went straight through and crashed right into my record cabinets! I said 'You are out of your mind!' But he didn't know how to stop, it was one of the first times he had done this thing."

Hardly—Johnnie was pulling the same free-wheeling, attention-getting prank he used to practice on Dallas High's football field. And enjoying it just as much. "When his house burned down and he was staying in the apartment," said Don, "he was so happy that I always asked him 'why don't you just sell the house and stay in the apartment?' The house was way up on the hill and since he wouldn't drive, he had no way of getting around, unless somebody went and got him or he called a cab. And he was always so happy down there, but he wouldn't do it."

Of course not. Johnnie, the country boy, knew the value of land, just as Johnnie, the showman, knew how swiftly it could become too difficult to make the monthly rent. He was determined to remain a property owner. His financial picture was better than it had been for the last ten years, and the Marmont home's re-building involved extensive improvements. He tailored it to his ideal, adding skylights and a swimming pool, making it his own kingdom—one with the privacy he would need when life turned dark and it became necessary to battle the fear and panic that followed his every step.

When the work was done in early 1976, Johnnie moved back in and felt even more comfortable than he had before. The remains of the gallery wall were still impressive; the "No Business Like Show Business" bathroom wall was undamaged. His personality demanded a Phoenix-like return. All that was missing were his gold records—the heraldic emblems of his nobility, physical representations of all he achieved and upheld, artistically and spiritually. The shipment from Columbia arrived not long after he moved back in.

He knew that they would bear not the classic red label, but the contemporary yellow and orange design. When he pulled the first one from its carton, his blood ran cold. "The Little White Cloud That Cried" read the type, vocal by "Johnny Ray."[13]

JOHNNY RAY? JOHNNY?

His name was misspelled on all of them. Not even Columbia could remember who the hell he was. Who he had been. Johnnie thought he might vomit. Instead, he cried. Then he got drunk.

Johnnie was fifty years old, an age which marked a final confrontation within himself. It was a year that he spent slugging and weaving through an ugly course of tumult, but by the end of it, he was able to thrash his fierce self-deprecation and resentment into an understanding and tenuous contentment. Before he reached it, there was one final Grand Guignol episode of on-stage self-destruction.

Johnnie elected metaphorically to "shit in his bed" at the single most high profile and affectionate setting as yet unsullied—a command performance before the Royal Family of Britain. In the summer of 1977, as the only American performer invited to appear at the Queen Mother's Silver Jubilee celebration at the Palladium, his subconscious yen for humiliation took control.

"Everybody's idea was that he would go back and re-create the same magic as he had in 1974, in 1954. That's what everybody expected," Bill Franklin, who accompanied Johnnie on the trip, said. "Maybe that's one of the things that got to him. Who knows? It was horrible—honky tonk time. He was just so . . . bad, like a total amateur. He came out and tripped over the mike cord, didn't fall down but sort of bounced off the piano.

"His voice was weak and wavering, the audience was embarrassed and you could hear some people in the house booing. It didn't become a crescendo of boos, but Johnnie caught on. I was backstage and I started crying. It was just a few, very short minutes and he stumbled through . . . it was horrible to see. And it wasn't booze, either, he was sober. It was just the demons in his head—he had so many of them. Elma and her husband had flown in for it, they were living in Italy at the time, and we sat in the bar afterward, Elma and I, and both cried.

"Elma didn't say anything about it to Johnnie and I couldn't get around to it, either. But the next night he asked 'Well, how did it really go?' And I said, 'You were no good—you were embarrassing. And I've got to tell you this, because if you get away with it, you're going to continue doing this.' And he said 'I couldn't hear the band,' started in on all that business and I told him 'That has nothing to do with it, Johnnie. It's just that whatever was in your head was not clicking. You weren't concentrating.' It was awful to have to say, but after seeing those kinds of things so many times . . . "

Franklin did not even finish recounting the story. There was nothing else to say; the Queen Mum fiasco was the unofficial end of their business and personal relationship. Johnnie rarely spoke to, or saw Bill after that tour. Yet it was almost as if by driving the final nail in the coffin that Johnnie became liberated. He succeeded in driving Franklin away, but not the Royal Family. Dyed in the wool fans, they prevailed upon Johnnie to give two more command performances, in 1980 and 1987.

When he returned home, Johnnie was not exactly free from his misgivings over losing Bill but had determined to lead life for himself. But his schedule for 1978 was almost as heavy as it was when working for Bernie.

He appeared in Reno, Tahoe, Chicago, up into Canada, back to Illinois, down to Houston, on to Denver. He had toured Australia twenty times, and went back for five weeks starting August 10. Back home in mid-September he saw several doctors, then flew to Britain on October 9.

He jumped back and forth from England to the continent for the next two months. Thanksgiving fell on the 23rd; his date book noted the anniversary of Kennedy's assassination and on Thanksgiving he wrote: "London! Thanksgiving! It would have been sixteen beautiful years . . . Just remember the good times." Johnnie struck out the 'w' in would and penned a 'c' above it. He was as hung up on Franklin as ever. His health was poor; by the time he arrived in Fort Lauderdale, "coughing up blood" and "no sleep" were frequent entries. When Hy Gardner (the veteran Broadway columnist who coined the "Prince of Wails" moniker) dined with him there on the 30th, Johnnie had not slept for five nights.[1]

The unvarying annual autumn pattern—tour Australia, home for a week, tour England, then back to the United States and straight into dates at the warm *boites* of Florida—was typically punishing. After another brief Marmont respite, it was straight back to work in Nevada.

Two years after the Silver Jubilee, Johnnie opened at London's Aphrodite's on September 3. Elma and David were in the house. "We did it," Johnnie wrote in his datebook, "Standing ovation." He was a harsh critic of himself; after his opener in Wales' Starlight Club, Johnnie deemed his performance "pure shit."

Yul Brynner was doing "The King & I" at the Palladium and he visited Brynner there several times. Johnnie was shocked to see they had changed the headliner dressing room ("Yuck!" he wrote). The next night, appearing at Croydon's Painfield Hall, fans rushed the bandstand. "Mobbed on stage—tux torn" he noted with satisfaction.

He worked like a dog in England and Wales for the next two months. It was rough, traveling from city to city on a string of one nighters, each of which required an afternoon rehearsal. Mobbed by autograph hounds, meeting the pop star likes of Gary Glitter, the road was as hectic and draining as ever. He persuaded Elma, through a series of phone calls, to return to England and accompany him.

Johnnie was enjoying it as much as possible, but he was worried. The entry "coughing up blood" appears in his date book three times during the last half of October. He closed the English tour on the 28th ("A night to remember—SRO Smash") and flew to Florida. His condition did not improve; on the 29th, "more blood. I'm worried." By November 7th, he seemed worn out "Long night, two stinking audiences, still lots of blood."

By the 10th, the blood ceased to flow. He was giving two shows a day, each in a different venue. Some audiences were good ("Yacht Club, SRO, Jerry jams, pretty people,") others disappointing, "Smash, but snobs." He was back home for Thanksgiving, a date which still meant only one thing to Johnnie. The datebook carries a bitter scrawl on the holiday: "Willie and J. Alvin Ray: 17 *years* of—WHAT!!" Within days, he was back at the Desert Inn, toiling in the lounge.

"And now ladies and gentlemen, we invite you to clap your hands and snap your fingers," Johnnie said, exactly as he had at his Copa bow, "to let the spirit move you while we do our old-time jubilee number, 'I'm Going to Walk and Talk with My Lord.'"

*   *   *

"You would never know that he had been as famous as he once was. He was never a good dresser, always wore K-Mart clothes, a short-sleeved shirt and a pair of khakis—but he had been one of the most famous people in the world. That's how down-to-Earth he was—very casual, very relaxed, very humble," John Thomas, a friend of Johnnie's, said. (Thomas grew up in Detroit, "a little kid who tried to act tough by smoking cigarettes and playing 'Whisky & Gin' on the juke box at the corner drug store".)

"He used to throw a big party at Christmas, with valet parking, bartenders, lots of celebrities, all kinds of people. Johnnie would get someone to play the piano and Martha Raye would sing, Richard Deacon would come, Jane Withers—Josephine the plumber—we'd have lots and lots of fun."[2]

The late 1970's saw Johnnie continue re-structuring his entire personal focus. The twinkle, twinkle syndrome was finally behind him—it was far too wearying. Up at Marmont, Johnnie played it strictly for laughs, concentrating all of his energies on enjoyment. While road work continued to send him around the world for at least half the year, Johnnie's social life kept him just as busy. He frequently dined with friends like Helen O'Connell, of "Green Eyes" fame, who accompanied Johnnie on several early tours Down Under, or Richard Deacon, the veteran actor who had appeared in everything from "Invasion of the Body Snatchers" to roles on television's "Leave It to Beaver" and "The Dick Van Dyke Show." Deacon was one of Johnnie's closest chums; they socialized a least once a week up until Deacon's death.

If Johnnie was publicly considered a figure of the past, it became his private pleasure to surround himself with colleagues from the same era. Their mutual warmth was insulation and sustenance, providing a deep vindication that transcended the ignorant carping reviewers often relied on when confronted by an assignment to cover Johnnie. These friends provided a context through which to reconcile his role in the trade, and the ability to recognize such a framework existed was something Johnnie badly needed. He relied even more on the close personal relationships which had survived the tempestuous years of his career.

Jim Low was a frequent companion; together, they sat and talked for hours, in precisely the same way they had as kids killing time on the banks of the Willamette. Stan Freeman moved to Los Angeles in 1977 and he, too, often hung around with Johnnie. Johnnie visited frequently at Jack Devaney's Palm Springs resort venture, Harlow's Haven (a former home of Jean Harlow which Devaney converted to a hotel/retreat). When Johnnie fell down now, it was simple over-indulgence, not an act of overt destruction.[3]

His drinking was still Olympic; Margaritas became the next entrant on his delusional fruity kid-stuff cocktail menu. "I've seen him sit down and drink fourteen double Margaritas in just a couple of hours," said Tito Adami, the Brooklyn fan whose persistent idolatry won him a place in Johnnie's "family." But this marathon drinking was as much because he simply loved to booze as it was an attempt to vanquish smoldering discontent.

Off the road, Johnnie was out to dinner an average of four nights a week, out for brunch most every Sunday. He attended an average of three nightclub shows or parties a week, often at Deke's (as he called Richard Deacon) or musician Page Cavanaugh's. He frequented West Hollywood's favorite gay nightspots, the Backlot, Studio One, the Cabaret, and often brought half of the nightclubbers back to Marmont for more drinks, more laughs. He often went out to Flipper's, the Rollerskate Disco. Johnnie can be seen there, whizzing past the camera in a 1979 episode of television cop show "CHiP's."

After the taping, he dined with Terry Moore, who had survived not only being romantically linked to Johnnie in 1955, but also a marriage to Howard Hughes—the pair howled over memories of their whirlwind romance. Fun was the order of the day.[4]

Johnnie had survived some of the worst campaigns to discredit and destroy ever mounted against a public figure, and he had outlived the majority of his enemies and friends. Whether show business acquaintances or soul mates, death was a constant. Billie Holiday, Marilyn Monroe, Lee Gordon, Johnny O'Keefe, Dorothy Kilgallen, both of his parents, soon joined by Sophie Tucker, Dan Dailey, Durante, Merman; Chris George and Betty Kean's passings were especially painful and untimely. Each loss saddened him, but Johnnie was never of a morbid nature; he rarely attended funerals.

Johnnie's nature-driven character remained. In his personal date books, he noted, by hand, each and every full moon; he also continued to mark every Thanksgiving with wistful entries on what could have been if he and Bill had stayed together. To friends, he was not as kind ("That bitch—she's getting a bit too long in the tooth to snag a sugar daddy," he told a delighted Jimmy Campbell during a Las Vegas reunion).

Franklin became the Daryl F. Zanuck of Johnnie's romantic history. Yet Johnnie would have taken him back in an instant. Losing Bill was one of the few failures he recognized as such; the career's fated twists were meaningless beside heartbreak.

Johnnie's artistic achievements were as profound and influential as they are obscure and forgotten, but his personal strength was even greater. Managing to survive the pit of being flat broke and in hock to the IRS was a Herculean effort, one he was able to get through only after seeing what the consequences could have been—looking into Garland's eyes as they shared a piano bench. As close as he came to toppling over that same volcano's rim, Johnnie would never do it. He realized it was a choice, that the fall came only when one let it happen. Johnnie would not allow weakness to destroy him.

The determination to lead life on his own terms was a fiercely demanding emotional conclusion. His career had always been so much like a war anyway, that to continue fighting back was still easier for Johnnie than going belly up. Only by keeping up a draining, globe-spanning itinerary could he hold himself together, financially and spiritually.

He slaved harder than anyone else in the trade. But he did so not only to save himself but to tithe, in a sense, to the weird fates that shaped him.

One of the most remarkable aspects of Johnnie's hectic campaign against penury was the fact that he never curtailed his charitable work on behalf of the deaf. Throughout the high hog days of the 1950's, Johnnie annually gave hundreds of thousands of dollars to organizations that worked with the hearing-impaired, both in the United States and Britain. Even as he struggled to get out from under the mid-1960's IRS whammy, Johnnie kept working and donating; he became a devoted supporter of the Pasadena-based HEAR organization, performing at benefits, donating personal items and cash up until the end of his life. Johnnie, in fact, probably donated more money to these interest groups than he had spent on liquor—an astronomical sum.[5]

Once his personal life was reconciled along specifically dictated lines, he turned to his act. By the early 1980's, Johnnie expunged most all of the contemporary material from his set list and simply concentrated on being himself. This meant "Whiskey & Gin," "Glad Rag Doll" and "Brokenhearted" went back in. As misunderstood as ever, when he appeared at New York City's Marty's in May 1981, reviewers pegged him as erroneously as ever: "A Different Johnnie Ray."

Of course, there was nothing different about Johnnie, except that he now worked with a quartet instead of a 12-piece orchestra. The one constant was his guarantee of going over a crowd's head. The only recognition afforded Johnnie was summed up in a review of his opener at Marty's:

> "He brings alive an era of pop music that has been largely forgotten because it was so quickly overwhelmed by the rock and roll outburst set off by Elvis Presley."[6]

That "outburst" was "set off" not by Elvis, but by Johnnie Ray—the one bad apple that spoiled the whole bunch. The irony of this typically sophomoric dismissal was by now an insult to which Johnnie was mostly immune. As Elma said, "I have never been able to understand why the entertainment industry has not accorded Johnnie his rightful place in how our music has evolved and how he partook in its development, that he was a vitally important link.

"He had a very strong influence—he took us from Crosby and Como, and as much as I don't like rock and roll, he took us down that road. Whether you are a J.R. fan or not is beside the point." She paused. "And, frankly, I am bitter because he has not been accorded that place. . . Well, maybe I do understand why, and I just don't want to talk about it, or face the reasons."

Johnnie was always a cultural enemy, doomed through warped perceptions instilled by trade revisionism to the pop bone yard. It was a bitter reality, but he turned it inside out and fashioned armor from it.

Like Elma, Johnnie understood. He understood that *no one* understood. That realization in itself brought a degree of melancholy resignation and satisfaction. He would never pander, lobby or trumpet his own artistic significance—why bother? It was too late.

Johnnie had a much greater stake and interest in private life, and whenever he was able to swing at Marmont, the orchestration of personal enjoyment took total precedence. Johnnie was freewheeling and feckless in his libertine duty; the parties there often assumed a much wilder tenor than they had even at 63rd Street. The guest list's guttersnipe quota grew ever higher, petty theft more common and bruises and scrapes from suddenly soured attempted romance were depressingly routine. He discounted all of these.

When he would finally reach a level of inebriation which moved him to sit before his piano and perform for the drunken crew awaiting the sunrise, he let the song flow with as much heat and emotion as he had when being fired from gin mills and strip joints in 1949. As Bill Franklin remarked, "Sitting alone at the piano and singing 'Whisky & Gin' was the only thing that remained natural for him."

That was where Johnnie belonged—lost in the didactic, primitive torch R&B style he had invented. But opportunities to drift through that opalescent idiosyncratic dimension were severely limited. He grew increasingly disenchanted with the numbing repetition of the road, but continued to play, after hours, as hard as he did when a young man. In 1984, working a Dallas hotel engagement that ran through Christmas, Johnnie, Jerry Blaine and road manager Tad Mann spent hours, at Johnnie's enthusiastic suggestion, holding elevator races, up and down. Up and down. Up and down. They then retired to Johnnie's room to drink. And drink. And drink.

"We're sittin' there drinkin' and watchin' tv," Tad Mann said. "This was Christmas Eve and there was nothin' on tv but hours of Sylvester the cat cartoons. Sylvester and Tweety Pie, I'll never forget it. About five in the morning, we all just sort of looked at each other and said, "My God, what are we doin' here? Three grown men, alone in a hotel on Christmas mornin', drinkin' wine and watchin Sylvester the cat . . . what are we doin'?"" (Johnnie provided an answer that particular Christmas—by spending thousands of dollars on food, liquor and flowers on a party he threw for the hotel's employees, capped by a Johnnie Ray performance.)[7]

In a sense, nothing had changed from the day Johnnie found himself in the Coconut Grove, thinking, "Well, you've got it all, but what have you got? You're still sitting alone in an empty nightclub on a Sunday afternoon . . . "

It was a question Johnnie had been asking himself since 1954.

*   *   *

His dogged road work continued unabated. By the mid-80's, he began to swear each Australian tour would be the final one. It never was. Between 1955 and 1989 he toured the country twenty-nine times, more than any other American performer. On his 1985 tour, he gave twenty-two performances in twenty-five days. Within hours of arriving, Johnnie had to endure four interviews, then rehearse and perform on a television show. An itinerary-designated "day off" meant, at the least, two interviews (Johnnie preferred it that way, and instructed his bookers to carry on; all of his international dates were handled through the Willard Alexander agency).[8]

In America, no one took Johnnie seriously except his fans, friends and his booking agent, Alan Eichler. Described by another client, Anita O'Day, as "a strange, brilliant cat—when I bugged him about what I owed him, he'd say 'Nothing,' or 'Oh, give me some money for my phone bill.'"[9] Eichler was a passionate fan of American pop music originals like Johnnie, Anita, Nellie Lutcher and Hadda Brooks. He was the first professional associate in Johnnie's career who worked to get him recognition as the influential R&B-based originator the Cry Guy was. Nobody wanted to hear about it.

Johnnie appreciated the effort, but knew it was pointless. He was far more interested in the romantic escapades of his friends and which dinner date was upcoming than he was in glory denied. On January 10, 1987, he wrote in his datebook "I am 60. What will I do on my birthday?" Concerned about Elma, who had undergone surgery two days earlier but called that afternoon ("Elma AOK!"), he dined at home with two couples, one of whom was calling their relationship quits. ("I saw it coming—of ALL days—Jim & Dennis split!! Din BBQ chicken, cake, 8:30 - 1 a.m. Looooong night.)

He toured and toured; Britain, all over the U.S., a long, unsuccessful run at the Golden Nugget in Las Vegas. Johnnie was boozing hard, and also popping Halcion, the powerful hypnotic tranquilizer, in an attempt to stave off insomnia. He dug the drug, noting in his datebook when the supply got low—a stash of forty pills was small enough to merit notation on June 27. August 2: "Drank 'til 8 a.m. Bang on the head."

September 14: "Halcion, [picked up] 100 Today." On October 21, he "ordered" more. On November 4, he noted "200 Halcions." In London on November 23 for the Royal Command Variety Performance, Johnnie wrote: "Sensational Perf. Be Proud!!" Back home on December 19 Johnnie was "Stoned! Quiet . . . Nebulous . . . Ephemeral . . . Gossamer . . . " The tolerance was growing. December 24: "12 Halcion today." On the 29th: "12 Halcion hypothetically consumed." On the 30th: "Order(ed) Halcion. I did." On January 1, 1988: "Saul & I go get 100 Halcion." On January 2nd, a note to call another doctor: "Halcion!" On his 61st Birthday: "Happy!! Still coughing up blood . . . "

Johnnie was winding down. The previous summer, on July 25, he wrote in his datebook "Dreamed my life finale!!" Johnnie had been meeting with a writer friend and done dozens of hours of interviews with him, in hopes of producing a book on the Cry Guy's life. Despite numerous sessions, it was fruitless. He notes that summer that the writer "is drunk, losing weight and on speed!" Nothing ever came of the project, and Johnnie ultimately kiboshed the entire deal.

By 1988, the once spindly wailer had begun to let himself go; his weight increased considerably. "He told me, 'They had a skinny Johnnie for years—Now they've got to take me fat!' He used to joke about that a lot, he'd always say, 'They can fix that in the pictures!'" said John Thomas. His health was poor; chills, colds, pain, no sleep, no food, a rotten tooth that got knocked out, constipation—Johnnie had run his physical self into the ground. But his spirit was as untrammelled as when he dyed his hair green fifty years before.

It all caught up with him in late 1989. Alan Eichler was on a roll with his career revitalization program for clients like R&B Empresses Ruth Brown and LaVern Baker, Little Miss Sharecropper herself, whom he helped persuade to return from decades of Officer's Club work at the Philippines' Mount Pinatubo US base. Both enjoyed substantially higher profiles, appearing in the Broadway musical "Black and Blue," as a result.

Now Eichler wanted to re-cast Johnnie as the R&B shouter he had been in the Flame Showbar. He booked Johnnie into New York's Ballroom and arranged to have Ruth Brown's band back him. Johnnie was nonplussed about the R&B angle, and unhappy that his accompanist Guy Pastor would not be in on the dates (Jerry Blaine had mysteriously disappeared, never to be heard from again, on the eve of an Australian tour). But he trouped on.

The Ballroom engagement was a disaster. The musicians set to back Johnnie dropped out at the last minute and he was stuck with a strange combo and no rehearsal time. It was ninety-five degrees. New York seemed to him "Dirty, smelly, Times Square empty, black and homeless." Johnnie was lackluster at his July 28 opener. "It was a fiasco," Marlin Swing grimly said. Johnnie, writing in his datebook, was more blunt, "A complete disaster." It did not improve, going, in his estimation from "Fair Show" to "Quiet show" to "Shit . . . barely made it."

He went to P.J. Clarke's, saw Thelma Carpenter, hung out with Hank Wesinger and Marlin Swing. But things at the Ballroom were getting very dicey. Worse, he noted on August 3, "Reviews are scathing . . ." They were the harshest of his career. The New York Times made Confidential sound like a fan club newsletter:

> "Mr. Ray, who is 62, still put odd rhythm spins on his mate-
> rial, but his singing has no emotional center. A delivery that
> once seemed driven by feeling sounded painfully mannered
> and at times scatterbrained as he struggled to remember
> words. At moments the singer, who pushes his voice very
> hard, simply bellowed. His vocal deterioration was under-
> scored by dreary, colorless band arrangements."[10]

On Saturday August 5th, Johnnie wrote: "Long Long day . . . Band bad . . . I was tired . . . " For the first time in his thirty-eight-year career, a Johnnie Ray engagement was cut short.

He wrote "Next week canceled . . . called Sol . . . No reply . . . midnight stomach hurts - back, right shoulder sore as hell . . . Liver grim *sore.*" Johnnie limped through the remaining dates. It was a hellish last week. On the 8th: "No Sleep. Pain." The 9th: "Up sore at 1:30 . . . sedated but living . . . SHOULDER really PAIN . . . ICM meeting agent usual bullshit—no offers—no encouragement—no advice . . . I am confused I think it's all the pills."

Being canceled was a blow Johnnie was totally unprepared for. He went home and laid low, not sleeping at night, cooking chili and watching soap operas by day. Johnnie was bored. Worse than bored. On September 15: "Depressing day! Suicide thoughts." On October 1st, a television special on the 1987 Royal Variety Performance aired: "I was cut out!"

*   *   *

On Friday, October 6th, 1989, Johnnie opened his final engagement, in Salem, Oregon, to benefit the city's Center for the Performing Arts. He had not appeared in Oregon for over ten years. "Aunt Bea! Great Show! Reception after . . . walked home," Johnnie wrote. The reviews were "great" the next day; unfortunately, "Elma was sick." Heartsick. Even on his natal stomping grounds, there was a problem. In Los Angeles, Jim Low got a telephone call from Marciel Shepard, the girl who used to listen to Johnnie grind out boogies by the hour when they were teenagers in Dallas.

"Marciel called me and said there was nobody there," Low said. "She was crying. I don't know if it was a failure to promote it, or what it was but Marciel was devastated, and I'm sure Elma was too. I really think that was a blow, because I spoke to John not long after he got back and he never mentioned it to me, never mentioned the shows once. And if anything would've broken Johnnie's heart, it was that."

Johnnie dropped out of sight almost completely, speaking only to Sol, Guy Pastor, Hank Wesinger and Elma. By October 27th, Johnnie knew it was serious: "Into Dr. for liver observation . . . Guy will take me thank god . . . feel like shit . . . 102 degree temperature . . . " On Thanksgiving, nothing about Franklin, just: "call Marvin's about Halcion."

Johnnie, still running a temperature, having hardly eaten or slept for weeks, took a cab to Marvin's Pharmacy to pick up his Halcion. Two days after that, Guy Pastor took him to Cedars Sinai. He was released five days later. Johnnie knew his liver had thrown in the sponge. He wanted to see if a transplant was possible.

His non-presence became a concern among friends. "He always liked to party, had lots of company, big social life, but I think he was realizing that he was getting sick, he didn't feel good and he became a lot quieter, a lot calmer," John Thomas said. "I hadn't heard from him in weeks, so finally I went up to visit. He was sitting in a big chair with his feet up and just looked like death. "He was very quiet, very calm and once he knew that I knew he was sick, Johnnie was close to me again—because he had been trying to hide it." When Johnnie marked his birthday on January 10, 1990, he still did not believe it was to be his last.

"I took him out to Farmer's Market, and I was scared to, because he was so weak and so top heavy, but he had loved it, had the time of his life. And he looked terrible, everybody was starin' at him, looking at him like he was really ill and they knew. And several people recognized him and one of the butchers came up and said 'Mr. Ray, I'm a fan . . . ' That always made him feel real good, he'd just light up."

By mid-January, it was clear even to Johnnie that a liver transplant for someone with his medical history was out of the question. He was furious—suicide thoughts of 1962 and 1989 notwithstanding, he did not want to die.

By February Johnnie was back in Cedars-Sinai. He would not come out under his own steam. Elma flew to Los Angeles. John Thomas stayed with him around the clock. "He was in a coma . . . the first few days I was there he just sat, with his eyes kind of glazed over. He was very yellow, and had lost lots of weight, he was very skinny," said Thomas. "And one day—I just couldn't believe it, because of the song and everything, this freaked me out. He was just sitting there staring . . . and all of a sudden this great big tear ran down his face."

Hours stretched into days. Elma was distraught. "He got real rambunctious a couple of times—kept trying to pull this tube out of his penis and jump out of the bed," Thomas recalled. "And oh my god, was he strong! Very strong, he was fighting to get up. I was scared to death, he had his legs stuck through those metal strips on the bed. I was hollerin' for help, and nobody heard me. I finally got somebody to come in and help. They had to tie him down and restrain him."

"Finally I was going to go home and rest, and the nurse, he had this wonderful black nurse, she really cared about him, and she told me, 'Don't go, baby. Don't go, because if you do when you come back, he won't be here.' Johnnie died about forty minutes later. Elma was out in the hall for a smoke, and she came back in the room just at the moment before he drew his last breath."

It was February 24, 1990. Back at 1654 Marmont, it was still and sunny. Upon the living room coffee table, surrounded by half a dozen brass Palladium record-breaker memorial plaques, his silver bowl was filled with pastel-colored, heart-shaped Valentine message candies.[12] They spelled out Johnnie Ray's last words:

Kiss Me Quick.

Be Mine.

I Love You.

NOTES

CHAPTER ONE: [1]45th Parallel designated by Oregon state signage Interstate 5. [2]Information on George Gay and early settlers from DAR marker, Hopewell, Oregon; also "WPA Writer's Project: Historic Tours of Oregon" 1939; also author interviews with Elma Ray, Salem, Oregon Jan. 10 1993; Beatrice Henry, Portland, Oregon, January 13, 1993. [3]Elma Ray author interview, January 10, 1993. [4]Elma Ray author interview, Salem, Oregon, April 13, 1993. [5]Beatrice Henry author interview. [6]Beulah Curtiss, letter to Salem Performing Arts Center, September 27, 1989. [7]Dorothy Shepard Ely, letter to Salem Performing Arts Center, September 27, 1989. [8]Naomi Brown, letter to Salem Performing Arts Center, September 28, 1989. [9]Johnnie Ray interview with John McNally KCRW, Santa Monica, California, November 11, 1984. [10]Jim Low author interview, Burbank, California, April 26, 1993. [11]Information on Logan Laam's Happy Hayseeds from Rich Nevins "Pioneers of Country Music" text, Yazoo Records, 1983. [12]Johnnie Ray interview, Arnold Shaw, "The Rockin' 50s" p55; New York: Hawthorn Books, 1974. [13]Johnnie Ray KCRW interview. [14]Marciel Shepard author interview, Salem, Oregon, January 11, 1993. [15]Betty Woodman, letter to Salem Performing Arts Center, September 27, 1989. [16]Marciel Shepard author interview. [17]See "The Inside Story of Johnnie Ray: His Life and Loves," by Phyliss Gray, TV & Movie Screen, July 1955. [18]Jim Smith, letter to Salem Performing Arts Center, September 28 1989. [19]Shaw, "The Rockin 50's," p55. [20]Jim "Snuffy" Smith author interview, Salem, Oregon, January 12, 1993. [21]Johnnie Ray KCRW interview. [22]"Johnnie Ray Comes Home," by Eric Apalategui, Salem Itemizer/Observer, Vol.114, #40, Oct. 4, 1989, p 1B.

CHAPTER TWO: [1]Daily News, Mon., May 10, 1993, Mary R. Hiller, Medical Adviser Column, L.A. Life Section, p 9. [2]Bill Franklin author interview, West Hollywood, California, August 6, 1993. [3]"Negroes Taught Me To Sing: Famous Cry Crooner Tells What Blues Taught Him" by Johnnie Ray, Ebony, March 1953. [4]Ray, "Negroes Taught Me To Sing." [5]Johnnie Ray KCRW interview. [6]"Johnnie Ray Is Back at East Side Club," by John S. Wilson, New York Times, Fri., May 22, 1981, p C17. [7]Bill Franklin author interview. [8]Gray, "Johnnie Ray," TV & Movie Screen, July, 1955. [9]"Mr. Emotion—His Inspiring story," Johnnie Ray souvenir program circa 1952. [10]Goldmine, April 1983, "Johnnie Ray: The $1,000,000 Teardrop" by Robert Cain, p 33. [11]Johnnie Ray KCRW interview. [12]Johnnie Ray author interview West Hollywood, May 11,

1989, [13]Shaw, "The Rockin' 50s" p 55. [14]Billboard, July 12 1952, "Johnnie Ray Case History Part I, Ray With $1,000,000 Remembers $500 in '49." by Joe Martin, p 33. [15]Dean Knupp author interview, Salem, Oregon, January 11, 1993. [16]Johnnie Ray KCRW interview. [17]Kay Starr speaking at Johnnie Ray's memorial service, Forest Lawn Hollywood Hills, Burbank, California, March 2, 1990.

CHAPTER THREE: [1]Dean Knupp author interview. [2]Johnnie Ray KCRW interview. [3]Johnnie Ray KCRW interview. [4]see "Mr. Emotion, his Inspiring Story." [5]Billboard, July 12 1952, Case History I: "Ray with $1,000,000 Remembers $500.00 in '49" By Joe Martin, p 1. [6]Big Jay McNeely author interview, Hollywood, California, May 24, 1993. [7]Dixie Evans author interview, Helendale, California, May 23, 1993. [8]see Shaw, "The Rockin 50s," p 56. [9]Herman Hover told author, June 12, 1993. [10]Variety, October 2, 1957, Johnnie Ray at Coconut Grove, live review by Helm, p 67. [11]see "Johnnie Ray in the Big Show, second Australian Tour souvenir program. [12]Ray to author, May 11, 1989. [13]see "Sweet Man The Real Duke Ellington" by Don George, New York: G.P. Putnam's Sons, 1981, pp 62-63. [14]Palomino owner Hank Penny told author. [15]Seymour & Billie Heller author interview, West Los Angeles, California, June 4, 1993. [16]Billie Rosenfield Heller interview, June 4, 1993. [17]20th Century Fox Johnnie Ray publicity file, Academy of Motion Picture Arts & Sciences Library. [18]Johnnie Ray interview, KCRW, November 11, 1984. [19]Los Angeles Daily News, October 23 1952, "A Few Notes On Johnnie Ray," by Marie Mesmer. [20]Johnnie Ray interview, KCRW, November 11, 1984. [21]Ray to author May 11, 1989. [22]Billboard, July 12, 1952, Johnnie Ray Case History I: "Ray With $1,000,000 Remembers $500 In '49." by Joe Martin, p 1. [23]TV & Movie Screen, July 1955, "Johnnie Ray His Life and Loves," by Phyliss Gray. [24]Billboard, July 12, 1952, Johnnie Ray Case History I: "Ray With $1,000,000 Remembers $500 In '49." by Joe Martin, p 1.

CHAPTER FOUR: [1]Elma Ray interview, January 10, 1993. [2]Goldmine, April 1983. [3]Billboard, July 12 1952, Johnnie Ray Case History I. [4]Billboard, August 2, 1952, Johnnie Ray Case History IV, "Ray Credits Those Who Helped Him Up," by Joe Martin, p 16. [5]Billboard, July 19 1952, Johnnie Ray Case History II, "Many Fingers Dip Into Ray Pie, Few Get Cuts," by Joe Martin, p 19. [6]Billboard, July 19 1952, Johnnie Ray Case History II; also Soupy Sales author interview, New York City, June 19, 1992. [7]Billboard, August 2, 1952, Johnnie Ray Case History IV. [8]Billboard, July 12 1952, Johnnie Ray Case History I. [9]"Johnnie Ray is back at East Side Club" by John S. Wilson, New York Times, Fri., May 22 page C 17. [10]Bill Franklin author interview. [11]Ebony, March 1953. [12]Johnnie Ray author interview. [13]Arnold Shaw, "Honkers & Shouters" p 443. [14]Physical description of the Flame from 1954 photo; billing at Flame from Billboard, August 2, 1952, Johnnie Ray Case History IV. [15]LaVern Baker told author April 27, 1991. [16]Ray, Ebony, March 1953. [17]Ray, Ebony, March 1953.

[18]Shaw, "Honkers & Shouters," p 365. [19]Johnnie Ray KGO radio interview, circa 1982. [20]LaVern Baker author interview, New York City, June 13, 1992. [21]New York Daily News, "Johnnie Ray's Back: After the Bawl" by Patricia O'Hare, August 1, 1990. [22]Jimmy Witherspoon author interview, Los Angeles, California, April 5, 1993. [23]All quotes on his performances at Flame from Johnnie Ray author interview, May 11, 1989. [24]Ray, Ebony, March 1953. [25]Billboard, July 26 1952, Johnnie Ray Case History III "Many Ventures Keep Ray Coffers Filled," by Joe Martin, p 18. [26]Bill Franklin author interview, West Los Angeles, California, August 6, 1993. [27]Shaw, "Honkers & Shouters," p 89. [28]Mitch Miller author interview, New York City, June 6, 1992. [29]"Stars of Country Music: Jimmie Rodgers," by Chris Comber & Mike Paris; Urbana: University of Illinois Press, 1975, p 121. [30]Danny Kessler author interview, Sherman Oaks, California, August 30, 1992. [31]Danny Kessler author interview; also Kessler in Shaw, "Honkers & Shouters," p 448. [32]Johnnie Ray author interview. [33]Billboard, August 2, 1952, Case History part IV. [34]Johnnie Ray author interview. [35]Titles courtesy of Columbia Archive. [36]Danny Kessler told author, April 26, 1990. [37]Billboard, July 19, 1952, Case History part II.

CHAPTER FIVE: [1]Johnnie Ray KCRW interview. [2]Ray, Ebony March 1953. [3]"The Life and Times of Little Richard," by Charles White, New York: Harmony 1984, p 26. [4]"We Demand A Pardon For Johnnie Ray," Lowdown, August 1955, p 8. [5]Billboard, July 19, 1952, Case History II. [6]Billboard Case, July 19, 1952, History II. [7]Danny Kessler told author, April 27, 1990. [8]Johnnie Ray author interview. [9]Shaw, "Rockin' 50s," p 37. [10]Tony Bennett author interview, New York City, September 1, 1992. [11]Johnnie Ray author interview. [12]Danny Kessler told author April 27, 1990. [13]Johnnie Ray author interview. [14]Shaw, "Rockin' 50s," pp 63-64. [15]Johnnie Ray author interview. [16]Johnnie Ray author interview. [17]"Mr Emotion His Inspiring Story." [18]Johnnie Ray KGO interview. [19]"Dino, Living High in the Dirty Business of Dreams," by Nick Tosches, New York: Doubleday 1992, pp 80-81, 134. [20]Soupy Sales author interview, New York City, June 19, 1992. [21]Variety, December 26, 1951, p 37. [22]Billboard R&B reviews, August 18, 1951, p 75. [23]Saturday Evening Post, July 26, 1952, "The Million Dollar Teardrop" by Robert Sylvester. [24]Cy Kertman author interview, Newport Beach, California, February 11, 1993. [25]Billboard, October 6, 1951 "The Ray Story: $90.00 to $1,750.00," p 1. [26]Shaw, "Honkers & Shouters," p 68. [27]Shaw "Honkers & Shouters," p 367; Kessler, Lang also told author. [28]"Mr. Emotion."

CHAPTER SIX: [1]Shaw, "Rockin 50s," pp 47-49. [2]Mitch Miller author interview, New York City, June 9, 1992. [3]Shaw "Rockin 50s,"pp 47-49. [4]Stan Freeman author interview, San Fernando Valley June 14, 1993. [5]Johnnie Ray author interview, May 11, 1989. [6]Johnnie Ray author interview. [7]Johnnie Ray author interview. [8]Johnnie Ray interview, "Off The Record" by Joe Smith, New York: Warner Books, 1988, p 69. [9]Tony Bennett author interview. [10]New York

Daily Mirror, April 17, 1952, "Only Human" by Sidney Fields. [11]Rolling Stone, June 28 1969, "Perspectives: Hank Williams, Roy Acuff and then God!" By Ralph J. Gleason, p 32. [12]"Sinatra," by Earl Wilson, New York: Macmillan 1976, p 79. [13]Charles Ostergrant author interview, Burbank, California, August 17, 1993.

CHAPTER SEVEN: [1]Bernie Lang described "the morning line" to author. [2]Downbeat, December 28, 1951, "Ray Humble About Sudden Success as Singer." [3]Saturday Evening Post, July 27, 1952,"The Million Dollar Teardrop" by Robert Sylvester. [4]Vanity Fair, March 1993, "Hidden Hoover," by Anthony Summers, pp 201-202. [5]Saturday Evening Post, July 27, 1952. [6]Variety, December 26, 1952. [7]Billboard, July 12, 1952 Case History I. At their five per-cent royalty rate, Johnnie would earn about $25,000 for every 500,000 records sold. When Bernie went back into Columbia and attempted to re-negotiate the re-negotiation, Johnnie wondered, "What's the matter with those guys? Do they want the whole company?" .[8]Jack Devaney author interview, Studio City, California, January 29, 1993. [9]Beatrice Henry author interview, Portland, Oregon, February 20, 1993. [10]Los Angeles Daily News, October 15, 1952, "None Other Than Bawling Ray" by Erskine Caldwell. [11]Tempest Storm author interview, Los Angeles, California, May 23, 1993. [12]Hollywood Citizen News, May 24, 1952 "Johnnie Ray Gets License, Will Wed Tomorrow." [13] Herman Hover author interview, Beverly Hills, California, June 12, 1993. [14]George T. Simon: "The Big Bands," p 400 New York: MacMillan, 1967. [15]Shaw, "Rockin' 50s," pp 54-55. [16]Voice of Broadway, Dorothy Kilgallen, New York Journal American, January 30, 1952. [17]Billboard, March 15 1952; as excerpted in "Sounds of the City," by Charlie Gillett, New York: Pantheon 1970. [18]New York Post, cited in editorial page notice of Ray's passing, February 25, 1993. [19]Melody Maker, Laurie Henshaw column, February 24, 1952, as excerpted in "Sounds of the City," by Charlie Gillett. [20]Variety, February 6, 1952. [21]Billboard, August 2, 1952, Case History IV. [22]Cliffie Stone author interview, Hollywood Musician's Union, May 24, 1993. [23]Billboard, August 2, 1952, Case History IV. [24]Life Magazine, March 24, 1952 pp 99-102. [25]Smith, "Off the Record," p 69. [26]"Sinatra," by Earl Wilson, p 100.

CHAPTER EIGHT: [1]Author visited Copacabana June 16, 1993, guided by the Copa's Arthur Meola; also author interviews with former Copa girls Lynn Shannon Kessler (Studio City, California, August 30, 1992), Toni Carroll (New York City, June 8, 1992) and Beck Steiner Gordon (Beverly Hills, California, November 13, 1993). [2]Billboard, April 19, 1952, "Johnnie Ray's Phenomenal Showmanship Wins Sophisticates in NY Club Bow," by Bill Smith, p 3. [3]Tosches, "Dino," p 134. [4]Copa audience info from various sources,including Saturday Evening Post, contemporary trade paper reviews, columns, "Sinatra" by Earl Wilson, and various author interviews. [5]Billboard, April 19, 1952. [6]Jane Kean author interview, Studio City, California, April 13, 1990. [7]Billboard, April 19, 1952. [8]On the QT, January 1956, "Why Johnnie Ray Likes To Go In Drag," p 36. [9]Billboard, April 19, 1952. [10]Bernie Lang told author; also Bill Franklin, Elma Money. [11]Saturday Evening Post, July 27, 1952. [12]"Sinatra" by Earl Wilson, p 100. [13]Look magazine, June 1952, "Prince of Wails," by Hy Gardner. [14]Mitch Miller author interview. [15]Press quotes as excerpted in Johnnie Ray official biography, from Sol Lazarow office, courtesy Johnnie Ray Estate; also see "Kilgallen," by Lee Israel. [16]Billboard, April 19, 1952. [17]"Jackie Gleason, an Intimate Portrait of the Great One" by W.J. Weatherby, New York 1992: Pharos Books, Scripps Howard, pp 183 & 189. [18]author interviews with Jane Kean, Billie Rosenfield Heller. [19]Saturday Evening Post, July 27, 1952. [20]Cy Kertman author interview, February 13, 1993. [21]New York Times, April 17, 1952, Howard Taubman column. [22]New York Daily Mirror, April 17, 1952, "Only Human" by Sydney Fields. [23]Billboard, August 2, 1952, Case History IV. [24]Billboard, July 26, 1952, Case History part III. [25]"Mr. Emotion." [26]Billboard, July 26, 1952, Case History part III. [27]Billboard August 2, 1952, Case History IV. Green, used to swindling ill-educated black artists, did not have an American Federation of Musicians license, which left his claim absolutely nowhere. [28]Billboard, July 26, 1952, Case History III. [29]Billboard, July 26, 1952, Case History III.

CHAPTER NINE: [1]Los Angeles Times, May 15, 1952 "Crooner Ray's Wedding Date Becomes Official." [2]Bernie Lang, Cy Kertman told author. [3]Billboard May 10, 1952, live review by Norman Wiser, p14. [4]Billboard May 10, 1952. [5]Charles Ostergrant author interview, Burbank, California, August 17 1993. [6]Los Angeles Examiner, May 14 1952 "Cry Girls Cry JR To Wed" by Louella O. Parsons. [7]Los Angeles Examiner, May 15, 1952 "Johnnie Ray says He's Confused. Weeping Singer Admits Doubt Over Approaching Nuptials." [8]Los Angeles Examiner, May 15, 1952. [9]Los Angeles Times, May 15, 1952 "Crooner Ray's Wedding Date Becomes Official." [10]Saturday Evening Post, July 26 1952, "The Million Dollar Teardrop" by Robert Sylvester. [11]United Press wire report, May 20, 1952, "Johnnie Ray: Tears Of Joy, Sweeps Fiancee Into Arms." Academy of Motion Picture Arts & Sciences Library Johnnie Ray clip file. [12]Los Angeles Daily News May 26, 1952, "Clouds Cry As Johnnie Ray Weds Hollywood Girl In New York." [13]New York Daily News, May 26, 1952, "Johnnie Ray Weds—Bride Cries" by Josephine Di Lorenzo. [14]New York Daily News, May 26, 1952. [15]Los Angeles Examiner, May 26, 1952, "Wedding Bells Dry Up Tears For Johnnie Ray," Associated Press wire report. [16]Los Angeles Times, May 26, 1952, "Little White Clouds Really Cry as Johnnie Ray Weds," United Press wire report. [17]Ray, Ebony Magazine, March 1953; also author interviews with La Vern Baker, June 13, 1992, Don Ovens, August 8, 1992. [18]Billboard, June 28, 1952, p 1, "Ray Receives 2 Gold Disks." [19]"Kilgallen," by Lee Israel, New York: Delacorte 1979, p 279. [20]Bernie Lang told author. [21]Voice of Broadway, Dorothy Kilgallen, New York Journal-American, July 13, 1952. [22]Saturday Evening Post, July 26, 1952. [23]Hollywood Citizen News, July 19,

1952 "Johnnie Ray and 4000 Others Gas Bombed." [24]Saturday Evening Post, July 26, 1952. [25]Saturday Evening Post, July 26, 1952. [26]Los Angeles Times, November 30, 1952, "Ray's Tears Joyful Now—It Wasn't Always That Way Though," by Edwin Schallert. [27]Los Angeles Examiner, August 23, 1952, "Johnnie Ray Expecting Baby," by Dorothy Manners. [28]Los Angeles Times, August 23, 1952 "Johnnie Ray Expects Baby," by Hedda Hopper. [29]Los Angeles Times, September 18, 1952 "Mrs. Johnnie Ray In Hospital, Loses Baby," by Hedda Hopper. [30]Jimmy Campbell author interview, Las Vegas, Nevada, May 20, 1992. [31]Johnnie Ray KCRW interview. [32]Los Angeles Daily News, October 23, 1952, "A Few Notes On Johnnie Ray" by Marie Mesmer. [33]Confidential, April 1953, "Johnnie Ray: Is It True?" by Jay Williams.

CHAPTER TEN: [1]Los Angeles Examiner, October 2, 1952, "Mrs Johnnie Ray Cries." [2]Los Angeles Times, October 3, 1952, "More Than 500 Attend Party of Marion Davies; Affair Honoring Johnnie Ray Most Lavish In Hollywood History" by Edwin Schallert. [3]"My Life" by Debbie Reynolds, New York: Morrow 1988, pp 99-100. [4]Newsweek, October 13, 1952. Academy of Motion Pictures Arts & Sciences Library, Johnnie Ray clippings file. [5]Los Angeles Times, October 3, 1952. [6]Jan Sterling author interview, Los Angeles, California, July 6, 1992. [7]Reynolds, "My Life", pp 99-100. [8]Reynolds, "My Life," pp 99-100. [9]Los Angeles Daily News, October 3, 1952, "Everyone Cried Along with Johnnie Ray—Marion Davies Gave A Wallop of a Party for the Singer," by Erskine Johnson. [10]Reynolds, "My Life," pp 99-100. [11]Newsweek, October 13, 1952. [12]George Schlatter author interview, Los Angeles, June 2, 1993. [13]Los Angeles Daily News, October 7, 1952 "Johnnie Ray's Car Stolen." [14]Johnnie Ray KCRW interview. [15]Speedy West author interview, Broken Arrow, Oklahoma, August 7, 1992. [16]Hadda Brooks told author, Glendale California, August 16 1993. [17]"Divided Soul," by David Ritz, New York: Da Capo Press 1985, p 29, 82. [18]Los Angeles Times, November 30, 1952, "Rays Tears Joyful Now" by Edwin Schallert. [19]Jimmy Campbell author interview, Las Vegas, Nevada, April 20, 1990. [20]Jim Low, Bill Franklin, Hank Wesinger, others told author. [21]Goldmine, April 1983. [22]Goldmine, April 1983. [23]Los Angeles Examiner, November 28, 1952, "Johnnie Ray Rift Denied," by Louella O. Parsons. [24]Los Angeles Times, November 30, 1952. [25]Los Angeles Daily News December 8, 1952 "Parents Squelch Report Ray, Wife Separated." [26]"Jimmie Tarantino's Hollywood Life Newsweekly of the West: San Francisco-Los Angeles," December 12, 1952; Academy of Motion Pictures Arts & Sciences Library, Johnnie Ray clippings file; this copy still bears the subscriber's address label: Hedda Hopper. [27]Johnnie Ray home movies courtesy Alan Eichler collection. [28]Los Angeles Daily News, December 16, 1952 "Johnnie Ray, Bride Reconciled," by Earl Wilson. [29]Tito Adami author interview, Las Vegas, Nevada, April 20, 1990. [30]Los Angeles Daily News, special reprint January 4, 1953, "Crier Takes Blame For Marital Breakup" by Earl Wilson. [31]Tad Mann author interview, Las Vegas,

Nevada, April 20, 1990. [32]Los Angeles Times, April 24, 1953, "Marion Davies Neglected to Pay $11,582 Bill, Suit Charges." [33]Los Angeles Times, April 25 1953, "Marion Davies to Fight 11,582 Bill For Party—Statement Through Secretary Gives Actresses version of Johnnie Ray Nuptial fete." [34]Wilson, "Sinatra," p 188. [35]Marilyn was too late; the two women were chatting after Johnnie's memorial service at Forest Lawn, Jane Kean told author.

CHAPTER ELEVEN: [1]Johnnie Ray author interview. [2]Variety, March 4, 1953, p 2. [3]Gray, TV & Movie Screen, July 1955. [4]"The mob shrieked and bellowed in a frenzy, with Ray heaping on the coals to keep them at white heat. . . maybe it was mass hysteria that drove Milton Berle out of his chair with his shoes in his hands, waving them madly aloft. Perhaps it was the same hysteria that drove Jan Murray out of his chair for an arm waving dance . . . " Billboard, February 14, 1953, "Ray Effect on Gotham Saloon set is Little Short of Electrifying," by Bill Smith, p 3. [5]Wilson, "Sinatra," p 162. [6]Kelley, "His Way," p 576. [7]Wilson, "Sinatra," p 138. [8]Tosches, "Dino," p 81. [9]Shaw, "The Rockin' 50s," p 56. [10]Variety, April 1, 1953, "London MU Bars Cry Guy Drummer," p 1. [11]"The Noel Coward Diaries," p 209. [12]Los Angeles Times, October 13, 1965. "For Crying Out Loud! Johnnie Ray Riding the Comeback Trail," by John L.Scott. [13]Voice of Broadway, Dorothy Kilgallen, New York Journal American, April 19, 1953. [14]Confidential, April 1953, "Johnnie Ray: Is It True?" by Jay Williams, p 37. [15]Confidential/Art Franklin caper: Bernie Lang, Danny Kessler told author. [16]Confidential, April 1953. [17]Confidential, April 1953. [18]Variety, June 24, 1953, "Johnnie Ray and Gary Morton Close Montreal's Sans Souci Venue," p 61. [19]Billboard, October 10, 1953, "Suit Charges Lang Assigned 50%." p 14. [20]Variety, December 25, 1953, "Pre-trial Exam for Publicist Art Franklin vs. Johnnie Ray," p 49.

CHAPTER TWELVE: [1]Billboard, September 28, 1953, by Abe L. Morris, p 134. [2]Variety, October 23, 1953, "Ray Squelched (1G Fine) For Quelling Riot." [3]Billboard, December, 26 1953, by Bill Smith, p12. [4]Los Angeles Examiner, January 12, 1954 "Johnnie Ray Divorce Nears in Mexico" by Louella O. Parsons; also January 14, 1954, AP wire report; also "Johnnie Ray Sued For Juarez Divorce." Johnnie Ray clippings file, Academy of Motion Picture Arts & Sciences Library. [5]UP wire report, January 15, 1954, "Cry Ray Shed by Wife in Juarez." Johnnie Ray clippings file, Academy of Motion Picture Arts & Sciences Library. [6]Gardner, Look Magazine, June 3, 1952. [7]Portland Sunday News, January 22, 1954. [8]Tad Mann interview Las Vegas, Nevada, April 20, 1990. [9]Boothroyd cited in Virginia Beach Ledger Star, March 30, 1979, "J.R. and Johnnie Ray: one a Show Biz legend the other a human being" by William Ruehlman, p C1. [10]Variety, April 27, 1955, "Johnnie Ray Returns to Palladium," p 54. [11]Variety, May 18, 1955, "Edinburgh Fans Mob Johnnie Ray at Airport," p 2. [12]Johnnie Ray KCRW interview. [13]Hollywood Citizen News, July 15, 1954 "Hollywood Is My Beat," Sidney Skolsky column. 14."I Got Rhythm, the Ethel

Merman Story" by Bob Thomas, New York: Putnam, 1985, pp130-131. [15]Thomas, "I Got Rhythm," pp 130-131. [16]"Johnnie Ray in the Big Show," second Australian Tour souvenir program. [17]Virginia Beach Ledger Star, March 30, 1979. [18]On the QT, January 1956, "Why Johnnie Ray Likes To Go In Drag." [19]Thomas, "I Got Rhythm," pp 130-131. [20]Thomas, "I Got Rhythm," pp 130-131. [21]Los Angeles Examiner, December 12, 1954, "Stage & Screen," Dorothy Manners column. [22]Johnnie Ray KCRW interview. [23]Johnnie Ray author interview. [24]Johnnie Ray KCRW interview. [25]Johnnie Ray clippings file, Academy of Motion Picture Arts & Sciences Library. [26]Los Angeles Examiner, December 18, 1954 "Johnnie Ray Gains in Stab of Toothpick." [27]20th Century Fox Studio Johnnie Ray Publicity file, Academy of Motion Picture Arts & Sciences Library. [28]Frank Laico author interview, New York, June 13, 1992. [29]Goldmine, April 1983. [30]Goldmine, April, 1983. [31]Bill Franklin described bracelet inscription to author, August 6, 1993. [32]Hollywood Citizen News, July 15 1954, "Hollywood is my Beat," Sidney Skolsky column. [33]Los Angeles Examiner, September 23, 1954 "Johnnie Ray, Divorced Wife to Try It Again" by Louella O. Parsons. [34]Beverly Hills Newsline, November 13, 1954, "In Hollywood" Aline Mosby column. [35]Los Angeles Examiner, December 18, 1954. [36]Virginia Beach Ledger Star, March 30, 1979. [37]Shake Books' Illustrated Price Guide To Scandal Magazines, New York; Shake Books, 1988. [38]Goldmine, April 1983; also see Variety, February 26, 1990, Johnnie Ray obituary. [39]Los Angeles Examiner, December 18, 1954.

CHAPTER THIRTEEN: [1]"Barbara Walters, an Unauthorized Biography" by Jerry Oppenheimer, p 15; New York: St Martin's Press, 1990. [2]Gold Coast Bulletin, December 10, 1988, p 53, "The Wild Days" by Douglas Kennedy. [3]Los Angeles Times, October 13, 1965, "For Crying Out Loud! Johnnie Ray Riding the Comeback Trail" by John L. Scott; also Gold Coast Bulletin, "The Wild Days." [4]Los Angeles Times, March 7, 1955, "Johnnie Ray Welcomed with Riot in Australia." [5]Variety, April 6, 1955, p 5. [6]Los Angeles Times, March 28 1955, "Johnnie Ray Saved From Fan Mob," Reynolds News Service item. [7]Anything Goes, May 1956, p 42, "Why Johnnie Ray Has To Get Half Stiff Every Night," Johnnie Ray interviewed by Paul Coates. [8]Screenland Magazine, March 1954, p 22, Dorothy Kilgallen's Exclusive Movie Gossip. [9]TV & Movie Screen, July 1955, p 14, "The Inside Story of Johnnie Ray, His Life and Loves" by Phyliss Grey. [10]Variety, April 6, 1955, p 5. [11]Variety, April 27, 1955, p 54. [12]Noel Coward Diaries, p 297. [13]Los Angeles Times, Reynolds News Service item, undated clipping; Academy of Motion Picture Arts & Sciences Margaret Herrick Library collection. [14]Jan Sterling author interview, Los Angeles, California, July 9, 1992. [15]Variety, June 18, 1955, p 51, review by Jose. [16]Oppenheimer, Barbara Walters, p 104. [17]Beck Steiner Gordon author interview, Beverly Hills, California, November 13, 1992. [18]1955 Australian tour program, "Lee Gordon Presents Johnnie Ray in the Big Show," courtesy of Alan Eichler collection. [19]Bill Franklin author interview, West Hollywood, California,

August 14, 1993. [20]Bernie Lang, Elma Money, Marlin Swing, Bill Franklin told author. [21]Lowdown, August 1955, p 8, "Lowdown Demands Michigan Governor Pardon Johnnie Ray!" by J. Alvin Kugelmass. [22]Shaw, "The Rockin' Fifties," p 57. [23]Variety, October 19, 1955, p 66, "Johnnie Ray Headache For Brit Gendarmes." [24]Variety, Nov 2, 1955, p 2. [25]1956 Australian tour program, "Lee Gordon Presents Johnnie Ray in the Big Show, Third Australian Tour 1956," courtesy of Alan Eichler collection. [26]Variety, November 9, 1955, review by Most. [27]Confidential, November 1955, "Knock, Knock! Who's There? . . . Why Did Johnnie Ray Try To Break Down Paul Douglas' Door?" by Francis Dudley. [28]Tito Adami author interview, April 20, 1990, Las Vegas, Nevada. [29]Uncensored, December 1955, p 48, "Why The Babes Still Cry For Johnnie Ray" by Bert Mason; Ray quoted in Shaw, "The Rockin' Fifties" p 57. [30]Los Angeles Times, November 1, 1976, "Johnnie Ray: Cry is no Sad Song," by Lynn Simross.

CHAPTER FOURTEEN: [1]Coates, Anything Goes, May 1956. [2]Variety, January 25, 1956, "Ray Whams South Africa." [3]"Ooh Ah Oh (This is Love)" was released in 1991 on German label Bear Family 1991 compact disc "Cry." [4]Variety, April 11, 1956, p 52, "Ray Really Weeps After Tokyo Flop." [5]Bill Franklin told author, August 8, 1993. [6]Johnnie Ray author interview. [7]Johnnie Ray author interview. [8]Variety, April 18, 1956, p 8, "Johnnie Ray at the Desert Inn" by Will. [9]Variety May 30, 1956, p 52 "Johnnie Ray at the Latin Quarter" nightclub review. [10]Johnnie Ray television appearances, video courtesy of Alan Eichler Collection. [11]Israel, "Kilgallen," p 222. [12]Israel, "Kilgallen," p 278. [13]New York Journal American, November 13, 1965, p 14, "The Dorothy Kilgallen Story, part 3" by Louis Sobol. [14]Sobol, New York Journal American, November 13, 1965. [15]Israel, "Kilgallen," p 472n. [16]Alan Eichler told author Johnnie often related this tidbit. [17]Israel, "Kilgallen," p 283. [18]Jimmy Campbell author interview, Las Vegas, Nevada, April 20, 1990. [19]Israel, "Kilgallen," pp 146, 155-156 and 174. [20]Time Magazine, November 24, 1961, television column, "Lambsy & Chopsy," Lincoln Center for Performing Arts Library collection. [21]Oppenheimer, "Barbara Walters," p 38. [22]New York Post Daily Magazine, April 28 1960, p 1, "The Dorothy Kilgallen Story," by David Gelman, with Beverly Carr, Peter J. McElroy, Sally Hammond and Richard Montague. [23]Time, November 24, 1961. [24]Israel, "Kilgallen," p 285. [25]see Wilson, "Sinatra," p 141; also Confidential, July 1957, p 6, "The Feud That Rocked the Copa: When Frank Sinatra Spit at Dorothy Kilgallen," by Ed Sinclair. [26]Wilson, "Sinatra," p 141. [27]Israel, "Kilgallen," pp 284-285; also Kelley, "His Way," pp 230-231 and Confidential, July 1957. [28]Louis Sobol quoted in Confidential July 1957. [29]Ray quoted in Israel, "Kilgallen," p 283; Kilgallen on Paar, Time, November 24, 1961. [30]Israel, "Kilgallen," pp 283-286.

CHAPTER FIFTEEN: [1]Johnnie Ray, Goldmine, April 1983. [2]Chart information and session data courtesy Columbia Records. [3]Shaw, "Honkers &

Shouters," pp 452-3. [4]Shaw, "Honkers and Shouters," pp 132-3. [5]Israel, "Kilgallen," p 288. [6] Israel, "Kilgallen," p 302. [7]Israel, "Kilgallen," p 301, 288. [8]Israel, "Kilgallen," p 283. [9]Israel, "Kilgallen," p 283. [10]Bill Franklin told author, August 8, 1993. [11]Ray itinerary information from Variety, July 17, 1957 p 3, "Johnnie Ray at Paul 'Skinny' D'Amato's Vermillion Room, 500 Club, Atlantic City," also Variety, July 24, 1957, p 64, "Johnnie Ray Booked Through Next Year." [12]Variety, March 6, 1957, p 57, "Johnnie Ray at Eden Roc Hotel." [13]Variety, May 15, 1957, p 67, "Johnnie Ray at Waldorf-Astoria" by Jose. [14]Oppenheimer, Barbara Walters, p 123. [15]Oppenheimer, Barbara Walters, p 166. [16]Oppenheimer, Barbara Walters, p 168. [17]Variety, May 15, 1957. [18]Tip Off, October 1956, p 12, "Why The Roman Rave Kicked Out Johnnie Ray," by Anthony Converro. [19]Revealed, July 1957, p 42, "London's Most Scandalous Nudie." [20]Variety, August 21, 1957, p 4, "Johnnie Ray on Presley: Giving Record Industry a Shot-In-Arm" by Hazel Guild. [21]Uncensored, July 1957, p 28, "When Marlon Brando and Johnnie Ray Flipped for That Paris Playgirl" by Gilbert Header. [22]Thelma Carpenter author interview, New York City, June 13, 1992. [23]Variety, October 27, 1957, p 65, "Johnnie Ray at the Desert Inn's Painted Desert Room" by Duke. [24]Variety, October 2, 1957, p 67, "Johnnie Ray at Coconut Grove" by Helm. [25]Variety, December 11, 1957, p 71, "Johnnie Ray at Town & Country" by Jose. [26]Ray to Murrow, CBS television's "Person To Person," May 1956.

CHAPTER SIXTEEN: [1]Billboard, July 12, 1952, p 1. [2]Undated clipping Academy Motion Picture Arts & Sciences Margaret Herrick Library Collection. [3]January 14, 1958, "Johnnie Ray Ear Miracle Thrills New York" by Earl Wilson, Margaret Herrick Library Collection. [4]Bill Franklin author interview, West Hollywood, California August 14, 1993. [5]New York Journal American, February 9, 1958, Voice of Broadway by Dorothy Kilgallen. [6]Dick Clark, "Rock Roll & Remember" p 163; New York: Popular Library 1978. [7]Oppenheimer, "Barbara Walters," pp 132-134. [8]Bill Franklin author interview, West Hollywood, California, November 11, 1990. [9]Hank Wesinger author interview, New York City, New York, March 22, 1993. [10]Bill Franklin interview, August 14, 1993. [11]Don Ovens author interview, Los Angeles, California, August 8, 1992. [12]Jim Low interview. [13]Allen Stokes quote; Israel, "Kilgallen," pp 346-47. [14]Marlin Swing author interview NYC, June 15, 1992. [15]Israel, "Kilgallen," p 303. [16]Don Ovens interview, August 8, 1992. [17]Bill Franklin author interview, West Hollywood, California August 20, 1993. [18]Israel, "Kilgallen," p 346. [19]Israel, "Kilgallen," p 345. [20]George, "Sweet Man: The Real Duke Ellington," pp 97-99. [21]Johnnie Ray KCRW interview. [22]Variety, October 29, 1958, "Johnnie Ray at Hotel Carrera, Santiago, Chile." [23]Israel, "Kilgallen," p 246. [24]New York Post Daily Magazine, April 28, 1960.

CHAPTER SEVENTEEN: [1]Johnnie Ray author interview. [2]Variety, February 18, 1959, "Johnnie Ray at Continental Room Shamrock Hilton,

Houston." [3]Variety, March 18 1959, p 87, "Johnnie Ray at Palace, London." Also Ray quote from author interview. [4]Gold Coast Bulletin, December 10, 1988. [5]Hank Wesinger author interview New York City, March 22, 1993. [6]Billboard, May 26 1958, p 7, "Sultan of Sob Solid Self Salesman." [7]Variety. June 10, 1959, "Johnnie Ray at Latin Quarter Follow Up" by Jose. [8]Jimmy Campbell, Tad Mann interviewed Las Vegas, Nevada , April 20, 1990. [9]Account of the trial is drawn from Los Angeles Mirror News, November 21, 1959, "Johnnie Ray Arrested On Vice Charge." Los Angeles Times, December 2, 1959 "Johnnie Ray Denies Vice Charge." Los Angeles Times, December 3, 1959, "Johnnie Ray Freed, Faints" (clippings in Academy of Motion Picture Arts & Sciences Margaret Herrick Library collection); also Israel, "Kilgallen," pp 304-305; Hush-Hush, May 1960, p 16, "Why Detroit isn't Home Sweet Homo For Johnnie Ray!" by Hal Clement; also previously cited author interviews with Marlin Swing, Hank Wesinger, Mitch Miller, Don Ovens, Tito Adami. [10]Bill Franklin author interview, West Hollywood, California, August 24, 1993. [11]Jimmy Campbell author interview, Las Vegas, Nevada, May 20 1992. [12]Variety, December 19 1959, p 55, "Johnnie Ray at Harrah's" by Long.

CHAPTER EIGHTEEN: [1]Hush-Hush, May 1960. [2]Israel, "Kilgallen," p 320. [3]Hank Wesinger, Alan Eichler related Dorothy's hospital hi-jinx to author. [4]All quotes from Johnnie Ray author interview. [5]Elma Ray author interview April 16, 1993. [6]Bernie Lang quoted in Johnnie Ray Australian Tour Program, "Bernie Lang, the Man who discovered 'The Cry Guy' talks about Johnnie Ray." [7]Variety, November 9, 1960, p 60, "Johnnie Ray at Basin Street East" by Herm. [8]Israel, "Kilgallen," p 301. [9]Bill Franklin interview, November 17, 1990. [10]Israel, "Kilgallen," p 345. [11]Johnnie Ray author interview. [12]Johnnie Ray KYA radio interview date unknown. [13]Johnnie Ray KYA interview. [14]Variety, May 17 1961, p 66, "Johnnie Ray at Angelo's, Omaha, Neb." by Trump. [15]Variety, July 5, 1961, p 53, "Johnnie Ray at Talk of the Town, London." [16]Bill Franklin interview, August 14, 1993. [17]Jimmy Campbell author interview, Las Vegas, Nevada, April 20, 1990. [18]Jimmy Campbell author interview Las Vegas, Nevada, May 20, 1992. [19]Israel, "Kilgallen," p 346. [20]Israel, "Kilgallen," p 347. [21]Israel, "Kilgallen," p 348. [22]Israel, "Kilgallen," p 349.

CHAPTER NINETEEN: [1]Variety, August 29, 1962, nightclub reviews, "Johnnie Ray at Holiday House, Pittsburgh." [2]Johnnie Ray KYA interview. [3]New York Times, May 22, 1981, p C17, "Johnnie Ray Is back At East Side Club" by John S. Wilson. [4]He does so, quite tartly, in the KYA interview cited above. [5]Israel, "Kilgallen," p 351. [6]Israel, "Kilgallen," p 351; also Bill Franklin interview November 1990. [7]Israel, "Kilgallen," p 352. [8]Israel, "Kilgallen," p 352. [9]Johnnie Ray author interview. [10]Johnnie Ray author interview.

CHAPTER TWENTY: [1]Johnnie Ray author interview. [2]Danny Kessler told author during a meeting in Pacific Palisades, California, April 26, 1990. [3]Los Angeles Times, April 24, 1953, "Marion Davies Neglected to Pay $11,582 Party

Bill, Suit Charges." [4]Bill Franklin quote, Israel, "Kilgallen," p 385. [5]Israel, "Kilgallen," p 367. [6]"Cry" sales figures in Sol Lazarow's official Johnnie Ray; courtesy Alan Eichler Collection. [7]Johnnie Ray author interview. [8]Oppenheimer, "Barbara Walters," pp 133-134, 142-143. [9]Oppenheimer, "Barbara Walters," pp 241-243. [10]Johnnie Ray author interview. [11]Bill Franklin told author, August 14, 1993. [12]Israel, "Kilgallen," pp 347, 349, 398. [13]Latin Quarter reviewers quotes appear in Johnnie Ray full page advertisement, Variety, September 27, 1965; also Israel, "Kilgallen," p 404. [14]Off the record source in New York told author; also Israel, "Kilgallen," p 385-387. [15]Variety, September 27, 1965. [16]Los Angeles Times, October 13, 1965, "For Crying Out Loud! JR Riding the Comeback Trail" By John L. Scott. [17]Israel, "Kilgallen," pp 404-405. [18]Israel, "Kilgallen," pp 312-313. [19]Israel, "Kilgallen," p 306. [20]Bill Franklin interview, November 17, 1990; also Israel, "Kilgallen," p 405. [21]Israel, "Kilgallen," p 405. [22]Israel, "Kilgallen," pp 260-274. [23]New York Journal American, September 3, 1965, "Voice of Broadway," column by Dorothy Kilgallen.

CHAPTER TWENTY ONE: [1]Bill Franklin interview August 8, 1993. [2]Israel, "Kilgallen," p 409. [3]Israel, "Kilgallen," p 415; Ruark on Ray cited in Saturday Evening Post, July, 1952 "The Million Dollar Teardrop" by Robert Sylvester. [4]Israel, "Kilgallen," p 423. [5]Israel, "Kilgallen," p 410, 412. [6]Israel, "Kilgallen," p 306. [7]New York Journal American, February 21, 1964 "Voice of Broadway" Dorothy Kilgallen column. [8]New York Journal American, February 22, 1964 "Nervous Ruby Feels Breaking Point Near." 9. Melvin Belli, Israel, "Kilgallen," pp 367-368. [10]Israel, "Kilgallen," pp 311-312. [11]Israel, "Kilgallen," p 372. [12]Israel, "Kilgallen," p 388. [13]Dorothy Kilgallen FBI File, U.S. Department of Justice, Freedom of Information Act request, pp 34-36, 38-39; also Israel, "Kilgallen," p 389. [14]New York Journal American, September 3, 1964 "Pre-Assassination Mystery Warren told Strange Trio Got Together" By Dorothy Kilgallen. [15]Israel, "Kilgallen," p 393. [16]New York Journal American, September 30, 1964 "Voice of Broadway" Dorothy Kilgallen column. [17]New York Journal American, September 30, 1964. [18]Mark Lane and the People's Temple information from "Journey to Nowhere: A New World Tragedy" by Shiva Naipul, pp 56, 103, 176; New York: Simon & Schuster 1980. [19]Israel, "Kilgallen," p 400. [20]Israel, "Kilgallen," p 398. [21]Israel, "Kilgallen," p 399. [22]Israel, "Kilgallen," p 403. [23]Israel, "Kilgallen," p 402. [24]Israel, "Kilgallen," p 403. [25]Israel, "Kilgallen," p 418. [26]Israel, "Kilgallen," p 421. [27]New York Journal American, November 9, 1965, "The Quiet Sadness of a City" by Alfred Robbins; also Israel, "Kilgallen," p 409. [28]Don Ovens told author; Tommy Sands, then Sinatra's son-in-law, related Sinatra's one-liner to Ovens. [29]"Dorothy Kilgallen's Funeral Mob Scene," clipping, Lincoln Center Library for the Performing Arts collection.

CHAPTER TWENTY TWO: [1]Tad Mann author interview Las Vegas Nevada, May 18, 1992. [2]Top Secret, August 1957, p 10, "What Happened when

Johnnie Ray was Noel Coward's House Guest" by Calvin Hunter. [3]Bill Franklin author interview West Hollywood, California, August 20, 1993. [4]Bill Franklin interview August 20, 1993. [5]Variety, August 1, 1966, "Reprise Ropes Ray," clipping in Margaret Herrick Library collection. [6]Wilson, "Sinatra," p 151. [7]Jimmy Bowen author interview, Nashville, Tennessee, February 8, 1991; Bob Merlis responded on Ostin's behalf December 10, 1993. [8]Variety, December 25, 1966, "Johnnie Ray Signed by Sheldon Cooper," clipping in Margaret Herrick Library collection. [9]Johnnie Ray KYA interview. [10]Variety, September 5, 1967, clipping in Margaret Herrick Library collection. [11]Los Angeles Times, December 27, 1967, Hal Humphreys column, clipping in Margaret Herrick Library collection.

CHAPTER TWENTY THREE: [1]Johnnie Ray author interview. [2]The Star, March 13, 1990, p 31, "Tormented Double Life of '50s Idol Johnnie Ray. [3]Derek Jewell, Sunday Times, excerpted in Weep No More, My Lady by Mickey Deans & Ann Pinchot, p 44, Variety citation p 49; New York: Pyramid 1972. [4]Deans, "Weep No More My Lady," p 56. [5]Deans, "Weep No More My Lady," p 23. [6]Sybil Burton, Arthur information from Jeff Gazall author interview, New York City, June 18, 1992. [7]Deans, "Weep No More, My Lady," p 50. [8]Deans "Weep No More, My Lady," p 150. [9]Deans, "Weep No More, My Lady," p 129-130. [10]Variety, March 19, 1969, p 69, "Garland and Ray Bow New Act in Sweden." [11]"The Last Performance" courtesy Alan Eichler collection. [12]Variety July 3, 1969, "Johnnie Ray Signs With Coast Artists" clipping.

CHAPTER TWENTY FOUR: [1]Johnnie Ray author interview; also Johnnie Ray KYA interview. [2]Goldmine, April 1983. [3]Johnnie Ray KCRW interview. [4]Johnnie Ray KGO interview. [5]Bill Franklin told author. [6]Johnnie Ray author interview. [7]Hollywood Reporter, September 11, 1972. [8]Village Voice, April 13, 1972, "Mr. One Time on the Rainbow Roof" by Randall Poe. [9]Village Voice April 13, 1972. [10]Jeff Gazall author interview, New York City, June 8, 1992. [11]Los Angeles Times, April 13, 1973 "Johnnie Ray at Westside Room." [12]New York Times, August 4, 1974, "Johnnie Ray Gets Standing Ovation." [13]Author saw misspelled labels at Ray's home in May 1989.

CHAPTER TWENTY FIVE: [1]Johnnie Ray's personal datebooks, 1978-81 and 1984-1989, courtesy of Alan Eichler collection, with permission from Johnnie Ray Estate; all references to datebooks entries are taken from Ray's original notations. [2]John Thomas author interview, Los Angeles California, June 14, 1993. [3]Jeff Gazall told author. [4]"CHiP's" taping and Terry Moore information from Johnnie Ray personal datebook entry August 8, 1979. [5]Details of Ray's donations and charity work contained in the 1956 Australian tour programs; see also Bill Franklin interview August 6, 1993, Variety, May 10, 1972, "Johnnie Ray Performs HEAR Benefit on Queen Mary." Hollywood Reporter, July 27, 1972, "Johnnie Ray Donates Two Truckloads of Clothes, Mementos to HEAR." [6]New York Times, May 21 1981, "A Different Johnnie Ray" by John S. Wilson. [7]Tad Mann interview May 1992. [8]Johnnie Ray's 1985 personal Australian Tour

Itinerary log, courtesy of Alan Eichler collection, with permission from Johnnie Ray Estate. [9]Anita O'Day with George Eells, "High Times Hard Times," p 294. [10]New York Times, August 4, 1989 "Johnnie Ray, Still Cry-ing," By Stephen Holden.

INTERVIEWS

Tito Adami author interview Las Vegas, Nevada, April 20, 1990.
LaVern Baker author interview New York City, June 13, 1992.
Tony Bennett author interview New York City, September 1, 1992.
Jimmy Bowen author interview Nashville, Tennessee, February 8, 1991.
Hadda Brooks author interview Glendale California, August 16 1993.
Jimmy Campbell author interviews Las Vegas, Nevada, April 20, 1990 and
    May 20, 1992.
Thelma Carpenter author interview New York City, June 13, 1992.
Toni Carroll author interview New York City, June 8, 1992.
Jack Devaney author interview Studio City, California, January 29, 1993.
Dixie Evans author interview Helendale, California, May 23, 1993.
Bill Franklin author interviews West Hollywood, California,
    November 11, 1990; August 6, 9, 14, 20, 1993.
Stan Freeman author interview San Fernando Valley, June 14, 1993.
Jeff Gazall author interview New York City, June 8, 1992.
Beck Steiner Gordon author interview Beverly Hills, California,
    November 13, 1992.
Seymour & Billie Heller author interview West Los Angeles, California,
    June 4, 1993.
Beatrice Henry author interviews Portland, Oregon, January 15 and
    February 20, 1993.
Herman Hover author interview Beverly Hills, California, June 12, 1993.
Jane Kean author interview Studio City, California, April 13, 1990.
Danny Kessler author interviews Pacific Palisades, California, April 27, 1990,
    Sherman Oaks, California, August 30, 1992.
Lynn Shannon Kessler author interview Sherman Oaks, California,
    August 30, 1992.
Cy Kertman author interviews Newport Beach, California,
    February 11 and 13, 1993.
Dean Knupp author interview Salem, Oregon, January 11, 1993.
Frank Laico author interview New York, June 13, 1992.
Bernie Lang author interviews Burbank California, September 6, 1992,
    Woodland Hills, California, June 2, 1993.
Jim Low author interview Burbank, California, April 26, 1993.

Tad Mann author interviews Las Vegas, Nevada, April 20, 1990, May 19, 1992.
Big Jay McNeely author interview Hollywood, California, May 24, 1993.
Mitch Miller author interview New York City, June 6, 1992.
Elma Money author interviews Salem, Oregon, January 10, 11, 13, 1993, April 16, 1993.
Charles Ostergrant author interview Burbank, California, August 17, 1993.
Don Ovens author interview Los Angeles, California, August 8, 1992.
Johnnie Ray author interview West Hollywood, May 11, 1989.
Soupy Sales author interview New York City, June 19, 1992.
George Schlatter author interview Los Angeles, June 2, 1993.
Marciel Shepard author interview Salem, Oregon, January 11, 1993.
Jim "Snuffy" Smith author interview Salem, Oregon, January 12, 1993.
Jan Sterling author interview Los Angeles, California, July 6, 1992.
Cliffie Stone author interview Hollywood, California, May 24, 1993.
Tempest Storm author interview Los Angeles, California, May 23, 1993.
Marlin Swing author interview New York City, June 15, 1992.
John Thomas author interview Los Angeles California, June 14, 1993.
Hank Wesinger author interview New York City, March 22, 1993.
Speedy West author interview Broken Arrow, Oklahoma, August 7, 1992.
Jimmy Witherspoon author interview Los Angeles, California, April 5, 1993.

BIBLIOGRAPHY

Clark, Dick and Robinson, Richard. *Rock Roll and Remember*. New York:Popular Library 1978.

Deans, Mickey and Pinchot, Ann. *Weep No More, My Lady*. New York: Pyramid 1972.

Dixon, Willie and Snowden, Don. *I am the Blues, the Willie Dixon Story*. New York: Da Capo 1989.

Drosnin, Michael. *Citizen Hughes*. New York: Holt, Rinehart & Winston 1985.

Fisher, Eddie. *Eddie, My Life, My Loves*. New York: Harper & Row 1981.

Gage, Nicholas, editor. *Mafia U.S.A.* Chicago: Playboy Press 1972.

George, Don. *Sweet Man, the Real Duke Ellington*. New York: G.P. Putnam's Sons 1981.

Gillett, Charlie. *The Sound of the City*. New York: Random House Pantheon reprint 1983.

Guralnick, Peter. *Lost Highway, Journeys and Arrivals of American Musicians*. New York: Random House Vintage Books reprint 1982.

Guralnick, Peter. *Feel Like Going Home, Portraits in Blues and Rock & Roll*. New York: Harper & Row Perennial Library reprint 1982.

Israel, Lee. *Kilgallen, a biography of Dorothy Kilgallen*. New York: Delacorte Press 1979.

Kelley, Kitty. *His Way, the Unauthorized Biography of Frank Sinatra*. New York: Bantam Books 1986.

Larkin, Philip. *All What Jazz, a Record Diary 1961-1971*. New York: Farrar, Straus, Giroux revised edition reprint 1985.

Lee, Peggy. *Miss Peggy Lee*. New York: Berkley reprint 1992.

Malone, Bill and McCulloh, Judy, editors. *Stars of Country Music*. Urbana: University of Illinois Press 1975.

Naipul, Shiva. *Journey To Nowhere, a New World Tragedy*. New York: Simon & Schuster reprint 1980.

O'Day, Anita and Eells, George. *High Times, Hard Times*. New York: Proscenium Limelight revised edition 1989.

Payn, Graham and Morley, Sheridan, editors. *The Noel Coward Diaries*. Boston: Little, Brown & Company 1982.

Oppenheimer, Jerry. *Barbara Walters, an Unauthorized Biography*. New York: St. Martin's Press 1990.

Reynolds, Debbie. *My Life.* New York: Morrow 1980.

Ritz, David. *Divided Soul, the Life of Marvin Gaye.* New York: Da Capo 1985.

Shaw, Arnold. *Honkers & Shouters, the Golden Age of Rhythm & Blues.* New York: Macmillan Collier Books edition 1978.

Shaw, Arnold. *The Rockin' Fifties.* New York: Hawthorn 1987.

Simon, George T. *The Big Bands* (fourth edition). New York: Macmillan Schirmer 1987.

Smith, Joe. *Off The Record, an Oral History of Popular Music.* New York: Warner 1988.

Storm, Tempest and Boyd, Bill. *The Lady is a Vamp.* Atlanta: Peachtree 1987.

Thomas, Bob. *I Got Rhythm, the Ethel Merman Story.* New York: Putnam 1985.

Tosches, Nick. *Dino, Living High in the Dirty Business of Dreams.* New York: Doubleday 1992.

Weatherby, W.J. *Gleason, an Intimate Portrait of the Great One.* New York: Scripps Howard 1992.

White, Charles. *The Life and Times of Little Richard, Quasar of Rock.* New York: Harmony 1982.

Wilson, Earl. *Sinatra, an Unauthorized Biography.* New York: Macmillan 1976.

Worth, Fred L. and Tamerius, Steve D. *Elvis, His Life from A to Z.* Chicago: Contemporary Press.

ARTICLES IN NEWSPAPERS AND MAGAZINES:

Anything Goes, May 1956, p 42, "Why Johnnie Ray Has To Get Half Stiff Every Night," Johnnie Ray interviewed by Paul Coates.

Beverly Hills Newsline, November 13, 1954, "In Hollywood" Aline Mosby column.

Billboard R&B reviews, August 18, 1951, p 75.

October 6, 1951, "The Ray Story: $90.00 to $1,750.00," p 1.

March 15, 1952; as excerpted in Gillett, "The Sound of the City."

April 19, 1952, "Johnnie Ray's Phenomenal Showmanship Wins Sophisticates in NY Club Bow," by Bill Smith, p 3.

May 10, 1952, live review by Norman Wiser, p1.

June 28, 1952, p 1, "Ray Receives 2 Gold Disks." Billboard, July 12, 1952, "Johnnie Ray Case History Part I, Ray With $1,000,000 Remembers $500 in '49," by Joe Martin, p 33.

July 19, 1952, Johnnie Ray Case History II, "Many Fingers Dip Into Ray Pie, Few Get Cuts," by Joe Martin, p 19.

July 26, 1952, Johnnie Ray Case History III "Many Ventures Keep Ray Coffers Filled," by Joe Martin, p 18.

August 2, 1952, Johnnie Ray Case History IV, "Ray Credits Those Who Helped Him Up," by Joe Martin, p 16.

February 14, 1953, "Ray Effect on Gotham Saloon set is Little Short of Electrifying," by Bill Smith, p 3.

September 28, 1953, by Abe L. Morris, p 134.

October 10, 1953, "Suit Charges Lang Assigned 50%" p 14.

December 26, 1953, by Bill Smith, p12.

May 26, 1958, p 7, "Sultan of Sob Solid Self Salesman."

Confidential, April 1953, "Johnnie Ray: Is It True?" by Jay Williams.

November 1955, "Knock, Knock! Who's There? . . . Why Did Johnnie Ray Try To Break Down Paul Douglas' Door?" by Francis Dudley.

July 1957, p 6, "The Feud That Rocked the Copa: When Frank Sinatra Spit at Dorothy Kilgallen," by Ed Sinclair.

Downbeat, December 28, 1951, "Ray Humble About Sudden Success as Singer." Lincoln Center for Performing Arts Library collection.

Ebony, March 1953 "Negroes Taught Me To Sing: Famous Cry Crooner Tells What Blues Taught Him" by Johnnie Ray; Lincoln Center for Performing Arts Library collection.

Gold Coast Bulletin, December 10, 1988, p 53, "The Wild Days" by Douglas Kennedy.

Goldmine, April 1983, "Johnnie Ray: The $1,000,000 Teardrop" by Robert Cain, p 33.

Hollywood Citizen News, May 24, 1952 "Johnnie Ray Gets License, Will Wed Tomorrow."

July 19, 1952 "Johnnie Ray and 4000 Others Gas Bombed."

July 15, 1954 "Hollywood Is My Beat," Sidney Skolsky column.

Hush-Hush, May 1960, p 16, "Why Detroit isn't Home Sweet Homo For Johnnie Ray!" by Hal Clement.

Life Magazine, March 24, 1952. "Again Shrieks & Swoons" pp 99-102

Look magazine, June 1952, "Prince of Wails," by Hy Gardner.

Los Angeles Daily News May 26, 1952, "Clouds Cry As Johnnie Ray Weds Hollywood Girl In New York."

October 3, 1952, "Everyone Cried Along with Johnnie Ray-Marion Davies Gave A Wallop of a Party for the Singer," by Erskine Johnson.

October 7, 1952 "Johnnie Ray's Car Stolen."

October 15, 1952, "None Other Than Bawling Ray" by Erskine Caldwell.

October 23, 1952, "A Few Notes On Johnnie Ray," by Marie Mesmer.

December 8, 1952 "Parents Squelch Report Ray, Wife Separated."

December 16, 1952 "Johnnie Ray, Bride Reconciled," by Earl Wilson.

January 4, 1953 special reprint, "Crier Takes Blame For Marital Breakup" by Earl Wilson.

Los Angeles Examiner, May 14, 1952 "Cry Girls Cry JR To Wed" by Louella O. Parsons.

May 15, 1952 "Johnnie Ray says He's Confused. Weeping Singer Admits Doubt Over Approaching Nuptials."

May 26, 1952, "Wedding Bells Dry Up Tears For Johnnie Ray,"

August 23, 1952, "Johnnie Ray Expecting Baby," by Dorothy Manners.

October 2, 1952, "Mrs Johnnie Ray Cries."

November 28, 1952, "Johnnie Ray Rift Denied," by Louella O. Parsons.

January 12, 1954 "Johnnie Ray Divorce Nears in Mexico" by Louella O. Parsons.

September 23, 1954 "Johnnie Ray, Divorced Wife to Try It Again" by Louella O. Parsons.

December 12, 1954, "Stage & Screen," Dorothy Manners column.

December 18, 1954 "Johnnie Ray Gains in Stab of Toothpick."

Los Angeles Mirror News, November 21, 1959, "Johnnie Ray Arrested On Vice Charge."

Los Angeles Times, May 15, 1952 "Crooner Ray's Wedding Date Becomes Official."

May 26, 1952, "Little White Cloud's Really Cry as Johnnie Ray Weds," United Press wire report.

August 23, 1952 "Johnnie Ray Expects Baby," by Hedda Hopper.

September 18, 1952 "Mrs. Johnnie Ray In Hospital, Loses Baby," by Hedda Hopper.

October 3, 1952, "More Than 500 Attend Party of Marion Davies; Affair Honoring Johnnie Ray Most Lavish In Hollywood History" by Edwin Schallert.

November 30, 1952, "Rays Tears Joyful Now-It Wasn't Always That Way Though," by Edwin Schallert.

April 24, 1953, "Marion Davies Neglected to Pay $11,582 Bill, Suit Charges"

April 25, 1953, "Marion Davies to Fight 11,582 Bill For Party - Statement Through Secretary Gives Actresses version of Johnnie Ray Nuptial fete."

March 7, 1955, "Johnnie Ray Welcomed with Riot in Australia."

March 28, 1955, "Johnnie Ray Saved From Fan Mob," Reynolds News Service item.

December 2, 1959 "Johnnie Ray Denies Vice Charge."

December 3, 1959, "Johnnie Ray Freed, Faints."

October 13, 1965, "For Crying Out Loud! Johnnie Ray Riding the Comeback Trail" by John L. Scott.

December 27, 1967, Hal Humprheys column.

November 1, 1976, "Johnnie Ray: Cry is no Sad Song," by Lynn Simross.

Lowdown, August 1955, p 8, "Lowdown Demands Michigan Governor Pardon Johnnie Ray!" by J. Alvin Kugelmass.

Melody Maker, Laurie Henshaw column, February 24, 1952, as excerpted in Gillett, "Sounds of the City."

New York Daily Mirror, April 17, 1952, "Only Human" by Sidney Fields.

New York Daily News, May 26, 1952, "Johnnie Ray Weds—Bride Cries" by Josephine Di Lorenzo.

New York Journal American, January 30, 1952, Voice of Broadway column by Dorothy Kilgallen.

July 13, 1952, Voice of Broadway, Kilgallen.

April 19, 1953, Voice of Broadway, Kilgallen.

February 9, 1958, Voice of Broadway, Kilgallen.

February 21, 1964 Voice of Broadway, Kilgallen.

February 22, 1964 "Nervous Ruby Feels Breaking Point Near" by Dorothy Kilgallen.

August 18, 1964 "Story of the Shocking Moment" by Dorothy Kilgallen.

August 23, 1964, "Kilgallen Reports Mix-Up in Dallas" by Dorothy Kilgallen.

September 3, 1964 "Pre-Assassination Mystery Warren told Strange Trio Got Together" By Dorothy Kilgallen.

September 30, 1964 Voice of Broadway, Kilgallen.

September 3, 1965, Voice of Broadway, Kilgallen.

November 9, 1965, "The Quiet Sadness of a City" by Alfred Robbins.

November 13, 1965, p 14, "The Dorothy Kilgallen Story, part 3" by Louis Sobol.

New York Post Daily Magazine, April 28, 1960, p 1, "The Dorothy Kilgallen Story," by David Gelman, with Beverly Carr, Peter J. McElroy, Sally Hammond and Richard Montague.

New York Post, cited in editorial page notice of Ray's passing, February 25, 1993.

New York Telegram & Sun, March 27, 1952, "Gone on Frankie in '42, Gone in '52—An open letter to Frank Sinatra," by Muriel Fisher.

New York Times, April 17, 1952, Howard Taubman column.

Fri., May 22, 1981, p C17 "Johnnie Ray Is Back at East Side Club," by John S. Wilson.

On the QT, January 1956, "Why Johnnie Ray Likes To Go In Drag," p 36.

Portland Sunday News, January 22, 1954 p 17, "When Johnnie Comes Home—Johnnie Ray That Is".

Revealed, July 1957, p 42, "London's Most Scandalous Nudie." Rolling Stone, June 28, 1969, "Perspectives: Hank Williams, Roy Acuff and then God!" By Ralph J. Gleason, p 32.

Salem Itemizer/Observer, Oct. 4, 1989, p 1B "Johnnie Ray Comes Home," by Eric Apalategui.

Saturday Evening Post, July 26, 1952, "The Million Dollar Teardrop" by Robert Sylvester.

Screenland Magazine, March 1954, p 22, Dorothy Kilgallen's Exclusive Movie Gossip.

The Star, March 13, 1990, p 31, "Tormented Double Life of '50s Idol Johnnie Ray.

Time Magazine, November 24, 1961, television column, "Lambsy & Chopsy" Lincoln Center for Performing Arts Library collection.

Tip Off, October 1956, p 12, "Why The Roman Rave Kicked Out Johnnie Ray," by Anthony Converro.

Top Secret, August 1957, p 10, "What Happened when Johnnie Ray was Noel Coward's House Guest" by Calvin Hunter.

TV & Movie Screen, July 1955, p 14, "The Inside Story of Johnnie Ray, His Life and Loves" by Phyliss Grey.

Uncensored, December 1955, p 48, "Why The Babes Still Cry For Johnnie Ray" by Bert Mason.

July 1957, p 28, "When Marlon Brando and Johnnie Ray Flipped for That Paris Playgirl" by Gilbert Header.

Vanity Fair, March 1993, "Hidden Hoover," by Anthony Summers, pp 201-202.

Variety, December 26, 1951, p 37.

February 6, 1952.

December 26, 1952.

March 4, 1953, p 2.

April 1, 1953, "London MU Bars Cry Guy Drummer," p 1.

June 24, 1953, "Johnnie Ray and Gary Morton Close Montreal's Sans Souci Venue," p 61.

October 23, 1953, "Ray Squelched (1G Fine) For Quelling Riot."

December 25, 1953, "Pre-trial Exam for Publicist Art Franklin vs. Johnnie Ray," p 49.

April 6, 1955, p 5.

April 27, 1955, "Johnnie Ray Returns to Palladium," p 54.

May 18, 1955, "Edinburgh Fans Mob Johnnie Ray at Airport," p 2.

June 18, 1955, p 51, review by Jose.

October 19, 1955, p 66, "Johnnie Ray Headache For Brit Gendarmes."

November 2, 1955, p 2.

November 9, 1955, review by Most.

January 25, 1956, "Ray Whams South Africa."

April 11, 1956, p 52, "Ray Really Weeps After Tokyo Flop."

April 18, 1956, p 8, "Johnnie Ray at the Desert Inn" by Will.

May 30, 1956, p 52 "Johnnie Ray at the Latin Quarter" nightclub review.

July 17, 1957 p 3, "Johnnie Ray at Paul 'Skinny' D'Amato's Vermillion Room, 500 Club, Atlantic City,"

July 24, 1957, p 64, "Johnnie Ray Booked Through Next Year."

March 6, 1957, p 57, "Johnnie Ray at Eden Roc Hotel."

May 15, 1957, p 67, "Johnnie Ray at Waldorf-Astoria" by Jose.

August 21, 1957, p 4, "Johnnie Ray on Presley: Giving Record Industry a Shot-In-Arm" by Hazel Guild.

October 2, 1957, p 67, "Johnnie Ray at Coconut Grove" by Helm.

October 27, 1957, p 65, "Johnnie Ray at the Desert Inn's Painted Desert Room" by Duke.

December 11, 1957, p 71, "Johnnie Ray at Town & Country" by Jose.

October 29, 1958, "Johnnie Ray at Hotel Carrera, Santiago, Chile."

February 18, 1959, "Johnnie Ray at Continental Room Shamrock Hilton, Houston."

March 18, 1959, p 87, "Johnnie Ray at Palace, London."

June 10, 1959, "Johnnie Ray at Latin Quarter Follow Up" by Jose.

December 19 1959, p 55, "Johnnie Ray at Harrah's" by Long.

November 9, 1960, p 60, "Johnnie Ray at Basin Street East" by Herm.

May 17 1961, p 66, "Johnnie Ray at Angelo's, Omaha, Neb." by Trump.

July 5, 1961, p 53, "Johnnie Ray at Talk of the Town, London."

August 29, 1962, nightclub reviews, "Johnnie Ray at Holiday House, Pittsburgh."

September 27, 1965, Johnnie Ray full page advertisement.

August 1, 1966, "Reprise Ropes Ray."

December 25, 1966, "Johnnie Ray Signed by Sheldon Cooper."

September 5, 1967, "A.C. Lyles Rogues Gallery."

March 19, 1969, p 69, "Garland and Ray Bow New Act in Sweden."

July 3, 1969, "Johnnie Ray Signs With Coast Artists"

Virginia Beach Ledger Star, March 30, 1979, "J.R. and Johnnie Ray: one a Show Biz legend the other a human being" by William Ruehlman, p C1.

Letters to Salem Performing Arts Center: Naomi Brown, September 28, 1989. Beulah Curtiss, September 27, 1989. Dorothy Shepard Ely,September 27, 1989. Jim Smith, September 28 1989. Betty Woodman, September 27, 1989. Johnnie Ray souvenir program circa 1952 "Mr. Emotion—His Inspiring Story," Australian tour programs 1954, 1955, 1956, 1957, 1958 "Lee Gordon Presents Johnnie Ray in the Big Show," and all personal date books, home movies and television appearances referred to courtesy of Johnnie Ray Estate/Alan Eichler collection.

Academy of Motion Picture Arts & Sciences Library, Margaret Herrick Library collection, Johnnie Ray clippings file: Johnnie Ray 20th Century Fox publicity file circa 1954;

United Press wire report, May 20, 1952, "Johnnie Ray: Tears Of Joy, Sweeps Fiancee Into Arms."

Jimmie Tarantino's Hollywood Life Newsweekly of the West: San Francisco-Los Angeles." December 12, 1952;

"Johnnie Ray Sued For Juarez Divorce," and "Cry Ray Shed by Wife in Juarez," UP wire reports, January 14-15, 1954.

January 14, 1958, "Johnnie Ray Ear Miracle Thrills New York" by Earl Wilson.

"Dorothy Kilgallen's Funeral Mob Scene," clipping in Lincoln Center Library for the Performing Arts collection.

INDEX

Blinstrub's Theater (Boston), 132
Boone, Pat, 239
Boothroyd, J.B., 175
Boscowitz, Hubie and Lillian, 225-26
Botkin, Nick, 100
Boulevard Club (Queens, New York), 93
Bowen, Jimmy, 351, 353
Bradley's Barn (Nashville), 259
Brady, Mary Lou, 6
Brando, Marlon, 83, 180, 232
Brandon, Joan, 44
Brass Rail (Chicago), 69
Britten, Sherry, 241
Bronowski, Dr. John, 196
Brooks, Hadda, 6, 39, 40, 143, 403
Brooks, Jack, 72
Brown, Charles, 39, 40
Brown, Horace, 138
Brown, Naomi, 14
Brown, Ruth, 52, 405
Bryant, Boudelaux, 259
Brynner, Yul, 111, 113, 181, 191, 200, 226, 228, 243, 397
Buchalter, Lepke, 158
Burton, Sybil, 368
Butera, Sam, 6
Butterfield, Billy, 252
Cafe de Paris (Miami), 230, 317
Cafe de Paris (New York), 241, 317
Cafe Slipper (New Orleans), 170
Cafe Society (New York), 46
Caldwell, "Uncle" Will, 13-14
Callaway, Candace, 6
Calthorpe, Gladys, 160
Campbell, Dee Dee, 284

Campbell, Jimmy, 135, 212, 281-305
    passim, 321-23, 330, 336, 400
Capitol Lounge (Chicago), 69
Capitol Theater (Washington, D.C.), 87
Capitol Theater (New York), 149
Capone, Al, 157
Carmichael, Hoagy, 40
Carney, Art, 208
Carpenter, Thelma, 6, 143, 233, 405
Carroll, Earl, 99
Carroll, Jimmy, 79, 80
Carroll, Toni, 6
Casey, Ruth, 80
Cassini, Igor, 219
Cavanaugh, Page, 399
Caviston, Eugene, 265-66, 268-69
Cerf, Bennett, 209, 336
Channing, Carol, 242, 322
Charioteers, 57
Chase Club (St. Louis), 169
Chase, Lincoln, 172
Chez Paree (Chicago), 169, 250-51
Chrisler, Christine, 6
Churchill, Savannah, 225
Ciro's (Los Angeles), 38, 39, 41, 98, 99, 100, 123, 124, 126, 129, 140, 178-79, 183
Clark, Dick, 58, 239-40
Clark, Wilbur, 158
Clooney, Rosemary, 60, 77, 78, 95, 97, 111, 173-74
Clover Club (Houston), 173
Club DeLisa (Chicago), 51, 53, 58, 69, 147, 224
Club Forty Niner (Detroit), 62